The Learning
of Liberty

American Political Thought

*edited by Wilson Carey McWilliams
and Lance Banning*

The Learning
of Liberty
The Educational Ideas of
the American Founders

Lorraine Smith Pangle
and
Thomas L. Pangle

 University Press of Kansas

Published by the University Press of Kansas (Lawrence, Kansas 66049), which was organized by the Kansas Board of Regents and is operated and funded by Emporia State University, Fort Hays State University, Kansas State University, Pittsburg State University, the University of Kansas, and Wichita State University

Library of Congress Cataloging-in-Publication Data

Pangle, Lorraine Smith.
The learning of liberty : the educational ideas of the American
    founders / Lorraine Smith Pangle and Thomas L. Pangle.
        p.   cm. — (American political thought)
    Includes bibliographical references and index.
    ISBN 0-7006-0581-9 (cloth)   ISBN 0-7006-0746-3 (pbk.)
    1. Education—United States—Philosophy—History—18th century.
    2. Education and state—United States—Philosophy—History—18th
    century. I. Pangle, Thomas L.   II. Title. III. Series.
    LA206.P36   1993
    370'.1–dc20   92-29956

British Library Cataloguing in Publication Data is available.

Printed in the United States of America
10 9 8 7 6 5 4 3 2

The paper used in this publication meets the minimum requirements of the American National Standard for Permanence of Paper for Printed Library Materials Z39.48-1984.

To Darwin and Jo Ann Smith

Contents

Acknowledgments

Our research into the educational ideas of the American Founders began with a senior thesis that Lorraine Smith wrote at Yale University entitled "Education and Liberty: A Study in the Thought of Thomas Jefferson." For useful suggestions at that time and encouragement in expanding that essay into a book, she wishes to thank Edmund Morgan, Jim Essig, Donald Kagan, and Walter Berns. Our editors, Lance Banning and Wilson Carey McWilliams, have been especially helpful with their critical comments. We are also indebted to the Library Company of Philadelphia for making available its fine collection of early American texts, and finally to Heather, who good-naturedly shared her parents with this project during her early years.

Introduction

The defenders of the dignity of mankind have long found in democracy both an object of aspiration and a source of apprehension. The American Founders were moved by both sentiments and felt themselves torn. Convinced that in the modern age, especially in America, government by the people could prove itself the best hope for stable public liberty and happiness, they were nevertheless keenly aware of the vices that had always before haunted republicanism and especially democratic republicanism. Those vices were starkly evident even or precisely in the most glorious historical examples of republics. As Alexander Hamilton put it in the ninth *Federalist Paper*:

> It is impossible to read the history of the petty republics of Greece and Italy without feeling sensations of horror and disgust at the distractions with which they were continually agitated, and at the rapid succession of revolutions by which they were kept in a state of perpetual vibration between the extremes of tyranny and anarchy. . . . If it had been found impracticable to have devised models of a more perfect structure, the enlightened friends to liberty would have been obliged to abandon the cause of that species of government as indefensible.[1]

The classic account of the reasons for the instability of republican government focused on education as the heart of the problem. Republics, it was argued, require an extraordinary degree of public-spiritedness, self-restraint, and practical wisdom in their citizens. To form such virtues of heart and mind, an especially intense and carefully supervised moral education of the young is essential. But such education, and the remarkable character traits at which it aims, represent a rare and fragile achievement, one that is bound to be easily undermined or corrupted.

Now the American Founders did not reject this analysis, but some of the

1

most thoughtful among them insisted that the problem of republicanism had to be approached from a new angle. Although they did not cease to rely on the moral character of the citizenry to help sustain and moderate self-government, they concentrated their attentions chiefly on new arrangements of legal and political institutions that would focus, check, and balance power in such a way as to foster the efficacious vigor of government while preventing its oppressive misuse. It was this distinctively modern approach Hamilton had in mind when he referred, in the passage just quoted, to "models of a more perfect structure."

John Adams, in his "Thoughts on Government" (1776) and *Defence of the Constitutions of Government of the United States* (1787–1788), provides perhaps the clearest articulation of the new perspective. Indeed, Adams's *Defence* may be said to be one long lesson in history and political theory aimed explicitly at educating "young Americans" in the new and correct conception of the relation between education and republican constitutionalism.[2]

Adams was convinced that virtue was a "principle and foundation" of the sort of republic to which Americans must aspire. He accordingly advocated "sumptuary" legislation (coercive restrictions on luxury and conspicuous consumption) as well as compulsory, universal military service aimed at promoting moderation, frugality, and manliness, and he never ceased to stress the importance of government expenditure for moral education of all classes of citizens, especially the poorest.[3] But Adams raised and pursued a question that must become paramount in any sustained reflection upon civic virtue and education. Which is prior, in order of fundamental importance: a good legal constitution, whose rules and practices regulate the actions of individuals in and out of office; *or* the inner spiritual disposition of the citizens, especially those who fill the highest offices? To what extent can individuals be made sufficiently trustworthy and thoughtful public servants by regulating and modifying behavior, through incentives and sanctions; and to what extent is character formation the essential presupposition of even the best legal institutions and regulations?

Classical republicanism had insisted that the priority belongs to inner spiritual disposition and character formation. In the words of Plato's Athenian Stranger:

> Presumably it's clear to everyone that although the giving of laws is a grand deed, still, even where a city is well equipped, if the magistrates established to look after the well-formulated laws were unfit, then not only would the laws no longer be well-founded, and the situation most ridiculous, but those very laws would be likely to bring the greatest harm and ruin to cities. . . . if the powers of office are to go to the correct persons, they and their families must each have been given a sufficient test—from the time

they were children until the time they are selected. Then again, those who are to do the selecting should be reared in lawful habits.[4]

The classical republicanism sprung from Plato had consequently put religion, music, and poetry at the center of public life: the cultivation of the specific moral qualities involved in civic virtue depends on those qualities being made to appear both divinely sanctioned and erotically attractive to the hearts of the young; and the key to the passions, the classical thinkers insisted, is music.

Thomas Jefferson, while largely jettisoning the religious and musical foundations of classical virtue, provides a dim echo of the classical view in a letter to Samuel Kercheval of 12 July 1816. After expressing severe doubts about the capacity of the institutions of the American regime to secure liberty, Jefferson asks, "Where then is our republicanism to be found?" "Not," he answers, "in our constitution certainly, but merely in the spirit of our people. That would oblige even a despot to govern us republicanly. Owing to this spirit, and to nothing in the form of our constitution, all things have gone well."[5]

But this extreme statement is hardly representative of the thinking of most of the prominent Founders. More characteristic is John Adams's insistence, in direct and emphatic opposition to the classical doctrine, that virtue in the citizenry is the product, more than the presupposition, of sound fundamental laws and institutions: "The best republics will be virtuous, and have been so; but we may hazard a conjecture that the virtues have been the effect of the well ordered constitution rather than the cause. And, perhaps, it would be impossible to prove that a republic cannot exist even among highwaymen, by setting one rogue to watch another; and the knaves themselves may in time be made honest men by the struggle." What is more, Adams contends that the best or most essential laws and institutions are not those that aim directly at the cultivation of virtuous behavior but those that aim at the mutual checking and balancing of vicious behavior.

Pythagoras and Socrates, having no idea of three independent branches in the legislature, both thought, that the laws could neither prevent the arbitrary oppressions of magistrates, nor turbulent insolence of the people, until mankind were habituated, by education and discipline, to regard the great duties of life, and to consider a reverence of themselves, and the esteem of their fellow-citizens, as the principal source of their enjoyment. In small communities, especially where the slaves are many, and the citizens few, this might be plausible; but the education of a great nation can never accomplish so great an end. Millions must be brought up, whom no principles, no sentiments derived from education, can restrain from trampling on

the laws. Orders of men, watching and balancing each other, are the only security; power must be opposed to power, and interest to interest. . . .
. . . Thus, experience has ever shown, that education, as well as religion, aristocracy, as well as democracy and monarchy, are, singly, totally inadequate to the business of restraining the passions of men, of preserving a steady government, and protecting the lives, liberties, and properties of the people. . . . Religion, superstition, oaths, education, laws, all give way before passions, interest, and power, which can be resisted only by passions, interest, and power.

Given a rule of law rooted in such constructive institutional antagonism, adequate and reasonable or well-grounded virtue will be, Adams is confident, the likely if not the necessary outcome. The discouragement of vicious behavior will promote the habitual practice of virtuous or relatively virtuous behavior, and such habituation will mold the character of the practitioners, constituting in them an effective, if not pure or sublime, sort of civic virtue: "A regular, well-ordered constitution, will never fail to bring forth men capable of conducting the national councils and arms; and it is of infinitely more importance to the national happiness, to abound in good merchants, farmers, and manufacturers, good lawyers, priests, and physicians, and great philosophers, than it is to multiply what are called great statesmen and great generals."[6]

Yet, to repeat, the new focus on institutional arrangements diminished but did not dissolve the concern for civic and moral education. It is true that education is never a subject of discussion in the *Federalist Papers*. Nonetheless, accompanying the Federalists' reliance on the "great improvement" in the science of politics, looming in the background of at least the wisest Founders' constitutional and political thinking, was continued meditation on the older and more problematic or perplexing republican theme: the question of how to create or encourage a specific moral character and tone in the citizenry and its leaders. Here again, however, the problem was viewed in a new light.

The classic discussions of republican (and, indeed, monarchic) education had stressed the need to form in the young a spirit of obedience to and respect for authority and tradition—familial, generational, communal, political, moral, and, above all, religious. Such reverence entailed two assumptions: the indebtedness of the inferior present to the superior past, and the subordination of the individual, and of individuality, to higher communal or collective social wholes. The firmest democracy was understood to be that in which equality meant primarily the equal subordination and devotion of all to the civic whole handed down from the sacred past.[7]

In contrast, the Founders, led by Jefferson and the modern philosophers whom they took as their guides, introduced a new stress on "enlightenment," and historical "progress" in enlightenment, as the heart of sound education. By the term *enlightenment*, they meant primarily modern philosophy's or modern science's liberation of mankind from age-old states of tutelage and subordination to authority—especially to religious authority rooted in the benighted or unenlightened past. This liberation was to be effected in the name of the individual's "natural rights" to security and to the "pursuit of happiness." The idea of enlightenment was thus grounded on the idea of the autonomy of the individual and on the attempt to derive all legitimate authority, and all healthy larger social wholes, from this autonomy. The social coalescence of enlightened individuals was to be facilitated by their developing, through a new sort of moral education, a sense of common "humanity": in becoming enlightened, individuals were to become aware of the similar rights and kindred needs (for security, liberty, and respect) that universally underlie the diversity among individuals and groups.

On the political level, enlightenment was to entail the collective awakening of individuals, as citizens, to a cooperative vigilance against government's overstepping of its strictly circumscribed legitimate bounds. Perhaps the most eloquent testimony to the meaning and centrality of enlightenment in this sense is Jefferson's last letter, reflecting on the significance of the Declaration of Independence.

> May it be to the world, what I believe it will be (to some parts sooner, to others later, but finally to all), the signal of arousing men to burst the chains under which monkish ignorance and superstition had persuaded them to bind themselves, and to assume the blessings and security of self-government. That form which we have substituted, restores the free right to the unbounded exercise of reason and freedom of opinion. All eyes are opened, or opening, to the rights of man. The general spread of the light of science has already laid open to every view the palpable truth, that the mass of mankind has not been born with saddles on their backs, nor a favored few booted and spurred, ready to ride them legitimately, by the grace of God.[8]

In this study, we take issue with a number of contemporary scholars who we believe blur or underestimate the fundamentally individualistic and egalitarian character of the Founders' conception of enlightenment.[9] We surely do not deny that the question of how to cultivate certain self-transcending moral and intellectual virtues judged essential for self-government—including piety, obedience to law, and farsighted prudence or judgment—remained a lively and troubling issue among the Founders. But this traditional republican preoccupation was enlarged and complicated by the new concern for education understood as the source of enlightenment, in the sense just described.[10]

This book is an exploration of the Founders' thoughts on the question of education, understood in the light of the complex duality of aim we have just sketched. Our intention is to resurrect and reassess some of the most important reflections on civic and personal education appearing in the writings of those among the Founding generation who spoke clearly and compellingly on the subject. A leading feature of this book is our effort to illuminate the Founders' thoughts on education by juxtaposing and contrasting them with the arguments of some of the most profound and influential earlier theorists and philosophers of education. The Founders drew from many diverse and opposing conceptions of education. With some they agreed, with some they disagreed, in a profitable dialectic. But more significant for us than any determination of influences or intellectual genealogies is the task of situating, defining, and assessing the value of the Founders' thought. It is this task that we seek to initiate by way of selective comparisons and contrasts with some worthy but competing views of education. Our aim is not merely to reconstruct, in the fashion of museum curators, what the Founders thought about education; we attempt also to reanimate, through the infusion of critical analysis and dialogue, the vein of living argument that once pulsed through the pages of the Founders' writings.

Our motivation in undertaking such a study is not, then, simply historical or scholarly. Currently the United States finds itself in a time of grave, ongoing public debate over education. It is not an exaggeration to say that a sense of crisis pervades the contemporary discussion. It seems to us that at the root of the present malaise are not simply concerns over the shortage of funds, or the insufficient number of teachers, or the inadequacies of teacher education, or, more generally, the incompleteness of our knowledge of how to implement the goals of education. The real seriousness of our situation is revealed when we recognize how uncertain Americans have become as to what the proper goals of education are.

We offer a wide array of subjects in our schools, and especially in our high schools, as we try to equip the next generation with skills that it may need for careers, many of which—given the uncanny character of technological development—do not yet exist; but we are more and more haunted by the suspicion that our educational theories and institutions have lost sight of the need to perpetuate a lasting core of moral and civic knowledge that is essential to true education for everyone. At the same time, in our attempts to articulate this educational ideal we sense is being forgotten, we become aware that we have great difficulty defining the content of the ideal, and thus the content of the curriculum that deserves to be perpetuated. We try to encourage tolerance and openness to all cultures, yet we wonder with growing uneasiness whether there is not a set of distinctly American, republican principles that children should be taught to believe in. Meanwhile, we find ourselves less and less confident that such principles can in any way be considered as simply and permanently true. We look to the schools to help solve our thorniest social problems, to root out racism and sexism, to reduce teenage pregnancy and venereal disease, to combat the spread of drug abuse, to redress the damages of broken homes. Yet amidst this profusion of programs aimed at specific moral ills, we too often stop short of addressing in a serious and sustained way the more fundamental questions that every conscientious parent and teacher feels must be at the very heart of moral education: what must one do to live well? What rights must children be taught to claim and honor, and what further principles, virtues, or habits do they most need if they are to become productive citizens and good parents? How can we help the young to go beyond fleeting amusements to find lasting and meaningful happiness in life?

Even at this most profound level of our contemporary perplexity, the Framers have something to teach us. This is not to imply that a study of their thoughts on education will supply formulas with which to resolve our difficulties. While there is much in the Founders' thought that will be found insightful and useful, a critical examination of their writings leads, on the whole, to perhaps more new questions than answers. We advance, therefore, this more modest contention: thoughtful reaction to or dialogue with the Founders' reflections on education may deepen our understanding of the basic problems that attend any effort to articulate the goals of education in a republican society such as ours; moreover, such an encounter with the Founders may broaden our awareness of some important alternative responses to those problems. At the very least, a study of the Founders' views of education will help us to see that the difficulties we now experience in trying to understand the goals of education are in some measure an outcome of unresolved tensions imbedded in the Founders' own conceptions of education, of republicanism, and of human nature. We will not discover practical solutions to contemporary problems simply by reading the Founders, but we may well find ourselves coming to grips with the current situation in a spirit that is less dogmatic or simplistic and more informed, circumspect, and moderate.

Moreover, through such a study we may gain a richer appreciation of the ambiguities of republicanism and of human nature, which may spur us in turn to investigate these great themes in a more philosophic way. For while the Founders were not philosophers in the strict sense, one of the most impressive accomplishments of men such as Thomas Jefferson and Benjamin Franklin was their ability to move gracefully from practical statesmanship to probing reflections on the nature of man and politics. In their habit of always approaching philosophical questions through genuine, living concerns, they provide the best kind of introduction to such questions. In their ability to combine deeply public-spirited careers with sustained theoretical interests, Franklin and Jefferson show how even intensely engaged lives can be made richer through a love of thought for its own sake. By living lives at once truly active and truly reflective, they make one of the greatest contributions that can be made to the education of any nation: that of furnishing models of fulfilled and happy human lives, whose fulfillment and happiness are rooted in self-knowledge.

Part One
The Legacy

1 · The Problematic Heritage of European Education

We will best appreciate the depth of the difficulties the Founders confronted when they turned their thoughts to education if we begin by considering the manifold and problematic educational legacy they inherited from the past. This legacy had been deeply influential in the Founders' own education and represented the natural point of departure for their reflections. Yet they recognized that the previously authoritative notions of education, including many of the notions on which they themselves had been bred, were at some tension not only with one another but, graver still, with the ethos of the new American democratic republic. The paramount educational challenge the Founding generation faced was that of preparing future generations to become democratic citizens who would sustain a regime of individual freedoms as well as responsible self-rule; and no fully satisfactory model of such a program was to be found in either the colonial past or its cultural matrix, the heritage of educational practice and theory derived from Europe.

For Americans in the eighteenth century, it was of course Western Europe that was the source from which learning and education emanated; and Western Europe, from the American perspective, was dominated by two kindred but competing political and cultural centers: Paris and London (with Edinburgh as a rather independent satellite). Great Britain naturally exercised the strongest influence over its colonists or former colonists, but France represented, especially in matters of education and culture, a major alternative. Montesquieu's authority as an educational as well as a political theorist was surpassed only by that of John Locke. The French nation had sided decisively with the Americans in their revolution, and a number of remarkable Frenchmen had fought beside the Americans as comrades in arms. Some of the Founders who were most preoccupied with educational questions—Franklin and Jefferson in particular—lived for years in Paris. They partook of French culture with zest and appreciation, forming close and enduring friendships with French aristocrats. They traveled extensively in France, witnessing firsthand both the charms and the blights of the "Old World."

Yet the American Revolution opened a fissure not only with England but with Europe generally, with repercussions not only in education but in culture as a whole. Noah Webster expressed the point somewhat dramatically in 1783, in the introduction to the school textbook he published as a contribution to the creation of a new, indigenous American education in language skills.

> Previously to the late war, America preserved the most unshaken attachment to Great-Britain: The king, the constitution, the laws, the commerce, the fashions, the books and even the sentiments of Englishmen were implicitly supposed to be the *best* on earth. . . . But . . . the political views of America have suffered a total change. . . . We find Englishmen practicing upon very erroneous maxims in politics and religion; and possibly we shall find, upon careful examination, that their methods of education are equally erroneous and defective. . . . Europe is grown old in folly, corruption and tyranny—in that country laws are perverted, manners are licentious, literature is declining and human nature debased. For America in her infancy to adopt the present maxims of the old world, would be to stamp the wrinkles of decrepid age upon the bloom of youth and to plant the seeds of decay in a vigourous constitution.[1]

Four years later, at the time of the ratification of the Constitution, Webster closed his essay "On the Education of Youth in America" by appealing to Americans to

> unshackle your minds and act like independent beings. You have been children long enough, subject to the control and subservient to the interest of a haughty parent. You have now an interest of your own to augment and defend: you have an empire to raise and support by your exertions and a national character to establish and extend by your wisdom and virtues. To effect these great objects, it is necessary to frame a liberal plan of policy and build it on a broad system of education. Before this system can be formed and embraced, the Americans must *believe* and *act* from the belief that it is dishonorable to waste life in mimicking the follies of other nations and basking in the sunshine of foreign glory.[2]

Benjamin Rush begins his "Address to the American People," published originally in January 1787 in the *American Museum*, by complaining that "there is nothing more common, than to confound the terms of *American Revolution* with those of *the late American War*." The "American war," Rush goes on to explain, "is over; but this is far from being the case with the American Revolution. On the contrary, nothing but the first act of the great drama is closed. It remains yet to establish and perfect our new forms of government, and to prepare the principles, morals, and manners of our citizens for these forms of government, after they are established and brought to perfection."[3] As Rush's words indicate, it remained to be seen whether the cultural revolution was to be as successful as the military one. Initially, there was at least as much evidence of disintegration as there was of new inspiration or construction.[4] Yet despite the loss of cultural moorings, Americans were inclined to the view that when it came to education there was no turning back to Europe, or at least to European practice.

If we are to ascend to the most fully reasoned analysis that informs this judgment, we need to turn to that educational and political theorist whom Webster repeatedly cites as authoritative: "the great Montesquieu."[5] For his understanding of the European spirit, and especially the spirit of European educational institutions, Webster, like so many of his contemporaries, takes his bearings from the *Spirit of the Laws*.[6] There Montesquieu analyzes the "Old World" of Europe, the world whose spirit so deeply shaped the Founding generation's own breeding, as a culture descended from feudalism and largely shaped by two coexisting and competing spiritual sources: hereditary nobility and Christianity.

European Education Grounded on Aristocratic Honor

According to Montesquieu, it is from its chivalric aristocratic heritage that European secular education has received its "soul," or "animating passion." That passion is "honor": a deep sense of prideful personal dignity, intimately bound up with a keen sensitivity to one's social place and rank within a rather rigid hereditary class structure. The code of honor is most brilliantly evident in the upper classes, but it spawns a preoccupation with personal and group dignity or prestige that permeates society, reaching down to the lowest echelons.

Montesquieu does not hesitate to unveil the injustice, conventionality, sloth, vanity, and dishonesty that lurk beneath the glittering surface of the European code of honor. But he insists nonetheless that education in honor plays a highly constructive role in a well-functioning monarchic society. So long as a social and political system reflects the principle of honor, it will be a system in which despotism is checked by competing centers of lawful power and authority. Honor generates and thrives on antagonism, but that antagonism also draws individuals together in a multitude of traditional family, class, regional, professional, and religious communities. Above all, honor breeds a specific sort of civic responsibility—one that is animated, broadened, and made farsighted by the sublimely selfish quest for a share in glory. As the conservative Virginian

Carter Braxton puts it in a remarkable essay inspired by Montesquieu, "In a monarchy limited by laws the people are insensibly led to the pursuit of *honour*, they feel an interest in the greatness of their princes, [and] unite in giving strength and energy to the whole machine."[7] Montesquieu's great disciple William Blackstone, author of the widely read and authoritative *Commentaries on the Laws of England*, was more enthusiastic in summarizing for English-speaking peoples the importance of education in honor.

> The distinction of rank and honours is necessary in every well-governed state . . . exciting thereby an ambitious yet laudable ardor, and generous emulation in others. And emulation, or virtuous ambition, is a spring of action which, however dangerous or invidious in a mere republic or under a despotic sway, will certainly be attended with good effects under a monarchy. . . . Such a spirit, when nationally diffused, gives life and vigour to the community; it sets all the wheels of government in motion . . . and thereby every individual may be made subservient to the public good, while he principally means to promote his own particular views.[8]

But if the Founders were well tutored in the advantages of honor for a monarchic system, they saw with unsentimental clarity how unsuited was this principle—and any education founded mainly on it—to a democratic system, or to what Blackstone dismissed as "a mere republic." No doubt monarchic honor could and would continue to play some role in the moral ethos of the new nation, but if honor was to survive as a wellspring for the American civic consciousness and education, it would have to be reconceived along republican lines. For this task, the conception of honor handed down from the republics of antiquity proved far more useful than the version available in contemporary European life. The *Federalist Papers*, in which the notion of honor has a significant part, strike the new keynote.[9] We shall later investigate how some notable Founders, especially George Washington, attempted to carry further the reconception of honor and direct it toward more explicit educational goals. But first we need to recognize how limited in applicability the contemporary European idea of education rooted in honor was bound to seem to anyone thoughtfully considering moral and civic education in postrevolutionary America.[10]

Christian Education: The Fear of Roman Catholicism

The alternative, religious pillar of European education appeared to offer more to the fledgling republic in the way of educational guidance. Yet it was by no means obvious that traditional Christian education harmonized with republicanism, and especially with the unprecedented form of republicanism aimed at in the American Founding. To begin with, it was not easy to free European Christian education from its feudal, aristocratic encrustations. As John Adams lamented in his "Dissertation on the Canon and the Feudal Law," the established church institutions of Europe—and not least the Anglican church that still exerted considerable influence in many of the colonies, especially Virginia—had become deeply imbued with the aristocratic principles of hierarchy and unrepublican honor.[11]

But the religious threat to which Americans in the Founding period were most keenly alive was the one that they saw posed by Roman Catholic education. Nowadays, and especially in the United States, we find it difficult to comprehend the profound suspicion with which Roman Catholicism was once regarded by principal Founders as well as by many of their English forebears. The Catholic church in the twentieth century has stood as an impressive bulwark against Marxist totalitarianism—particularly in Eastern Europe. Within the United States, the parochial school system has served as an essential refuge for discipline, decency, and intellectual standards in an era when the public school system in urban areas has verged on moral collapse. But we forget, or, as Americans, we never experienced in its most shocking forms, the vast political and educational designs—defensive as well as offensive—of the papacy and the Jesuits in the days when the memory of religious warfare, with all its atrocities on both sides, was still fresh. It is easy to forget how late in the day it was before the papacy finally made its peace with "modernism" or liberalism and, above all, how severe and lasting were the struggles throughout Europe over the role of the church in education. As the historian A. J. P. Taylor has put it, in the context of a discussion of Bismarck's *Kulturkampf* with the Roman Catholic church:

> The modern liberal state came everywhere into conflict with the Church. Education, for instance, could be a matter for compromise so long as it was limited to a few. It was bound to cause bitter dispute as soon as it became universal; and after 1871 universal elementary education was everywhere the order of the day. Disputes over religious education dominated the politics of every European country in the last thirty years of the nineteenth century—not merely Germany, but England, France, Belgium, and Austria-Hungary, to name a few at random.[12]

Certainly among Americans of the Founding era the view was widespread that the political and educational role of the Roman Catholic church in Europe had tended to promote, at least in the most recent centuries, despotic ambition in the few, supine slavishness among the many, and hypocrisy, conspiracy, and cruelty generally. The papacy disavowed the quest for temporal suzerainty; but

again and again (and not least in the course of English history) it had inter-
vened to undermine the legitimacy of non-Catholic rulers and boost that of
Catholics, seeming to show a tireless energy in defending and advancing the political power of its admittedly often persecuted adherents. Locke, in his famous
Letter Concerning Toleration (1689), had suggested that so long as the Roman
church continued to resemble Islam, inspiring in its adherents a divisive and
subversive political allegiance to the papacy, Catholicism could not be afforded
the protection of toleration.[13] Echoing Locke, Samuel Adams wrote in 1772:

> In regard to religion, mutual toleration in the different professions thereof,
> is what all good and candid minds in all ages have ever practiced; . . . Mr.
> Lock has asserted, and proved beyond the possibility of contradiction on
> any solid ground, that such toleration ought to be extended to all whose
> doctrines are not subversive of society. . . . The Roman Catholicks or Pa-
> pists are excluded by reason of such doctrines as these: that princes excom-
> municated may be deposed, and those they call *Hereticks* may be destroyed
> without mercy; besides their recognizing the Pope in so absolute a manner,
> in subversion of Government, by introducing as far as possible into the
> states, under whose protection they enjoy life, liberty, and property, that
> solecism in politicks, Imperium in imperio, a Government within a Gov-
> ernment, leading directly to the worst anarchy and confusion, civil dis-
> cord, war and blood shed.[14]

Two years later, on 21 October 1774, the Continental Congress complained to
"the people of Great Britain" for allowing Parliament to make Roman Catholicism the established religion of Quebec—"a religion, fraught with sanguinary
and impious tenets, . . . that has deluged your island in blood, and dispersed
bigotry, persecution, murder and rebellion through every part of the world."
The Congress likewise protested Parliament's opening Quebec to more Catholic
immigrants, "fit instruments in the hands of power, to reduce the free Protestant
colonies to the same state of slavery with themselves."[15]

Yet because the Americans were, at least in the late eighteenth century, under
no immediate threat from the vicinity of powerful Catholic states, and because
the colonies contained only a small minority of Catholics, who at any rate were
quiescent and comparatively liberal, the fear of active Catholic subversion and
tyranny remained abstract and somewhat histrionic.[16] More concrete was the
Founders' unease at the hierarchical and authoritarian character of the Catholic
priesthood and the education it seemed to attempt to inculcate in the people.
As they gloomily observed the struggle for liberty in South America, and the
apparent incapacity of the people to escape their tutelage to a priesthood that allied itself with undemocratic government, Adams and Jefferson felt driven to

wonder, "Can a free Government possibly exist with a Roman Catholic Religion?"[17]

The Church of England

For many Americans in the eighteenth century, respectable religion meant the established religion, the Church of England. The meaning and the educational function of "established religion," and therefore the arguments in support of it as an institution, had undergone a long and complex evolution since the term was first introduced. Originally, the term *established religion* referred to the new situation created by the founding of the Episcopal Church of England by Henry VIII and Elizabeth. The monarch, associated in some crucial matters with Parliament, replaced the pope as the head of the religious hierarchy and either confiscated or became final arbiter of all the possessions of the church—including, in particular, the previously Catholic educational system. Henceforth the bishops, who sat with other nobles in the House of Lords, were appointed by, or through the authority of, the throne, and no changes could be effected in church doctrine except by sanction of an act of Parliament.

Initially, then, religious "establishment" was an English institution directed squarely against Roman Catholicism and Roman Catholic education and, more obliquely, against the perceived ambitions of various Protestant sects to control education. Only later and gradually did the notion of "establishment of religion" become relaxed and broadened to include officially supported Catholic or non-Episcopalian Protestant denominations in other countries (notably, the Presbyterian church as the "Established Kirk of Scotland" in 1690). And only much later, in particular in some of the American states, did "establishment" connote state support for *multiple* sects, irrespective of their power over education of the young.

Religious establishment in its original sense came to be fervently embraced in the seventeenth century by English advocates of the divine right of kings, like Sir Robert Filmer; but it received an earlier and much more sober and profound justification in the Elizabethan masterpiece of theology and political theory, Richard Hooker's *Laws of Ecclesiastical Polity* (1594). Hooker, a disciple of Thomas Aquinas, transplanted the Thomistic synthesis of biblical and Aristotelian political theory into the Anglican communion.[18] Hooker supported, with fervor but also with some melancholy, the newly established national church as the best means of saving sensible Christian piety and Aristotelian politics in a dire age "full of tongue and weak of brain." He saw piety, education, and civic spirit mortally threatened, and not only by Roman Catholicism. There was in addition the poor morale, waning faith, and moral laxity poisoning the clergy and the laity within the Church of England itself. Still graver, in some respects, was the danger in the Calvinist or Presbyterian reaction, for in Hooker's eyes, much of this reformist zeal represented a lurch toward fanatic biblical theocracy and moralism, insufficiently advised and checked by reason and respect for tradition. Last, and in a way most sinister of all, Hooker discerned in the spiritual underbrush around him the growth of a new, sophisticated atheism, eager to take advantage of the disarray within Christendom caused by the Reformation. The great fountainhead of the new atheism was that "wise malignant," Machiavelli, who taught that all religion ought to be conceived as a manmade instrument of political education or indoctrination that could be used to work on the people's fears in order to make them more law-abiding and pliant in the hands of their "wiser" atheist rulers.

Hooker argues that a state-sponsored religion is necessary for good government because good government requires just men in office. Justice requires the devotion of the individual to the common good; justice, especially among public officials, policemen, and soldiers, demands transcendence, and sometimes even sacrifice, of self-interest. The experience of the centuries teaches that, apart from a heroic or saintly few, officials and citizens cannot be relied upon to overcome self-interest unless they believe the command to do so is divinely sanctioned, unless they see office as a sacred trust. Yet experience also shows that no religion will long endure if it cannot be believed in as the *true* religion—and believed in by the highest authorities and rulers, not just by the "ignorant" masses. One may, in Machiavellian fashion, hoodwink the common people, but the "ignorant" masses—who, Hooker insists, are not so ignorant as the Machiavellians suppose—will not remain hoodwinked for very long. Hooker therefore dismisses as "a strange kind of madness" the Machiavellians' attempt to treat religion as merely a useful tool in the hands of unbelieving but shrewd leaders.

Christianity, then, is uniquely beneficial to political life above all because it is the true religion, the only religion which requires no lies. In addition, since it was not invented by men for worldly purposes, Christianity is not a mercenary religion, and the civic virtues it supports and inspires are not merely utilitarian. This indeed is one great testimony to the truth of Christianity: Christianity is the only faith that adequately responds to the human soul's deepest moral and spiritual longing—for a meaning, task, and destiny that cannot be reduced to mundane calculation of interest.

A just society, Hooker argues, is sincerely and actively concerned not simply with the material but primarily with the spiritual welfare of its citizens; and the welfare of the spirit means the eternal salvation of the soul through Christian repentance and love. A politics that fails to make such redemption its highest priority is neglecting the genuine well-being of its citizenry. In the final analysis, such a politics is one of indifference rather than of love, of collective selfishness rather than of fraternal justice.

On the other side, establishment of religion is essential to the health of religion itself. If Christianity is to maintain its moral force, a world dominated by economic and political might, the church must have solid economic and legal buttresses. If Christian belief is to be honored by all and successfully implanted in the young, it must be exemplified in the most honored public officials and instilled through public as well as private education. Moreover, adults are not so different from youths when it comes to what imbues them with a sense of respect: they will reliably respect and obey only that authority whose word is backed up by the capacity to coerce.

Last but not least, if priests and bishops are to be truly pious, then they must be men of good works, and politics is the place for the doing of good works. No doubt bishops and lower clergy need to enter the political arena with a special sense of caution. They must be wary of the vices of ambition that have corroded Roman Catholicism. Yet the higher episcopacy should aim at attaining an economic wealth and political preeminence that makes them the highest estate of the realm, in the first rank of the nobility. In the House of Lords, the bishops should play an active part in maintaining the balance of power between monarch and Parliament, Commons and Lords. The clergy should conceive itself to be the conscience of society, and bishops should make that conscience vocal, especially in the realm of education and educational policy. Ecclesiastical courts, governed by canon law, should retain and defend their full traditional jurisdiction. Dissenting views based on the Scriptures are to be tolerated but not encouraged. Heretical views that deny the Trinity, Creation, Providence, Resurrection, or Heaven and Hell are to be actively discouraged. As for idolatry and atheism, they are to be ruthlessly rooted out.

One may well wonder whether the Church of England, from its inception in the machinations of Henry VIII and Thomas Cromwell, was not inspired as much by a Machiavellian as by a Hookerian spirit. Certainly many of the philosophers of the subsequent century who spoke for, as well as those who spoke against, the establishment of religion on the English model reflected an outlook expressed most bluntly by John Locke in his *Letter Concerning Toleration*:

> The commonwealth seems to me to be a society of men constituted solely for the preservation and advancing of civil goods. Civil goods I call life, liberty, the integrity and freedom from pain of the body, and the possession of external things, such as estate, money, furniture, and so forth. . . . in truth the whole jurisdiction of the magistrate reaches only to these civil goods, and all civil power, right, and dominion terminates in and is limited to the care and promotion of these things alone.[19]

Those Enlightenment philosophers (such as Montesquieu, David Hume, William Blackstone, and Adam Smith)[20] who praised the English religious establishment tended to do so on the grounds that this establishment made the dominant religion in England tepid, worldly, and undogmatic; at the same time, it tolerated Catholicism and the more fervent Protestant sects, while leaving them under disadvantages that kept them small and fragmented. In other words, the establishment of religion was viewed as a way to soften the dominant religiosity while channeling into harmless rivulets those geysers of religious enthusiasm that inevitably erupt in the populace from time to time.

None of this is meant to deny that there were many fervently pious Anglicans, in America as in old England. But the relative dearth of any educational inspiration or concern arising from Anglicanism in the New World seems to lend some credence to Montesquieu's and Hume's suggestions as to the most widespread consequence of this type of established religion. In those southern states like Virginia where orthodox Anglicanism was strongest, there was little in the way of public or private schooling. The rural dispersion of the population in the South does not by itself explain the relative silence on educational policy, especially in comparison with New England. Indeed, the pattern of settlement of New England—in compact villages rather than scattered farms—was a deliberate decision taken in order to create close-knit communities of educated Christians. The concern or lack of concern with education was as much a cause as it was an effect of the varying patterns of settlement in colonial America.

On the other hand, those rare Anglican political thinkers who did articulate passionate defenses of their religion and its educational mission spelled out a vision of politics, society, and religion that was far too intimately interwoven with European aristocracy to be congenial to the temper of the new American people. The greatest example at the time of the Founding is Edmund Burke, the eloquent friend of the American revolutionaries.

Stung into action by the French Revolution and its assault on traditional religious institutions linked to the crown and the aristocracy, Burke issued a ringing defense of the Church of England. Like Hooker, Burke anchored the case for established religion in the classical republican tradition. But unlike Hooker, Burke stressed the benefits of establishment to political life much more than the benefits to ecclesiastical and contemplative life. Burke also went well beyond both the classical and the Christian traditions in striving to show the harmony between the established religion and the modern preoccupations with economic growth and individual liberty.[21]

Established religion, Burke argues, has an especially important role to play in an age and in a regime grounded on popular sovereignty. For such a religious institution is the surest and sanest check on the inevitable proclivity of the people to neglect its long-range responsibilities to future generations and, worst of all, to fall prey to the delusion that a people or a majority has the moral right to do as it pleases. Only an educational system guided by a deeply rooted church and staffed by clergymen can be relied upon to insist that the people recall all that it owes to the future and all that it has to learn from a study of the past. Religious establishment is the most reliable source of habits of deference—deference to high moral principle, to venerable traditions, and to men of superior moral and intellectual virtue. At the same time, religious establishment is the most certain way to instill in the more powerful few a sense of their obligations and ultimately humble origins.[22]

This line of argument lays down a plausible and perhaps compelling ground for religious establishment in a mixed or limited monarchy such as the English system. But as Thomas Paine insisted in *The Rights of Man*, his famous reply to Burke, the views here summarized fail to comport with the principles of equality, toleration, and liberation from traditional authority, which Americans believed they had fought for in their Revolution. Besides, the loyalty to the Crown of the Anglican clergy and many of the laity during the Revolution left the Anglican church under a cloud of suspicion. Although at the time of the Founding many Americans remained members of the Anglican communion (two-thirds of the delegates to the Constitutional Convention were at least nominally Episcopalians), Americans found in that allegiance little that could illuminate their educational reflections.

The Puritans

Altogether different was the status and significance, for the Founding generation, of the educational heritage derived from the Calvinist wing of the Church of England. Under Cromwell, "Puritanism"[23] had proved its capacity to overthrow traditional monarchy, aristocracy, and church hierarchy—purging educational establishments, especially the universities, in the process. But the Puritans' positive, alternative vision of civic life and education remained ambiguous, particularly in regard to the question of the status of republicanism and the meaning of citizenship. Nothing testifies more vividly to this ambiguity than the remarkable blend of devotion to individual liberation, egalitarianism, and repressive authoritarianism that characterizes the careers of both Oliver Cromwell and John Winthrop—respectively the greatest of the English and American Puritan leaders.[24]

Calvinism called on every individual conscience to struggle, in awareness of the miserable equality of all sinful men before God and under the guidance afforded by constant study of the Scriptures, for inner signs of God's predestined and unmerited election; and then to exemplify that election through energetic sanctification of the world in public service and laborious vocation. This call dictated an unprecedented concern for education of oneself and one's brethren. As many as possible must become both literate and also trained in some calling, while a few must be afforded the leisure and erudition that would enable them to lead the rest through the intricacies of the sacred word and the thicket of worldly temptations. Accordingly, the first New England colonists had barely settled before they began to establish public schools, and Harvard College was founded within a decade of the establishment of Massachusetts Bay Colony. The curricula of these institutions were by no means limited to biblical or theological studies. Classical languages and literature were judged essential to an informed reading of the Bible and an intelligent judgment of the world.[25]

Yet the distinctive character of this Calvinist emphasis on education indicates the new foundation for hierarchy and exclusivity. Illumination by faith sets apart the tiny societies of the chosen from the vast unregenerate majority of mankind. Within the company of the chosen, learning and special grace distinguish a God-given elite, which is authorized and obliged to lay down coercive moral and religious legislation.[26] No one has captured so well as Ernst Troeltsch the paradox of Calvinism as a social-historical force: its combination of a profoundly pre- or even antimodern central teaching with a capacity to fuel the most vigorous modern social action.

> The Calvinist is filled with a deep consciousness of his own value as a person, with the high sense of a Divine mission to the world, of being mercifully privileged among thousands, and in possession of an immeasurable responsibility. This idea of personality, however, which arises out of the idea of predestination, must not be confused with modern individualistic and democratic ideas. Predestination means that the minority, consisting of the best and the holiest souls, is called to bear rule over the majority of mankind, who are sinners.

Writing in 1911, Troeltsch goes on to observe that "down to the present day, the peculiar nature" of the Calvinist conception of community

> stamps the life of the Calvinistic peoples with a unique emphasis on the cultivation of independent personality, which leads to a power of initiative and a sense of responsibility for action, combined with a very strong sense of unity for common, positive ends and values, which are invulnerable on account of their religious character. This explains the fact that all Calvinistic peoples are characterized by individualism and democracy, combined with a strong bias towards authority and a sense of the unchangeable nature of law. . . . the Divine Ruler of the world has ordained that some

should serve, and some should rule, as part of the essence of human life, and not as a result of the Fall.[27]

As Michael Walzer has shown, the English Puritans, in contrast to the continental (especially Huguenot) Calvinists, forged a powerful revolutionary ethos and organization. The key features of what Walzer calls the "revolution of the saints" included "a well-disciplined citizens' army in which representative councils arose and 'agitators' lectured or preached to the troops, teaching even privates to reflect upon political issues"; the writing and rewriting of constitutions; "the public presentation of whole sets of clamorous demands, many of them from previously passive and nonpolitical men," for the reorganization of church, state, and educational system; "the formation of groups specifically and deliberately designed to implement these demands, groups based on the principle of voluntary association"; the emergence of a popular and vigorous political journalism; and "above all, the sharp, insistent awareness of the need for and possibility of *reform*."[28] This revolutionary politics, carried to New England and mitigated and modified over several generations, played an incalculable part in the evolution of the American spirit of stubborn opposition and eventually independence. And yet the mitigations and modifications are at least as important as the original Puritan ethos in the shaping of the distinctive conception of republican politics and citizenship that underlies the American Constitution.

The classic American Puritan statement on democracy and the relations between church and state is that of John Cotton—whose "many writings on church polity were," in Perry Miller's words, "looked upon both in New England and in England as the standard expositions of the Congregational system."

> It is better that the commonwealth be fashioned to the setting forth of Gods house, which is the church: than to accommodate the church frame to the civill state. Democracy, I do not conceyve that ever God did ordeyne as a fitt government eyther for church or commonwealth. If the people be governors, who shall be governed? As for monarchy, and aristocracy, they are both of them clearly approved, and directed in scripture, yet so as referreth the soveraigntie to himselfe, and setteth up Theocracy in both, as the best forme of government in the commonwealth, as well as in the church.[29]

On the voyage to New England in 1630, John Winthrop preached a sermon on charity in which he reminded his fellow refugees that "God almightie in his most holy and wise providence hath soe disposed of the Condicion of mankinde, as in all times some must be rich some poore, some highe and emi-

nent in power and dignitie; others mean and in subiection."[30] The same principle was reiterated in a broader framework a half century later by William Hubbard, one of the most venerated ministers in the colony:

> It suited the wisdom of the infinite and omnipotent Creator, to make the
> world of differing parts, which necessarily supposes that there must be dif-
> fering places, for those differing things to be disposed into, which is Order.
> The like is necessary to be observed in the rational and political World,
> where persons of differing endowments and qualifications need differing
> stations to be disposed into, the keeping of which, is both the beauty and
> strength of such a society. . . . are not some advanced as high above others
> in dignity and power, as much as the cedars of Lebanon the low shrubs of
> the valley? It is not then the result of time or chance, that some are
> mounted on horseback, while others are left to travel on foot. . . . Is it not
> found by experience, that the greatest part of mankind, are but as tools and
> Instruments for others to work by, rather than any proper Agents to effect
> any thing of themselves . . . ? Nothing therefore can be imagined more re-
> mote either from right reason, or true religion, than to think that because
> we were all once equal at our birth, and shall be again at our death, there-
> fore we should be so in the whole course of our lives.[31]

For the Puritans, to be sure, government rests on consent, on a compact between rulers and ruled that echoes the covenant between God and man. Yet just
as God's covenant does not for a moment imply his political or moral equality
with man, so the consent of the ruled in politics is their acknowledgment of
their superiors in Christian virtue and wisdom. This, as Winthrop explains in
one of his most solemn and public articulations of Puritan political theory, is
"civil or federal liberty," in contrast to that "natural corrupt liberty," which so
far from entailing any natural right, "makes men grow more evil, and in time to
be worse than brute beasts."[32] Government, in this perspective, is not conceived
as "representative" of the people but as ruling over the people; and the giving of
unanimous consent does not imply the moral hegemony of majority rule. Well
into the eighteenth century, even the relatively liberal (and unusually Aristotelian) Puritan divine John Barnard rejected majoritarianism and described the
end of government in these terms:

> If the Good of the Subject, considered as distinct from that of the Ruler,
> were the End of Government, what would the Consequence of this be, but
> Anarchy, wild Disorder, and universal Confusion? Which would be as de-
> structive to Government as the hottest Tyranny could be. For the civil
> Rulers of a People have not only their Interests in many respects, twisted to-

gether with the Subjects, but some things which belong to them, in a peculiar Manner, as Rulers, which are very essential to the Support of Government; I mean, their distinguishing Honour, their Authority and Power, their more special Security, and the like.[33]

John Winthrop characteristically draws a parallel between the rule of magistrate over consenting subject and the rule of husband over consenting wife: "the woman's own choice makes such a man her husband; yet being so chosen, he is her lord, and she is to be subject to him, yet in a way of liberty, not of bondage; and a true wife accounts her subjection her honor and freedom." Still, the Puritans hesitate to ground patriarchal authority, in family or state, on simply natural excellence or preeminence. For fallen man, it is not so much natural superiority as it is God-given grace and inspiration (and terror) that truly and adequately distinguish, among the equally miserable sinners, those qualified to assume the responsibilities of office and education in home and society. As Winthrop asserts, "Noe man is made more honourable then another or more wealthy etc., out of any particular and singular respect to himselfe but for the glory of his Creator and the Common good of the Creature, Man; Therefore God still reserues the propperty of these guifts to himselfe."[34]

It is not surprising, then, that the legislative, coercive promotion of education and conduct in accordance with the true faith is seen as perhaps the highest duty of the magistrate. Warning "Anabaptists and other Enthusiasts" "to keep away from us," Nathaniel Ward proclaims in 1647 that "God doth no where in his word tolerate Christian States, to give Tolerations to such adversaries of his truth, if they have power in their hands to suppresse them." The sufferance of false religion is "far worse" than the persecution of true religion, since persecution strengthens faith while toleration saps it. Toleration is inevitably accompanied by doubt and religious insincerity, by the preference for comfort and peace and ageeableness over truth, salvation, and dedication. "It is almost pathetic," Perry Miller remarks, "to trace the puzzlement of New England leaders at the end of the seventeenth century, when the idea of toleration was becoming more and more respectable in European thought. They could hardly understand what was happening in the world." For example, he reports, when Massachusetts Bay was criticized by Anabaptists in 1681 for its policy of intolerance, on the grounds that intolerance was a departure from the faith of the Puritan fathers who fled persecution in England, Samuel Willard, pastor of Old South Church in Boston, wrote of the critics, "I perceive that they are mistaken in the design of our first Planters, whose business was not Toleration; but were professed Enemies of it."[35]

As late as 1745, Yale College appealed to the view that Christian charity prohibits toleration of religious diversity as the basis for expelling two students who had, while at home on vacation and in the company of their parents, attended Separatist religious services.

There's scarce any thing more fully and strictly Enjoin'd in the Gospel than Charity, Peace, and Unity among Christians; and scarce any thing more plainly and frequently forbidden than Divisions, Schisms and Separations; And therefore nothing can justifie a Division or Separation, but only some plain and express Direction in the Word of God; which must be understood as a particular exception from the general Rule. . . .

Whereupon it is Considered and Adjudged by the *Rector* and *Tutors*, That the said *John* and *Ebenezer Cleaveland*, in Withdrawing and Separating from the publick Worship of God, and Attending upon the Preaching of a Lay-Exhorter, as aforesaid, have acted contrary to the Rules of the Gospel, the Laws of this Colony and of the College; and that the said *Cleavelands* shall be publickly Admonished for their Faults, aforesaid; And if they continue to Justifie themselves and refuse to make an Acknowledgement they shall be Expelled.

And since the principal End and Design of Erecting this College (as declared in the Charter) was, *To Train up a Succession of Learned and Orthodox Ministers*, by whose Instruction and Example people might be directed in the ways of Religion and good Order; therefore to Educate persons whose principles and practices are directly Subversive of the Visible Church of Christ, would be contrary to the Original Design of Erecting this Society. And we conceive that it would be a Contradiction in the Civil Government, to Support a College to Educate Students to trample upon their own Laws, and brake up the Churches which they Establish and Protect.[36]

The keynote of Puritan life and education was discipline, in government, in the family, and in labor at one's vocation. The natural consequence for Puritan economics was an unprecedented honor ascribed to work and a considerable rise in prosperity. But here again it is a far cry from Puritan industriousness to the commercial and eventually capitalist outlook that was to characterize the political economy of the new American nation. Calvin and his faithful American followers were as severe in their condemnation of lending money at interest ("usury") as had been the medieval scholastics. Lawyers, as Miller says, "were held in contempt," and merchants were viewed with suspicion. Devotion to the accumulation of material wealth beyond a modest competence was condemned as sinful: "It was not intended that work should bring wealth; the ministers had little sense of the possibility of rapid increases in productivity. Instinctively, they tended toward a kind of economic restrictionism. Men should be content, [the

Puritan divine William] Perkins wrote, 'if they have as much as will provide them food and raiment, and thus much lawfully may they seek.' "[37]

In education, as we have noted, the Puritans looked to classical literature and to the models there presented as well as to the biblical tradition; but here too a powerful hesitation is evident. The discipline, devotion, Stoicism, public spirit, and strict censorship found in the classical city met with strong approval among the Puritans. But the heathenism, pride, and unqualified exaltation of political and merely moral or philosophic virtue tended to be viewed with grave reserve. It was often the perceived republican or even democratic tendencies of classical political philosophy that awakened unease. In Milton's *Paradise Lost*, the classical civic and philosophic virtues are most conspicuous among the fallen angels in Hell, and it is Satan who delivers the great speech appealing to equality and liberty, while the angels Raphael and Abdiel preach obedience.[38] In 1641 Nathaniel Ward gave an election sermon that caused something of a stir, for reasons that become evident in Jonathan Winthrop's account:

> In his sermon he delivered many useful things, but in a moral and political discourse, grounding his propositions much upon the old Roman and Grecian governments, which sure is an error. . . . Among other things, he advised the people to keep all their magistrates in an equal rank, and not give more honor or power to one than to another, which is easier to advise than to prove, seeing it is against the practice of Israel.[39]

Once we recognize how great a distance separates the Puritan ethos from that of the American Founding, we are prepared to understand why some of the New England leaders of the Revolution and Founding felt compelled to declare their independence not only from England but from the Puritan legacy. Nevertheless, it seems too much to claim, as does Rush Welter, that "the purposes and practices of colonial education stand historically as a kind of false start from which it was necessary to turn away before education could become a key principle of the American democratic faith."[40] This judgment overlooks, in the first place, what Bernard Bailyn and Samuel Morison stress: the importance, for subsequent American history, of the Puritan commitment to public schooling, which Bailyn describes as "in the context of the age . . . astonishing" and Morison calls "truly extraordinary."[41] Welter also disregards the significance of Puritan discipline for the formation of the private and public habits of industry and service presupposed by a commercial republic. Above all, his assessment fails to take into account the complex development by which original Puritan preaching and teaching were transmogrified in the course of the eighteenth century.

In the eighteenth century, Perry Miller writes, as the original doctrine "ceased to arouse their loyalties," the people "went seeking after gods that were utterly strange to Puritanism." But this search was in some measure led and inspired by Puritan divines. The crucial transformation in Puritan preaching surfaces most clearly in the otherwise rather obscure figure John Wise. As Miller points out, Wise's *Vindication of the Government of New-England Churches* (1717), with its appeal to the authority of Hobbes's student Samuel Pufendorf, embodies nothing less than a "real revolution in thought" regarding the relation between reason and revelation, natural and divine law, rulers and ruled, and society altogether.[42]

Discourses such as Wise's set the stage for the enormous civic educational impact of Protestant preachers in the generations leading up to the Revolution. These preachers sowed some of the most potent seeds of the Revolution by propagating among the masses Lockean natural religion and natural rights. In doing so, admittedly, they allowed traditional Christian doctrine to be reshaped by a new philosophic rationalism and secular republicanism. Some drifted far and fast from the traditional subordination of reason and republicanism to biblically based authority. But others succeeded, at least for a time, in integrating revolutionary principles of freedom into authentically biblical doctrines, thus tempering and elevating pure Lockean republicanism. If in the long run they were more co-opted than co-opting, they left nevertheless an indelible and vital tincture on American popular culture and self-consciousness.[43]

Rush Welter's major error, however, is one that is all too common in our time, and that hence deserves more searching scrutiny. The error consists in assimilating the "American democratic faith" to an outlook that remained foreign to Americans (and, for that matter, to all great democratic societies) until the late nineteenth century: namely, the view that democracy entails unrestricted "social leveling" and the jettisoning of all habitual obedience to authority. Adopting so narrowly egalitarian and libertarian a notion of the "American democratic faith" inevitably leads Welter to reject even the Founders' educational ideas as alien to this anachronistic standard.

> Early republican commitments to education were limited in other senses that are particularly striking to anyone who expects to discover a democratic orientation in the founding fathers' demands for a universal dissemination of knowledge. . . . many of the national plans for education emphasized the importance of instruction in common obligations to government and to the established institutions of society. Within the areas to which common agreement limited government, an informed obedience on the part of the people was at least as important as their particular freedoms.[44]

If, contrary to Welter, we avoid the pitfalls of simplistic notions of democratic liberty and equality and instead keep clearly in sight the healthy, organic relation between effective democratic republicanism and both "common obligations" and "informed obedience" to law, we will preserve a more balanced understanding of the continuing, though over time steadily diminishing, contribution of the Puritan educational heritage to the "American democratic faith." Writing to John Adams in the fall of 1790, Samuel Adams laments the sorry history of human liberty, or the lack thereof. With a view to the present and future of liberty in America, he asks rhetorically:

> What then is to be done?—Let Divines, and Philosophers, Statesmen and Patriots unite their endeavours to renovate the Age, by impressing the Minds of Men with the importance of educating their *little boys*, and *girls*— of inculcating in the Minds of youth the fear, and Love of the Deity, and universal Phylanthropy; and in subordination to these great principles, the Love of their Country—of instructing them in the Art of *self* government, without which they never can act a wise part in the Government of Societys great, or small—in short of leading them in the study, and practice of the exalted Virtues of the Christian system, which will happily tend to subdue the turbulent passions of Men, and introduce that Golden Age beautifully described in figurative language.[45]

Six weeks later, in response to John Adams's favorable response to this letter, Samuel Adams continues:

> Should we not, my friend, bear a gratefull remembrance of our pious and benevolent Ancestors, who early laid plans of Education; by which means Wisdom, Knowledge, and Virtue have been generally diffused among the body of the people, and they have been enabled to form and establish a civil constitution calculated for the preservation of their rights, and liberties?

To be sure, Adams then introduces a new chord:

> This Constitution was evidently founded in the expectation of the further progress, and "extraordinary degrees" of virtue. . . . It is allowed, that the present age is more enlightened than former ones. Freedom of enquiry is certainly more encouraged: The feelings of humanity have soft'ned the heart: The true principles of civil, and religious Liberty are better understood.[46]

Samuel Adams thus limns one of the greatest puzzles of educational thought in the Founding period: to what extent and in what ways were traditional—especially traditional religious—educational ideals to be integrated constructively into the new republican regime?

Benjamin Rush's Christian Republican Education

The ambivalence of thoughtful Americans of the Founding period towards traditional Christian education is nowhere more vividly expressed than in the capacious if somewhat incoherent ruminations of Benjamin Rush. In his essay, "The Bible as a School-Book," Rush argues that all children should be steeped in biblical readings from the earliest possible moment. Insisting that prejudice and habit are all-important in forming the opinions of men, Rush contends that the Bible is a precious reservoir of morally sound opinion, and he stresses that those who do not read the Bible in their youth probably never will. As he puts it in his "Thoughts upon the Mode of Education Proper in a Republic":

> The first impressions upon the mind are the most durable. They survive the wreck of the memory and exist in old age after the ideas acquired in middle life have been obliterated. Of how much consequence then must it be to the human mind in the evening of life to be able to recall those ideas which are most essential to its happiness, and these are to be found chiefly in the Bible.[47]

Yet Rush is on the defensive, gripped by the fear that Christianity is losing its hold on American hearts. He comes to the aid of the flagging faith with every argument he can muster, emphasizing in particular the social utility of the biblical teachings. "If the Bible," he insists, "did not convey a single direction for the attainment of future happiness, it should be read in our schools in preference to all other books, from its containing the greatest portion of that kind of knowledge which is calculated to produce private and public temporal happiness." Rush attacks the deists for weakening religion and paving the way to agnosticism, and he complains that "they have rendered instruction in the principles of Christianity by the pulpit and the press, so unfashionable, that little good for many years seems to have been done by either of them." In speaking of the deists' attempts to get the Bible out of the schools, he warns that "if they proceed in it, they will do more in half a century, in extirpating our religion, than Bolingbroke or Voltaire could have effected in a thousand years." He consoles himself with the rather gloomy hope that teaching the Bible in Sunday schools "will give our religion (humanly speaking) the chance of a longer life in our country."[48]

Simultaneously, however, Rush endorses the very enlightenment spirit, the very love of progress and innovation and skeptical thinking, that has allowed Deism to flourish. Indeed, in contrast to the pessimism just cited, he sometimes expresses hope that scientific investigation will lend new support to the authority of the Bible: "The time, I have no doubt, will come, when posterity will view and pity our ignorance of these truths [of the Bible], as much as we do the ignorance of the disciples of our savior, who knew nothing of the meaning of those plain passages in the Old Testament which were daily fulfilling before their eyes."[49] Most strikingly, Rush so confidently takes the side of independent, critical thinking against the stultifying hold of "traditional error" that he expresses a wish to see schools established to teach "the art of forgetting"—an art whose first students ought to be America's teachers, legislators, and ministers. Rush cannot quite make up his mind. Convinced of the truth and goodness of Christian faith, he wants it to be taught by traditional authority—and wants to free men from the shackles of traditional authority at one and the same time.

But it would be oversimplifying to portray Rush as content with a simply Christian education, for he is keenly aware that such a program is quite inadequate to prepare Americans for their new political role as republican citizens. For this preeminent task of civic education, Rush insists, guidance has to be sought in an altogether different historical quarter.

2 · Classical Republican Educational Ideals

To find models of educational systems whose direct and unambiguous goal was the fostering of republican citizenship, many Americans in the Founding era turned back to the republics of antiquity and to the educational writings of the classical republican theorists. No one was more conspicuous in this respect than Benjamin Rush, and no one spoke as emphatically as Rush did about the need for Americans to use the lever of classical republican educational thought to break the chains of colonial ways of thinking about education. In 1786 Rush published a proposal outlining a new, republican system of education for his state of Pennsylvania, and appended his general reflections on education in America, framed as a message to his fellow citizens in all thirteen states.

After calling upon Americans to undertake a self-critical uprooting of their previous habits in education, Rush proceeds boldly to declare that, as regards the great task of instilling a distinctively republican patriotism in the youth, "the policy of the Lacedamonians is well worthy of our imitation." More specifically, Rush suggests:

> Let our pupil be taught that he does not belong to himself, but that he is public property. Let him be taught to love his family, but let him be taught at the same time that he must forsake and even forget them when the welfare of his country requires it.
>
> He must watch for the state as if its liberties depended upon his vigilance alone. . . . These are practicable lessons, and the history of the commonwealths of Greece and Rome show that human nature, without the aids of Christianity, has attained these degrees of perfection.[1]

The example of the Spartan institution is to apply in physical education as well:

To assist in rendering religious, moral, and political instruction more effectual upon the minds of our youth, it will be necessary to subject their bodies to physical discipline. To obviate the inconveniences of their studious and sedentary mode of life, they should live upon a temperate diet, consisting chiefly of broths, milk, and vegetables. The black broth of Sparta and the barley broth of Scotland have been alike celebrated for their beneficial effects upon the minds of young people. They should avoid tasting spiritous liquors. They should also be accustomed occasionally to work with their hands in the intervals of study and in the busy seasons of the year in the country. Moderate sleep, silence, occasional solitude, and cleanliness should be inculcated upon them, and the utmost advantage should be taken of a proper direction of those great principles of human conduct—sensibility, habit, imitation, and association.

Regarding the demeanor of teachers, Rush goes beyond even Spartan discipline.

In the education of youth, let the authority of our masters be as *absolute* as possible. The government of schools like the government of private families should be *arbitrary*, that it may not be *severe*. By this mode of education, we prepare our youth for the subordination of laws and thereby qualify them for becoming good citizens of the republic. I am satisfied that the most useful citizens have been formed from those youth who have never known or felt their own wills till they were one and twenty years of age, and I have often thought that society owes a great deal of its order and happiness to the deficiencies of parental government being supplied by those habits of obedience and subordination which are contracted at schools.

Naturally, military training will be emphasized in any such republican educational program: "In a state where every citizen is liable to be a soldier and a legislator, it will be necessary to have some regular instruction given upon the ART OF WAR and upon PRACTICAL LEGISLATION. These branches of knowledge are of too much importance in a republic to be trusted to solitary study or to a fortuitous acquaintance with books."[2]

Yet this extraordinary celebration of Spartan self-sacrifice is far from being Rush's last word on the nature of the education required in the American states. Insofar as he does give way here to an almost febrile enthusiasm for classical educational principles, Rush goes well beyond most or all of the other Founders who voiced their views on education.[3] Indeed, when examined more closely, not only in comparison with other pronouncements of the time but even with an eye to internal consistency, Rush's essay begins to appear somewhat bizarre. For the essay's invocation of Spartan discipline and sacrifice appears hand in hand with a call for education in precisely those sorts of habits, preoccupations, and studies which the Spartan and other similar classical systems regarded as virulent germs of corruption: commercialism, consumerism, the accumulation of private wealth, and progressive scientific investigation leading to theological criticism as well as to technological innovation in the machines of war and peace.

Immediately after invoking the Spartan model, Rush adds that the youth he has in mind "must be taught to amass wealth"—although "it must be only to increase his power of contributing to the wants and demands of the state." The student, Rush continues, "must be indulged occasionally in amusements, but he must be taught that study and business should be his principal pursuits in life." "Above all," Rush proclaims in his curious fashion, the student must learn to "love life and endeavor to acquire as many of its conveniences as possible by industry and economy"—always with the proviso that the student is to be "taught that this life 'is not his own' when the safety of his country requires it." "In a state which boasts of the first commercial city in America," Rush declares, "I wish to see [knowledge of our language] cultivated by young men who are intended for the counting house, for many such, I hope, will be educated in our colleges. The time is past when an academical education was thought to be unnecessary to qualify a young man for merchandise." "I wish likewise," he adds,

> to see the numerous facts that relate to the origin and present state of COMMERCE, together with the nature and principles of MONEY, reduced to such a system as to be intelligible and agreeable to a young man. If we consider the commerce of our metropolis only as the avenue of the wealth of the state, the study of it merits a place in a young man's education, but, I consider commerce in a much higher light when I recommend the study of it in republican seminaries.[4]

The more closely it is considered, the more Rush's essay will be found to exhibit an all-too-common syncretistic turn of mind: a hopefulness that deeply discordant but attractive principles and ways of life can somehow be combined in a synthetic mixture that will preserve all their appealing features while washing out the unappealing.

Other prominent Americans sometimes evinced milder versions of this rather incoherent embrace of antiquity. Rush's essay is reminiscent of the vision adumbrated by Samuel Adams in his famous if puzzling aspiration to a "Christian Sparta" as the hoped-for future destiny of Boston after the Revolution.[5] But by and large the more thoughtful commentators in the 1780s and 1790s were impressed by the gulf that separated America from Sparta or republican Rome. Their admiration for the civic virtues of antiquity was therefore controlled by a keener sense than Rush seemed to possess of the distance between their situation and that of the classical lawgivers. Even while expressing deep regard for the Stoic virtues, the Founders were more likely to exhibit great classical learning than severe manners and morals. They could more easily imagine themselves at home with Plutarch than with Lycurgus or the Spartan hoplites honored by Plutarch. The Founders sympathized most with those classical authors—the prosaic more often than the poetic, the historians and orators more often than the philosophers—who looked back with admiration to the glories of an austere republican life but who themselves lived in "soft," more "civilized" societies. The Founders accordingly sought in practice a much-relaxed version of classical civic virtue. Few Americans were as self-conscious or frank as Samuel Knox, but he formulates the more general attitude toward the classics with an ingenuous clarity.

So circumscribed was the state of literature in those times and such the circumstances of those commonwealths that their plans of education were rather military schools preparing them for the camp, either for self-defense or for butchering the human species, than seminaries suited to literary acquisition, the conduct of life, or the improvement of the human mind.

This observation, however, extends no farther than as it applies to institutions of national education and is by no means considered as applicable to the schools of the philosophers or of many celebrated orators, grammarians, and rhetoricians of the ancient world.[6]

But Knox is too complacent. The difficulty in an attitude such as his is this: how can one genuinely follow or respect the political judgment and moral taste of the classical educators like Isocrates, yet shrink from their explicit and emphatic political and moral preferences—for Sparta over Athens (or for old, taciturn Athens over new, talky Athens), for selfless austerity and piety over sophisticated enlightenment? It is one great merit of Benjamin Rush's essay that it compels us to confront this problem. As we read and reflect on Rush, we are forced to recognize that the Americans' admiration for classical republicanism was not merely ornamental. Rush's essay may be bizarre, but in its moral and political seriousness—in the earnestness with which it looks to the classics, through searching if not always welcoming eyes—Rush's discussion brings to the fore the most important dimension of the Founders' concern with classical texts and authors. The Founding generation's posture toward the classical republican tradition mingles real respect and some serious attachment with criticism so severe as to suggest a sense of alienation. The most reflective of the Founders take the classics too seriously, and struggle with them too intensely, to have regarded them simply from an "aesthetic" point of view.

Our first task must be to clarify the precise character of this complex, uneasy blend of kinship and antagonism between the principles of American and classical republicanism. To do so, we need to examine briefly the relationship between the theory of classical republicanism and the new, competing republican theory that arose in the centuries immediately preceding the American Founding—the theory that captivated and "corrupted" the originally Puritan spirit of New England. Then, on the basis of this contrast, we will try to attain a more vivid understanding of the educational implications of these two antagonistic conceptions of republicanism.

Modern in Contrast to Classical Republicanism

At first sight, the disagreements between the American and the classical republicans appear to be over means rather than ends, for the goals of all republican government seem obvious and indisputable. All republics seek freedom from foreign domination and from internal oppression. Now it suffices to read a few pages of Thucydides or Aristotle to note that the massive threat to freedom and security in the classical republic was the prevalence of selfish, violent, factional conflict, especially between rich and poor. "The friend of popular governments," Madison writes at the start of the tenth *Federalist Paper*, "never finds himself so alarmed for their character and fate as when he contemplates their propensity to this dangerous vice." Are not the discoveries in political science that Madison and Hamilton extol in the *Federalist Papers* new cures for the old republican diseases of factionalism and consequent instability? Let the republic be so large and so diverse, let factions become so numerous, Madison and Hamilton argue, that no faction will be widespread and thus powerful enough to oppress the others. Let tyranny, of the mighty ruler or of the entrenched governmental faction, be prevented through the separation of powers and a system of checks and balances, so that "ambition [may] be made to counteract ambition." Let the people's views be filtered and moderated by representatives elected from diverse constituencies at diverse times, to prevent the passionate excesses of the populace from coalescing in direct, mob democracy goaded on by demagogues.[7]

There is considerable and by no means shallow truth to this assimilation of the ends of the American Founders to the ends of the classical republics. Nevertheless, a closer and more searching analysis reveals how incomplete the truth is that this picture captures. The new "means" the Founders adopt and employ in order to secure good government entail in fact a profound shift—more precisely, a profound constriction—in the very meaning of "good government," growing out of a new conception of the proper ends of civil society.

The philosophers of classical republicanism (Thucydides, Socrates, Plato,

Xenophon, Aristotle, Cicero, etc.) begin not from theories about republics or about human nature but instead from direct observation of republics and of men living as republican citizens. This firsthand experience prompts them to start by trying to conceive human beings as naturally at home, and naturally seeking their fulfillment, not as independent individuals but as participants in and dutiful contributors to the civic community: a community that, to be healthy or fulfilling, must be a small, homogeneous, and fraternal city. Republics, so conceived, necessarily put great demands on all of their citizens, for they require remarkable courage and discipline in their citizen armies, and justice, good judgment, and self-restraint in their councils and assemblies. But, the classics insist, to say that republics strive to foster these virtues as means, in order to survive or even to remain free, is to characterize republicanism too narrowly. Serious republican citizens recognize virtue as one of the chief aims, perhaps *the* chief aim, of civic life. Although they indeed see in virtue a bulwark of safety and freedom, these citizens also see security and liberty as gaining their full dignity in providing the opportunity for the exercise of virtue.

In the seventeenth and eighteenth centuries, this understanding of republican virtue was deeply and decisively challenged in the name of a revolutionary and radically unclassical conception of politics first put forth by Machiavelli and subsequently modified in diverse and competing ways by Hobbes, Spinoza, Locke, Montesquieu, and Hume. It was the teachings of these modern political philosophers that issued in the "liberal" republican or democratic outlook of the American Founders.[8] The new republicans argue that the virtues and the virtuous community extolled by the classical republicans are unreasonable, because such virtues and such community demand a self-transcendence, a sacrifice of material and individual interests, a subordination of commerce and acquisitiveness, that is simply contrary to human nature. Classical civic virtue was inspired and in fact only made tolerable by the ceaselessly belligerent condition of the ancient cities in which that virtue flourished. "Ancient policy was violent, and contrary to the more natural and usual course of things," David Hume argues.

> The Roman and other ancient republics were free states; they were small ones; and the age being martial, all their neighbors were continually in arms. Freedom naturally begets public spirit, especially in small states; and this public spirit, this *amor patriae*, must encrease, when the public is almost in continual alarm, and men are obliged, every moment, to expose themselves to the greatest dangers for its defence. A continual succession of wars makes every citizen a soldier. . . . This service is indeed equivalent to a heavy tax. . . . Now, according to the most natural course of things, industry and arts and trade encrease the power of the sovereign as well as the

happiness of the subjects; and that policy is violent, which aggrandizes the public by the poverty of individuals.

. . . Could we convert a city into a kind of fortified camp, and infuse into each breast so martial a genius, and such a passion for public good, as to make every one willing to undergo the greatest hardships for the sake of the public; these affections might now, as in ancient times, prove alone a sufficient spur to industry, and support the community. It would then be advantageous, as in camps, to banish all arts and luxury; and by restrictions on equipage and tables, make the provisions and forage last longer than if the army were loaded with a number of superfluous retainers. But as these principles are too disinterested and too difficult to support, it is requisite to govern men by other passions, and animate them with a spirit of avarice and industry, art and luxury. . . . The harmony of the whole is still supported; and the natural bent of the mind being more complied with, individuals, as well as the public, find their account in the observance of those maxims.[9]

It was John Locke who articulated most fully the principles of justice and morality underlying this new theory of human nature and of legitimate republican government. Locke's political teaching was transmitted to the Americans in large part directly, through their reading and study of his works, but it also made an impact by way of two of his most eloquent followers—John Trenchard and Thomas Gordon, whose famous journalism, published under the name of *Cato's Letters*, provided a blunt, simplified, and somewhat coarsened version of the key Lockean teachings.[10] The new political doctrine, elaborated most fully in Locke's *Two Treatises of Government*, takes as its foundation the idea of the "State of Nature," or the proposition that human beings are all essentially free and independent beings, equally possessed of inalienable personal freedoms, claims, or "rights" that, it is argued, are implicit in the natural independence of every individual. All obligations, and in particular all civic obligations, are understood to flow from the rational contractual consent of the free and by nature independent individuals seeking to protect and augment their personal interests.

Government (as opposed to individuals and their rights) is therefore held to be artificial, the product of human contrivance. Government finds its only legitimate basis in the consent of the governed and contracting individuals, and it finds its overriding legitimate purpose in securing their rights. The individual rights whose protection thus defines the common good include notably the right to life, or secure self-preservation, as most basic; the right to lawful liberty, or liberty of speech and deed limited only by restrictions necessary to insure the congruent liberties of all; and the right to what Locke taught Americans to call "the pursuit of happiness,"[11] i.e., the liberty of every individual to decide for oneself, within the confines of legitimate law, the ends of life and the good for one's own soul, including especially one's religious vocation or otherworldly destiny and duty. The most reasonable and, within a reasonable society, the most naturally prevalent expression of the pursuit of happiness is the exercise of the right to acquire, produce, and increase property or material possessions without any restraint except law enacted by consent. In the service of all these ends, public policy ought to allow and encourage science and free inquiry—less as ends in themselves than as means to the ever-increasing prosperity, comfort, health, liberty, and safety of society.

With this skeleton of Lockean liberalism in view, we are better able to appreciate the distance that separates the new from the classical republican conception. For Locke, government or politics has no legitimate authority to promote the health or excellence or salvation of men's souls: "The care of the soul belongs to each individual, and it is to be left to each." Or as he said in a rather bold and early (unpublished) work, "Give me leave to say, however strange it may seem, that the law-giver hath nothing to do with moral virtues and vices."[12]

According to classical republicanism, however, "politics" is defined as "the art whose business it is to care for souls."[13] As a result, classical republicanism places far less emphasis on toleration, property rights, commercial growth, and provision for material and technological progress. Yet this is not to say that classical republican theorists are unalive to the charms of such "progressive" hopes, for that would posit a too-simplistic contrast between classical republican theory and the new republican theory that chiefly inspired the Founders. The best antidote to such oversimplification is a perusal of the educational writings of Xenophon, the most obviously radical, or most willing to experiment, of the classical republican educational theorists.

Xenophon presents his sustained reflections on civic education in a work of fiction entitled *The Education of Cyrus*. The novel depicts a conceivable best regime founded on a dynamic leader's liberation of an oppressed poor population. His efforts are directed to the steady elimination of ethnic, religious, class, and even to some extent sexual discrimination, to the creation of a far-reaching equality of opportunity, to the unleashing of unlimited military and economic growth, and finally to the attainment of universal peace and security through large-scale bureaucratic planning, commercialism, and elaborate economic interdependence in a vast and ethnically heterogeneous nation or empire.

Yet while painting, often in glowing colors, the wonderful benefits such a society would bring, especially to the underprivileged and impoverished masses, Xenophon portrays in no less dramatic hues the severe costs, especially to those from all classes who care passionately about human dignity and an education in dignity. In other words, Xenophon never abandons what may be said to be the great positive theme of classical republicanism: the theme of virtue or excellence and its cultivation. Cyrus, the "hero" of Xenophon's novel and the genius who creates the new and liberated society, builds his project on the corruption of the small, austere, inegalitarian republic in which he was born and educated. That republic was dedicated to civic or moral virtue as an end; Cyrus corrupts it in the name of a society that conceives of virtue as a means and that attempts to make prosperity, freedom, and glory its ends. It is the doubt as to the viability, in the long run, of such a ranking of priorities—it is the insistence that a sound political society must base itself on an explicit, shared dedication to nonutilitarian nobility—that is the leitmotif of authentically classical republicanism.

But if we are to understand more precisely the ramifications of the classical dedication to "virtue," if we are thereby to begin to understand the alternative, but still dialectically derivative, notion of civic life that guides the educational thought of the American Founders, we need to penetrate a bit deeper into the theory of classical republicanism. We need above all to try to understand the grounds for the *aristocratic* bent of the classical republican tradition. The preference for aristocracy over democracy, at least in principle, follows from the classical preoccupation with virtue understood as the noble end of political life. For if the healthy republic exists chiefly to foster and give opportunities for the exercise of virtue, then such a republic will seek to give fullest recognition and scope to the activity of those who prove themselves most virtuous. One may go so far as to say that "popular sovereignty," or government understood as deriving its just authority solely from the consent of the governed, is never a doctrine of classical republicanism. Classical republicanism stubbornly insists that there are two necessary but competing sources of legitimacy: consent, and wisdom or virtue. And the latter is the more authoritative of the two.[14]

Still, one cannot leave it at this. For the classical theorists are fully aware of the difficulties involved in trying to identify the few who are truly virtuous or wise and therefore truly deserving of the highest offices and honors. As a result, they readily concede that republican life is compelled in almost all practical situations to settle for rulers who at best exemplify some kind of bastardization of genuine virtue or wisdom. On the other hand, they observe that consent, since it is consent of the less than wise, is almost always colored by deception and self-deception. The complex task of constitution making and of ruling, in the classical understanding, is therefore the weaving together of two necessarily mutilated strands of political authority, through the arbitration and regulation of the rule of law. But this means to say that, in the classical view, there is something radically imperfect, even questionable, about all actual political authority.

It would therefore be leaving a rather false impression of classical republicanism, and of its contrast with American or modern, liberal republicanism, if we were not to add that the classical political philosophers insist on presenting civic virtue, and political legitimacy rooted in virtue, *as a problem*. This dimension of classical republican political and educational theory has been very severely neglected and misunderstood in almost all the present-day scholarly accounts of the history of educational thought. The drama of *The Education of Cyrus* lies in Xenophon's fascinating portrayal of how a virtuous citizenry is corrupted by a gifted, enchanting, and supremely talented leader; and it is precisely the ease with which Cyrus is shown to corrupt his virtuous fellow citizens that illuminates the fragility of civic virtue.

It is only when we recognize this fragile or problematic character of republican virtue, as it is treated by classical educational and political thought, that we begin to discern the deepest—and usually ignored—contrast between classical and American republicanism. For it seems likely that in the final analysis the classical writers would have rebuked the American Founders—and their great teachers, even Machiavelli—not for having been too skeptical about virtue but for having failed to question or probe virtue sufficiently. The classics teach that the profound questioning—and hence the true *understanding*—of morality and of moral education have as their essential prerequisite a powerful but also thoughtful attachment to conventional virtue, an attachment that is capable of becoming deeply troubled by the question of whether the virtue society teaches is according to nature. The classics might well have criticized the Founders for too quickly and easily assimilating the moral to the expedient in their thinking; the Founders thereby failed to recognize the depth of the attachment that they still felt for nonutilitarian virtue and failed to ponder sufficiently the powerful hold that morality has on the human heart altogether. They thus never fully understood the problematic character of that attachment, and the consequent tendency of man's moral feelings, when not cultivated by a careful education, to be alternately weak and dangerously explosive. The ancient philosophers might thus censure the Founders for having taken virtue a bit too much for granted, for having assumed that, at least in an attenuated form, it could always somehow be counted upon as a kind of necessary concomitant of political freedom.

The classical philosophers' more quizzical posture towards virtue goes hand in hand with the very elevated place the theme of law (and the kindred theme of piety) occupies in their educational thinking. Civic virtue, the classics will not let us forget, is emphatically dependent on law and law-enforced communal habituation and education. The classics have in mind here not merely the indirect encouragement of virtue through the institutional checking and channeling of passions; they mean the use of legally supervised artistic talent, law-enforced mores, and legally sanctioned religion to form souls, to mold character. As Aristotle stresses in the conclusion to the *Nicomachean Ethics*, moral as well as civic virtue and education has to be legislated and backed up by official praise and blame, as well as lawful reward and penalty, or it will wither, despite the naturally inspiring quality of nobility. This linkage between virtue and lawful fear or coercion sharply distinguishes ˹classical˺ republicanism from all Kantian and neo- or post-Kantian conceptions of virtue and education in virtue, for the outlooks inspired by Kant hold that virtue ceases to be virtue if it is not rooted in the free choice or "commitment" of the "autonomous" individual.

Conversely, no feature of classical republicanism is so close to the biblical political and educational tradition. In the Bible, the love of God, and the commandment to love God and to love one's neighbor for the sake of God, are inseparable from the fear of God as the punisher as well as the redeemer. In the words of Mary's Magnificat, "His mercy is on those who fear him from generation to generation" (Luke 1:50). Christ speaks chilling words in Luke 12:5: "I will warn you whom you should fear: Fear Him who, after he has killed, has power to cast into Hell; yes, I say unto you, fear Him!" His admonition receives a mighty echo in early American educational thought in Cotton Mather's leading pronouncement on the subject: "*Come, ye Children, Hearken to me, I will teach you,* what you ought to do. You ought, *First,* To be *Willing* to be *Taught the Fear of the Lord.* . . . *Children,* 'Tis your *Dawning* Time. It may be your *Dying Time.* . . . Go unto the *Burying-place*; There you will see many a *Grave* shorter than your selves. . . . And what needs any more be said, for your Awakening, to Learn the *Holy Scriptures!*"[15] A later and milder insistence on the importance of fear in the Christian education of very young children is John Witherspoon's influential *Letters on Education* of 1765 (printed in the *Pennsylvania Magazine* in 1775 and reprinted five times in the United States before 1822):

> I despise the foolish refinement of those, who, through fear of making children mercenary, are for being very sparing of the mention of heaven or hell. . . . I know no circumstance from which your opinion of the necessity of religion will appear with the greater clearness, or carry it in greater force, than your behavior towards and treatment of your children in time of dangerous sickness. Certainly there is no time in their whole lives when the necessity appears more urgent, or the opportunity more favorable, for impressing their minds with a sense of the things that belong to their peace. What shall we say then of those parents, who, through fear of alarming their minds, and augmenting their disorder, will not suffer any mention to be made to them of the approach of death, or the importance of eternity?[16]

For the classical philosophers, however, the observation that virtue and education in virtue, depend on law—and hence, in crucial respects, on coercion and fear—casts a long shadow over virtue. How can that which hinges essentially on conventional habit, shame, coercion, and fear be fully natural? How can a republic that has at its heart the rule of law ever be the true response to the deepest spiritual needs of human nature? In short, the "rule of law" is in the classical analysis fraught with grave questions, which culminate in one crucial query: Are the virtues as they are known in political life, even at its highest, the fulfillment or perfection of human life, or are they not in fact pale reflections of a kind of excellence and a way of life that is, as Aristotle has it, "divine," "set apart," truly noble, and therefore "blessed?"[17] With these words Aristotle refers to the philosophic or contemplative or theoretical life, which is always in one way or another brought to the fore in classical republicanism as a challenge and an alternative that transcends whatever can be achieved in political existence.

Now since, in the classical understanding, the philosophic or political-philosophic life is inevitably attended by a questioning and probing of civic virtue, of civic education, and of the law, the relations between the philosophic and the civic realms are of the utmost danger and delicacy to both parties. The gingerly but sustained exploration of this tension-filled relationship between philosophy and law may be said to be the very highest theme of classical republicanism and classical political philosophy.

That theme is pursued above all through the depiction and exploration of Socrates and his way of life—the way of life of a man who was *the* citizen-philosopher and *the* educator par excellence. Socrates and the philosophers who followed him became famous for constantly raising and pursuing, in dialogues or conversations with the young, questions about morality and happiness: What is virtue? Can it be taught? How? What is a statesman? What is a friend? Who or what is worthy of passionate love? In other words, the moral and political prudence that the classical political philosophers distilled and offered to statesmen and citizens was a wisdom always infused with new and ever deeper sources of wonder and thought. It is the downplaying or even the absence of this theme—the Socratic life, the friendly tension between the life of action and the life of philosophic inquiry, the uneasy but mutually fruitful relation between theory and practice—that marks the widest departure of the Americans from classical republicanism.

Classical Education Theory and Its Modern Disciple Milton

John Milton's short tract "Of Education" (1644), especially when read in the light of his famous *Areopagitica*, published in the same year, represents the best brief introduction to the modern tradition that attempted to carry on classical republican educational theory in the English-speaking world. Moreover, Milton's political thought as a whole stands as a high point in the endeavor to combine classical republicanism with the Puritan faith. His work therefore helps illuminate both the affinities and the tensions between the classical and the Protestant Christian outlook, at its most astute, while also preparing us to appreciate the sharp break Locke managed to effect with both classical and Puritan educational ideas. Milton's educational writings were well known and influential in America.[18]

But to understand Milton, and the Americans he influenced, we need to share with him and them, in some small degree at least, the experience of reading the most vivid classical accounts of education as found above all in Xenophon as well as Plato. Xenophon figures large in Milton's various recommended curricula, and Xenophon's influence as well as his reputation were infinitely higher in the seventeenth and eighteenth centuries than they are today. If we wish to see classical republican educational theory from the eighteenth century perspective, we do well to start by looking at Xenophon.[19]

Xenophon presents his famous account of the best sort of republican public education through his depiction, in the second chapter of *The Education of Cyrus*, of the Old Persian civic order that the "hero" Cyrus corrupted and transformed. The leitmotif is struck at the outset, when Xenophon draws a contrast between the Old Persian *polis* and most Greek cities (except Sparta):

> Most cities permit everyone to train his own children just as he will, and the older people themselves to live as they please; and then they command them not to steal and not to rob, not to break into homes, not to strike one they have no right to strike, not to commit adultery, not to disobey a magistrate, and so forth. And if someone transgresses in any of these respects, they levy punishment. The Persian laws, however, anticipating, take care that from the first their citizens shall not be of such a character as ever to be inclined toward a wicked or shameful deed.[20]

At the center of the city, Xenophon goes on to explain, is located what is called "the Square of Liberty." There are found the government buildings, where public affairs are handled, and there is where education takes place. All commerce is prohibited from this square, and no one who engages in business or merchandising can be a citizen or participate in government. The need for trade, banking, and so forth is kept to a minimum by severe sumptuary laws forbidding all luxury or conspicuous consumption and by legislation placing strict ceilings on the amount of property individuals may own. All the male citizens and the boys who are being educated to be future citizens must leave their farms (which are worked by tenants) and appear at the Square of Liberty every morning at dawn, to spend the entire day in public fellowship and the performance of political or educational duties.[21]

The youngest boys, Xenophon says, "go to school and spend their time learning justice; and they say that they go there for this purpose, just as among us they say boys go to school to learn to read and write." The boys are constantly engaged in prosecuting and defending one another in miniature trials, learning the laws and the meaning of investigation, law enforcement, prosecutorial and defense rhetoric, and civic responsibility. There are no lawyers or distinct police force or prosecutor's office in such a republic. At the same time, the boys are habituated, through constant trials and tests, to strict obedience to lawful rulers and to stoic self-control regarding food and drink, physical endurance, and the mastery of anger. Their food in particular is of the utmost austerity and equality.

> They bring from home bread for their nourishment, watercress for a relish, and, for drink, when they need it, a cup for drawing water from the river. . . . and if you think their meals are not enjoyable, when all they get is bread with watercress, or that their drinking is not enjoyable, when they drink just water, think back to how sweet barley bread and wheat bread taste when you are famished, and how sweet it is to drink water when you are parched.[22]

As they get older, the boys are introduced to weapons and begin to learn the military skills so necessary for the collective defense of a tiny country whose survival depends on a reputation for hornetlike resistance to foreign domination, and which scorns reliance on a hired or professional army. For ten years, the adolescents spend not only all their days but all their nights camping around the public square with their weapons. They have the responsibility (under adult supervision) for guarding as well as policing the country, night and day. Every week or so, half the population of adolescents and mature citizens under fifty go out on great public hunts led by the king. These hunts are in fact the equivalent of military maneuvers and are meant to test and develop physical courage, stamina, and shrewdness. In the stress of action against ferocious beasts, the youths as well as their elders are honed in cooperation, leadership, discipline, and rapid, tricky thinking. They thus prepare for the day when, at the age of twenty-five, the young men assume their places among the little band of brothers that takes responsibility for administering and defending the city through constant committee and platoon work.

Milton's design for the public schools he would have established in every city in England proposes a mitigated version of the military discipline of Xenophon. For an hour and a half each day the boys are to be at "exercises," beginning with swordsmanship. In addition to promoting health, strength, endurance, and agility, this will

> inspire them with a gallant and fearless courage, which being tempered with seasonable lectures and precepts to them of true fortitude and patience, will turn into a native and heroic valor, and make them hate the

cowardice of doing wrong. They must be also practiced in all the locks and grips of wrestling, wherein Englishmen were wont to excel, as need may often be in fight to tug, to grapple, and to close.

At unpredictable occasions in the evening, the students are

> by a sudden alarum or watchword, to be called out to their military motions, under sky or covert, according to the season, as was the Roman wont; first on foot, then, as their age permits, on horseback, to all the art of cavalry; that having in sport, but with much exactness and daily muster, served out the rudiments of their soldiership in all the skill of embattling, marching, encamping, fortifying, besieging, and battering, with all the helps of ancient and modern stratagems, tactics, and warlike maxims, they may as it were out of a long war come forth renowned and perfect commanders in the service of their country.[23]

Plato's *Republic* and *Laws* in no way diminish Xenophon's emphasis on the need for training in law, self-control, gymnastics, and military skill; if anything, Plato lays greater stress on wrestling and the rough-and-tumble arts of manly self-defense. But Plato adds also a complementary accent on music education. "Music" means here all those arts presided over by the goddesses called the Muses: poetry, choral performance, dance, and the study of literature and history. With the pleasing adornment of rhythm, harmony, poetic metaphor, and dramatic vivacity, the models of virtuous men and virtuous behavior become more compelling and more attractive. The arts induce a grace, delicacy, and sensitivity that soften the otherwise overly harsh tendencies of the stern gymnastic and military civic education. In the words of Milton, religious, martial, and political songs, "if wise men and prophets be not extremely out, have a great power over dispositions and manners, to smooth and make them gentle from rustic harshness and distempered passions."[24]

Moreover, as the young people mature, thought-provoking problems can be cautiously introduced by way of poems and plays and histories that depict virtuous men struggling against evil or confronted by perplexing moral and political choices; thus practical wisdom, together with pleasure and grace, may insensibly come to adorn, deepen, and elevate the habitual attachment to the civic virtues. Milton has his students' course of studies commence with "some easy and delightful book of education," of which "the Greeks have store, as Cebes, Plutarch, and other Socratic discourses." But his curriculum culminates (after the students have learned to read ancient Greek) in the "Attic tragedies of stateliest and most regal argument, with all the famous political orations," which, "if they were not only read but some of them got by memory and solemnly pronounced with right accent and grace, as might be taught, would endue them even with the spirit and vigor of Demosthenes or Cicero, Euripides or Sophocles." Then, "lastly, will be the time to read with them" what the ancient philosophers have written about the science of language, to the point where "Logic" will

> open her contracted palm into a graceful and ornate rhetoric taught out of the rule of Plato, Aristotle, Phalerus, Cicero, Hermogenes, Longinus. To which poetry would be made subsequent, or indeed rather precedent, as being less subtle and fine, but more simple, sensuous, and passionate. I mean not here the prosody of a verse, . . . but that sublime art which in Aristotle's poetics, in Horace, . . . teaches what the laws of a true epic poem, what of a dramatic, what of a lyric. . . . This would make them soon perceive what despicable creatures our common rhymers and play-writers be, and show them what religious, what glorious and magnificent use might be made of poetry, both in divine and human things. From hence, and not till now, will be the right season of forming them to be able writers and composers in every excellent matter, when they shall be thus fraught with an universal insight into things.[25]

At the heart of the music Plato and Milton have in mind is the civic piety that inspired the poets and now inspires their readers. In Plato's best city, frequent festivals of the gods become the occasion for constant communal artistic endeavors, and the gods themselves become, in some measure, models for as well as stern enforcers of the virtuous life. Moreover, "theology," or the encouragement of some discussion of the nature of the gods, may be the guise in which philosophy and the philosophic virtues can to some extent safely insinuate themselves into the otherwise rather closed public life of a virtuous city such as Plato envisages. For according to Plato the virtuous city is necessarily a closed rather than an open society. Plato argues that all theological discussion and all work of the artists must be subject to very strict censorship on the part of the communal authorities. The enormous educational responsibility assigned to the poets and artists, and the very grave consequences of their work in a society where the moral qualities of the future citizens depend on the passionate tastes shaped by the communal dedication to the arts, make it necessary that the poets work hand in hand with, and under the watchful eye of, the elected older supervisors of education and morals.

Yet to say that Platonic educational philosophy endorses censorship is to say too little and at the same time too much. It is more accurate to observe that Plato's discussion of the central educative role of poetry, of literature, and of the fine arts generally is inseparable from his famous condemnation of the greatest actual poets for their failure to live up to their educative responsibilities. This denunciation, culminating in the banishment of the poets from the best regime, is justly shocking to the sensibilities of every serious first-time reader of the *Republic* and the *Laws*. Yet upon further reflection, one cannot help but become aware of the extraordinarily paradoxical and hence thought-provoking character of Plato's condemnation of the poets. Certainly Milton, at any rate, insists that precisely Plato's discussions of censorship reveal clearly that Plato never seriously intended either the *Republic* or the *Laws* to be prescriptions for actual cities. According to Milton, Plato was depicting in those works the absurd lengths to which one would have to go to create a society so morally pure as to entail the censorship of writings through licensing, or prior restraint on publication. Plato was after all himself a poet, who as composer of "wanton dialogues" transgressed simultaneously the laws of poetry he had the characters in those dialogues propose.

> That Plato meant this law peculiarly to that commonwealth which he had imagined, and to no other, is evident. Why was he not else a lawgiver to himself, but a transgressor, and to be expelled by his own magistrates, both for the wanton epigrams and dialogues which he made, and his perpetual reading of Sophron Mimus and Aristophanes . . . he knew this licensing of poems had reference and dependence to many other provisoes there set down in his fancied republic, which in this world could have no place; and so neither he himself, nor any magistrate or city, ever imitated that course.[26]

Milton's *Areopagitica*, the work in which this remarkable suggestion as to how to read Plato appears, is the most famous plea for freedom of the press ever written, but it is a kind of appeal profoundly unfamiliar to us nowadays. For it is a classical republican plea, an oration (in imitation of Isocrates) written by a very great poet deeply indebted to Plato and Aristotle, as well as to the Bible, for his understanding of poetry and of education through poetry. Milton does not rest his case on an appeal to natural rights, and he certainly does not advocate artistic "self-expression" or even "freedom of speech." The argument is rooted in a keen awareness of the poet's civic duties and educative responsibilities and of the consequent need for limits on what a poet or any writer can or ought to say. The question for Milton is how to set and police those limits in the republican community: "I deny not but that it is of greatest concernment in the church and commonwealth, to have a vigilant eye how books demean themselves as well as men; and thereafter to confine, imprison, and do sharpest justice on them as malefactors: for books are not absolutely dead things, but do contain a potency of life in them to be as active as that soul was whose progeny they are."[27]
In the rare worst cases—of libel, blasphemy, and obscenity—books may be

banned and their authors punished, but only after publication and hence scrutiny by the public. For this is the core of a truly civic censorship, as taught by Plato when his books are read with the proper care.

> Those unwritten or at least unconstraining laws of virtuous education, religious and civil nurture, which Plato there mentions as the bonds and ligaments of the commonwealth, the pillars and sustainers of every written statute; these they be which will bear chief sway in such matters as these, when all licensing will be easily eluded. Impunity and remissness, for certain, are the bane of a commonwealth; but here the great art lies, to discern in what the law is to bid restraint and punishment, and in what things persuasion only is to work.[28]

Persuasion, counterargument, honor, and dishonor are the proper communal rewards and punishments for all works that appear to advocate falsehood or to challenge on insufficient grounds the accepted principles of politics and religion: so long as they contain no libel, blasphemy, or outright wickedness, the books should be free to enter the lists in the struggle to find and express the truth.

Milton does indeed criticize Plato for having published, in the guise of an account of the "best city," his fantastic vision of what would be required to create a totally—and hence impossibly—pure society. These speculations "they who otherwise admire him wish had been rather buried and excused in the genial cups of an Academic night sitting," for they are written in such a way as too much tempts the reader to take them seriously, as Plato's actual proposals or wishes. In Milton's judgment, Plato was not statesmanlike enough in his self-censorship.[29]

But even if we grant Milton's remarkable interpretation, with its claim that Plato in his *Republic* sought to delineate the limits of politics rather than to lay down its proper goals, we may still wonder whether Plato meant to offer exactly the teaching on censorship and education through books, that Milton here offers. Milton differs from Plato not only in his concern to publish only what serves a constructive civic purpose but also in the confidence with which he trusts that truth will ultimately grow stronger and emerge more clearly in the public contest of words and books; for Milton writes in the light of what he believes is the dawn of a magnificent English "reformation of the reformation," under God's providence. At least in the context in which he publishes his oration (England in 1644), Milton's faith may allow him greater confidence than Plato could afford that the religious and moral truth discerned by the philosopher is on the road to triumph in the world, and neither threatens the foundations of existing society nor needs to be protected and nurtured as something fragile.

When one looks a bit more closely at Plato's works, provoked and guided by Milton's startling interpretative suggestions, one observes that the poet Plato has his chief characters condemn the poets on two different and rather contradictory grounds. In the second book of the *Laws*, the "Athenian Stranger" criticizes the poets for being insufficiently moralistic or civic-spirited—for speaking too frankly and thus failing to write poetry whose "noble lies" or myths strengthen the attachment of citizens, and especially young citizens, to the laws and ethos of the political community. In book 2 of the *Republic*, Plato has Socrates reiterate this verdict—although Socrates adds the reflection that the immoral stories about the gods are perhaps necessarily false, given the premise that the gods must be wholly good. But in the last book of the *Republic*, Socrates bans the poets because of their lack of concern for education in the truth, or nature, especially the nature of the human soul, as opposed to convention and lawful or conventional beliefs about the soul. The poets' failure as educators is now said to be most evident in their excessive docility before what is respectable according to the traditional laws or conventions. For the poets to make good on their claim to be educators, they would have to succeed in revolutionizing society with new laws more in accord with nature; or, failing to achieve political reform, they would have to found independent sects of followers whose way of life was more in tune with nature and therefore departed strikingly from what is conventionally respectable in any civil society. In the *Laws*, the Athenian Stranger eventually presents a criticism of the narrowness and rigidity of civic or legal language and thought—in the name of the superior flexibility of poetic speech. Poetic speech, the Athenian Stranger observes, can truly educate because in the same speech the poet can say contradictory things, thus addressing different messages adapted to the radically different types of people in his audience.[30]

The paradoxical character of the Platonic criticism of the poets may indicate that Plato's preeminent objective is to teach the enormous difficulty (perhaps the impossibility, in the strict sense) of civic education. Civic education at its intellectual peak is education in thinking, guided by books—above all, the books of great poets (and, following Milton, of great historians and orators). Those books have a threefold and tension-ridden educational goal. They seek in the first place to edify and inspire loyal, self-sacrificing, and reliable citizens. Next, they attempt to instill prudence, or shrewd and versatile practical wisdom, in leaders who emerge out of the decent and reliable citizens. To this end, good books compel the reader to witness and share vicariously some of the burden of agonizing deliberations over fundamental questions of public policy. Finally, and as a sort of sequel to the preceding, good books try to awaken in some individuals, including at least some of the leadership, a more or less profound awareness of the essential limitations on what may be expected from all political life or action. Among the most important effects of such an awareness of limitations is the dissolving or at any rate diminution of false hopes and fears that may otherwise distort a clear-eyed view of the potentialities and pitfalls of political existence. The roots of these limitations are to be found in the seemingly insuperable conflicts or contradictions that define human existence—for example, the tension between private erotic or familial love and public civic duty; or the tension between the happiness of the individual and the good of the community, to which the individual is duty-bound on occasion to sacrifice his or her happiness; or the tension between societies like Sparta that stress the communal nature of humanity and societies like Athens that give much greater scope or encouragement to the competitive ambitions of individuals.

It is difficult to judge the extent to which Americans were alive to the complexities, tensions, and paradoxes of the authentic classical republican educational legacy. As has been noted, the Americans praised most often the grace and style of classical literature. They also lauded the moral edification conveyed by the heroic examples contained in the classical histories; and they spoke, with more qualified praise, of the practical wisdom or political science the historians could offer—especially through their stirring portrayals of the evils of despotism and the attractions of liberty. Very rarely, however, does one find an American putting stress on students' vicarious participation in classical political debate, or the moderation of political hopes and dreams that is inculcated through a study of the most thoughtful—and most austere (one is tempted to say most tragic)—of the classical historians. Milton has his educational curriculum culminate in a thorough study and assimilation of the "Attic tragedies of stateliest and most regal argument"; in the educational writings of the American Framers, there will be found little reference to ancient tragedy.[31]

The Leading Eighteenth-Century Academic Representative of Ancient Education

To get a better sense of how the Founding generation may have viewed, or been taught to view, the challenge posed by classical educational thought, it is useful to cast a glance at the most authoritative contemporary academic interpreter of the classical educational texts—the famous Sorbonne professor of ancient history, Charles Rollin, who completed his influential treatise on education in 1731.[32] Rollin's treatise was immediately translated into English, went through numerous English editions, and was referred to frequently by the colonists. Benjamin Franklin, in particular, cites "the much admired Mons. Rollin" in his 1749 *Proposals Relating to the Education of Youth in Pennsylvania*.[33]

As a faithful Roman Catholic, a loyal subject of the French monarchy, and a favorite of Jacobites, Rollin could hardly champion the rebirth of classical republicanism; but he could insist on the supreme value of the academic study of the classics, and, with an eye to his favorite author, Xenophon, he could assert the continuing relevance of classical political and educational theory even under monarchic systems of government. In this respect, Rollin may be said to have carried on the scholastic tradition, though under the shadow of, and to some extent in opposition to, the increasingly dominant current of the Enlightenment.

In making the case for classical education, Rollin takes his cue from the preamble to the educational legislation of Henry IV. Following that great king, he says not a word about enlightenment or the rights of man but instead stresses the education of the young in "their inviolable duties to God, their parents, and their country, with the respect and obedience which they owe to Kings and Magistrates." But lest obedience be confused with slavery, Rollin turns immediately to what he calls "the first object of instruction": "forming the mind." The exemplar of a well-formed mind is that possessed by Roman statesmen like Aemilius and his son Scipio, who relied on Xenophon for their wisdom in the ways of the world. For the education of men of practical affairs, there is a unique value in the study of historians like

> Caesar, Polybius, Xenophon, and Thucydides, who by their lively descriptions carry the reader into the field of battle. . . . The same may be said of negotiations, magistracies, offices of civil jurisdiction, commissions, in a word, of all the employments which oblige us either to speak in publick or in private, to write, or give an account of our administration, to manage others, gain them over, or persuade them. And what employment is there, where almost all these things are not necessary?

Even more important than the forming of the mind for Rollin is the forming of the character that underlies the mind. Here Rollin commends the classical authors for avoiding preaching, precepts, or moralizing and instead employing vivid example accompanied by laconic or even allusive lessons, sometimes communicated by pregnant silences.

> Nothing is more apt to inspire sentiments of virtue, and to divert from vice, than the conversation of men of worth, as it makes an impression by degrees, and sinks deep into the heart. The seeing and hearing them often will serve instead of precepts, and their very presence, tho' they say nothing, speaks and instructs. And this advantage is chiefly to be drawn from the reading of authors. It forms a kind of relation between us and the great-

est men of antiquity. We converse with them; we travel with them; we live with them; we hear them discourse, and are witnesses of their actions; we enter insensibly into their principles and opinions. . . . When I talk thus, it is not that I think moral reflections should be largely insisted on. If we would make an impression, our precepts should be short and lively, and pointed as a needle. . . . 'Tis with these reflections, says Seneca, as with seed, which is small in itself, but if cast into a well-prepared soil, unfolds by degrees, till at last it insensibly grows to a prodigious increase. Thus the precepts we speak of are oft but a word, or a short reflection, but this word and reflection, which in a moment shall seem lost and gone, will produce their effect in due time.[34]

Though Rollin speaks with force and some penetration about the peculiarly thought-provoking manner in which the classical texts convey their lessons in statecraft, his comprehension of the substance of the classical teaching (and especially of the higher, more problematic, reaches of classical educational thought) is limited. Rollin tends to assume that the advent of the Catholic faith has resolved whatever fundamental difficulties may be found in the classical accounts concerning the relation between philosophy and piety or between poetry and morality, and that what is best in classical philosophy, poetry, and education anticipates and is completed by that faith. Yet despite this easygoingness, Rollin does afford his readers at least an echo, however faint and tremulous, of certain key debates or questions raised in the original classical texts on education.

Rollin, we have said, is a partisan of the ancients, understood to be subordinate to the revealed truths of the Roman Catholic tradition. Even so, Rollin cannot help but acknowledge that the educational treatise of John Locke has offered to all humanity an unprecedented fund of wisdom regarding the methods (though not the ultimate goals) of education. Rollin concedes that no one before Locke so closely observed and so accurately described the peculiar nature of the young. Rollin therefore does not hesitate to transcribe long sections of Locke's treatise, even while voicing unmistakably his reservations as to the intention that guides Locke, as well as his reservations about Locke's attitude toward study of the classics.[35] All the more impressive, given these reservations, is Rollin's bow to Locke, a bow which testifies to the overwhelming influence, the striking innovation, and the deep penetration of Locke's treatise on education. For it is indeed the case that when we turn from the classics celebrated by Rollin to the educational reflections of John Locke, we find ourselves, as it were, in a different world.

3 · The Lockean Revolution in Educational Theory

The wide gulf separating Locke from his predecessor Milton is evident at the first glance. Milton describes an education conducted in boarding schools at which boys would live together for years in "troops" of a hundred or more. Locke describes an emphatically private moral education, in the bosom of the private home, under the loving and painstaking supervision of the parents, and with the assistance of a carefully selected and well-paid private tutor. In effect, this means that Locke's treatise, *Some Thoughts Concerning Education*, is immediately directed toward that small minority of the population constituted by the gentry and the nobility. Nonetheless, as Pierre Coste, Locke's French translator, stresses, the actual substance of Locke's educational prescriptions is "universal" in scope, applying to "all sorts of children."[1] Locke aims his message at the upper class partly because he sees no prospect in the foreseeable future of families in a lower station possessing the leisure and financial resources required to carry out the time-consuming, difficult, and complex labor that Locke conceives to be necessary for a truly sound and effective moral education. But Locke makes it clear that he hopes and expects that a reform, under his auspices, of upper-class education, character, and outlook will have an indirect but profound long-run impact on the way of life of the whole nation. As Locke says in the epistle dedicatory to the treatise:

> The well Educating of their Children is so much the Duty and Concern of Parents, and the Welfare and Prosperity of the Nation so much depends on it, that I would have every one lay it seriously to Heart; and after having well examined and distinguished what Fancy, Custom or Reason advises in the Case, set his Helping Hand to promote every where that Way of training up Youth, with regard to their several Conditions, which is the easiest, shortest, and likeliest to produce vertuous, useful, and able Men in their distinct Callings: Though that most to be taken Care of, is the Gentle-

man's Calling. For if those of that Rank are by their Education once set right, they will quickly bring all the rest into Order.[2]

Locke's Attack on Schooling in the Name of Education

In the passage just quoted, as in his numerous references to education in the *Two Treatises of Government*, Locke reveals his paradoxical and radically unclassical view: although education is of supreme importance to the nation and therefore to the government, it is not a responsibility or a "duty" of government, but rather, "the duty and concern of parents."[3] For education is above all moral education, which in turn is inseparable from some sort of religious education or at the least some distinct posture toward religion; and, as we have seen, morality and religion are according to Locke not the legitimate business of coercive governmental authority.

Locke is not dogmatically opposed to state schools; in the case of the very poor, he advocates state intervention and support with a view to providing the minimal moral and religious discipline required for guiding destitute young people to gainful employment and hence survival.[4] But the basic thrust of his conception of the political community is toward individual, familial, and private responsibility for the essential moral formation of the souls of the young.

It is not merely Locke's concern with liberating individual souls from the coercive hand of governmental authority that leads him to recommend private education at home, for he is as severely critical of private schools as he is of public ones. Schools, Locke argues, are not the proper place to carry on effective childhood education.[5] On the negative side, Locke draws attention to the pernicious influence crowds of boys have upon one another's character development, and he deduces the advantages that might accrue from an educational reform that would assimilate the education of boys to that traditionally bestowed on girls.

He that considers how diametrically opposite the Skill of living well, and managing, as a Man should do, his Affairs in the World, is to that malapertness, tricking, or violence learnt amongst Schoolboys, will think the Faults of a Privater Education infinitely to be preferr'd to such Improvements; and will take care to preserve his Child's Innocence and Modesty at home. . . . Nor does any one find, or so much as suspect, that that Retirement and Bashfulness, which their Daughters are brought up in, makes them less knowing or less able Women. Conversation, when they come into the World, soon gives them a becoming assurance; and whatsoever, beyond that, there is of rough and boisterous, may in Men be very well spared too. . . .

Vertue is harder to be got, than a Knowledge of the World; and if lost in a Young Man is seldom recovered. Sheepishness and ignorance of the World, the faults imputed to a private Education, are neither the necessary Consequents of being bred at home, nor if they were, are they incurable Evils. . . .

. . . Boys will unavoidably be taught assurance by Conversation with Men, when they are brought into it; and that is time enough.

. . . But how any one's being put into a mixed Herd of unruly Boys . . . fits him for civil Conversation, or Business, I do not see. And what Qualities are ordinarily to be got from such a Troop of Play-fellows as Schools usually assemble together from Parents of all kinds, that a Father should so much covet, is hard to divine. . . .

. . . Gentlemen's Houses are seldom without Variety of Company: They should use their Sons to all the Strange Faces that come there, and ingage them in Conversation with Men of Parts and breeding, as soon as they are capable of it. (*Some Thoughts Concerning Education*, sec. 70)

Locke is keenly aware that the company of the servants who inhabit an upper-class home may be at least as dangerous as the influence of schoolboys, and therefore he stresses that by an education in the home he means an education in which the children are "kept as much as may be *in the Company of their Parents*, and those to whose care they are committed" (sec. 69). The selection of the latter, and especially of the tutor, Locke regards as a matter of the gravest moment. For, and here we come to the positive side of his argument against schools, Locke insists on the need for the most sensitive attention to the individual development, needs, and circumstances of each child being educated, and furthermore, he insists on the need for a constant regard to the sort of model being set for the young person under one's charge. It is the practical impossibility of such individually tailored education in schools that forms Locke's most serious reason for rejecting schooling, despite its admitted virtues.

Being abroad, 'tis true, will make him bolder, and better able to bustle and shift amongst Boys of his own age; and the emulation of Schoolfellows, often puts Life and Industry into young Lads. But till you can find a School, wherein it is possible for the Master to look after the Manners of his Scholars, and can shew as great Effects of his Care of forming their Minds to Virtue, and their Carriage to good Breeding, as of forming their Tongues to the learned Languages; you must confess that you have a strange value for words. . . .

. . . For let the Master's Industry and Skill be never so great, it is impossible he should have 50. or 100. Scholars under his Eye, any longer than they are in the School together: Nor can it be expected, that he should instruct them Successfully in any thing, but their Books: The forming of their Minds and Manners requiring a constant Attention, and particular Application to every single Boy, which is impossible in a numerous Flock; And would be wholly in vain (could he have time to Study and Correct every one's particular Defects, and wrong Inclinations) when the Lad was to be left to himself, or the prevailing Infection of his Fellows, the greatest part of the Four and twenty Hours. . . .

. . . In all the whole Business of Education, there is nothing like to be less hearken'd to, or harder to be well observed, than what I am now going to say; and that is, that Children should from their first beginning to talk, have some *Discreet, Sober*, nay, *Wise* Person about, whose Care it should be to Fashion them aright, and keep them from all ill, especially the infection of bad Company. I think this province requires great *Sobriety, Temperance, Tenderness, Diligence*, and *Discretion*; Qualities hardly to be found united in Persons, that are to be had for ordinary Salaries; nor easily to be found any where. (secs. 70, 90)

The Contrast with Classical Communal Education

To form a just estimate of the import, the strength, and the difficulties of Locke's famous attack on schooling in the name of education, it is helpful to draw out a bit the contrast with classical republican educational theory. At first sight, it seems obvious that a version of precisely the sort of "herd" education that Locke deplores lies at the very heart of the rather militaristic classical educational ideal. As Plato's Athenian Stranger puts it near the conclusion of the most elaborate classical proposal for a system of public education:

The most important thing is that no one, male or female, should ever be without a ruler, and that no one's soul should acquire the habit of doing something on its own and alone, either seriously or in play; at all times, in war and in peace, it should live constantly looking to and following the ruler, governed by that man in even the briefest matters—such as standing when someone gives the order, and walking and exercising in the nude and washing and eating and getting up at night to guard and carry messages, and in dangers, not pursuing someone or retiring before another without an indication from the rulers. In a word, one should teach one's soul by habits not to know, and not to know how to carry out, any action at all apart from the others; as much as possible everyone should in every respect live always in a group, together, and in common—for there is not nor will there ever be anything stronger, better, and more artful than this for producing security and victory in war. This ought to be practiced during peacetime, from earliest childhood: ruling the rest and being ruled by others.[6]

As Locke notes, the classical authors are far from scorning the crucial role played by family and especially parents in the education of the young. But the classical educational theorists are impressed by the fragility and weakness of even the most determined parental education in the face of the overwhelming strength of the customs and models created by the specific, reigning political "regime" or "culture" (*politeia*), under whose coercive legal and moral authority the family always finds itself.[7] Besides, weighing at least equally heavily against the family as custodian of moral education are the oft-repeated classical animadversions on the family as the most deeply rooted source of private interest—including both private property or acquisitiveness and private emotional attachment. Plato goes so far as to have Socrates experiment with the abolition of the private family and of parenthood (in anything other than the biological sense), and there is in all classical educational writing a deep wariness of the family's capacity and tendency to draw men away from the public and common to the private and personal.

Yet because of the ultimately profound reservation the classical philosophers harbor against all life that is limited to the horizon of politics or the city, there is also in the classical texts an unobtrusive but in the final analysis telling reservation against the platoonlike character of civic education. Near the outset of the same *Laws* in which he develops so regimented a civic educational scheme, Plato has the Athenian Stranger say of the regimentation in education practiced by Sparta and Crete: "You keep your young in a flock, like a bunch of colts grazing in a herd. None of you takes his own youngster apart, drawing him, all wild and complaining, away from his fellow grazers. None of you gives him a private groom and educates him by currying and soothing him, giving him all that is appropriate for child rearing."[8] The Athenian Stranger thus indicates his knowledge of a superior, private education which presupposes the public and herdlike education but which requires—at the age of adolescence—an enforced separation of the youngster from the herd.

Here is yet another facet of the fundamental paradox that runs throughout classical republican educational thought. The human being is that animal who is the political animal, but the human being is also that animal whose nature, rooted in and springing out of politics or the city, has the potential radically to transcend politics. Civic education must therefore be distinguished from a higher, philosophic education. The latter is necessarily private and informal and is indeed preoccupied with the diversity and individuality of students. But only for rare human beings and only under rare circumstances will such meticulous attention to individuality and transcendence of civic life result in virtue and fulfillment. Furthermore, the nature of such human beings and their potential to be affected by a personal, philosophic, or proto-philosophic educative experience emerge only in adolescence and are at best dimly foreshadowed in the earlier years of childhood. Accordingly, while the classical philosophers admit the importance of private education of very young children within the home, they say relatively little about it, though they try to give some constructive advice and guidance to heads of families and cities. Moreover, they do not expect heads of households to devote much attention to the education of the potential philosophers. The existence of a distinct class of philosophers is to be recognized and its interests attended to, but in the interstices or even at the margins of organized educational institutions.[9] The Socratic philosophers reveal their most serious educational concern only in a somewhat reserved way, by expressing their aspiration to educate "gentlemen": men who rise above ordinary citizenship through a partially independent moral seriousness and an attendant capacity for mature reflection that enables them to be open to at least the more superficial charms of philosophy.

Locke, in striking contrast, says practically nothing about the dichotomy between philosophic and subphilosophic education. He elevates to the center of educational attention the individuality of human beings in general and puts the focus from the outset on the education of the vast majority of people who are less than supremely gifted. His treatise on education, with its painstaking attention to the character of young children, certainly has no equivalent in the classical literature. This new and, from the classical perspective, meticulous concern with human infancy is grounded in Locke's new conception of human nature. Locke's famous denial of all innate moral ideas, and his equally famous and correlative doctrine of the state of nature, entail the notion that man is endowed with practically no mental or spiritual natural inclinations which may serve as moral guidelines. Mankind by nature exhibits no steady positive goal, no reliable conscience, no universal principles of social organization. If, and only if, we accept this denuded conception of human nature, we become open to the recognition that man is a being with hitherto undiscerned potential malleability and even perfectibility. Human beings are by nature almost pure potential. Because humanity is so little defined by nature, humanity can largely define itself—once we acknowledge the absence of essential or natural or predestined character and recognize the molding power of education.[10]

According to Locke, human nature is directed neither toward citizenship nor toward philosophy; but, being potentially rational, or capable of making reason the mighty tool of the passions, mankind can direct itself toward cooperative labor, protection, and comfort. By accepting humanity's diversity and lack of natural organization or directedness, thinking humans can set to work reshaping their existence by working on the passions and thus—especially if the very young are gotten hold of in the right way—may create societies that are "natural" in the peculiar sense of being rational responses to the poverty and disharmony of our given natural condition.

Locke's philosophy of education thus carries to new heights that extraordinarily ambitious and public-spirited Baconian enterprise, in which philosophy does not simply contemplate the truth, nor manipulate and exploit it, but instead, from the truth, generates or procreates a humane life. In the richly metaphorical words of Francis Bacon,

> The greatest error of all the rest is the mistaking or misplacing of the last or furthest end of knowledge. . . . as if there were sought in knowledge a couch whereupon to rest a searching and restless spirit; or a terrace for a wandering and variable mind to walk up and down with a fair prospect; or a tower of state for a proud mind to rest itself upon; or a fort or commanding ground for strife and contention; or a shop for profit or sale; and not a rich storehouse for the glory of the Creator and the relief of man's estate. . . . Neither is my meaning, as was spoken of Socrates, to call philosophy down from heaven to converse upon the earth; that is, to leave natural philosophy aside, and to apply knowledge only to manners and policy. But as both heaven and earth do conspire and contribute to the use and benefit of man; so the end ought to be, from both philosophies to separate and reject vain speculations, and whatsoever is empty and void, and to preserve and augment whatsoever is solid and fruitful: that knowledge may not be as a courtesan, for pleasure and vanity only, or as a bondwoman, to acquire and gain to her master's use; but as a spouse, for generation, fruit, and comfort.[11]

To appreciate the radicalism of Locke's treatise on education, it will be illuminating to contrast it, as we proceed, not only with Milton, but also with two other influential educational treatises that had appeared in English in the previous couple of generations and that continued to be read by Americans in the eighteenth century. The first of these is Obadiah Walker's *Of Education, Especially of Young Gentlemen.* Though Walker was a Roman Catholic, his treatise was calculated to have a universal appeal to English gentlemen, and it certainly spoke to their typical domestic situation in the late seventeenth century much more aptly than anything Milton had written. The success of Walker's *Of Education* is indicated by the fact that it went through six editions in the seventeen years after its first publication in 1673. But equally or more revealing is the fact that after 1700 Walker was not again reprinted: Locke's treatise swept the field (though Walker's "excellent Treatise" is still cited twice by Benjamin Franklin in his *Proposals Relating to the Education of Youth in Pennsylvania*).[12] Our second comparative benchmark will be the influential discussion of early childhood education in the "Letters on Education" of the Presbyterian teacher and divine John Witherspoon. Witherspoon's work is deeply indebted, sometimes to the point of paraphrase, to Locke; all the more striking and illuminating are those respects in which Witherspoon departs from Locke, in the name of Christianity and the conscience.[13]

Education as the Mastery of Nature

The goal of Lockean education is an enlightened self-interest grounded in rational self-control; the self-control is buttressed and the self-interest enlarged by a sense of dignity rooted in the recognition bestowed by similarly rational fellow citizens. In Nathan Tarcov's felicitous formulation:

> The gentleman's education Locke advocates is supportive of the politics he taught. It forms men of business and affairs. They are physically fit and courageous, able to be soldiers if necessary. But, much more important, they are willing and able to concern themselves with their estates, perhaps even with trade, and to be active and informed in public affairs. . . . They are well formed to further the public interest by attending to private property while being at the same time vigilant observers of government, awake to the danger of tyranny while being no source of such danger themselves, and plausible representatives of the people should the need arise.[14]

With a view to this goal, the principal task of moral education, in Locke's estimation, is instilling in children a capacity to master their natural inclinations—"their natural wrong Inclinations" (sec. 90). As we have already remarked, for Locke the human being naturally needs the inner rule of reason to escape from a kind of chaotic sociability, but the human animal does not automatically possess or even naturally develop such rule. As a consequence, the human being is by nature, or originally and spontaneously, a dangerous creature both for itself and for others.

> I told you before that Children love *Liberty*; . . . I now tell you, they love something more; and that is *Dominion*: And this is the first Original of most vicious Habits, that are ordinary and natural. This love of *Power* and Dominion shews it self very early. . . .
>
> We see Children as soon almost as they are born (I am sure long before they can speak) cry, grow peevish, sullen, and out of humour, for nothing

but to have their *Wills*. They would have their Desires submitted to by others; they contend for a ready compliance from all about them. (secs. 103–4)

Or as Locke says in the rather more brutal *Essay Concerning Human Understanding*: "*Robberies, Murders, Rapes*, are the Sports of Men set at Liberty from Punishments and Censure. . . . Principles of Actions indeed there are lodged in Men's Appetites, but these are so far from being innate Moral Principles, that if they were left to their full swing, they would carry Men to the over-turning of all Morality."[15]

These drastic defects or disorders of the mind to which education must respond Locke does *not* ascribe to sin or to the Fall; accordingly, he never suggests that the remedy for them is to be found in fear of God or supplication for divine grace and redemption. For Locke's first readers, the contrast in this fundamental respect with Obadiah Walker as well as John Milton would have been vivid. Walker speaks repeatedly of the need for divine grace, while urging constant prayer for this grace on the part of children, tutors, and especially parents. Walker stresses piety and daily religious worship as the first "calling" or "duty" of a gentleman; what is more, the Roman Catholic Walker anticipates the Puritan Cotton Mather in recommending frequent reminders to children of death, judgment day, and the awesome alternatives of either everlasting punishment or everlasting bliss in the afterlife.[16]

It is also in this respect that Witherspoon takes his greatest distance from Locke. Witherspoon opens his first letter on education by emphasizing that education is to be regarded as the "duty" of a "Christian" as well as a "citizen." As he reminds his addressee, "You and I have chiefly in view the religious education of children." This means primarily, Witherspoon goes on to say, that one "desires to educate his children in the fear of God." "The end I consider as most important," Witherspoon declares in the third letter, "is, the glory of God in the eternal happiness and salvation of children."[17]

Locke's stark departure from the well-beaten track concerning the role of religion in family life and education needs to be stressed, given contemporary scholars' misunderstanding of this central aspect of his educational philosophy and influence. For example, Lawrence Cremin has somehow come away from his perusal of Locke's text with the impression that it is "a devotional manual in the tradition of [Lewis Bayly's] *The Practise of Pitie*" and has depended on this gross error in his attempt to understand the impact of Locke's treatise on the educational ideas of Americans in the eighteenth century. Cremin makes the astounding claim that Locke advises parents, in his treatise on education, to "ensure that the Bible itself is systematically studied as the foundation of all morality."[18] Since Cremin provides no specific citations to the text of Locke, it is impossible to ascertain what passages led him to such a misreading.

The fact is that Locke expresses grave reservations about children's reading, let alone studying, the Bible; the Fables of Aesop, Locke says, is "the only Book almost that I know fit for Children" (sec. 189). Locke was as good as his word: He arranged to have a new edition of Aesop published, and recent research has discovered both the previous edition by Hoole and the pattern in the changes that Locke introduced into his own. According to Robert Horwitz and Judith Finn, Locke "eliminated two fables that portrayed reliance upon religion as a wise or advantageous policy, as well as several fables portraying women in an unfavourable light. Perhaps the most noteworthy change made by Locke and Grigg in their rendition of the Hoole fables is that classical references were somewhat diminished, while appeals to the authority of the classics were largely omitted." As a replacement for the Bible, Locke recommends substituting a brief catechism of "moral rules scattered up and down in the Bible" (sec. 159), and "a good History of the Bible, for young people to read: wherein if every thing, that is fit to be put into it, were laid down in its due Order of Time, and several things omitted, which are suited only to riper Age, that Confusion, *which is usually produced by promiscuous reading of the Scripture, as it lies now bound up in our Bibles* would be avoided" (sec. 190, italics added).[19]

Locke indeed insists that "there ought very early to be imprinted on [the child's] Mind a true Notion of God, as of the independent Supreme Being, Author and Maker of all Things, from whom we receive all our Good, who loves us, and gives us all Things." To this "true" God, children are to pray morning and evening in "some plain and short Form of Prayer." But this unitarian God of Nature, who "made and governs all things, hears and sees every Thing, and does all manner of Good to those that love and obey him," is the sum and substance of divinity. There is no mention here of Jesus Christ, the Messiah, the Second Coming, sin, grace, redemption, the resurrection of the body—or, for that matter, any miracle of any sort, any reference to the soul, heaven and hell, or divine punishment of any kind. Locke in fact repeatedly exhorts parents to make every effort to keep their children from associating fear, including fear of punishment, with God. Locke boldly adds, "I think it would be better if Men generally rested in such an Idea of God" (sec. 136); and he has the audacity to sum up his educational teaching using Juvenal's counsel against prayer as something either superfluous or mischievous: "*Nullum numen abest si sit prudentia* [No divine spirit is absent where there is prudence]" (sec. 200).[20]

The disorder of the human personality is, according to Locke, natural. The proper remedy is consequently a contra-natural, artificial implantation, beginning at an early age, of habits of self-control resting initially on fear of parents and eventually on a reconstruction of the natural lust for power and a modulation of the natural desires for liberty and pleasure. "*Reward* and *Punishment*," Locke insists, "are the only Motives to a rational Creature: these are the Spur and Reins, whereby all Mankind are set on work, and guided, and therefore they are to be made use of to Children too" (sec. 54). The specific reward and punishment that give virtue its strength in the human heart are "*Esteem* and *Disgrace*," which "are, of all others, the most powerful Incentives to the Mind, when once it is brought to relish them" (sec. 56).[21]

The mind can be brought to such a point because the natural desire for power can easily be linked to prestige, whose conventional character allows it to be shaped by praise and blame. In a rational Lockean environment, praise and blame will always be closely correlated with the display or lack of display of reasonableness. Children

> love to be treated as Rational Creatures sooner than is imagined. 'Tis a Pride should be cherished in them, and as much as can be, made the greatest instrument to turn them by.
>
> But when I talk of *Reasoning*, I do not intend any other, but such as is suited to the Child's Capacity and Apprehension. No Body can think a Boy of Three, or Seven Years old, should be argued with, as a grown Man. . . . there is no Vertue they should be excited to, nor Fault they should be kept from, which I do not think they may be convinced of; but it must be by such *Reasons* as their Age and Understanding are capable of. (sec. 81)

The appeal to "reason," then, is in fact a benevolently duplicitous appeal to the childish appearance of being reasonable or to the childish pleasure of being reputed to be reasonable, and this appearance or reputation is exhibited through behavior that is grounded at least as much in habituation as in deliberation: "habits working more constantly, and with greater Facility than Reason: Which, when we have most need of it, is seldom fairly consulted, and more rarely obey'd" (sec. 110). One may appropriately contrast here Witherspoon's words in his fifth letter on education: "Let not human reasonings be put in the balance with divine wisdom. . . . It is not the native beauty of virtue, or the outward credit of it, or the inward satisfaction that arises from it, or even all these combined together, that will be sufficient to change our natures and govern our conduct; but a deep conviction, that unless we are reconciled to God, we shall without doubt perish everlastingly."[22]

Locke's focus on the grounding of virtue in habits instilled in early childhood echoes Aristotle's teaching in book 2 of the *Nicomachean Ethics*, but Locke sharply disagrees with Aristotle over the natural basis and hence the actual substance of the virtuous habituation. Locke rejects the notion, handed down from the Greco-Roman classics but also from the biblical tradition, that virtue conceived as noble or sublime (and not merely as useful, pleasant, or prestigious) has an intrinsic attraction to and rootedness in human nature, as part of an essential human longing for self-transcendence and self-overcoming for the sake of higher sources of meaning and devotion. The artificial sense of shame, Locke avers, "is the only true Restraint belonging to Virtue" (sec. 78). Nowhere in Locke's education are children oriented toward heroism, self-sacrifice, or sublime asceticism. There is no hint of a call to imitate the sufferings and labors of Christ, and very little if any reference to the great classical civic educational themes of patriotism, military heroism, and passionate friendship or love. The inspiration of poetry and the other fine arts occupies at best a subordinate place in Locke's educational doctrine; and Locke does not suggest that an attachment to specific heroes or heroic models, in history or literature, ought to figure prominently in moral education.

The contrast with both Obadiah Walker and John Witherspoon, as well as John Milton, is again sharp. Walker speaks repeatedly of the need to appeal to the child's sense of honor and conscience as something above and beyond a sense of shame or a desire for repute and fame: When teaching the child "to carry himself decently, tell him, not that the people will think better of him, *that* he shall be more accepted in conversation; but tell him *that* he ought to carry himself as the noblest and sublimest of God's creatures." Awe for the sublime, yearning for heroism, and reverence, not merely respect, for one's self and soul are to be cultivated through the call and the experience of self-sacrifice; Christ's sufferings are to be held up as exemplars of the sufferings, including disgrace and shame, that the child should be prepared to endure in adult life. Of course, only a handful can be saints or heroes, but those few are relevant models for everyone, and the preparation for the call to heroism must be unceasing. Every child should strive for a life of "*more* leisure for devotion, *more* severity towards our selves, *more*, and *more* heroicall, acts of virtues, *which* approach nearest to the life of our Lord."[23]

It is worth recalling here the classic statement of the pre-Lockean view as found in the oft-cited essay "On the Education of Children," attributed to Plutarch. After recommending the examples of Socrates, Plato, and Archytas in their mastery of anger and moral indignation, the author says:

> But someone will say these things are hard, and difficult to imitate. I too know that. But one must try as much as possible, using these as models, to rein in the greater part of unrestrained and raging anger; for in other respects as well we are not really comparable to those men, in experience or in gentlemanliness. But since we too are, no less than they, priests, as it were, of divine mysteries, and torchbearers for Wisdom, we attempt, as much as is in our capacity, to imitate and come within hailing distance in these respects.[24]

Witherspoon, in letter 3, observes, "You cannot easily believe the weight that it gives to family authority, when it appears visibly to proceed from a sense of duty, and to be itself, an act of obedience to God."[25] Locke explicitly criticizes moral upbringing that devotes great energy to the attempt to instill in children a sense of duty or an adherence to rules. As much as possible, parents should induce in the child a desire to do what ought to be done; the appeal should be not only to the child's primitive "reasoning" about what is good or pleasant for him but also to the natural delight all humans feel in freedom from constraint or rule.

> None of the Things they are to learn should ever be made a Burthen to them, or imposed on them as a *Task*. Whatever is so proposed presently becomes irksome. . . . Is it not so with grown Men? What they do chearfully of themselves, do they not presently grow sick of, and can no more endure, as soon as they find it is expected of them, as a Duty? Children have as much a Mind to shew that they are free, that their own good Actions come from themselves, that they are absolute and independent, as any of the proudest of you grown Men, think of them as you please. (sec 73)

Locke recognizes pitfalls in this advice, but he insists that with great care they are avoidable. He does not mean that children should be indulged or allowed to do just as they wish at every moment. They should be led by habit, praise, and example to learn to enjoy exercising the mental self-control that enables one to shift from one occupation or train of thought to another that is less immediately enjoyable or inviting, but recognized as advantageous. Even turning away from what one enjoys can become a matter of enjoyment, if the education is well managed: "You cannot imagine of what Force Custom is" (sec. 14). The most powerful lever of custom is example, especially the example set by the parents in every moment of their lives. Many have said this, or something similar, but no one before Locke went so far in reducing the natural inclinations of man toward zero, thereby transforming human beings, especially in childhood, into moral and spiritual chameleons.

> Children (nay, and Men too) do most by Example. We are all a sort of Camelions, that still take a Tincture from things near us.
> . . . He that will have his Son have a Respect for him, and his Orders, must himself have a great Reverence for his Son. *Maxima debetur pueris reverentia* [Boys are owed the greatest reverence—Juvenal, *Satires* 14]. You must do nothing before him, which you would not have him imitate. . . . if you assume to your self the liberty you have taken, as a Privilege belonging to riper Years, to which a Child must not aspire, you do but add new force to

your Example, and recommend the Action the more powerfully to him. For you must always remember, that Children affect to be Men earlier than is thought. (secs. 67, 71)

Through example, rough-and-tumble play, and well-gauged praise and blame, children may be habituated to considerable pain and discomfort: "They should be harden'd against all Sufferings, especially of the Body, and have no Tenderness but what rises from an ingenuous Shame, and a quick Sence of Reputation" (sec. 113). In this way, though "true fortitude" is something "so few Men attain to, that we are not to expect it from Children," children may nevertheless take the first steps toward "noble and manly Steadiness," especially if one is careful "to keep Children from Frights of all kinds" and "by gentle degrees, to accustom Children to those things, they are too much afraid of"—bearing in mind that "the only thing, we naturally are afraid of, is Pain, or loss of Pleasure" (sec. 115).

But, just as there is no particular place in Locke's political theory for the right to keep and bear arms, so there is no place in Locke's moral education for the practice of hunting. In the classical republican tradition, hunting with weapons had been a crowning feature of adolescent education.[26] In Locke's scheme, what replaces the promotion of hunting is a strong endorsement of kindness to pets and all animals, while the celebration of military virtue is replaced by the sober praise of "humanity" and "preservation."

Children should from the beginning be bred up in an Abhorrence of *killing*, or tormenting any living Creature; and be taught not to *spoil* or destroy any thing, unless it be for the Preservation or Advantage of some other, that is Nobler. And truly, if the Preservation of all Mankind, as much as in him lies, were every one's Persuasion, as indeed it is every one's Duty, and the true Principle to regulate our Religion, Politicks and Morality by, the World would be much quieter, and better natur'd than it is. (sec. 116)

Given the marked deemphasis on training the youngster in either weaponry or politics and public speaking, and given the domestic character of the education and the private life of family and business for which the education prepares the youth, it is much easier for Locke than it was for Xenophon, Plato, and Milton to suggest that his educational proposals ought to be applied, with small variation, to daughters as well as sons. In opposition to the prevailing custom of the time, especially in the upper classes, Locke writes concerning girls that "the nearer they come to the Hardships of their Brothers in their Education, the greater Advantage will they receive from it all the remaining Part of their Lives" (sec. 9).[27]

It is appropriate to add here that Locke's political philosophy, as presented in the *Two Treatises of Government*, may be said to represent one long theoretical polemic against patriarchy and all forms of authority, both familial and extrafamilial, rooted in or derived from patriarchy. Locke attacks the traditional authority of fathers not simply in the name of maternal authority but, more radically, in the name of the liberty and equality of all human beings, even in their relations as parents and offspring. Locke is of course well aware that children "are not born in this full state of *Equality*, though they are born to it"; initially, parents must have an awesome and fearful sway over children, for the sake of the children's incipient and future education. But Locke therefore insists that this authority is "but a temporary one. The Bonds of this Subjection are like the Swadling Cloths they are wrapt up in, and supported by, in the weakness of their Infancy. Age and Reason as they grow up, loosen them till at length they drop quite off, and leave a Man at his own free Disposal."[28]

It is hard to imagine a political or educational thesis more deeply opposed to Locke's in spirit than that of the early eighteenth-century Englishman Lord Kames. Kames praises the "absolute dependence" of children on their parents, because such dependence "produces a habit of submission to authority, a fine preparation for the social life. The authority of the magistrate succeeds to that of the parent; and the submission paid to the latter is readily transferred to the former." In this as in several other fundamental respects, Thomas Jefferson and other Founders unequivocally reject Lord Kames's patriarchal educational and civic views in the name of Lockean principles. This repudiation needs to be stressed, given the misleading and exaggerated claims advanced by scholars in the past generation about the influence of Lord Kames on Jefferson or about the purported congruity between the views of Jefferson and Kames. Thus, for example, Wilson Smith, apparently bedazzled momentarily by the prevailing scholarly fad, excerpts precisely the passage on authority just quoted in a brief reading entitled "Lord Kames's Educated Man Anticipates the Jeffersonian View."[29]

Education in the Social Virtues

Lockean education culminates in the inculcation of the social virtues, which represent the rational, constructed antidote to the naturally vicious proclivities of human sociability.

> Children who live together often strive for Mastery, whose Wills shall carry
> it over the rest: Whoever begins the *Contest*, should be sure to be crossed in

it. But not only that, but they should be taught to have all the *Deference, Complaisance and Civility* for one another imaginable. This, when they see it procures them respect, Love and Esteem, and that they lose no Superiority by it, they will take more Pleasure in, than in insolent Domineering; for so plainly is the other. (sec. 109)

Justice in the strict sense depends on the respect for private property, and since children can, strictly speaking, own no property, they can know no justice. However, they can be guided toward a sense of justice by being taught generosity, or the evil of covetousness. The appeal to love or to sacrifice is not, in Locke's opinion, the proper method to instill this virtue. One succeeds in making children reliably generous by showing them that they will eventually profit and acquire more if they are first generous: "Let them find by Experience, that the most *Liberal* has always most plenty, with Esteem and Commendation to boot, and they will quickly learn to practise it. . . . This should be encouraged by great Commendation and Credit, and constantly taking care, that he loses nothing by his *Liberality*. Let all the Instances he gives of such Freeness, be always repaid, and with Interest" (sec. 110).[30]

The keystone of the social virtues is what Locke calls *"civility"*—a word to which he gives a new and unprecedentedly elevated significance. Before Locke we may identify two major clusters of meaning for this crucial term in the history of educational thought. "Civility" comes from the Latin term *civilitas*, which stems from the Latin word for city, understood as the equivalent of the Greek *polis*. As the Oxford English Dictionary remarks (sv. "civility"), the Latin *civilitas* is analogous to the Greek *politikē*: It denotes the political art, or statesmanship, understood as the craft of ruling and being ruled in a small classical republic like early Rome or Athens.

The first cluster of meanings of civility in English, now mostly obsolete, stems from this classical republican signification. So conceived, the term is central to such works as Thomas Elyot's *Boke Named the Governour* (1531) which, as Lawrence Cremin remarks, "set the tone for an immense literature devoted to the education of those who would qualify for positions of leadership in Tudor and Stuart England." The stress in these works was on education to the calling of politics or public service in the classical mold, and Cremin has argued that Locke's treatise on education is "a civility manual in the tradition of *The Governour*."[31] Viewed in this deceptive light, Locke's educational teaching appears to be the crucial bridge between the classical republican tradition and the American Founding generation. But here again Cremin's characterization is wide of the mark and contributes to a misunderstanding of the fundamentally unclassical thrust of Lockean educational theory and its impact on the colonists.

Locke's use of the term is in fact rooted in a different, though not totally unrelated, cluster of meanings.

From a very early period, civility had another connotation, deriving from the classical notion that life in the *polis* or the republican city was the distinguishing mark of a humane as opposed to a barbaric existence. By the late medieval period and the Renaissance, this meaning of civility, understood as opposed to barbarism, had been broadened and diluted through educational works such as Baldesar Castiglione's *Book of the Courtier*, which applied it to monarchic political systems. As a result, in sixteenth- and seventeenth-century English the word "civility," in this second sense, became nearly the equivalent of the French word *politesse*, with connotations, not of republican virtue, but of courtly polish or politeness, gentility and social grace, "breeding." To be sure, the word could at the same time refer, as it does in Obadiah Walker, to the inner sense of humanity, the respect for one's fellowmen, that dictates or ought to dictate the outward expression of politeness.[32] It is *this* meaning of civility that Locke picks up and enlarges in significance.

Civility, as Locke uses the term, does not refer to political leadership, statecraft, or even citizenship: it is a social rather than a civic or political virtue. But at the same time, Locke departs from Walker in dissociating civility and courtiership, for Locke's civility embodies a more egalitarian sentiment of humanity. And, of course, Locke makes the desire for recognition from others, rather than piety or pride or a sense of one's inner nobility, the motive underlying the virtue. Accordingly, the difference between Walker's notion of civility and Locke's is most marked in Walker's insistence that the first rule of civility governs behavior before God, in church. John Witherspoon characteristically remains closer to Walker than to Locke when, in his fourth letter, he emphasizes the intimate connection between civility and piety: "I cannot help thinking that true religion is not only consistent with, but necessary to the perfection of true politeness. . . . politeness can scarcely be attained in any other way."[33]

Although Lockean civility is observant of conventional distinctions of rank and station, this social virtue may be understood to replace the Christian virtues of humility and charity in the lists as the opponent of the vice of vainglory—and also the vice (the Aristotelian virtue) of pride.

> We ought not to think so well of our selves, as to stand upon our own Value; and assume to ourselves a Preference before others, because of any Advantage, we may imagine, we have over them; but modestly to take what is offered, when it is our due.
>
> . . . Civility of the Mind . . . is that general Good will and Regard for all People, which makes any one have a care not to shew, in his Carriage, any contempt, disrespect, or neglect of them. (secs. 142–43)

Learning as the Least Important Part of Education

Locke's education is predominantly a moral education, and the erudition that usually bulks so large in thoughts or writing about education is treated almost dismissively by Locke:

> You will wonder, perhaps, that I put *Learning* last, especially if I tell you I think it the least part. This may seem strange in the mouth of a bookish Man, and this making usually the chief, if not the only bustle and stir about Children; this being almost that alone, which is thought on, when People talk of Education, makes it the greater Paradox.
> . . . Reading, and Writing, and *Learning*, I allow to be necessary, but yet not the chief Business. (sec. 147)

Nevertheless, Locke bends his amazing mind to the discovery of wonderfully clever and in fact deeply insightful methods for the teaching of linguistic and scientific skills, and he does not cease before he has sketched the outlines of a capacious and humane learning. Throughout this discussion, Locke's eye is on what will be truly useful to the young in adult life. He therefore stresses competence in one's native tongue above all. Latin remains essential for a gentleman, but Locke doubts whether it is not a waste of time for youngsters who are destined for trades and farming. Greek can be dispensed with, for all except those who (like Locke himself) intend to be scholars or "bookish." Nowhere in the treatise on education does Locke suggest the superiority of his own philosophic or contemplative life, or make any attempt to lead the young to revere that way of life from afar.[34] Locke does add, with an apology and as a kind of afterthought, "the Thoughts of a Judicious Author," "for the sake of those who are designed to be Scholars," or for "all who desire to be truly Learned" (as is Locke himself):

> The Study, *says he*, of the original text can never be sufficiently recommended. 'Tis the shortest, surest, and most agreeable way to all sorts of Learning. Draw from the spring head, and take not things at second hand. Let the Writings of the great Masters be never laid aside, dwell upon them, settle them in your Mind, and cite them upon occasion; make it your Business thoroughly to understand them in their full Extent, and all their Circumstances: Acquaint yourself fully with the principles of Original Authors; bring them to a consistency. . . . and then do not you rest till you bring your self to the same. (sec. 195)

Locke was extraordinarily reticent about his own life as a philosopher, but he was always too much a philosopher ever wholly to overlook the existence among his readership of readers akin to himself.

As for the life of the poet—classically the great competitor of the philosophic life for the garland of wisdom, bliss, and favor from God—Locke reflects that if a child "have a Poetick Vein, 'tis to me the strangest thing in the World, that the Father should desire, or suffer it to be cherished, or improved. Methinks the Parents should labour to have it stifled, and suppressed, as much as may be. . . . and there are very few Instances of those, who have added to their Patrimony by any thing they have reaped from thence" (sec. 174). In contrast, we find Walker asserting that, "when Poetry is despised, other Sciences are also on the wane."[35]

Geography, arithmetic, astronomy, geometry, and chronology form an ascending path of study that culminates in history, political science, and law. But much of what passes for history is in Locke's view worse than useless: "All the Entertainment and talk of History is of nothing almost but Fighting and Killing. . . . by these Steps unnatural Cruelty is planted in us" (sec. 116). The study of history ought to be guided and controlled by the political theory that teaches "the natural Rights of Men, and the original and Foundations of Society, and the Duties resulting from thence. This *general Part of Civil-law* and History, are Studies which a Gentleman should not barely touch at, but constantly dwell upon, and never have done with" (sec. 186). Locke's treatise on education leads to the threshold of the *Two Treatises of Government* and the new conception of legitimate republican government there elaborated.

Part Two
Schools for the Emerging Republic

4 · Benjamin Franklin and the Idea of a Distinctively American Academy

By the middle of the eighteenth century, the influence in America of Locke's educational treatise, partly by way of intermediaries such as John Clarke and Isaac Watts, was massive. Older educational writings and theories, especially those stemming from the Christian tradition, were surely not cast into oblivion, but, just as surely, they were under relentless pressure either to reinterpret themselves in Lockean terms or to take up a rather desperate struggle against the new wave of Lockean and post-Lockean educational thinking.[1]

Testifying vividly to this state of affairs is the most remarkable American contribution to the discussion of education in midcentury: Benjamin Franklin's *Proposals Relating to the Education of Youth in Pennsylvania* (1749), coupled with his "Idea of the English School" (1750). Franklin later revisited these writings near the end of his life in "Observations Relative to the Intentions of the Original Founders of the Academy in Philadelphia" (1789). In these essays, Franklin cites Obadiah Walker and John Milton, but it is manifestly taken for granted that the supreme authority for Franklin and his readers is John Locke—and this estimation gains added certainty when we note that the two recent authorities other than Rollin to whom Franklin appeals (David Fordyce and George Turnbull) are themselves followers of Locke.[2] Yet however numerous and substantial his explicit borrowings from and implicit dependence upon Locke's theory of education and of human nature, we cannot fail to notice that Franklin's whole project departs in a decisive respect from Locke, and the nature of the departure may be said to be archetypical of the distinctively American path in education.

Franklin's objective was the establishment of an academy. This academy was intended to serve as the vanguard of a grand new army of private (and eventually public) secondary schools to which Americans were to entrust the education of the leading citizens of the future. In the near term, Franklin's proposals met with only limited success. The founding of Phillips Andover Academy in 1778, however, initiated a period of steadily growing enthusiasm for boarding schools whose curricula and vision of educational goals were in considerable measure shaped by the spirit of Franklin's suggestions.[3]

As they followed Franklin's lead, Americans who spoke out about education became increasingly conscious that in advocating and designing formal schooling, they were shaping a new synthesis of Lockean and classical educational principles. They recognized, moreover, that this new synthesis was of a more transformative and perplexing character than the relatively modest innovations offered by such English schoolteachers or writers on schoolteaching as John Clarke, whose *Essay upon the Education of Youth in Grammar Schools* had shown how Locke's pithy thoughts on "learning"—especially the learning of languages—could be felicitously expanded and applied to small Latin school situations.

To some extent, the American concern with formal schooling builds on the peculiarly strong traditions of public schooling of the New England states, especially Massachusetts and Connecticut; but a closer look shows how greatly the genius set in motion by Franklin differs from the spirit of the earlier colonial schools. In 1647 Massachusetts had passed a law, copied verbatim by Connecticut in 1650, that had mandated publicly supported schools to combat "the old deluder, Satan," by teaching the reading skill needed to study the Bible. From these and other kindred laws had grown not only a system of elementary schools aimed at Bible study but also a small number of secondary ("grammar") schools; the latter taught a classical curriculum similar to the course of study in England's numerous secondary schools, which was intended to prepare men for the ministry as well as other learned professions.[4] The new outlook spearheaded by Franklin parted company with this official New England conception in two crucial (and Lockean) respects.

The New Status of Religion in the School

In the first place, the cultivation of Puritan religious spirituality, as well as the Quaker spirituality that was more familiar in the existing schools of Philadelphia, ceased to be a goal.[5] This is not to say that the new academic notion entailed the total expulsion of religion from the academy. But Franklin treated religion as a necessary supplement to, rather than the inspiration and guiding light for, morality. And the religion in question was "public" or "civil" religion; i.e., that minimal popular creed which history showed to be essential for social health. When Franklin sent his *Proposals* to the great evangelist preacher George Whitefield and asked for comment, Whitefield replied:

> Your plan I have read over, and do not wonder at its meeting with general approbation. It is certainly well calculated to promote polite literature; but I

think there wants *aliquid Christi* in it, to make it so useful as I would desire it might be. It is true, you say, "The youth are to be taught some public religion, and the excellency of the christian religion in particular:" [This passage is in fact nowhere to be found in the *Proposals* as we have them; did the wily Franklin send a "doctored" version to Whitefield for his approval?] but methinks this is mentioned too late, and too soon passed over. As we are all creatures of a day; as our whole life is but one small point between two eternities, it is reasonable to suppose, that the grand end of every christian institution for forming tender minds, should be to convince them of their natural depravity, of the means of recovering out of it, and of the necessity of preparing for the enjoyment of the supreme Being in a future state. These are the grand points in which christianity centers. Arts and sciences may be built on this, and serve to embellish and set off this superstructure, but without this, I think there cannot be any good foundation. . . . I think also in such an institution, there should be a well-approved christian orator, who should not be content with giving a public lecture in general upon oratory, but who should visit and take pains with every class, and teach them early how to speak, and read, and pronounce well. . . . It would serve as an agreeable amusement, and would be of great service, whether the youth be intended for the pulpit, the bar, or any other profession whatsoever. . . . I hope your agreement meets with the approbation of the inhabitants, and that it will be serviceable to the cause of vital piety and good education. . . . But all this depends on the integrity, disinterestedness, and piety of the gentlemen concerned. An institution, founded on such a basis, God will bless and succeed; but without these, the most promising schemes will prove abortive, and the most flourishing structures, in the end, turn out mere Babels.

Whitefield's very polite complaint acquires greater force when we observe that in the sole passage where Franklin does make a passing nod to "publick religion," he does not in fact say or imply that the students are to be taught any such religion in the school. The reference to "public religion" occurs in a paragraph under the rubric of "History": "*History* will also afford frequent Opportunities of showing the Necessity of a *Publick Religion*, from its usefulness to the Publick; [and] the Advantages of a religious Character among private Persons."[6]

There is no indication that Franklin attempted to change the school's goals or program in response to Whitefield's protest. On the other hand, Franklin later felt compelled to make some qualified concessions. In 1751, he replied to a letter (now lost) from the Anglican divine Samuel Johnson, subsequently president of King's (Columbia) College, whom Franklin hoped would accept the post of first rector of the new school: "I received your Favour of the 11th Inst. and thank you for the Hint you give of the Omission in the Idea. The Sacred Classics are read in the English School, tho' I forgot to mention them: And I shall propose at the Meeting of the Schools after the Holidays, that the English Master begin and continue to read select portions of them daily with the Prayer, as you advise."[7]

The rather radical deism that Lawrence Cremin has attributed to Franklin's educational thinking is nowhere more gracefully or sinuously evident than in the closing words of his *Proposals*. There he discusses the end of education, virtue, which he defines as service to one's fellowman; and virtue so conceived, he insists, encompasses the whole of piety. To sanction this transformation of the idea of love of God, Franklin appeals to the authority of none other than Milton!

> The Idea of what is *true Merit*, should also be often presented to Youth, explain'd and impress'd on their Minds, as consisting in an *Inclination* join'd with an *Ability* to serve Mankind, one's Country, Friends and Family; which *Ability* is (with the Blessing of God) to be acquir'd or greatly encreas'd by *true Learning*; and should indeed be the great *Aim* and *End* of all Learning. [Franklin's Note:] To have in View the *Glory* and *Service of God*, as some express themselves, is only the same Thing in other Words. For *Doing Good to Men* is the *only Service of God* in our Power; and *to imitate his Beneficence* is to *glorify* him. Hence Milton says, "The *End* of Learning is to repair the Ruins of our first Parents, by regaining to *know God aright*, and out of that Knowledge to *love him*, to *imitate him*, to be *like him*, as we may the nearest by possessing our Souls of true Virtue."

What Franklin omits is Milton's crucial final clause: "by possessing our souls of true virtue, *which being united to the heavenly grace of faith makes up the highest perfection.*"[8]

The New Curriculum

But there is a second major break with Milton—and also with prior American tradition, at least at the official level. Franklin deepened and made respectable previously emerging challenges to the Latin and Greek philological and literary training that had bulked so large as the secular component of the "liberal" education offered in the "Latin Grammar" schools of New England and Britain. He did so in the name of a more practical education, emphasizing instruction in English usage, writing, drawing, calculation, and modern history and thought. Massachusetts laws had dictated (with mixed success) the establishment of Latin schools in counties throughout the state; but it was the so-called writing schools—private for-profit and nonprofit schools that sprang up in New England as well as in Philadelphia and elsewhere to train adolescents in the practical use of their mother tongue and arithmetic—that were in some key respects the precursors of Franklin's new notion of secondary schooling.[9]

Elaborating his aims in the "Idea of the English School," Franklin writes that students should come out of his academy

> fitted for learning any Business, Calling, or Profession, except such wherein Languages are required; and tho' unacquainted with any antient or foreign Tongue, they will be Masters of their own, which is of more immediate and general Use; and withal will have attain'd many other valuable Accomplishments; the Time usually spent in acquiring those Languages, often without Success, being here employ'd in laying such a Foundation of Knowledge and Ability, as, properly improv'd, may qualify them to pass thro' and execute the several Offices of civil Life, with Advantage and Reputation.[10]

Franklin thus shifts away from the traditional Latin school toward a model of schooling that attempts to give children skills that will help them find employment in professions other than divinity, law, teaching, and medicine; in doing so, he retains only a tenuous link to the old Puritan concern that children be readied for a "calling." In the new outlook, no longer should the young prepare for a vocation in a spirit of humility and radical dependence on God's grace, hoping for success blessed by and signifying divine election; instead, young people should seek to make a place for themselves in the world so as to achieve independence, repute, and a justified pride in their own accomplishments. The most obvious testimony to the change is the disappearance of Bible study as an essential part of the preparation for every calling.

The curricular sections of Franklin's *Proposals* commence under the explicit guidance of Locke, and specifically with the latter's recommendation that youngsters be taught not only to write but to draw clearly, "a Thing very useful to a Gentleman on several Occasions."

> How many Buildings may a man see, how many *Machines* and Habits meet with, the Ideas whereof would be easily retain'd, and communicated by a little Skill in Drawing; which being committed to Words, are in Danger to be lost, or at best but ill retained in the most exact Descriptions?

Second comes arithmetic, joined with what Franklin calls "Accounts"—a conjunction he explains by quoting as follows from Locke:

Merchants accounts, he says, if it is not necessary to help a Gentleman to *get* an Estate, yet there is nothing of more Use and Efficacy to make him *preserve* the Estate he has. 'Tis seldom observed that he who keeps an Account of his Income and Expenses, and thereby has constantly under View the Course of his Domestic Affairs, lets them run to Ruin: and I doubt not but many a Man gets behind-hand before he is aware, or runs farther on when he is once in, for want of this Care, or the Skill to do it. I would therefore advise all gentlemen to learn perfectly Merchants Accounts; and not to think 'tis a Skill that belongs not to them, because it has received its Name, and has been chiefly practis'd by Men of Traffick.[11]

Franklin then turns to the core of the curriculum, the study of "our own" English language. Tacitly following Locke, Franklin assigns a translation of the fables of Aesop as the reading for the first grade in the English school. Under the new dispensation there is of course no longer any need to have even older students practice English by reading the King James Bible. The highest level of reading is to be in contemporary English literature, including substantial modern political theory: "Some of our best Writers, as Tillotson, Addison, Pope, Algernon Sidney, Cato's Letters, &c. should be Classicks: the Stiles principally to be cultivated, being the *clear* and *concise*." For this crucial innovation of making English grammar and literature his focus instead of Latin and Greek, Franklin invokes the authority of Locke.

Mr. Locke, speaking of *Grammar*, p. 252. says, "That to those the greatest Part of whose Business in this World is to be done with their Tongues, and with their Pens, it is convenient, if not necessary, that they should speak properly and correctly. . . . *Grammar is necessary*; but it is the Grammar *only of their own proper Tongues*. . . . If this be so (as I suppose it is) it will be Matter of Wonder, why young Gentlemen are forc'd to learn the Grammars of foreign and dead Languages, and are never once told the Grammar of their own Tongues. . . . Nor is their own language ever propos'd to them as worthy their Care and Cultivating, tho' they have *daily Use* of it, and are not seldom, in the future Course of their Lives, judg'd of by their handsome or awkward Way of expressing themselves in it."[12]

Continuing explicitly to follow the lead of Locke, Franklin's *Proposals* recommends that practice in letter writing be a chief means of familiarizing youngsters with English composition and clear and graceful expression of their thoughts. To appreciate the radicalism of this suggestion, we need to remind ourselves of what Milton had proposed in the way of instruction in language. Milton had recommended that after students began to master the rudiments of grammar, "some easy and delightful book of education would be read to them, whereof the Greeks have store, as Cebes, Plutarch, and other Socratic discourses," and "after evening repast, till bedtime, their thoughts will be best taken up in the easy grounds of religion and the story of Scripture."

> But here the main skill and groundwork will be to temper them such lectures and explanations, upon every opportunity, as may lead and draw them in willing obedience, inflamed with the study of learning and the admiration of virtue, stirred up with high hopes of living to be brave men and worthy patriots, dear to God and famous to all ages; that they may despise and scorn all their childish and ill-taught qualities, to delight in manly and liberal exercises.

The full implications of Franklin's notion of the benefits of instruction in letter writing emerge in the amplification he provides in his essay on the English school. There he makes it clearer that, far from aspiring to imitate heroes, the boys are to practice formulating their own opinions, tastes, and "common" experiences, as well as the types of letters that will be useful in future business dealings: "The Boys should be put on Writing Letters to each other on any common Occurences, and on various Subjects, imaginary Business, &c., containing little Stories, Accounts of their late Reading, what Parts of Authors please them, and why. . . . Some of the best Letters published in our own Language, as Sir William Temple's, those of Pope, and his friends, and some others, might be set before the Youth as Models."[13]

Yet immediately after this striking endorsement of repeated practice in expressing the Lockean "self," Franklin reminds us of his steady attachment to the classical tradition Milton represents. For in the private home situation that Locke envisages as the environment for education, there is of course little place for declamation. Franklin, however, has in mind a school or schoolroom filled with an audience of other boys, and he advises that "they may be put on making Declamations, repeating Speeches, delivering Orations, &c." One of the school's goals is to cultivate the skills of public oral communication that are native to self-governing communities.[14]

This concern with oratory would become more pointed in discussions of education at the time of the Revolution. "Eloquence is the child of a free state," David Ramsay proclaimed in 1778.

> In this form of government, as public measures are determined by a majority of votes, arguments enforced by the arts of persuasion, must evermore be crowned with success. . . . In royal governments, where the will of one or a few has the direction of public measures, the orator may harangue, but

most probably will reap persecution and imprisonment, as the fruit of his labor: Whereas, in our present happy system, the poorest school boy may prosecute his studies with increasing ardor, from the prospect, that in a few years he may, by his improved abilities, direct the determinations of public bodies, on subjects of the most stupendous consequence.[15]

The ebullient Ramsay does not pause to reflect on the new dangers from demagoguery and from the arts of deceit that are in our time called "public relations." More sober minds, like Franklin's, call for a training in rhetoric that would enable discrimination between sophistry and eloquently reasoned public discourse. Models are to be sought in the great classical teachers and practitioners. The stress by Franklin and others on oratory or rhetoric echoes the great tradition of rhetoric and of educating gentleman-orators, which derives from Isocrates, Cicero, and Quintilian. This heritage remained alive, if in enfeebled and routinized versions, in the Middle Ages and sprang to vigorous life again in the Renaissance. Even in Puritan New England, but to a greater extent among the Anglican southern gentry, the traditional model of the noble orator continued to provide some of the inspiration for what vitality there was in the classical education.

But while reaching back to the past, Franklin as usual keeps his eye on the present and future. Perhaps the most important aspect of rhetoric in the contemporary world, he notes, is that expressed by the pen and the printed page: "Modern Political Oratory being chiefly performed by the Pen and Press, its Advantages over the Antient in some Respects are to be shown; as that its Effects are more extensive, more lasting, &c." In Franklin's new vision, journalism, conceived as a high civic calling within the republic, replaces or grows out of the ancient Isocratian oratorical vocation. The text to which Franklin and others return again and again as a model for students is *The Spectator*. Franklin links the training in oral public expression to an encouragement of the reading of newspapers, and he calls for the cultivation of a vivid reading voice as a vehicle for bringing to life and disseminating the written word, in circles as small as family gatherings and as large as public meetings. Moreover, he evidently means to encourage youngsters to enjoy and learn from participating in the give-and-take of argument and discussion that might accompany and intensify the drama of historic occasions.

Accustoming Boys to read aloud what they do not first understand, is the Cause of those even set Tones so common among Readers, which when they have once got a Habit of using, they find so difficult to correct: By which means, among Fifty readers we scarcely find a good One. For want of good Reading, Pieces publish'd with a view to influence the Minds of Men for their own or the publick Benefit, lose half their Force. Were there but one good Reader in a Neighbourhood, a publick Orator might be heard throughout a Nation with the same Advantages, and have the same Effect on his Audience, as if they stood within the reach of his Voice.

On *Historical* Occasions, Questions of Right and Wrong, Justice and Injustice, will naturally arise, and may be put to Youth, which they may debate in Conversation and in Writing. When they ardently desire Victory, for the Sake of the Praise attending it, they will begin to feel the Want, and be sensible of the use of *Logic*, or the Art of Reasoning to *discover* truth, and of Arguing to *defend* it, and *convince* Adversaries. This would be the Time to acquaint them with the Principles of that Art. Grotius, Pufendorf, and some other Writers of the same Kind, may be used on these Occasions to decide their Disputes. Publick Disputes warm the Imagination, whet the Industry, and strengthen the natural Abilities.[16]

Integrated into the study of English is to be history, "as a constant Part of their Reading, such as the Translations of the Greek and Roman Historians, and the modern Histories of antient Greece and Rome, &c." Here again Franklin cites Locke, but this time with a significant counterfeit: Locke had indeed, as Franklin quotes him, praised history as the most "delightful" study and therefore "the fittest for a young Lad"; but in Locke this was a prelude to a very different argument, namely, that history was then the way to introduce one's son to Latin. By reading "the plainest and easiest *Historians*" rather than "Books beyond their Capacity, such as are the *Roman* Orators and Poets," the youth might be led "by a gradual Progress" to "read the most difficult and sublime of the *Latin* Authors, such as are *Tully*, *Virgil*, and *Horace*." For while Locke deplored the ignorance of English grammar and usage, and questioned whether young people, including the younger sons of gentlemen, who were destined for trades and agriculture needed to waste their time learning Latin, he was nonetheless certain that Latin was "absolutely necessary to a Gentleman." With a view to educating gentlemen, he offered fascinating new methods of learning Latin, with a stress on beginning by way of daily conversation and reading aloud, especially when very young with the mother (who Locke was sure could teach herself Latin as they went, "if she will but spend two or three hours in a day with him") and later with the tutor.[17]

The distance between Locke's gentlemanly education and Franklin's academic education is particularly evident here. (It is pertinent to observe that Franklin himself, in sharp contrast to Locke, was not well-educated in the classical languages.) By a sly distortion of Locke's text, Franklin invokes the great philosopher's authority while quietly erasing the purely gentlemanly dimension of the master's concern with education in history. Still, one may argue that Franklin's alteration of the sense of Locke's remarks is for the sake of their spirit, as applied in new circumstances. For Locke may be understood to have insisted on the necessity of a gentleman's learning Latin on utilitarian grounds: Latin at the turn of the eighteenth century remained the lingua franca of European discourse and of many major publications. Moreover, Franklin's break with traditional canons does not imply his intention to abandon training in the classical languages altogether. His *Proposals* goes on to affirm that history should indeed be taught in such a way as to arouse the appetite for learning the classical languages, that all who wish should be allowed to do so, and that those who are to be divines, doctors, or lawyers *must* do so:

> When Youth are told, that the Great Men whose Lives and Actions they read in History, spoke two of the best Languages that ever were, the most expressive, copious, beautiful; and that the finest Writings, the most correct Compositions, the most perfect Productions of human Wit and Wisdom, are in those Languages, which have endured Ages, and will endure while there are Men; that no Translation can do them Justice, or give the Pleasure found in Reading the Originals; that those Languages contain all Science; that one of them is become almost universal, being the Language of Learned Men in all Countries; that to understand them is a distinguishing Ornament; &c. they may be thereby made desirous of learning those Languages, and their Industry sharpen'd in the Acquisition of them. All intended for Divinity should be taught the Latin and Greek; for Physick, the Latin, Greek and French; for Law, the Latin and French; Merchants, the French, German, and Spanish: And though all should not be compell'd to learn Latin, Greek, or the modern foreign Languages; yet none that have an ardent Desire to learn them should be refused; their English, Arithmetick, and other Studies absolutely necessary, being at the same time not neglected.[18]

The study of history is to be both a central feature of the curriculum in its own right and the vehicle for introducing such useful studies as geography, chronology, ancient customs, languages, and morality. These all lead up to constitutional law and the political theory that teaches "how Men and their Properties are protected by joining in Societies and establishing Governments; their Industry encouraged and rewarded, Arts invented, and Life made more comfortable: The Advantages of *Liberty*, Mischiefs of *Licentiousness*, Benefits arising from good Laws and a due Execution of Justice, &c. Thus may the first Principles of sound *Politicks* be fix'd in the Minds of Youth." Here Franklin cites both Milton, who appeals first to Moses and then to the classics, and Locke, who appeals to those modern theorists by whom the student may be "instructed in the natural Rights of Men."[19]

Franklin breaks notably with Locke, however, when he makes human history the prelude to a study of natural history. Locke had warned that an inquiry into nature by itself, without some prior study of a compendium of the Bible or its teachings, was likely to issue in materialism: "Matter being a thing, that all our Senses are constantly conversant with, it is so apt to possess the Mind, and exclude all other Beings, but Matter, that prejudice, grounded on such Principles, often leaves no room for the admittance of Spirits, or the allowing any such things as *immaterial Beings in rerum natura*."[20] Franklin either does not heed, or does not care about, the danger. As authorities for the study of nature, he does indeed cite Rollin and Milton, who, more sanguine than Locke, advocate this study without hesitation. They recommend it as conducing to natural religion and providing medicinal benefits for soldiers in war and for heads of families in peace. What Franklin does not note is that these two authorities intended the study of nature to be guided by the works of Aristotle rather than (as in Locke) by Descartes, Boyle, and Newton.

Franklin himself blazes a new trail in his *Proposals* by expatiating upon the commercial and technological grounds for the study of natural history or science. Such study

> would not only be delightful to Youth, and furnish them with Matter for their Letters, &c. as well as other History; but afterwards of great Use to them, whether they are Merchants, Handicrafts, or Divines; enabling the first the better to understand many Commodities, Drugs, &c. the second to improve his Trade or Handicraft by new Mixtures, Materials, &c. and the last to adorn his Discourses by beautiful Comparisons, and strengthen them by new Proofs of Divine Providence. . . . *Natural History* will also afford Opportunities of introducing many Observations, relating to the Preservation of Health.

As Franklin puts it in his essay on the English school, "next to the knowledge of *Duty*, this Kind of Knowledge is certainly the most useful." In fact, the curriculum sketched in the *Proposals* culminates with the study of the history of commerce, leading to "mechanical philosophy."

> The History of *Commerce*, of the Invention of Arts, Rise of Manufacturers, Progress of Trade, Change of its Seats, with the Reasons, Causes, &c. may also be made entertaining to Youth, and will be useful to all. And this, with the Accounts in other History of the prodigious Force and Effect of Engines and Machines used in War, will naturally introduce a Desire to be instructed in *Mechanicks*, and to be inform'd of the Principles of that Art by

which weak men perform such Wonders, Labour is sav'd, Manufactures ex-
pedited, &c. &c. This will be the Time to show them Prints of antient and
modern machines, to explain them, to let them be copied, and to give Lectures in Mechanical Philosophy.[21]

It is at this point in the *Proposals* that Franklin adds his exhortation to inculcate and cultivate constantly the Lockean virtue of civility and its expression in
"good breeding." Franklin thus seems to contend that the study of natural science with practical ends clearly in view is much more closely tied to the study of
duty or morality than has hitherto been recognized. As Franklin here notes,
Locke had praised learning about trades and had recommended that even gentlemen master at least one trade, and preferably more than one. Milton had not
advocated the learning of a trade but did urge that the school procure "the helpful experiences of hunters, fowlers, fishermen, shepherds, gardeners, apothecar-
ies; and in the other sciences, architects, engineers, mariners, anatomists."
Given their desire to encourage a spirit of humanity, Franklin and Locke of
course do not recommend that students spend time with hunters and fowlers.
But Franklin goes well beyond even Locke's remarks to introduce a motif that
looks back to Bacon and anticipates some of the most striking and innovative
passages of Montesquieu's *Spirit of the Laws*. It is in the course and on the basis
of the study of the history of commerce and technology, Franklin seems to suggest, that the higher moral themes Locke broaches in a rather different context
in his treatise on education ought to be fully elaborated. Political history leads
naturally to the discussion of morality, justice, and the legitimate foundations of
government; but it is only when the student has studied the history of commerce, and begun to grasp the significance of the flowering of science and trade
under sound regimes, that he will begin fully to appreciate "that *Benignity of
Mind* which shows itself in *searching for* and *seizing* every Opportunity *to serve*
and *to oblige*." Just as in Bacon's New Instauration, so here in Franklin's new academic curriculum, there is a new understanding of the kind of individuals who
should be set up as models for emulation. The greatest heroes of history are to
be the captains of commerce and the argonauts of scientific inquiry and technological innovation. Their path is cleared, but only cleared, by the lesser heroes of
political and military history, who had been brought forward as models of the
second rank by Milton. The religious heroes to whom Milton had assigned pre-
eminence have no significant place in Franklin's academy.[22]

The Organization of the School

As we have seen, however, Franklin's new political project was also in large measure a very old political project, in that it sought to recreate some of what was

best in ancient public life. The precise character of the appeal to classical prece-dent prior to the rise of the full-blown revolutionary republican outlook be-comes clearer in the essay through which Franklin initiated his public campaign for the creation of a local academy. He proceeded in a manner that is both highly characteristic of his foxlike political style and revealing as to the nature of his conception of schooling.

Franklin arranged to have reprinted in the *Pennsylvania Gazette*, with a brief anonymous introduction arguing the immediate relevance of the document, a translation of a letter from Pliny the Younger to Tacitus on the subject of the founding of an academy. Pliny wrote asking his friend to help him locate in Rome candidates for tutorial positions in a school he hoped to see established by the fathers of his native provincial town. On a recent visit, Pliny had discovered that the sons were being sent far away to school in Milan, at considerable ex-pense, inconvenience, and—Pliny thought—risk to their morals. He urged the local fathers to use the money to hire tutors chosen by themselves, in a school set up in the town, so that their sons could live at home "under the eye of their parents." He further volunteered to put up a third of the money required, not-ing that he could easily afford to put up all the money but that he thought it was essential "to have the choice of the masters entirely in the breast of the par-ents, who will be so much the more careful to determine properly, as they shall be obliged to share the expense of maintaining them: for tho' they may be care-less in disposing of another's bounty, they will certainly be cautious how they apply their own." Pliny added that Tacitus was to make no engagements with the candidates since he "would leave it entirely free to the parents to judge and choose as they shall see proper."[23] The essence of Franklin's proposal as bor-rowed from Pliny is, then, a school that allows sons of citizens of a vast monar-chic empire who live far from the imperial center to be educated at home under the guidance of their parents—who are to be induced by economic incentives, as well as parental love or duty, to take an active and continuous part in selecting the local academy's teachers.

Yet the organization of the academy in Franklin's actual *Proposals* differs sig-nificantly from that foreshadowed in the anonymous letter in the *Pennsylvania Gazette*. The Pennsylvania academy is to be founded, financed, and supervised not by parents but instead by "some Persons of Leisure and publick Spirit." They are to become in a very diluted sense parental in their care for the school and the students, by making

> it their Pleasure, and in some Degree their Business, to visit the Academy often, encourage and countenance the Youth, countenance and assist the Masters, and by all Means in their Power advance the Usefulness and Rep-utation of the Design; that they look on the Students as in some Sort their

Children, treat them with Familiarity and Affection, and when they have
behav'd well, and gone through their Studies, and are to enter the World,
zealously unite, and make all the Interest that can be made to establish
them, whether in Business, Offices, Marriages, or any other Thing for their
Advantage, preferably to all other Persons whatsoever even of equal Merit.

And if Men may, and frequently do, catch such a Taste for cultivating
Flowers, for Planting, Grafting, Inoculating, and the like, as to despise all
other Amusements for their Sake, why may not we expect they should acquire a Relish for that *more useful* Culture of young Minds.[24]

Education here comes close to sounding like a spare-time hobby of the
wealthy trustees, and the quasi-parental care that is most stressed is that lav-
ished on mature and successful students rather than on those still needing acute
assistance in their adolescent moral development. There is no little irony—and
no slight vindication of both Pliny and Locke—in the fact that Franklin himself
in later years admitted that the academy had strayed far from its original aims
and that his own personal neglect of its management was largely responsible.
The trustees, and especially Franklin, who remained on the board until 1789
and served as the first elected president, had failed almost from the very start to
visit the academy, let alone to "cultivate" or assist the students there. Franklin
quotes at length from the minutes of the trustees' meetings to show that he and
his fellows had no idea what was going on at the school and had openly confessed during these sessions their total ignorance. Citing the passage just quoted
regarding the visitations and solicitations of the trustees, Franklin indignantly
comments: "these splendid promises dazzled the eyes of the public," but in fact
the trustees "shamefully broke through and set at naught the original constitutions"; "the subscribers have been disappointed and deceived."[25] We can discern
in the outcome of Franklin's proposal the sobering precedent for the very mixed
success that has attended so many American high hopes as to what might be expected from projects for institutional education, conceived as a substitute or
supplement for parental and communal rearing of adolescents.

But this was not the only respect in which Franklin's plan failed to materialize
as he had hoped. The modern, practical thrust of the academy Franklin envisioned was seriously blunted from the outset. "The Constitutions of the Publick
Academy in the City of Philadelphia," drafted by Franklin and Tench Francis
and signed on 13 November 1749, created a dual academy: one branch was to be
a Latin grammar school, but the other and, Franklin tried to insist, equally important and respected branch was to be the new sort of English grammar school.
That this bifurcation issued in a severe setback for Franklin becomes evident in
Franklin's own lament of 1789. Franklin there declares that he personally never
wanted a Latin school and agreed to one only because the more wealthy and

hence more influential subscribers insisted. He recalls the early signs that the English branch of the academy would not be put on an equal footing.

> When the Constitutions were first drawn, Blanks were left for the Salaries, and for the Number of Boys the Latin Master was to teach. The first Instance of Partiality, in favor of the Latin Part of the Institution, was in giving the Title of rector to the Latin Master; and no Title for the English one. But the most striking instance was, when we met to sign, and the blanks were first to be fill'd up, the votes of a majority carryied it to give twice as much salary to the Latin Master as to the English, and yet require twice as much duty from the English master as from the Latin, viz. 200 pounds to the Latin Master to teach 20 Boys; 100 pounds to the English Master to teach 40! . . . Another instance of the partiality above mentioned was in the March preceding, when 100 pounds sterling was voted to buy *Latin* and *Greek* books, . . . and nothing for the *English* books.[26]

Yet if Franklin's own academy slipped from his grasp, his was the spirit that slowly but surely gained ground in the American version of the "battle of the books" that occurred in the late eighteenth and early nineteenth centuries.[27] To repeat, this spirit was not one that sought to leave classical education wholly behind. On the contrary, it was to classical education that appeal was made, precisely for authorizing the deemphasis, if not the abandonment, of the study of the classical languages. For, as Franklin pointed out, quoting Turnbull and Locke, the study of dead or even foreign languages played no role whatsoever in Greek civic education; and among Romans, the study of Greek, though prized in the later, decadent ages of Rome, never became an essential part of a Roman citizen's or gentleman's education—as one of Pliny the Younger's letters on education attests.[28] What was important for the classical citizen, in contrast to the later classical grammarians and scholars, was less belles lettres than the development of the capacities appropriate to an economically independent and politically public-spirited member of society. In other words, the Americans turned from the secondhand, ornamental or scholarly, study of classic texts to a reenactment—in a wholly new setting, and with a much-changed script—of a portion at least of the civic spirit those texts depicted. That spirit, the Americans insisted, was sufficiently available in translations and resumes—such as Rollin's. At any rate, American educators were beginning to pay much less attention to philology in teaching the classics; their chief concern was that students should learn and take to heart some of the maxims of the ancients, suitably modified. "It would be well," says Franklin at the start of his description of the proposed curriculum of the academy, "if they could be taught *every Thing* that is useful, and *every Thing* that is ornamental: But Art is long, and their Time is short. It is therefore propos'd that they learn those Things that are likely to be *most useful* and *most ornamental*, Regard being had to the several professions for which they are intended."[29] It was this spirit of respect for learning, combined with a stubbornly practical and political purpose, that was to pervade all the Founders' discussions of schooling.

5 · The American Insistence on Public Schooling as Essential to Democracy

The Americans' departure from Locke, to some extent in the name of the classics, became more pronounced after the Revolution, as they tried to devise a civic education that would harmonize with a polity rather different from that of the monarchic, imperial (if increasingly liberal) England to which Locke had directly addressed his thoughts on education. Hesitantly in midcentury, and becoming ever more pronounced as the pressure of events increased the radicalness of reflection, there appeared an insistence on public, government-sponsored and -supported schools as an essential foundation of a truly self-governing republic.

The Case for Schools

Most fundamentally, American leaders made arguments—sometimes explicitly against Locke—for the superior moral merits of a school education, where the collective student life could help form the habits and tastes of republican citizens. Although schools were admittedly subject to the moral dangers Locke so cogently delineated, it was argued that they nevertheless compensated with unique moral opportunities unavailable in the private home even in the best of cases. George Washington, never one to underestimate the importance and difficulty of moral education, acknowledged the value of a parent's or private tutor's close observation, but he believed that the more rigorous discipline of schools could replace it, while providing spurs to ambition and a knowledge of men that private study could not give.[1] Locke himself had conceded that a certain emulation or stimulating competition was more readily found in a schoolroom than in a private home; the Americans suggested, however, that Locke had underemphasized the value and indeed the necessity of such emulation.

Three writers who comment incisively on this matter are Samuel Harrison Smith and Samuel Knox, co-winners of a prize given in 1797 by the American

Philosophical Society for an essay on a national system of education, and the French immigrant Lafitte du Corteil. As Smith remarks in his critique of Locke, "The great argument which may be called the center of all others urged is the production of emulation by a public education." The awarding of prizes of varying magnitude at varying intervals, the daily distribution of students into teams, and the good-natured rivalries between close friends are all seen as incomparably valuable incentives to study and excellent exercises for learning how to compete in a humane and fair spirit. Lafitte du Courteil supplements these reflections with the observation that emulation among teachers as well as students can be a beneficial feature of public schooling, especially where there is some regular and justly distributed public recognition for outstanding teachers. Taking Lafitte du Courteil's thought a step further, Samuel Knox points out that lawfully established educational institutions lend to education the majesty of the law and the moral authority of governmental suasion; the whole moral weight of the community is thrown behind education, with profoundly encouraging effects on the outlook of both children and parents.[2]

Another major set of arguments for the moral advantages of schooling revolves around the ways in which the school experience can enlist youngsters in important bonds of fellowship with other children. In childhood, Knox observes, "the youthful breast glowing with every generous, friendly, and benevolent feeling is generally most attached to those who discover the same amiable qualities and disposition. Hence friendships have been formed and cemented which no circumstance or accident during their future lives could entirely dissolve." The civic value of personal friendships formed in public school is enhanced when the school mixes youths of diverse backgrounds, thus making possible a discovery of affectionate ties that counteract the social dynamic tending to alienate classes, religious persuasions, and ethnic groups. Homogenizing and fraternal effects of a weaker but still appreciable sort may even extend across and between states, if young Americans grow up all possessing some roughly similar educational experiences, the outcome of a roughly uniform system of schooling.[3]

Samuel Harrison Smith goes further in praise of collective education; he appeals not only to Milton and Quintilian but, most emphatically, to the example of Sparta to support his plan for public education in boarding academies. Such academies, he argues, will not only teach republican virtues but will remove students from the often stultifying prejudices of parents. In this, Smith of course overlooks the fact that Sparta and the other Greek republics were urban, not rural, societies and that the young therefore lived at home even while attending the most platoonlike schools. Few are as enthusiastic as Smith in praising the separation of children from their parents, but others do note the potential for civic education that comes with living together and especially the benefits of boarding academies located out in the country, away from the corrupting atmosphere of large towns and cities.[4]

Benjamin Rush, on the other hand, makes a more plausible appeal to classical republicanism when he protests

> against the custom which prevails in some parts of America (but which is daily falling into disuse in Europe) of crowding boys together under one roof for the purpose of education. The practice is the gloomy remains of monkish ignorance and is as unfavorable to the improvements of the mind in useful learning as monasteries are to the spirit of religion. I grant this mode of secluding boys from the intercourse of private families has a tendency to make them scholars, but our business is to make them men, citizens, and Christians. The vices of young people are generally learned from each other. The vices of adults seldom infect them. By separating them from each other, therefore, in their hours of relaxation from study, we secure their morals from a principal source of corruption, while we improve their manners by subjecting them to those restraints which the difference of age and sex naturally produce in private families.

Like Rush, many Americans continued to prefer the kind of academy implied in Franklin's initial borrowing from Pliny—a school that would be local, administered at least in part by parents and the community, and attended by children who should not board at school but "might," in Noah Webster's words, "live in decent families, be subject in some measure to their discipline, and even under the control of those whom they respect."[5] Semiprivate or tuition-supported boarding academies did remain common in America and formed a part of most comprehensive educational plans, including Jefferson's. The country's widely scattered, largely rural population seemed to make such an arrangement necessary in most areas. But for Jefferson and Rush, as for many others among the Founders, the goal was to move toward a system of universal, free public schools that allowed all students to remain as close to home as possible.

Education and Equality

With this demand for universal schooling, the Americans made their most far-reaching departure from Locke and his assumption of a rather rigidly stratified society. Locke's hopes for the long-range democratizing consequences of his educational proposals were modest and decidedly of the "trickle-down" variety. In the best foreseeable case, the well-educated sons and daughters of the new Whig upper classes would set examples that would induce the parents of the less fortunate to modify, in dimly-echoed imitation, the very limited education they were able to afford for their children. Meanwhile, the clergy and the upper classes were to undergo an intellectual transformation in the latitudinarian and radically this-worldly direction set forth in Locke's *Reasonableness of Christianity* and commentaries on the Epistles of St. Paul; this change would gradually rationalize, moderate, and make more economically productive the spiritual outlook of the working classes. As the division of labor intensified, as technology took firmer root, as the tide of economic growth rose, all levels of humanity except the slothful and stubborn would from generation to generation steadily approximate a greater and greater homogeneity of moral, spiritual, and educational attainment and outlook.

Americans, however, believed themselves to be already inhabiting a society far more egalitarian than any previous, in terms of education as well as wealth and influence. As John Adams put it during the Revolution, responding publicly to "a great Dutch capitalist" who had wondered whether "the common people in America" might not be able and inclined "to frustrate by force the good intentions of the skillful politicians"—and thus bring about a surrender to England:

> There is no country where the common people, I mean the tradesmen, the husbandmen, and the laboring people, have such advantages of education as in that [the United States]; and it may be truly said, that their education, their understanding, and their knowledge are as nearly equal as their birth, fortune, dignities, and titles. It is therefore certain, that whenever the common people shall determine upon peace or submission, it shall be done. But of this there is no danger. The common people are the most unanimously determined against Great Britain of any; it is the war of the common people.[6]

The Americans after the Revolution intended to carry on and strengthen the egalitarian forces at work in the new nation, so as to create a society in which the ranks and stations that inevitably emerged would be much less fixed, much more fluid over time, much more determined by the dynamic of equality of opportunity and of careers open to talents and merit, than any society previously known. In addition, as their revolutionary ethos matured, they sought to bring into being a form of government in which the full rights and duties of citizenship would be available to the children, or at least the descendants, of almost every rank or station. As a result, they were unwilling to await the glacial pace of change with which Locke seems to have rested satisfied.

In the southern states, private education through tutors in the home was widespread among the dispersed plantation and slaveholding class, with many of the Founders themselves having received much of their education in such a fashion. Nevertheless, the system had left its most distinguished beneficiaries distinctly unimpressed.[7] At least among the first generation of southern American republicans, there is evidence that some leaders had a genuine belief or hope that equal, if not integrated, education would one day be spread even to the freed descendants of black slaves. David Rice, one of the founders of both Hampden-Sydney College and Transylvania University, was an elected delegate to the Kentucky state constitutional convention in 1792 and pleaded there for the abolition of slavery, arguing that abolition and widespread education would complement each other and bring great blessings to the country.

> Emancipation on some such plan as above hinted, would probably in many instances, be a real advantage to children in point of wealth. Parents would educate them in such a manner, and place them in such circumstances, as would be more to their interest, than possessing such unproductive estates as slaves are found to be. The children would imbibe a noble independent spirit, learn a habit of managing business, and helping themselves. They would learn to scorn the mean and beggarly way of making a living, at the expence of others, living in splendour on plunder of the innocent. . . . The children of the slaves, instead of being ruined for want of education, would be so brought up as to become useful citizens. The country would improve by their industry; manufacturers would flourish; and, in time of war, they would not be the terror, but the strength and defence of the state.

To be sure, Rice's was a minority view, and Rice himself never freed his own slaves. Indeed, apart from Franklin it is hard to find a leading Founder who made any effort to advance the education of blacks, slave or free. Hamilton, Webster, and other northerners certainly tried to promote emancipation, but among the great southern leaders, including notably the Virginians, Robert Mc-Colley's assessment holds: they "were in the peculiar position of repeatedly describing an evil and then proceeding to insist that nothing could be done about it."[8]

But however uncertain or divided their views on black slavery, or on the future education of black Americans, the Founders were united and firm in the conviction that their modifications of Lockean political theory made a safe and reasonable democratic republic possible, at least under the conditions prevailing in America. At the same time, the Founders were troubled by the sense that these conditions were perhaps temporary and surely somewhat fortuitous. They included a level of education that was in great measure due to the influence of English aristocratic and theocratic traditions, now dying out. But they included also, according to Jefferson and others, a moral purity and a freedom from the "ignorance and prejudices" that characterized the mass of people in Europe's aristocratic or monarchic countries. This lucky advantage of education and civic virtue among the populace could be transformed into a more permanent condition if government, harking back to classical republicanism and building on the New England tradition of activism, stepped in to assume the burden the vast majority of parents could not afford and educated the young in groups at school. If government failed to meet this challenge, the future prospects of democracy looked, to say the least, considerably more grey. As John Adams observes in 1778:

> Children should be educated and instructed in the principles of freedom. Aristotle speaks plainly to this purpose, saying: "that the institution of youth should be accommodated to that form of government under which they live; forasmuch as it makes exceedingly for the preservation of the present government, whatsoever it be." . . . The instruction of the people, in every kind of knowledge that can be of use to them in the practice of their moral duties, as men, as citizens, and Christians, and of their political and civil duties, as members of society and freemen, ought to be the care of the public, and of all who have any share in the conduct of its affairs, in a manner that never yet has been practised in any age or nation. The education here intended is not merely that of the children of the rich and noble, but of every rank and class of people, down to the lowest and the poorest. It is not too much to say, that schools for the education of all should be placed at convenient distances, and maintained at the public expense.

In 1785 Adams takes up the theme again.

> The whole people must take upon themselves the education of the whole people, and must be willing to bear the expenses of it. There should not be a district of one mile square, without a school in it, not founded by a charitable individual, but maintained at the public expense of the people themselves.[9]

Crucial to this vision is the education in particular of the poor. As Adams states in his "Thoughts on Government" of 1776, "Laws for liberal education of youth, especially of the lower class of people, are so extremely wise and useful, that, to a humane and generous mind, no expense for this purpose would be thought extravagant." Even Franklin's proposal calls from the beginning for scholarships to be awarded to talented poor children at the academy, and from almost the first days of the actual establishment of the academy, an affiliated charity school offered instruction in literacy and basic arithmetic to poor children. Jefferson writes likewise of the need for scholarships, "to avail the state of those talents which nature has sown as liberally among the poor as the rich, but which perish without use, if not sought for and cultivated." At the end of the century, Noah Webster and Samuel Knox hinted at the dangers that lurked in a situation where the poor as a class lacked enlightened awareness of the relative advantages they enjoyed under the American Constitution. Consequently, Webster and Knox made the need to provide education for the poor one of the chief arguments in their proposals to establish public schooling in the states, or even a national system of government-supported education. As Webster observes:

> In several states we find laws passed establishing provision for colleges and academies where people of property may educate their sons, but no provision is made for instructing the poorer rank of people even in reading and writing. Yet in these same states every citizen who is worth a few shillings annually is entitled to vote for legislators. This appears to me a most glaring solecism in government. The constitutions are *republican* and the laws of education are *monarchical*. The *former* extend civil rights to every honest industrious man, the *latter* deprive a large proportion of the citizens of a most valuable privilege. In our American republics, where government is in the hands of the people, knowledge should be universally diffused by means of public schools. . . . When I speak of a diffusion of knowledge, I do not mean merely a knowledge of spelling books and the New Testament. An acquaintance with ethics and the general principles of law, commerce, money, and government is necessary for the yeomanry of a republican state. . . . In Rome it was the common exercise of boys at school to learn the laws of the twelve tables by heart, as they did their poets and classic authors. What an excellent practice this in a free government!

On the same theme, Knox reasons:

> It is certainly of the highest importance in a country like this that even the poorest or most uninstructed of its citizens be early impressed with a knowledge of the benefits of that happy constitution under which they live and of the enormity of their being corrupted in their right of suffrage.[10]

The quest for government financial support for schools, linked to the perceived need to educate the poor, was also foreshadowed in Franklin's earlier proposal for a private academy. Although Franklin wrote in 1750 that "from our Government we expect nothing," he had opened his *Proposals* with a strong reminder of the great tradition of governmentally sponsored public education.

The good education of youth has been esteemed by wise Men in all Ages, as the surest Foundation of the Happiness both of private Families and of Common-wealths. Almost all Governments have therefore made it a principal Object of their Attention, to establish and endow with proper Revenues, such Seminaries of Learning, as might supply the succeeding Age with men qualified to serve the Publick with Honour to themselves, and their Country.

And in July 1750, Franklin presented to the governing council of the city of Philadelphia his "Paper on the Academy" as part of a request (successful, in the event) for financial help. Among the four main civic benefits to be expected from the academy, he listed the preparing of local young men to become magistrates,

there being at present great Want of Persons so qualified in the several Counties of this Province. And this is the more necessary now to be provided for by the English here, as vast Numbers of Foreigners are yearly imported among us, totally ignorant of our Laws, Customs, and Language.

He added immediately a closely allied benefit.

That a Number of the poorer Sort will hereby be qualified to act as Schoolmasters in the Country, to teach Children Reading, Writing, Arithmetick, and the Grammar of their Mother Tongue; and being of good Morals and known Characters, may be recommended from the Academy to Country Schools for that Purpose; The Country suffering at present very much for want of good Schoolmasters, and oblig'd frequently to employ in their Schools, vicious imported Servants, or concealed Papists, who by their bad Examples and Instructions often deprave the Morals or corrupt the Principles of Children under their Care.

The talented and educated among the poor were thus to become in some measure the custodians of the morals of the state.[11]

Franklin's proposal is far from advocating the kind of public school or public school system with which we have become familiar. It is rather a proposal for a private school rooted in the community and sanctioned and supported (in part) by local government, a school having as a cardinal goal the preparation of youngsters for public service to the community. It was this model that prevailed in American practice until the mid-nineteenth century.

Education and Natural Rights

The most outspoken American commentators on education during the Founding period sought to go further, however, toward a public school system with a more democratic goal. Although Franklin spoke, in a traditional vein, of the need to educate a cadre of the young for public service, other commentators, like Jefferson in his preamble to the proposed Bill for the More General Diffusion of Knowledge, added a strong emphasis on educating all individuals in their "natural rights" as well as duties. Others pointed out the collective interest that all should take in protecting children from the negligence of those parents who might leave them too unenlightened to be capable of contributing to the intelligent mass vigilance required for defending everyone's rights. A few went so far as to interpret the social contract as implying that civic education was indeed a fundamental duty of government and even a basic right of individuals. It is not clear whether Jefferson's friend Joel Barlow was aware that his famous public critique of the French Constitution of 1791 might be read as drawing into question the legitimacy of the American Constitution:

> In raising a people from slavery to freedom, you have called them to act on a new theatre; and it is a necessary part of your business, to teach them how to perform their parts. By discovering to a man his rights, you impose upon him a new system of duties. Every Frenchman, born to liberty, must now claim, among the first of his rights, the right of being instructed in the manner of preserving them. This the society has no authority to refuse; and to fail of enjoining it on the legislative body, as a part of its constant care, would be to counteract the principles of the revolution, and expose the whole system to be overturned.

But in a somewhat less famous letter from France to his fellow Americans, Barlow appealed to the sorry experience of the French in warning:

> We must not content ourselves with saying, that education is an individual interest and a family concern; and that every parent, from a desire to promote the welfare of his children, will procure them the necessary instruction, as far as may be in his power, which will be enough for their station. These assertions are not true; parents are sometimes too ignorant, and often too inattentive or avaricious, to be trusted with the sole direction of their children; unless stimulated by some other motive than a natural sense of duty to them. Neither is it merely a family concern; it is a civil and even a political concern. The legislator and the magistrate neglect an essential part of their duty, if they do not provide the means and carry them into effect, for giving instruction to every member of the state.[12]

In 1791, at almost the same time that Barlow published his critique of the French Constitution, Robert Coram adopted a significant Rousseauian modification of Locke's property doctrine to advance a radical argument: the right to private property guaranteed by the social contract is only valid if accompanied by a right of every individual to receive the minimal education requisite for earning a living, or acquiring the property essential for secure survival, in the society in which he finds himself.

> If in adverting from a state of nature to a state of civil society, men gave up their natural liberty and their common right to property, it is but just that they should be protected in their civil liberty and furnished with means of gaining exclusive property, in lieu of that natural liberty and common right of property which they had given up in exchange for the supposed advantages of civil society; otherwise the change is for the worse, and the general happiness is sacrificed for the benefit of a few.
>
> . . . Society should then furnish the people with means of subsistence, and those means should be an inherent quality in the nature of the government, universal, permanent, and uniform, because their natural means were so. The means I allude to are the means of acquiring knowledge, as it is by the knowledge of some art or science that man is to provide for subsistence in civil society. . . . the education of children should be provided for in the constitution of every state. . . . Education, then, ought to be secured by government to every class of citizens, to every child in the state. . . . Education should not be left to the caprice or negligence of parents, to chance, or confined to the children of wealthy citizens.

Coram goes on to advocate that government compel parents to bind children out as apprentices, so as to force the children to learn a specific trade away from home—"that they may be enabled to support themselves with becoming independency when they shall arrive to years of maturity." It is fascinating to observe how Coram's "advanced" egalitarianism and expansive conception of fundamental rights—anticipating what we now call "economic and social" rights—goes together with a somewhat menacing willingness to countenance the use of governmental authority to coercively break up families and assign to individuals their ways of life.[13]

Few were willing to go so far as Coram, most writers confining themselves to stressing the enormous benefit of education or the urgent need for it rather than elevating it into a universal right. But by tying education both to the property right and to civic duties, Coram illuminates with unique lucidity the new duality of purpose in the curriculum of the public education that the Americans envisaged. For their chief educational goals were twofold: on the one hand, moral or civic, and on the other hand, vocational or economic. Piety as Milton conceived it, as the ascent toward meditation on God and the poetry centered on God, was eclipsed by a piety that could be fulfilled through the betterment of one's own and others' material welfare. This lessened emphasis on religious devotion, in turn, made possible the nonsectarian schooling that most of the Founders sought as a politically unifying force in the heterogeneous country. What Franklin called "ornamental" education—the forming of taste and of the habits and passions of a life devoted in some considerable measure to contemplation and reflection for its own sake, while not forgotten, receded into the background. The young were to be trained as citizens who understood their rights and were prepared to meet their civic responsibilities; but they were to meet those responsibilities as persons chiefly devoted to work and business rather than to leisure and the "beautiful and useless things" that adorn the life of Aristotle's man of greatness of soul.[14]

Female Education

However cogently the Americans may have argued for the moral merits of public schooling, they never supposed that the meticulous care called for by Locke in the supervision of the young could be wholly matched by school education. Accordingly, the Americans continued to highlight the importance of education before and beyond schooling—education in the home but also education through a variety of informal or sub- and supra-institutional means.

But the Americans added to this concern for nonschool education a characteristic twist. If education in the early years before schooling is of the utmost importance, especially with a view to morals, taste, habit, and the formation of character; if, as Simeon Doggett puts it, "as soon as the powers and capacities of the mind begin to unfold, the directing and fostering hand of education should be applied"; if "the turn which the young mind receives while it is tender and pliable and its powers and capacities are unfolding and maturing is very stubborn"; then we must "urgently recommend early education." And in a democratic republic such as the United States, where the vast proportion of the sovereign people cannot afford and do not wish to consign their infants to servants for upbringing, this critical early education must be carried out by the mothers.

> Has the mother been well-educated, is the tender parent a good preceptress, the fortunate child is at the best school in the universe while in its mother's lap. . . . The pupil, being constantly with and strongly attached to the mother, will assume her as an example of perfection and imitate her every look, word, and gesture. These imitations will soon grow into habits and probably fix traits upon the child's mind, speech, and manners which will be as durable as life. Hence the maxim, as is the parent, so is the child; and hence the inconceivable consequences of female education.[15]

What principles are to guide the education of these all-important maternal educators? Noah Webster puts the key point succinctly.

> In a system of education that should embrace every part of the community the female sex claim no inconsiderable share of our attention.
>
> The women in America (to their honor it is mentioned) are not generally above the care of educating their own children. Their own education should therefore enable them to implant in the tender mind such sentiments of virtue, propriety, and dignity as are suited to the freedom of our governments. Children should be treated as children, but as children that are in a future time to be men and women. . . . In order to prevent every evil bias, the ladies, whose province it is to direct the inclinations of children on their first appearance and to choose their nurses, should be possessed, not only of amiable manners, but of just sentiments and enlarged understandings.

Or, as Benjamin Rush writes, "The equal share that every citizen has in the liberty and the possible share he may have in the government of our country make it necessary that our ladies should be qualified to a certain degree, by a peculiar and suitable education, to concur in instructing their sons in the principles of liberty and government."[16]

As Webster goes on to argue, it is not only in the light of their fundamental role in shaping the characters of children that women's own education assumes awesome significance.

> Their influence in controlling the manners of the nation is another powerful reason. Women, once abandoned, may be instrumental in corrupting society, but such is the delicacy of the sex and such the restraints which custom imposes upon them that they are generally the last to be corrupted. . . . A fondness for the company and conversation of ladies of character may be considered as a young man's best security against the attractives of a dissipated life. . . . For this reason, society requires that females should be well educated and extend their influence as far as possible over the other sex.

But these observations only compound the necessity for a reform of women's education in the direction of a new sense of civic mission.

> A distinction is to be made between a *good* education and a *showy* one, for an education, merely superficial, is a proof of corruption of taste and has a mischievous influence on manners. The education of females, like that of

males, should be adapted to the principles of the government and correspond with the stage of society. Education in Paris differs from that in Petersburg, and the education of females in London or Paris should not be a model for the Americans to copy.[17]

Webster further asserts that this extensive new educational task cannot safely be trusted to private efforts, because tutors and family members are too likely to be still imbued with the traditional notions of women's roles as viewed in an aristocratic or monarchic society.

Webster himself does not draw out the implications of these remarks so fully or so clearly as does Benjamin Rush in his "Thoughts upon Female Education." Rush begins from the observation that if mothers are to inspire a sense of dignity in a society where independence is grounded on competence in economic matters and where most families require the close cooperation of husband and wife in managing family finances and property, then women must be educated to possess such competence.

> The state of property in America renders it necessary for the greatest part of our citizens to employ themselves in different occupations for the advancement of their fortunes. This cannot be done without the assistance of the female members of the community. They must be the stewards and guardians of their husbands' property. That education, therefore, will be most proper for our women which teaches them to discharge the duties of those offices with the most success and reputation.

Accordingly, women are to study English, bookkeeping and arithmetic, geography, the history of the nation (particularly its struggle for freedom), and the principles of modern political theory. Some women at least are to gain "a general acquaintance with the first principles of astronomy and natural philosophy." While praising training in vocal music, especially the preparation for church singing, and allowing instruction in dancing ("in our present state of society and knowledge, I conceive it to be an agreeable substitute for the ignoble pleasures of drinking and gaming"), Rush advises against the expensive and time-consuming training in instrumental music. In the place of this aristocratic adornment, he seeks to substitute the cultivation of a habit of serious reading: "How many useful ideas might be picked up in these hours from history, philosophy, poetry, and the numerous moral essays with which our language abounds!"

> The attention of our young ladies should be directed as soon as they are prepared for it to the reading of history, travels, poetry, and moral essays.

These studies are accommodated, in a peculiar manner, to the present state
of society in America, and when a relish is excited for them in early life,
they subdue that passion for reading novels which so generally prevails
among the fair sex. I cannot dismiss this species of writing and reading
without observing that the subjects of novels are by no means accommodated to our present manners. They hold up *life*, it is true, but it is not yet
life in America.

"It will be necessary," Rush concludes, to "connect all these branches of education with regular instruction in the Christian religion." For Rush differs from
many of his contemporaries in insisting on the need for a common religion as a
common foundation for morality; and in this regard women have a uniquely important role to play, given that "the female breast is the natural soil of Christianity." The reading and study of the Bible is "improperly banished from our
schools," and most improperly of all from schools for girls.[18]

Benjamin Rush's vision and views found their most powerful advocate in a
woman born the year that he delivered the address that later was published as
"Thoughts on Female Education." In 1819 Emma Willard presented a long-med-
itated and well-honed proposal for the creation of a system of state-supported
seminaries for women to the governor of New York for transmission to the legislature. In essence, the "Address to the Public, Particularly to the Members of the
Legislature of New York, Proposing a Plan for Improving Female Education"
draws together the arguments of Rush and others like Webster and takes them
one further, crucial step.[19] For Willard argues that the education begun in the
home by mothers educated in state seminaries must continue in state-estab-
lished primary schools, where the most apt and available teachers would be
women, not men. In other words, Willard spearheaded what was to become the
most striking new feature of school education, a feature almost completely unforeseen by Americans in the Founding period: the transformation of the educational profession, particularly in the primary grades, by the overwhelming predominance of women as teachers. When Willard's petition failed, she went on
to establish (in 1821) the Troy Female Seminary, the first permanent collegiate-
level school for women in the United States. This institution pioneered, with
enormous success, the unprecedented notion of educating women for a learned
profession—to wit, teaching.

Emma Willard thus contributed perhaps more than did any other American
of her time to the amelioration of the gravest practical problem recognized and
lamented by almost all those who wrote about the future of schooling in the
country: the shortage of dedicated professional teachers, caused by the low salaries and the limited esteem accorded men who entered the vocation. As Webster
describes it:

The principal defect in our plan of education in America is the want of good teachers in the academies and common schools. . . . From a strange inversion of the order of nature, the cause of which it is not necessary to unfold, the most important business in civil society is in many parts of America committed to the most worthless characters. The education of youth, an employment of more consequence than making laws and preaching the gospel, because it lays the foundation on which both law and gospel rest for success, this education is sunk to a level with the most menial services.

Still, the relief afforded by the gradual entry of women into the profession hardly constituted a solution.[20] The frustration Willard encountered in her attempt to induce New York State to establish seminaries for the training of women teachers parallels the more general failure to establish public school systems throughout the United States in the generations immediately after the Founding. Nowhere was that failure more tragic than in Virginia, for nowhere had a more worthy plan been devised.

6 · Thomas Jefferson on the Education of Citizens and Leaders

If it was Benjamin Franklin who led the way in articulating the character and curriculum of the new American academy, it was Thomas Jefferson who conveyed most lucidly and compellingly the vision of a system of public schooling for the new republic. While perhaps the most eloquent proponent of the liberal principles on which the country was founded, Jefferson was nevertheless one of the Constitution's less ardent supporters, not only because he wanted a bill of rights, but because he placed relatively little faith in institutional structures to preserve freedom, and took more seriously than most the education and moral temper of the citizens. In a 1787 letter to Madison detailing his assessment of the Constitution, he concludes:

> It is my principle that the will of the Majority should always prevail. If they approve the proposed Convention in all it's parts, I shall concur in it chearfully, in hopes that they will amend it whenever they shall find it work wrong. I think our governments will remain virtuous for many centuries; as long as they are chiefly agricultural. . . . Above all things I hope the education of the common people will be attended to; convinced that on their good sense we may rely with the most security for the preservation of a due degree of liberty.[1]

Earlier, when the struggle to separate from England was only beginning, Jefferson was leading the work of a committee appointed by the Virginia legislature to revise the state's laws and adapt them to the spirit and conditions of a republic; the keystone of his proposed revision was a plan for a comprehensive system of schools and academies for the state. Eventually reaching the floor as the 1779 Bill for the More General Diffusion of Knowledge, this paper is probably Jefferson's most important writing on education.[2] Although it was aimed at the immediate needs of Virginia, the bill, like all of Jefferson's educational efforts, was

106

also intended to serve as a model for the rest of the country. With its well-reasoned arguments and carefully structured plan, it stands as a permanent testimony to the clarity and subtlety of Jefferson's political theorizing, and as a text in political theory, it elicits and rewards the closest scrutiny.

Jefferson's Theory of Civic Education

In classic Jeffersonian fashion, the bill opens with a preamble that grounds the case for public schooling on fundamental political principles. In this way Jefferson sought to educate the legislature even as he called on it to champion education. If the bill had been passed, the preamble, taken together with the Declaration of Independence and the Virginia Declaration of Rights (which are manifestly presupposed in the immediate background) would have stood as the introduction, for all citizens, to republican education and its place in authentic republican government. The preamble sums up clearly the political or civic educational goals that were uppermost in Jefferson's mind and, more nebulously, in the minds of most other Founders.

> Whereas it appeareth that however certain forms of government are better calculated than others to protect individuals in the free exercise of their natural rights, and are at the same time themselves better guarded against degeneracy, yet experience hath shewn, that even under the best forms, those entrusted with power have, in time, and by slow operations, perverted it into tyranny; and it is believed that the most effectual means of preventing this would be, to illuminate, as far as practicable, the minds of the people at large, and more especially to give them knowledge of those facts, which history exhibiteth, that, possessed thereby of the experience of other ages and countries, they may be enabled to know ambition under all its shapes, and prompt to exert their natural powers to defeat its purposes; And whereas it is generally true that the people will be happiest whose laws are best, and are best administered, and that laws will be wisely formed, and honestly administered, in proportion as those who form and administer them are wise and honest; whence it becomes expedient for promoting the publick happiness that those persons, whom nature hath endowed with genius and virtue, should be rendered by liberal education worthy to receive, and able to guard the sacred deposit of the rights and liberties of their fellow citizens, and that they should be called to that charge without regard to wealth, birth or other accidental condition or circumstance; but the indigence of the greater number disabling them from so educating, at their own expence, those of their children whom nature hath fitly formed

and disposed to become useful instruments for the public, it is better that such should be sought for and educated at the common expence of all, than that the happiness of all should be confided to the weak or the wicked.

Jefferson speaks first and foremost of the enlightenment of the mass of the citizenry, so as to instill in them not only an awareness of their individual rights but also a shrewd vigilance against tyranny. It is assumed that legitimate government has its basis in the protection of individuals' natural rights, and this is by implication the primary lesson of civics. As Jefferson later wrote to Joseph Cabell, his friend and collaborator in the campaign for public education, "Equal right . . . is the polar star to be followed."[3] But the threat to natural rights from government, or from "ambition" perverting government, is the second and most urgent lesson. Education in "forms of government," issuing in an appreciative understanding of those institutions that check and balance while yet enabling government, is necessary; but the stress is on the limited safety of even the "best forms," and hence the decisive importance of a spirit of informed watchfulness in the populace at large. In Jefferson's view, that spirit cannot be presumed—as the *Federalist Papers* seems to imply—but must be cultivated and its grounds carefully articulated.

Jefferson therefore delineates with great care the rather complex knowledge or awareness of political theory that is to be the goal of popular education. The end of government is the securing of natural rights that inhere in human beings as individuals, yet the final shield of these rights is the "natural powers" that characterize not individuals as such but individuals gathered in "the people at large." The enlightenment at which education aims is therefore an enlightenment of the people as a whole, or of the individuals gathered into a people. To quote the Declaration, "Whenever any Form of Government becomes destructive of these ends, it is the Right of *the People* to alter or abolish it." Yet "the People," though it possesses "natural powers" once it is formed, is never said to be itself a "natural" entity or to possess natural rights above and beyond the rights of the individuals who constitute the people. Jefferson never suggests that the people have an organic unity, or that the people somehow possess one mind or spirit or "general will": to enlighten the people is to enlighten "their minds," not "its mind." As Jefferson sums up the major goal of his educational proposals in 1810, it is "to enable every man to judge for himself what will secure or endanger his freedom."[4] "The people" is, then, created by unanimous contractual consent of naturally independent individuals, whose rights as individuals remain the only basic rights and whose consensual combination into a people governed by majority rule never transcends the moral primacy of their distinctive individuality. Taken one by one, the individuals are practically powerless in

the face of government and therefore lack the right to alter or overthrow government—for no one has a right to attempt what is impossible or mad. But once
the individuals are made aware of the possibility of deliberately combining their
powers, the united individuals can discover "natural powers"—the powers in
collectivity governed by the principle of majority rule—that can alter or overthrow government and that therefore allow the emergence of the natural right
to alter or to overthrow government.

Institutions are of great importance, but the natural powers of the people constitute the bedrock of healthy society. Yet paradoxically, to become truly effective, these natural powers require conventional law, devised by a superior and
unusual individual, that establishes an educational system for the leader's natural inferiors. Only in retrospect, as it were, and under proper guidance, do the
people become aware of what they essentially seek and need and hence ought to
claim. This first part of the preamble breathes the radical but paradoxically theoretical spirit of Locke's *Second Treatise of Government*, with its famous teaching
on the right to revolution inherent in the people—i.e., the majority—as a result
of their natural rights as individuals, which are known to the people only
through the teaching of the philosopher Locke.[5]

Locke never proposes a system of public education, however, and he seems to
suppose that the written words of philosophy or of the followers and gentlemen-
supporters of philosophy will suffice to awaken the mass of men to their natural
condition and to the rational behavior in society dictated by that awareness. In
addition, Locke has very little to say, even in his treatise on education, about
the specific recruitment or training of political leaders who would promulgate
his message. Jefferson not only sees government as having an essential role to
play in educating the governed to guard against the misuse of government; he
sees as the second vital purpose of public education the cultivation, in a spirit
reminiscent of the classical tradition, of the "natural aristocracy." As he writes
later to John Adams:

> The natural aristocracy I consider as the most precious gift of nature, for
> the instruction, the trusts, and government of society. And indeed it would
> have been inconsistent in creation to have formed man for the social state,
> and not to have provided virtue and wisdom enough to manage the con-
> cerns of the society. May we not even say that that form of government is
> the best which provides the most effectually for a pure selection of these
> natural aristoi into the offices of government?[6]

Locke's teaching on the radically individualistic and disconnected, not to say
antagonistic, state of nature implies that there is no natural political ordering of
mankind and no person who is by nature intended to exercise civil rule over an-

other. Hence, it is necessary to maintain ceaseless vigilance as regards those in power, who will inevitably and naturally use the power for their own advantage, and will do so at the expense of others unless they are checked and channeled by the proper rewards and punishments. Jefferson in the preamble does not contradict any of this teaching, but he supplements it with the observation that a few are by "nature" endowed with politically relevant superior capacities for rule, and that these individuals must be recognized and drawn into service in a republic.

One might at first suppose that in the letter to Adams, Jefferson verges on suggesting that some men are by nature intended to rule others. But not only does Jefferson argue that "the mass of mankind has not been born with saddles on their backs, nor a favored few booted and spurred, ready to ride them legitimately, by the grace of God." He also insists that all political rule, if legitimate, is a form of service—of dedication to guarding the "sacred deposit of the rights and liberties of their fellow citizens." The unalienable natural right to liberty would be violated the moment anyone was said to be by nature intended for such servitude: "It were contrary to feeling, and indeed ridiculous to suppose that a man had less rights in himself than one of his neighbors, or indeed all of them together. This would be slavery, and not that liberty which the [Virginia] bill of rights has made inviolable, and for the preservation of which our government has been charged. . . . [I] think public service and private misery inseparably bound together." Accordingly, among his own relations and in his advice to aspiring young statesmen, he insists on the superiority of the pleasures of the private over the duties of the public life.[7]

Now the virtues of the natural *aristoi* would presumably include a deep patriotism or concern for one's fellowmen, qualities to which the electorate naturally pays special attention in choosing its leaders. Jefferson does seem to trust that nature has endowed mankind as a whole with enough virtue—or, as he writes elsewhere, a strong enough moral sense—to meet the requirements of life in civil society. But as we shall see, it is not clear how far this moral sense may actually go in inducing individuals to sacrifice their own interests.[8] Given Jefferson's unappealing portrait of the political life, it remains a question whether decent men with the wisdom truly to understand what is good for themselves have sufficient motives to devote themselves to politics. Jefferson was always distrustful of the motives of those in power, convinced that any elite, even one based on personal merit, must be watched closely. Nor did he share the classical notion that a proper education, moral and religious, of the most gifted is the best armor against their corruption. After all, on Jefferson's principles, are not the truly wise likely to avoid politics, and does not Jefferson come close to suggesting that those who are gifted and also devoted to politics are necessarily somehow unhealthy or misguided? It is the education of the masses, rather than the education of the few, that is the only effective safeguard against the corruption, by temptations to exploitation, of the gifted minority who become political leaders. Not the fostering of the rare virtues of the few, but the instilling of restless vigilance and wariness in the many, even with all their mistaken judgments and lack of information or political experience, is the best guarantee of the morality of the few.

One of the principal aims of the education of the few, then, is to awaken in them a self-knowledge that will allow them to recognize their own dependence, for moral decency or dignity, and in the long run for liberty and security, on the checking and wary watchfulness of the less wise majority of their fellow citizens. The fate that awaits an elite that fails to grasp its own need to be watched by the people was brought home to Jefferson with special force during his service as minister to France (1784-1789), when he saw such an untrammeled ruling class firsthand. As he argues in a letter written from Paris during this period:

The people are the only censors of their governors; and even their errors will tend to keep these to the true principles of their institution. To punish these errors too severely would be to suppress the only safeguard of the public liberty. The way to prevent these irregular interpositions of the people, is to give them full information of their affairs through the channel of the public papers, and to contrive that those papers should penetrate the whole mass of the people. The basis of our government being the opinion of the people, the first object should be to keep that right; and were it left to me to decide whether we should have a government without newspapers, or newspapers without a government, I should not hesitate a moment to prefer the latter. But I should mean that every man should receive those papers, and be capable of reading them. I am convinced that those societies (as the Indians) which live without government enjoy in their general mass an infinitely greater degree of happiness than those who live under European governments. Among the former, public opinion is in the place of law, and restrains morals as powerfully as laws ever did any where. Among the latter, under pretence of governing, they have divided their nations into two classes, wolves and sheep. I do not exaggerate. This is a true picture of Europe. Cherish, therefore, the spirit of our people, and keep alive their attention. Do not be too severe upon their errors, but reclaim them by enlightening them. If once they become inattentive to the public affairs, you and I, and Congress, and Assemblies, Judges, and Governors, shall all become wolves. It seems to be the law of our general nature, in spite of individual exceptions; and experience declares that man is the only animal which devours his own kind; for I can apply no milder term to the governments of Europe, and to the general prey of the rich on the poor.[9]

Jefferson brings to the fore and lays unqualified stress on a feature of republican theory that the classical philosophers keep in the background and hedge in with qualifications. In elaborating his theory of democracy at its best and worst, Aristotle observes that "with regard to equality and justice, though it is very difficult to discover the truth in these matters, it is nonetheless easier to hit upon it than it is to win over those who have the power to take advantage of others; for it is always the case that the weaker people seek equality and justice, while the stronger don't give these things a thought." From this Aristotle draws the conclusion that "to be hemmed in, and not to be able to do whatever one opines, is advantageous; for the capacity to do whatever one wishes does not adequately keep in check what is base in every human being." Yet Aristotle does not for a moment fall into the delusion of supposing that just because the weak always seek justice, while the strong always ignore it, the weak are thereby more noble or disinterested in their attachment to justice than are the strong. The weak always seek justice because it is always in their interest to do so. The populace, or the mass of the weaker citizens, is characterized by its own sorts of oppressive lusts and vices, and needs in turn to be hemmed in by the officeholders and the laws. Aristotle therefore recommends a democracy in which access to office is restricted to the propertied but officeholders are selected and audited by the populace.[10]

This other dimension, neglected by Jefferson, of the problem of a judiciously tempered democracy was more evident to Jefferson's critics among the Founders. They warned of the dangers in directing the core of public education toward the inculcation of a suspiciously vigilant stance toward authority; they argued that Jefferson, perhaps partly out of his misguided enthusiasm for the French Revolution, was insufficiently aware of these dangers. In the *Federalist Papers*, Madison criticizes Jefferson's recommendation for new conventions to correct deficiencies in the Constitution: "Frequent appeals would, in a great measure, deprive the government of that veneration which time bestows on everything, and without which perhaps the wisest and freest governments would not possess the requisite stability." For the same reason, he opposes Jefferson's radical proposal that, because "the earth belongs to the living," no law should be in force for more than a generation unless expressly renewed.[11]

But Alexander Hamilton provides the most clearly contrasting alternative to Jefferson's position. Before and during the revolutionary war, Hamilton took a courageous stand in defense of the civil rights of unpopular minorities, which in his time were chiefly Tories. As a champion of the freedom of the press, he defended a Tory printer whose shop had become the target of mob fury in 1775. On that occasion he wrote:

In times of such commotion as the present, while the passions of men are worked up to an uncommon pitch, there is great danger of fatal extremes.

The same state of the passions which fits the multitude, who have not a sufficient stock of reason and knowledge to guide them, for opposition to tyranny and oppression, very naturally leads them to a contempt and disregard of all authority. The due medium is hardly to be found among the more intelligent; it is almost [im]possible among the unthinking populace. When the minds of these are loosened from their attachment to ancient establishments and courses, they seem to grow giddy and are apt more or less to run into anarchy.[12]

The remedy Hamilton calls for is firm adherence by the leaders to the rule of law, upholding rights when it is unpopular to do so and resisting the temptation to act without proper authority. Hamilton hated unchecked majority action precisely because he loved liberty and saw liberty's foundation in the rule of law. To minimize oppressive mob or moblike behavior and secure individual liberty, Hamilton sought to remove government from the close control of the people, while keeping it ultimately dependent on them.

Characteristically, it is George Washington who harmonizes the Jeffersonian and Hamiltonian views on the proper place of public vigilance. In his First Annual Message to Congress, he gives an admirably brief and incisive summary of the civic goal of popular education in a republic, focusing on the problem of balancing vigilance with self-control and forbearance.

There is nothing which can better deserve your patronage, than the promotion of Science and Literature. Knowledge is, in every country, the surest basis of public happiness. In one in which the measures of Government receive their impression so immediately from the sense of the Community as in ours it is proportionably essential. To the security of a free Constitution it contributes in various ways: By convincing those who are entrusted with the public administration, that every valuable end of Government is best answered by the enlightened confidence of the people: and by teaching the people themselves to know and to value their own rights; to discern and provide against invasions of them; to distinguish between oppression and the necessary exercise of lawful authority; between burthens proceeding from a disregard to their convenience and those resulting from the inevitable exigencies of Society; to discriminate the spirit of Liberty from that of licentiousness—cherishing the first, avoiding the last; and uniting a speedy, but temperate vigilance against encroachments, with an inviolable respect to the Laws.[13]

Washington's statement compels us to note with unease the absence, in Jefferson's preamble, of any reference to the virtues of obedience to and reverence for law. It is a high level of political wisdom that Washington wants to instill in the nation's citizens. Such a moderate, discriminating spirit requires that the people understand well both human nature and the nature of politics. They must comprehend the basis of the rights they cherish, so that they can judge how far individual rights extend and where government can justly assert the rights of the community in limiting individual freedom. In calling for counterweights to popular vigilance, Washington has no disagreement with what we will see to be Jefferson's belief in the value of history in the curriculum; but Washington would use history to teach perhaps deeper lessons about the need for proud obedience, moderation, and sober expectations in politics, as well as the need for resistance to oppression.

Jefferson's System of Education: Elementary Schools

Because Jefferson relied mainly on the common people to preserve both the country's liberty and the integrity of its leaders, he placed special emphasis on the education of the masses through public elementary schools. This concern was accompanied by a lifelong interest in higher education. Jefferson's 1779 school bill, and a similar measure he introduced in 1817, both included plans for a state university to train the gifted for leadership in all fields. In the event, the only portion of his design that saw fruition in his lifetime was the University of Virginia, the apex of the system and therefore its most constricted element. Jefferson was delighted to succeed in establishing the university, and he welcomed the prospect of being remembered as its founder; but, given the importance of popular enlightenment in the preamble to his initial bill, it is not surprising to find that for Jefferson the most critical aspect of the system always remained not the highest but the lowest level of education. As he wrote late in life to Joseph Cabell, in the midst of the eventually successful struggle to establish the University of Virginia: "Were it necessary to give up either the Primaries or the University, I would rather abandon the last, because it is safer to have a whole people respectably enlightened, than a few in a high state of science, and the many in ignorance. This last is the most dangerous state in which a nation can be."[14]

Jefferson's Bill for the More General Diffusion of Knowledge envisages primary schools in every village or ward of the state, where "all the free children, male and female, resident within the respective hundred, shall be entitled to receive tuition gratis, for the term of three years, and as much longer, at their private expense, as their parents, guardians, or friends shall think proper." The curriculum is to consist of reading, writing, arithmetic, and history. Literacy is important for individuals' economic independence, but it is crucial as a means of participating in politics. It is indicative of Jefferson's seriousness in this regard that his 1817 proposal includes a provision that "no person unborn or under the age of twelve years at the passing of this act, and who is *compos mentis*, shall, after the age of fifteen years, be a citizen of this commonwealth until he or she can read readily in some tongue, native or acquired." Jefferson entertained the idea of making education compulsory, but he preferred this restriction on the franchise as less coercive and more suited to the spirit of the people.

A question of some doubt might be raised on the latter part of this section as to the rights and duties of society toward its members, infant and adult. Is it a right or a duty in society to take care of their infant members in opposition to the will of the parent? How far does this right and duty extend?—to guard the life of the infant, his property, his instruction, his morals? The Roman father was supreme in all these; we draw a line, but where?—public sentiment does not seem to have traced it precisely. Nor is it necessary in the present case. It is better to tolerate the rare instance of a parent refusing to let his child be educated, than to shock the common feelings and ideas by the forcible transportation and education of the infant against the will of the father. What is proposed here is to remove the objection of expense, by offering education gratis, and to strengthen parental excitement by the disfranchisement of his child while uneducated. Society has certainly a right to disavow him whom they offer, and are not permitted to qualify for the duties of a citizen. If we do not force instruction, let us at least strengthen the motives to receive it when offered.[15]

It is not, however, a sufficient guarantee of liberty that children be taught to read. They must acquire habits of choosing useful and edifying books, and habits of attending thoughtfully to public affairs. Partly because he conceives the fundamental purpose of the schools to be laying "the principle foundation of future order," Jefferson rejects the time-honored practice of using the Bible to teach children to read "at an age when," as he puts it, "their judgments are not sufficiently matured for religious enquiries." Most Christian parents, following the biblical injunction to "train up a child in the way he should go, and when he is old, he will not depart from it," taught biblical readings and catechisms *before* the child was old enough to understand them fully, so that the habit of faith might take deep root and the child would not be left with only his fallible reason to guide him. Locke advocates teaching only as much of the Bible as is suited to a child's interest and capacity—such as the stories of Joseph and David—but Jefferson prefers to wait until the powers of judgment are developed before introducing the Bible at all. He recommends that a young person should first have some acquaintance with history and science before confronting the miraculous claims of the Old and New Testaments. Jefferson maintains that the speeches of Jesus contain sublime moral truths, but argues that these teachings have been so mutilated and disfigured in transmission, so interlaced with the sophistical subtleties of his followers, that the whole is far beyond a child's capacity to evaluate fairly. Such an evaluation he does encourage in his seventeen-year-old nephew Peter Carr, whom he enjoins to "fix reason firmly in her seat, and call to her tribunal every fact, every opinion." But in the schools, especially the primary schools, Jefferson's desire to minimize religious teaching extends (in his 1817 version of the school bill) to prohibiting ministers of the gospel from serving as "visitors" to the schools and forbidding teachers to give any religious instruction that is contrary to the beliefs of any sect—in effect limiting religious teaching to the most simple tenets of deism.[16]

What reading material, then, does Jefferson consider most suitable for children? Both to train the judgment and to impart the knowledge most essential for citizens, he proposes that the books used to teach reading "shall be such as will at the same time make them acquainted with Graecian, Roman, English, and American history." These volumes will give examples not only of republics in full flower but of republics being subverted, corrupted, and overthrown. They will acquaint students with the sources of their own political tradition and with the rights and liberties for which their revolutionary leaders fought. Above all, by availing the people of "the experience of other times and other nations," history "will qualify them as judges of the actions and designs of men; it will enable them to know ambition under every disguise it may assume; and knowing it, to defeat its views."[17]

Yet Jefferson knew that there was always a cost in getting one's knowledge secondhand: specifically, the biases and distortions that are especially dangerous to unformed minds. To minimize these distortions, he recommended the study as much as possible of primary sources—and of authors of a liberal or republican outlook. Jefferson worried a great deal about what he saw as the unfairness of John Marshall's *Life of Washington*, and he sought to persuade Joel Barlow to write a Republican history of the period to answer it. He was likewise chary of David Hume's *History of England*, which he urged should be among the last histories of England to be read: "If first read, Hume makes an English Tory, from whence it is an easy step to American Toryism." Hence Jefferson advised that even the university use a bowdlerized version. At times he expressed despair at ever getting to the truth in history, when he saw how much falsehood was being written about his own country even by men close to the facts and how readily it was believed abroad. Yet he continued to recommend the study of history, under the guidance of soundly republican teachers, and in his 1817 school bill, he paired history with geography as a subject particularly appropriate for the children of a diverse and growing nation.[18]

Over time, however, there appeared a certain change in Jefferson's way of describing the proper aims and course of study for the elementary schools. Especially when one compares his 1779 school bill to Franklin's educational writings, one cannot help but be struck by how highly charged is its political tenor, and how correspondingly silent it is about vocational or professional education. In 1818, when Jefferson headed a commission that met at Rockfish Gap to lay the groundwork for the University of Virginia, he took the opportunity to restate his educational aims for primary and secondary education as well. In the report he drafted, Jefferson spoke more specifically about elementary schooling, in terms that brought to the fore its vocational aspects. The goals of elementary education as he conceived them were:

> To give to every citizen the information he needs for the transaction of his own business;
> To enable him to calculate for himself, and to express and preserve his ideas, his contracts and accounts, in writing;
> To improve, by reading, his morals and faculties;
> To understand his duties to his neighbors and country, and to discharge with competence the functions confided to him by either;
> To know his rights; to exercise with order and justice those he retains, to choose with discretion the fiduciary of those he delegates; and to notice their conduct with diligence, with candor, and judgment;
> And, in general, to observe with intelligence and faithfulness all the social relations under which he shall be placed.[19]

The fact that Jefferson dropped the original preamble in his revised education bill of 1817 and in this 1818 report substituted a less strictly political description of the aims of education, gives pause. Could Jefferson have regarded the first statement as too political, a product of the noble but extreme fervor of the Revolution? Or did he simply sense a practical need, two generations after the Revolution, to adjust his rhetoric to the temper of a Virginia grown less generous and less civic-spirited? It seems likely that, in the course of his unsuccessful struggle for public education, Jefferson was chastened by the discovery that stinginess, religious and regional parochialism, envy, and plain sloth in the vast majority were all but intractable obstacles to what he saw as the obvious need to create new republican educational institutions.

Nevertheless, Jefferson's 1818 summary of the aims of elementary education is more than an accommodation to grim political realities. In this carefully articulated statement, Jefferson's stated aims ascend from the minimally required economic knowledge, to a more capacious economic self-reliance (rooted in arithmetic and literacy), to a personal enrichment, and thence to civic duty, culminating finally in the understanding of individual rights and the virtues needed for the proper exercise and defense of those rights; Jefferson then concludes with a summary stressing the social character of human existence. This progression of goals helps illuminate the connection between economic self-reliance and liberty that lies at the heart of Jeffersonian republicanism. Jefferson's observations of Europe and the United States convinced him that only independent-minded, self-reliant people could make good citizens in a liberal republic. Those who were poor and dependent, unaccustomed to thinking or acting for themselves, could only become the pawns of the rich and powerful, or else break loose as a destructive mob.[20] Jefferson wanted the majority of citizens to support themselves as competent managers of their own farms or businesses, because this was equally good for prosperity, for individual dignity, and for public liberty. Thus even the most apparently private aspects of education, such as the basic mathematics needed to keep one's accounts, have a political function also, in promoting the habits of prudence and forethought that successful democracy requires. Perhaps by 1818 Jefferson saw that there was more work to be done in laying the vocational and economic foundation for liberty, and in teaching citizens the connection between their own well-being and the political health of the country, than he had hitherto realized.

This same effort to encourage self-reliance is even more evident in the device Jefferson proposed for organizing elementary schools in Virginia: the establishment of "wards" or "hundreds" throughout the state. Jefferson's plan was to divide every county into smaller wards, each of which would have enough men for one company of the militia and enough children for one school. Each section would be in effect "a little republic within the republic of the county." It would first be called together to build a schoolhouse and appoint a school board. Jefferson hoped that eventually each ward might also establish its own police, provide juries and a judge for the county court, and take responsibility for warrants, roads, and provisions for the poor. "Divide the counties into wards," he wrote. "Begin them only for a single purpose; they will soon show for what others they are the best instruments." These wards or hundreds were clearly modeled in part after the New England townships that Jefferson admired (but also found alarmingly effective in opposing his policies as president). By using the old English term *hundred*, Jefferson also harks back to the Anglo-Saxon tradition of local self-government, later appealed to by Whigs as the source of English liberties in their struggle against what they regarded as the encroachments of the monarchy after the Norman Conquest. Jefferson found, in this rural model of self-government, an inspiration more congenial to American conditions than that offered by the urban, martial, and largely aristocratic republics of Greece and Rome. He never succeeded in implementing this part of his plan, but his defense of it was unflagging. In 1814 he wrote that ward government and education were two subjects he would try to further as long as he lived: "I consider the continuance of representative government as absolutely hanging on these two hooks."[21]

Why was this project of political subdivision so necessary when all of these functions were or could be performed adequately at the county level? Jefferson contends, first of all, that decentralization is the key to safe government.

> What has destroyed liberty and the rights of man in every government which has ever existed under the sun? The generalizing and concentrating all cares and powers into one body. . . . Where every man is a sharer in the direction of his ward-republic, or of some of the higher ones, and feels that he is a participator in the government of affairs, not merely at an election one day in the year, but every day; when there shall not be a man in the State who will not be a member of some one of its councils, great or small, he will let the heart be torn out of his body sooner than his powers be wrested from him by a Caesar or a Bonaparte.[22]

But Jefferson does not even concede that this arrangement means sacrificing wise and efficient management for the sake of security against oppression, so great is his confidence in the abilities of ordinary people to handle serious matters. "My partiality for that division" into wards, he writes to Governor Nicholas in 1816, "is not founded in views of education solely, but *infinitely more as the means of a better administration of our government*, and the eternal preservation of its republican principles" (italics added). Or as he writes to Cabell, "If it is believed that these elementary schools will be better managed by the governor and council . . . than by the parents within each ward, it is a belief against all experience. Try the principle one step further, and . . . commit to the governor and council the management of all our farms, our mills, and merchants' stores."[23] The safest and most effective government comes from dividing responsibility, giving to each body the functions it is competent to perform and delegating as little as possible to the central authorities, who must be elected and held responsible.

But Jefferson believed in the decentralization of power for yet another reason, which includes safety and competence but goes beyond them. The autonomy that he strove to promote was, for him, utterly essential to human freedom and dignity. Although Jefferson described political service as drudgery and was always suspicious of men who had an ambition to rule, he had nothing but respect for the public-spiritedness that shows itself in local initiative and collective self-reliance. His goal in allocating maximum powers to the smallest local bodies is not merely to frustrate schemes for tyranny but to change the lives of individuals, involving all citizens in public affairs and so expand their lives and visions. Thus Jefferson's school bills are designed to serve a double purpose: teaching literacy and history to the children through the schools and teaching civic-mindedness and collective self-reliance to the adults through the wards. This same desire to maximize free and rational self-direction lies behind Jefferson's defense of state sovereignty and of a sharply limited federal government with only expressly delegated powers, as articulated in his Kentucky Resolutions of 1798. It is likewise the philosophy that prompted him, when asked to give some practical rules for daily life to a young namesake, to emphasize self-discipline and self-reliance and to put high on the list the maxim, "Never trouble another for what you can do yourself."[24] That advice he might just as easily have given to a fellow planter, a town, or a state government. Such independence at every level was good not only because it brought safety but because it would give the new nation and its citizens a greater dignity, a fuller happiness, and the capacity for unfettered advancement.

The Academies

In the same commission report in which Jefferson spells out his more practical goals for elementary education, he elaborates the aims that should govern the training of the few destined for positions of leadership in society.

> To form the statesmen, legislators and judges, on whom public prosperity and individual happiness are so much to depend;
> To expound the principles and structure of government, the laws which regulate the intercourse of nations, those formed municipally for our own government, and a sound spirit of legislation, which, banishing all arbitrary and unnecessary restraint on individual action, shall leave us free to do whatever does not violate the equal rights of another;
> To harmonize and promote the interests of agriculture, manufactures and commerce, and by well informed views of political economy to give a free scope to the public industry;
> To develop the reasoning faculties of our youth, enlarge their minds, cultivate their morals, and instill into them the precepts of virtue and order;
> To enlighten them with mathematical and physical sciences, which advance the arts, and administer to the health, the subsistence, and comforts of human life;
> And, generally, to form them to habits of reflection and correct action, rendering them examples of virtue to others, and of happiness within themselves.

These objectives were to be fully attained only at the university, but the groundwork for them must be laid at the intermediate level of education—the regional grammar schools or colleges, whose curriculum was to be primarily classical. Some such academies were already scattered throughout Virginia; they were woefully uneven in quality and served almost exclusively the sons of well-to-do planters. Jefferson's plan was to establish better ones under state auspices, "one within a day's ride of every man's door," and to open them to all who could afford to pay as well as to a small number of promising students who could not.[25]

This project of winnowing out talent was dear to Jefferson's heart and a key part of his plan to disestablish what he called the "artificial aristocracy" that rested only on wealth and birth. Through revised laws of inheritance and broader access to education, Jefferson hoped to bring more power to the "natural aristocracy" of virtues and talents, so that it might be able to "defeat the competition of wealth and birth for public trusts." Jefferson's rather exaggerated expectations for a fluid class structure are seen in a letter to Cabell in which he explains why the rich should be willing to bear a major part of the cost of maintaining ward schools: when their own descendants become poor, which in the absence of a law of primogeniture "they generally do within three generations," they too will benefit from free public education.[26]

In order to help society's most worthy members rise to the top as the fortunes of their unenterprising cousins sink, Jefferson's proposals stipulate that two or more boys from the primary schools in each collegiate district should be chosen for their "promising genius and disposition" and sent on to the grammar school at public expense, with a smaller number of these to be continued at the university. "By this means," he explains in *Notes on the State of Virginia*, "the best geniuses will be raked from the rubbish annually." Accommodating to the parsimony he had discovered in the Virginia public, his later plans provide for considerably fewer students to be schooled at public expense. But surely Jefferson also counted on these scholarships to excite emulation and interest in education that would spread their benefit beyond their immediate recipients. Looking for ways to reward merit at minimal cost, he added to his 1817 Bill for the Establishment of District Colleges and a University a clause calling on the academies' visitors to examine the students and award honors that might "encourage or excite to industry and emulation." And Jefferson was always hopeful that as the ideas of free schools and scholarships for advanced study gained ground, others would build upon any slender beginnings that he could make.[27]

Despite his love of progress and his constant concern with utility in education, Jefferson expected the core of the curriculum at the academies to remain Latin and Greek. To this extent he was consciously more conservative than Franklin. As he argues in *Notes on the State of Virginia*:

The learning Greek and Latin, I am told, is going into disuse in Europe. I know not what their manners and occupations may call for: but it would be very ill-judged in us to follow their example in this instance. There is a certain period of life, say from eight to fifteen or sixteen years of age, when the mind, like the body, is not yet firm enough for laborious and close operations. If applied to such, it falls an early victim to premature exertion; exhibiting indeed at first, in these young and tender subjects, the flattering appearance of their being men while they are yet children, but ending in reducing them to be children when they should be men. The memory is then most susceptible and tenacious of impressions; and the learning of languages being chiefly a work of memory, it seems precisely fitted to the powers of this period, which is long enough too for acquiring the most useful languages antient and modern. I do not pretend that language is science. It is only an instrument for the attainment of science. But that time is not lost which is employed in providing tools for future operation: more especially as in this case the books put into the hands of the youth for this purpose may be such as will at the same time impress their minds with useful facts and good principles.

Elsewhere, Jefferson defends the study of classical languages for their contribution to a clear and pure English style, for the "elegant luxury" of "reading the Greek and Roman Authors in all the beauties of their originals"—an especially charming and comforting recreation for one's declining years, he observes—and for "the stores of real science deposited and transmitted us in these languages." When he describes classical reading as a luxury, he does not mean to suggest that there is anything frivolous in it but, rather, that it is one of the pleasures that make a private and leisured life sublimely enjoyable. At the threshold of old age, Jefferson was to write, "I thank on my knees him who directed my early education, for having put into my possession this rich source of delight, and would not exchange it for anything I could then have acquired, and have not since acquired."[28]

Nevertheless, on one occasion Jefferson seems to have shown great impatience with the classical grammar-school education, scoffing at

the petty *academies*, as they call themselves, which are starting up in every neighborhood, and where one or two men, possessing Latin, and sometimes Greek, a knolege of the globes, and the first six books of Euclid, imagine and communicate this as the sum of science. They commit their pupils to the theatre of the world with just taste enough of learning to be alienated from industrious pursuits, and not enough to do service in the ranks of science.[29]

Did Jefferson at some point change his mind and determine that the traditional curriculum was useless or even dangerous? While he always conceded that a classical education was not for everyone, his quarrel here seems to have been with the spirit of snobbery without excellence, which regards a modicum of knowledge as an end in itself rather than as a foundation for proficiency in the sciences that will be truly useful. Jefferson unapologetically defended what he called luxury in learning, yet he always believed that this luxury should take its place in a life that strove to be of service to others, and in which the learned languages would also create a foundation for other, more practical studies, preferably at the university.

In order to insure that students would learn some of what is useful as well as beautiful and, just as importantly, would learn to seek applications for their knowledge, Jefferson added several modern subjects to the traditional academy fare of Latin, Greek, and mathematics. His 1779 bill added only English grammar, but his proposals of 1817 and 1818 included other modern languages, as well as geography, surveying, and navigation. Indeed, in an 1814 letter to Peter Carr, Jefferson described a "college" curriculum that would begin where the primary schools left off and encompass ancient and modern languages and history, grammar, belles-lettres, rhetoric and oratory, higher mathematics, several branches of modern science, philosophy, government, and political economy. But as Roy Honeywell has persuasively argued, this plan was specifically intended for "our institution," Central College, of which Carr and Jefferson were both trustees and which they hoped to set on the way to becoming the state university.[30] Jefferson thus outlined in this letter the first four professorships that he thought most appropriate for an expanded grammar school that might attract statewide attention and patronage. When the Virginia legislature eventually approved funds to transform Central College into the University of Virginia, Jefferson reverted to his three-tiered plan of primary schools, grammar schools focusing on language instruction, and a full-fledged university.

It is striking, however, given the prominence of political concerns in both Jefferson's 1779 preamble and his 1818 statement of aims for the education of the elite, that politics and history receive almost no mention in his simpler plans for the academies.[31] Jefferson of course expected that many of the Greek and Latin works studied would be histories and would be taught so as to support republican principles. But since a major justification for state-supported academies and universities was that they would train leaders, it is odd that Jefferson had nothing to say about how the grammar-school students might be encouraged to revere political heroes and to aspire to lives in public service. Apparently he simply assumed that there would be no lack of ambition for high office among talented youths or that the moral sense would suffice to draw good people into the nation's service, and that consequently, no special cultivation of future leaders was necessary.

Jefferson's discussions of the academy always remained sketchy, and he gave few specific suggestions of any kind as to how the hearts and minds of the students were to be cultivated. Of the three levels of education in his system, this was the one that engaged him the least. In contrast to the primary schools and the university, he did not see the academies as offering instruction that was immediately essential for the country's happiness. While classical studies were personally delightful to Jefferson, they never fired his imagination in quite the way that securing liberty or the progress of the sciences did. And he was aware that the academies, supported as they would be by wealthy parents, were the part of his system least in need of public funding.[32] Nevertheless, he always valued them as an integral part of his carefully structured framework. By drawing talented youths out of the local schools, sending the best on to higher education, and preparing some of their own less talented graduates to become teachers themselves, the academies could help fill what all acknowledged to be a serious shortage of worthy instructors for the young, and thereby help to produce a population more literate and learned than that of which any other nation could boast.

7 · The Unfulfilled Visions for a System of Public Schooling

Jefferson's educational plans, comprehensive though they were, did not represent his ideal of republican popular education. Although the success of free government was to rest on people of ordinary means and talents, his proposals allow only three years of free schooling for this majority—a span that scarcely seems sufficient for achieving true literacy, let alone mastering the science, history, and moral principles that Jefferson thought citizens needed to become independent and judicious supporters of republican government. The record of Jefferson's dogged and, within his lifetime, fruitless struggle to secure at least a minimal public education for all confirms that he did not consider his scheme an optimal arrangement, but only the best that could be accomplished as a start—and, as his hopes grew more dim, the best that could be wrung out of a stingy and short-sighted legislature. Jefferson's school bills therefore describe the bare skeleton of an education comprising only those elements that he thought most necessary. To this extent, his writings are more politic, and hence less revealing of their author's full thought, than the more speculative and theoretical proposals that were made from time to time by others in the years after Jefferson drafted his 1779 bill. Through essays and through texts that they wrote for students, men such as Noah Webster, Samuel Knox, and Samual Harrison Smith fleshed out their more elaborate visions of a common education for Americans. In so doing, they carried on from Franklin and Jefferson the debate as to what should be the core of education for all citizens and who should be responsible for ensuring that it was taught.

Vocational versus Liberal Education

One of the early republic's most tireless champions of education was the young teacher, essayist, lecturer, editor, author of schoolbooks, legislator, reformer, and

125

philologist, Noah Webster. His interests were as far-ranging as Franklin's and Jefferson's, although his mind was not as deep. A youthful acquaintance described him as hopelessly dull and unoriginal, but hardworking and sure to make his mark; it is no accident that his most lasting achievement was his painstakingly compiled, monumental *American Dictionary of the English Language*, finished toward the end of a long life of scholarly and patriotic labors. Much earlier, in 1787, Webster wrote an influential essay that helped win ratification for the Constitution. In that piece he stressed the relatively high level of education, especially in civics, that was already present and that needed to be sustained in the American citizenry. In the same year, he began a series of essays laying out his views on the kind of educational system required by the new nation.

> It is an object of vast magnitude that systems of education should be adopted and pursued which may not only diffuse a knowledge of the sciences but may implant in the minds of the American youth the principles of virtue and of liberty and inspire them with just and liberal ideas of government and with an inviolable attachment to their own country. It now becomes every American to examine the modes of education in Europe, to see how far they are applicable in this country and whether it is not possible to make some valuable alterations, adapted to our local and political circumstances.[1]

Two generations after Franklin first proposed curricular changes in American schools, Webster lamented the tenacity of traditional programs of study that failed to teach boys the sciences they would need in life and instead burdened them with languages that most would forget as soon as they left school.

> What advantage does a merchant, a mechanic, a farmer, derive from an acquaintance with the Greek and Roman tongues? . . . This absurdity is the subject of common complaint; men see and feel the impropriety of the usual practice, and yet no arguments that have hitherto been used have been sufficient to change the system or to place an English school on a footing with a Latin one in point of reputation. . . . there is scarcely an institution to be found in the country where the English tongue is taught regularly.

Webster adds that it is not his wish "to discountenance totally the study of the dead languages," that in fact he hopes to "urge a more close attention to them among young men who are designed for the learned professions." "But my meaning is that the dead languages are not necessary for men of business, merchants, mechanics, planters, etc." He argues for a common elementary education in English and arithmetic, followed by diversification according to the different employments the young people are destined to pursue.[2]

Webster's own experience as a country schoolmaster made him keenly aware of the frustrations, boredom, and idleness with which most students' lives were fraught. In keeping with his desire to make education as useful as possible, he argues that the students' programs can be so individually tailored, and the organization of the whole school so arranged, that learning may progress much more efficiently for everyone. While still a teacher, he wrote several essays on American country schools, deploring the false economy that kept schools unhealthy and poorly equipped. In place of the harsh discipline that was traditionally used to drive students forward, he made it his motto that "the pupil should have nothing to discourage him."

In his later essay "On the Education of Youth in America," Webster points out three major defects in the organization of schools, beginning first with the practice of bewildering students with material unsuited to their age. "The principles of any science afford pleasure to the student who comprehends them. . . . Examples should be presented to the senses, which are the inlets of all our knowledge." But unfortunately, schools are all too often

> putting boys into difficult sciences while they are too young to exercise their reason upon abstract subjects. For example, boys are often put to the study of mathematics at the age of eight or ten years and before they can either read or write. . . . those sciences a knowledge of which is acquired principally by the reasoning faculties should be postponed to a more advanced period of life.

In the second place, he criticizes the practice of having the same person teach different subjects.

> For suppose the teacher to be equally master of all the branches which he attempts to teach, which seldom happens, yet his attention must be distracted with a multiplicity of objects and consequently painful to himself and not useful to the pupils. Add to this the continual interruptions which the students of one branch suffer from those of another, which must retard the progress of the whole school. It is a much more eligible plan to appropriate an apartment to each branch of education, with a teacher who makes that branch his sole employment.

Third, Webster suggests that greater leeway be given for students to progress at their own pace from grade to grade, both as a recognition of distinctive talents and as a spur to competition and hence greater achievement: "Classing is necessary, but whether students should not be removable from the lower to the higher classes as a reward for their superior industry and improvements is submitted to those who know the effect of emulation upon the human mind."[3]

Such flexibility will allow youngsters to proceed more quickly to the completion of their common elementary studies and thence to preprofessional or prevocational education. In this regard, Webster advocates a sharp distinction between those students destined for the university, viewed strictly as a preparation for one of the learned professions, and those more numerous youths headed for farming, trade, and business.

> There are some arts and sciences which are necessary for every man. Every man should be able to speak and write his native tongue with correctness and have some knowledge of mathematics. . . . But besides the learning which is of common utility, lads should be directed to pursue those branches which are connected more immediately with the business for which they are destined.
>
> It would be very useful for the farming part of the community to furnish country schools with some easy system of practical husbandry. . . .
>
> Young gentlemen designed for the mercantile line, after learning to write and speak English correctly, might attend to French, Italian, or such other living language as they will probably want in the course of business. These languages should be learned early in youth, while the organs are yet pliable; otherwise the pronunciation will probably be imperfect. These studies might be succeeded by some attention to chronology, and a regular application to geography, mathematics, history, the general regulations of commercial nations, principles of advance in trade, of insurance, and to the general principles of government. . . .
>
> Such a system of English education is also much preferable to a university education, even with the usual honors, for it might be finished so early as to leave young persons time to serve a regular apprenticeship, without which no person should enter upon business. But by the time a university education is completed, young men commonly commence *gentlemen*; their age and their pride will not suffer them to go through the drudgery of a counting house, and they enter upon business without the requisite accomplishments. Indeed it appears to me that what is now called a *liberal education* disqualifies a man for business. . . . the mind may contract a fondness for ease, for pleasure or for books, which no efforts can overcome. . . .
>
> The method pursued in our colleges is better calculated to fit youth for the learned professions than for business. But perhaps the period of study required as the condition of receiving the usual degrees is too short. Four years, with the most assiduous application, are a short time to furnish the

mind with the necessary knowledge of the languages and of the several sciences. . . . it may be worthy of consideration whether the period of academic life should not be extended to six or seven years.[4]

Why is Webster's focus so strictly vocational? He is not only concerned to provide young men with the best possible means to earn a livelihood; he also has moral reasons for wanting all men, including those of independent means, to establish from their youth habits of industrious labor and to follow a trade or profession when grown.

> We are all the creatures of habit; a habit of *acquiring* property should always precede the *use* of it, otherwise it will not be used with credit and advantage. Besides, business is almost the only security we have for moral rectitude and for consequence in society. It keeps young people out of vicious company; it operates as a constant check upon the passions . . . it strengthens the mind by exercise, and puts a young person upon exerting his reasoning faculties. In short, a man bred to business loves society, and feels the importance of the principles that support it. On the other hand, mankind respect him; . . . the ladies uniformly despise a man who is always dangling at their apron strings, and whose principal excellence consists in singing a good song.[5]

One may wonder whether there is any place left in Webster's scheme for what Milton would call a liberally educated young citizen. Education is to prepare the young for their various walks of life; but is there any way of life, any genuine art of leadership, whose purpose it is to guide and unify their disparate existences? Moreover, the question arises whether the tracking Webster advocates might not introduce too early and rigid a classification of the young—denying to many the exposure, during adolescence, to alternative opportunities to try out their talents; sequestering the intellectually gifted in professional schools removed from the practical life of their fellow citizens; and rendering the majority of citizens ignorant of crucial skills required in an increasingly scientific age.

The Irish clergyman, pamphleteer, and academy principal Samuel Knox begins to confront the last of these considerations in his prize-winning essay, as he takes up the subject of mathematics instruction. He expresses some worry about the increasing distance between the specialists who comprehend the modern mathematics underlying so much of science and its products, and the vast majority, even among the literary, for whom the path toward higher mathematics was never opened: "One great deficiency in modern education, it must be allowed, is that as the sciences have been enlarged and improved, especially such as depend on mathematical knowledge, a proportionable attention to a preparatory introduction by mathematics has been, too generally, either dispensed with altogether or at best inculcated in a very superficial manner." Instruction, Knox concedes, ought "to be well accommodated to every different genius whether classical or mathematical. . . . It will be found, however, that there are few who have good natural abilities for one species of literature who may not also make competent proficiency to whatever part of it the mind may be directed. All, then, who should be considered as liberally educated ought to be well instructed in the mathematical sciences."[6]

Indeed, few who commented on American education were more concerned than Samuel Knox about the dangers of religious, ethnic, regional, and class diversity (fostered, possibly, by economic growth), and few looked more avidly to the public schools to introduce a countervailing, homogenizing force within the republic. Knox not only argues strenuously for a national system of education, with standardized textbooks, curricula, and requirements; he also contends that in substance the nation's education should include a common liberal core that will imbue all those educated beyond elementary school with some experience of and taste for "that refined and sublime knowledge on which the improvement of genius, science, and taste, rather than worldly circumstances, chiefly depends." Knox heartily agrees that "it is certainly laudable to pay due regard to those sciences that tend to enlarge the sphere of worldly interest and prosperity and without which the various and complicated business of human life cannot be transacted." But he insists that too much will be lost if the older ideals of reading works in the classical languages and cultivating the mind for its own sake are jettisoned. These older notions are essential not only for the elevation of the human spirit but for the establishment of a shared sense of national dignity and pride on which alone an enlightened patriotism and a national sense of community can grow, welding together the otherwise competitive and potentially conflict-ridden populations of the states. "To confine" education, Knox warns,

> to a system that comprises only the knowledge of mechanical, commercial, or lucrative arts; or even a knowledge of the world as far as it can be attained by literary accomplishments, would be to view its advantages in a very narrow and illiberal light. The nation that would conceive such a system as sufficiently entitled to its patronage could neither be considered as enlightened in itself nor as meriting the refined improvement of a liberal and cultivated course of education. In proportion, then, as a nation hath formed a just sense of its own dignity and importance, in proportion, also, as it hath formed just conceptions of the importance of virtue and science, founded on the enlightened improvement of the human mind, so must

that nation be influenced to patronize or establish such a system of literary education as may bid fairest for the acquisition of these important ends.

. . . it might be justly observed that a narrow or illiberal system of education from lucrative views would not ultimately tend to the prosperity or happiness of any nation. Were the human soul taught to cultivate only the sordid dictates of avarice or the knowledge of lucrative speculations, soon must that community lose a taste for whatever is most excellent in science or best calculated to refine and improve the faculties of the mind. Where such a taste hath become prevalent in any state, it is rather an evidence of its degeneracy than reformation and is commonly the forerunner of whatever may tend to enervate the patriotism, corrupt the virtue, or contaminate the morals of the community. . . .

It is remarked, with concern, that in this country, at least in some considerable share of it, such a false taste in education becomes more and more prevalent. The study of the English language only by those means it affords of itself, a smattering of French, arithmetic, and those branches connected with it, are considered by many as an abundant competence of literary acquisition.[7]

The Training of Citizens

If Webster failed to support liberal education, he was nevertheless wholly sympathetic to Knox's concern for civic education, and in his numerous schoolbooks he worked to provide a common core of moral, political, and historical lessons for Americans. To be sure, it is Webster who discounts the political importance of morals in his "Examination into the Leading Principles of the Federal Constitution."

A general and tolerably equal distribution of landed property is the whole basis of national freedom: The system of the great Montesquieu will ever be erroneous, till the words *property or lands in fee simple* are substituted for *virtue,* throughout his *Spirit of Laws.*

Virtue, patriotism, or love of country, never was and never will be, till men's natures are changed, a fixed, permanent principle and support of government. But in an agricultural country, a general possession of land in fee simple may be rendered perpetual, and the inequalities introduced by commerce, are too fluctuating to endanger government. An equality of property, with a necessity of alienation, constantly operating to destroy combinations of powerful families, is the very *soul of a republic.*

Yet these rather abrasive words ought not to be taken out of their context. Webster immediately adds a most pregnant "but":

> But while *property* is considered as the *basis* of the freedom of the American yeomanry, there are other auxiliary supports; among which is the *information of the people*. In no country is education so general—in no country, have the body of the people such a knowledge of the rights of men and the principles of government. This knowledge, joined with a keen sense of liberty and a watchful jealousy, will guard our constitutions.

Thus it is also Webster who, in his contemporaneous educational essays, quotes approvingly Montesquieu's corollary to his assertion that republics rest on virtue: "In a republican government, the whole power of education is required." Though Webster does not agree with Montesquieu that republicanism requires devotion to the point of constant and painful self-renunciation, he still concedes the necessity of that degree of civic devotion that is entailed in the people's knowing and loving the laws. And in contrast to the passage quoted above, Webster writes a few pages later in the essay that "education, in a great measure, forms the moral characters of men, and morals are the basis of government. Education should therefore be the first care of a legislature, not merely the institution of schools but the furnishing of them with the best men for teachers."[8]

In denying that virtue is the basis of freedom, then, Webster does not mean that republics ever can or should be indifferent to the morals of the citizenry. Rather, he is indicating, with perhaps misleading or excessive emphasis, the distance between the modern and the ancient conceptions of republican morals. Instead of demanding a Spartan self-sacrifice, Webster seeks to cultivate a gentler, more rational, and more interested devotion to the laws. Like Franklin and Jefferson, he sees in the new vocational bent of education the promise of a new and firmer foundation for civic health. Commerce and science are to liberate humanity from the blinders of religious sectarianism, peasant obtuseness, and aristocratic sloth, illuminating for all men their common neediness and mutual advantage in pacific trade. The new attentiveness to self-interest is to be enlightened by an awareness of the importance of fidelity to the collective interest, to the institutions and laws of representative government that are the best defense of the deepest interests shared by all individuals. The pride of the individual as a self-reliant and independent being is to be softened and civilized by his awareness of the dignity that arises from the sense of being in good repute with fellow-citizens whose respect he values because he looks upon them as respectable equals. No one expresses the moral goal of the new trend in education more eloquently than the young Jeffersonian Samuel Harrison Smith, in describing the hoped-for "enlightened conviction of the intimate connection between duty and interest."

> The citizen, enlightened, will be a free man in its truest sense. He will know his rights, and he will understand the rights of others; discerning the connection of his interest with the preservation of these rights, he will as firmly support those of his fellow men as his own. Too well informed to be misled, too virtuous to be corrupted, we shall behold man consistent and inflexible. Not at one moment the child of patriotism, and at another the slave of despotism, we shall see him in principle forever the same. Immutable in his character, inflexible in his honesty, he will feel the dignity of his nature and cheerfully obey the claims of duty.[9]

Noah Webster's Schoolbooks

What, specifically, could the schools do to cultivate such an outlook? Noah Webster believed that much could be accomplished by producing a carefully crafted series of texts that would, as Jefferson recommended, teach moral and civic lessons in the course of teaching English. Through the numerous schoolbooks that he wrote, and especially through his best-selling "blue-backed speller," Webster did more than perhaps any other American to give a distinctive tone and substance to the young nation's education. His spelling book first appeared in 1783 under the lofty title *A Grammatical Institute of the English Language, Part I,* and was followed shortly thereafter by parts two and three, a grammar and a reader. Declaring in his introduction a cultural independence from a Europe "grown old in folly," Webster set out in his slender spelling book to purify and standardize the American language, to fill children's minds with virtuous precepts, and in so doing to promote national unity and strength. While the grammar and reader both sold reasonably well, the speller was an instant and phenomenal success. It quickly supplanted all rivals to become for a time the most common book in the United States after the Bible. It went west with the settlers and was often the first work to be printed by the small presses of frontier towns. Even intense political opposition to Webster and his Federalist party was unable to dislodge it from the schools, so that by the end of the nineteenth century it had sold as many as 100 million copies.[10]

Such popularity was possible for a spelling book because, at the time Webster's became established, spellers were the chief texts used to teach children to read. Novice readers were instructed to spell each word out aloud and then to pronounce it, and they were expected to learn long tables of words by rote before they ever encountered them in prose selections. Webster's book was an improvement over its most popular predecessors, Daniel Fenning's *Universal Spelling Book* and especially Thomas Dilworth's *A New Guide to the English Tongue*, mainly in terms of its organization and syllabic division of words and in the attention given to pronunciation. To Webster, however, such things were far from trivial. "It is important that all the people of this country should follow one dictionary & Spelling book, that all may speak & write alike," he wrote late in his life. "This is a matter of national importance." He wanted to foster a uniformity of language that would help eradicate divisions and prejudices based on region and class.[11]

Webster took the speech of the people at large as his standard for dictionaries and spellers, rejecting alike the novelties of stylish affectation and the aberrations of ignorance. Similarly, in his grammar, he broke with the practice of imposing Latin rules on the English language and instead sought to describe English as it was actually spoken and written. He believed that the American people, with their generally high level of education, already used an exceptionally pure and correct form of English, but he also argued that the early period of our national life was the time for further improvements, when many conventions were in flux and people were receptive to change. In particular, Webster, like Franklin, proposed reducing all English spelling to a simple phonetic system. He saw advantages not only in the ease with which English could then be learned by both natives and immigrants but also in the spur to indigenous publishing and writing that would come from having a nationally distinct language. In later life he reversed himself, accepting the tenacity of custom and seeking instead to unify the language of Britain and the United States. His more radical spelling innovations he prudently kept out of his schoolbooks, but he did introduce there those modest changes that he thought most valuable, which have endured and which distinguish American English to this day.[12]

Along with their tables of words, previous English spellers had included lists of English place-names and short selections in prose and verse. Webster substituted a list of American place-names; and while he adopted many readings directly from Dilworth and Fenning, he replaced those that supported English monarchic patriotism with others more appropriate to America. He also cut back somewhat on the religious material of his predecessors, eliminating most references to the name of God. The reasons he gives for this are curious, however, and reveal an outlook quite different from that of Jefferson or Franklin.

Nothing has a greater tendency to lessen the reverence which mankind ought to have for the Supreme Being, than a careless repetition of his name upon every trifling occasion. . . . To prevent this profanation, such passages are selected from scripture, as contain some important precepts of morality and religion, in which that sacred name is seldom mentioned. Let *sacred things* be appropriated to *sacred purposes*.

In the preface to the first edition of his reader, Webster likewise objects to the nearly universal practice of using the Bible as a schoolbook, both because of its archaic language and because such a use seems to prostitute divine Scripture to secular purposes. This argument shocked the pious Benjamin Rush, among others, and was deleted from later editions. It does fit Webster's pattern of introducing each book with a denunciation of all competitors, but even so there is little reason to doubt the sincerity of his professed concerns. Though not in the 1780s as religious as he was later to become, Webster was always a faithful communicant of the Congregational church. This same delicacy or fastidiousness regarding language was to reappear in the absence of coarse words in his dictionaries and most strikingly in a bowdlerized version of the Bible that he produced late in life. Yet even as he preserved the sacred name from careless use, Webster fell in with a broad secularizing trend in eighteenth-century thought—a trend away from viewing religion as the only thing that ultimately mattered to man, and toward viewing it as an excellent, perhaps indispensable support of human morality.[13]

The change in tone that Webster helped bring to American schoolbooks is best seen by examining the first great American reading book, *The New England Primer*, in the light of Webster's speller and other elementary texts, including his own revision of the primer. Beginning in 1690, *The New England Primer* had been the first reading book for generations of American children. With its unwavering seriousness, it embodies the heart of the Calvinist teachings and the single-minded piety of the early Puritans. Frequent quotations from the King James Bible lend the work a certain stern beauty, but its message of sin and predestination is nonetheless a threatening one. Together with the Lord's Prayer, the Ten Commandments, the Apostle's Creed, and the Westminster Shorter Catechism, the book contains many brief verses, beginning with (for the letter "A") "In Adam's Fall / We Sinned All," and includes numerous references to death, even explicitly the death of children: "I in the Burying Place may see / Graves shorter there than I." It is hard to imagine the child who could study such a text and remain wholly unmoved and untroubled by it.[14]

Webster, by contrast, makes more attempts to appeal to childhood's delights. He uses occasional descriptions of apple pie and animals to engage children and delivers constant reminders of all the good things that virtue will bring. While his speller still contained many scriptural passages, especially those with a moral teaching, he added short moral precepts and, after 1787, when the title was changed to the simpler *American Spelling Book*, several popular fables with woodcut illustrations. The flat morality tale of Tommy and Harry, though not wholly original with Webster, typifies his approach. Dutiful Tommy is heaped with love, respect, and property; his disobedient, truant, gaming, and swearing brother Harry meets with every conceivable earthly disgrace. In dialogues intended for pupils to read aloud, Webster puts into children's mouths such unlikely utterances as "I believe that thousands ruin their constitutions by idleness," "I hope that we shall both take pains to correct our faults," and, after one child has heard another describe his parents' unremitting strictness, "It would be well for us all, if we were kept in such subjection to our parents."[15] In answer to *The New England Primer*'s Calvinist catechism, Webster appended to his 1794 speller a "Moral Catechism." Going through each of the Beatitudes, he here explains the Christian virtues in terms of both duty and worldly advantage, softening the most difficult demands of Jesus to allow *some* fighting on one's own behalf, *some* resentment of injuries, and *some* prudent constraints on charity. Webster's own revision of *The New England Primer* similarly makes a much more worldly case for virtue than the Puritan version had done. His last major reworking of his spelling book went further. Introduced in 1829, *The Elementary Spelling Book* was designed to replace the now old-fashioned-looking *American Spelling Book*; despite his own deep piety, Webster reduced the religious content from around half to perhaps 10 percent, as part of a successful bid to recover his dwindling share of the market. The new speller, whose main strenghs lay in the skillful teaching of orthography, had few stories to captivate children but more information on nature that would be of interest to them. Nonetheless, he managed to work his rather stifling moralisms into nearly every paragraph. Also in abundance are such pithy sayings as the following:

Seek a virtuous man for your friend, for a vicious man can neither love long nor be long beloved. The friendships of the wicked are conspiracies against morality and social happiness.

More persons seek to live long, though long life is not in their power, than to live well, though a good life depends on their own will.[16]

Webster wrote two other short "catechisms" for use by beginning students that are of special interest. One is his "Federal Catechism," first included in a 1790 grammar text and later in *The American Spelling Book*, which gives a simple account and defense of the Constitution, of federalism, and of representative government. Webster clearly differentiates a representative republic from democracy, which he, like the *Federalist Papers*, treats as a defective form of government. The catechism justifies both property qualifications for voters, as a way to exclude irresponsible vagabonds, and salaries for representatives, so that others besides the wealthy may serve. Taken together, the catechism's simple explanations constitute the first American civics text.

In the same year, Webster produced an introductory reading book called *The Little Reader's Assistant*, to which he added "A Farmer's Catechism," aimed at supporting republican virtue by keeping citizens on the farm and giving them the first agricultural lessons that they would need to prosper there. It begins:

Q. What is the best business a man can do?
A. Tilling the ground or farming.
Q. Why is farming the best business?
A. Because it is the most necessary, the most helthy, the most innocent, and most agreeable employment of men.[17]

Webster goes on to attribute the innocence of farmers to their freedom from temptations and bad examples, and he also extols what Jefferson does not stress in his praise of farming—the power of nature's beauty, harmony, and purity to lead the heart to God. But important as these little works were, the main thrust of Webster's civic education came in his more advanced text, the reader that completed his original trilogy of schoolbooks.

Webster's reader of 1785, part three of *A Grammatical Institute*, was the first book of its kind, directed toward putting a collection of extracts from great writings and speeches in the hands of children. Beginning with instructions for reading aloud, it continues with many pages of sententious, edifying statements from Swift, Shakespeare, Johnson, Pope, Bacon, Dryden, Addison, and Franklin, and a variety of longer English and American selections, especially dialogues for practice in oral reading. An expanded edition of 1787, renamed *An American Selection of Lessons in Reading and Speaking*, has a far more political purpose: the promotion of American patriotism and the new national government then being framed. In every edition Webster includes a substantial amount of Shakespeare, thereby introducing the great dramatist's poetry to common folk who otherwise would have little exposure to him; but many passages are taken out of context so as to give more unambiguous support for virtue and piety than the plays themselves do. Among the stories Webster includes is one about a philosopher named La Roche, which contrasts the life of a proud and somewhat selfish philosopher with the greater happiness of those who are simple but moral and religious. Equally disapproving of learning for its own sake is the aphorism, "To endeavour all one's days to fortify our minds with learning and philosophy, is to spend so much in armour, that one has nothing left to defend." These ideas correspond with the moralistic, rather authoritarian, and less emphatically intellectual definition of "education" given in Webster's 1828 dictionary:

The bringing up, as of a child: instruction; formation of manners. Education comprehends all that series of instruction and discipline which is intended to enlighten the understanding, correct the temper, and form the manners and habits of youth, and fit them for usefulness in their future stations; to give children a good *education* in manners, arts and sciences, is important; to give them a religious *education* is indispensable; and an immense responsibility rests on parents and guardians who neglect their duties.

Many other selections in the reader celebrate, in one way or another, the simple virtues, from Rousseau's description of the modest and captivating Sophie in *Emile* to Webster's own, utterly cloying portrait of "Juliana." In general, however, the volume maintains a high tone, and several excerpts from ancient authors in defense of republican liberty add to its dignity.[18]

What is most distinctive about editions after 1787, however, is not the ancient selections but the copious political material about the United States. On the title page is a quote from Mirabeau: "Begin with the infant in the cradle; let the first word he lisps be Washington." With his unflagging nationalism, Webster was one of the first to recognize the importance of preserving and teaching American history. He saw history lessons as an indispensable means to convey the political principles, love and respect for the country, and the sense of a common past that might bind together the disparate people of the several states who so recently had looked up chiefly to England and had regarded one another almost as foreigners. As editor of the *American Magazine* in 1787 and 1788, he reprinted portions of significant early American historical records and urged his readers to collect others. Here he also published his educational essays, which called for much more of the kind of instruction he was promoting in his reader.

Every child in America should be acquainted with his own country. . . . As soon as he opens his lips, he should rehearse the history of his own country; he should lisp the praise of liberty and of those illustrious heroes and statesmen who have wrought a revolution in her favor.

A selection of essays respecting the settlement and geography of America, the history of the late revolution and of the most remarkable characters and events that distinguished it, and a compendium of the principles of the federal and provincial governments should be the principal schoolbook in the United States. These are interesting objects to every man; they call home the minds of youth and fix them upon the interests of their own country, and they assist in forming attachments to it, as well as in enlarging the understanding.[19]

Webster's reader was especially influential in building the country's historical consciousness because it set the pattern for many others that followed—even if the imitators that supplanted it by 1800 responded to the waning of patriotic fervor by including rather more literary and less political material. Webster's text contained accounts of the discovery and settlement of North America and the revolutionary war; Washington's farewell orders to the army; a number of other famous American orations and state papers, including the Declaration of Independence; and Webster's own "Remarks on the Manners, Government, Laws, and Domestic Debt of America." In this essay he calls for industry, frugality, and self-respecting American independence from Europe in fashions, language, and manners. He also voices his lifelong concern for the restoration of a proper deference toward authority; though conceding that this was rightly disrupted by the Revolution, he emphasizes the need for stable laws that can restore trust in government. For a time Webster also had in his reader a unit on the geography of the United States, and he contributed a synopsis of American history to Jeddediah Morse's more complete 1789 *American Geography*. After 1795, when Morse's text attained widespread adoption, Webster removed the geography section from his own book. He later expanded his treatment of American history and geography into two more-advanced volumes, as part of his four-volume series for academy students entitled *Elements of Useful Knowledge*. These works, like the reader, had only a brief popularity but a wide influence, spawning many imitators. Altogether, as his chief biographer has plausibly argued, Webster's collection of schoolbooks played a decisive part in creating a unified American culture and spirit, and they "shaped the destiny of American education" far into the future.[20]

As the final stage of a thorough civic education for young Americans, Webster advocated travel within the United States. Like other patriots, he deplored the practice of sending youth abroad for their education, where they would contract foreign vices and foreign attachments. Ever the champion of national unity, Webster was also anxious to see young men move beyond their parochial circles to gain an understanding of the conditions and institutions of other states, so that regional jealousies might be removed and a stronger federal union might ensue.

But such travel, like the reading of history, was intended to serve a deeper purpose than the mere fostering of unity. This goal was adumbrated by Webster and others, but it was most clearly delineated by John Adams, who saw the knowledge of one's own country as the basis of a new species of self-respect. As he wrote in a 1785 letter on education:

The people must be taught to reverence themselves, instead of adoring their servants, their generals, bishops, and statesmen. . . . If Thebes owes its liberty and glory to Epaminondas, she will lose both when he dies, and it would have been as well if she had never enjoyed a taste of either. But if the knowledge, the principles, the virtues, and the capacities of the Theban nation produced an Epaminondas, her liberties and glory will remain when he is no more. And if an analogous system of education is established and enjoyed by the whole nation, it will produce a succession of Epaminondases.[21]

No one can suppose that when John Adams speaks here of the people learning to have reverence for themselves he could mean their learning to be satisfied with themselves, much less their learning to enjoy flattering themselves or hearing themselves flattered. For the people to reverence themselves, the people must be capable of reverence: They must learn from history to avoid the extremes of worship of authority and simplistic or resentful egalitarianism. The people must look up to themselves—i.e., to the "better angels of our nature," in Abraham Lincoln's indelible phrase—which means that the people must maintain, as democrats, a sense of rank, an awareness of higher and lower, of noble and base, of what is to be admired and what is to be despised, within themselves. In short, the people must be democrats who do *not* believe that all kinds of people, all ways of life, and all outlooks are equal. They must be democrats who have not lost the fundamental and predemocratic human capacity for shame, for self-contempt—and hence for aspiration and self-overcoming.

We must pause and wonder, however, whether the tone that Webster set in his schoolbooks, and especially in his best-selling spellers, was one truly conducive to such noble self-reverence. *The New England Primer*, despite its faults, did teach awe toward God, and hence a seriousness about one's soul, but Webster's elementary books are as likely to teach moral smugness as reverence. These texts are rife with sound advice, useful facts, and well-heeded warnings. But, particularly in the speller, Webster appeals mainly to a child's fear of failure and disgrace, to the quintessentially American desires to get ahead, win approval, and be well-liked. Timid children may read such books and congratulate themselves on their obedience and diligence, but high-spirited youths can find in Webster's writings no models of passionate individuals who wrestle with hard questions and overcome real temptations and obstacles to make something splendid of their lives. Nowhere in Webster do we find the erotic longing for human excellence that Milton expressed so eloquently, in a passage cited earlier, when he discusses the classics and Scriptures that he thought students should read.

But here the main skill and groundwork will be to temper them such lectures and explanations, upon every opportunity, as may lead and draw them in willing obedience, inflamed with the study of learning and the admiration of virtue, stirred up with high hopes of living to be brave men and worthy patriots, dear to God and famous to all ages; that they may despise and scorn all their childish and ill-taught qualities, to delight in manly and liberal exercises: which he who hath the art and proper eloquence to catch them with, what with mild and effectual persuasions, and what with the intimation of some fear, if need be, but chiefly by his own example, might in a short space gain them to an incredible diligence and courage, infusing into their young breasts such an ingenuous and noble ardor as would not fail to make many of them renowned and matchless men.[22]

A strictly practical education, with practical moral, civic, and vocational training, however important, is not enough to infuse this valiant spirit. In American society, with its economic preoccupations and its rather prosaic political principles, what is required to nourish a noble spirit of self-reverence is precisely a *liberal* education in something like Milton's sense, an education that brings students to the finest examples of American leadership and thought—but also to challenging alternatives beyond them. Those who will eventually set the tone for society need to be given the leisure to ponder, and to be touched by, the examples of Achilles and Socrates, of Abraham and David, of Joan of Arc and Napoleon. Only then can they acquire a self-reverence that is not self-satisfied, a reverence that takes justifiable pride in our nation's virtues but one that is qualified by the knowledge of how hard political and moral questions really are, and how high above us the greatest human beings have stood.

Webster's marked lack of enthusiasm for liberal education goes with his rather pedestrian spirit, but it also reflects an unusual awareness of the dangers of learning—especially "a little learning." If Webster did not understand the soul's need for great books to rouse its highest aspirations, he did have at least an inkling of the classical understanding of how problematic it can be to try to make intellectuals into good citizens.

Far more typical in the Founding era was the outlook of Samuel Harrison Smith, who wrote confidently that "knowledge itself cannot possibly be too extensively diffused." Smith makes the case for the utility of all knowledge, even that which seems at first purely speculative. He trusts that reason will teach the perfect convergence of our social duty and our natural interest, that an "enlightened understanding" will create a spirit of universal philanthropy and brotherhood, even though, with a confusion characteristic of his day, he also concedes that natural man "scarcely merits the epithet of a social being." Smith felt but never fully grasped the challenge to the Enlightenment posed by Rousseau, who had published a perverse and astounding work called, in its English translation of 1761, *A Discourse upon the Origin and Foundation of Inequality among Mankind.* In that work and its companion, the *Discourse on the Sciences and the Arts*, Rousseau dares to take the side of sentiment against reason and science, and dares to argue that in all but the rarest individuals science or enlightenment corrupts virtue and debases liberty. Smith, while calling Rousseau "a philosopher of great distinction," regretted what he saw as the "inexplicable feelings" powering his admittedly "noble intellect." The American polity, built on reasoned arguments, could not reject reason without undercutting itself. Fortunately for the political unity and vigor of the new republic, few Americans appreciated the magnitude and the radicalness of Rousseau's attack on the Enlightenment.[23]

Obstacles to an Adequate System of Education

If the American people were mostly unaware of the deepest arguments against liberal education, neither were they enthusiastic supporters of it. Thoughtful writers such as Webster and Knox might debate the relative merits of liberal and vocational studies, but they recognized that the immediate challenge was far more rudimentary. Most of the country still had no public schools at all, and the ones that existed were often woefully neglected and staffed by ex-convicts, alcoholics, and other unsavory characters who commanded little respect and hence often had to rule the students by brute force. The quality of teachers reflected the low esteem in which all learning was generally held. As Jefferson wearily observed during his unsuccessful battle to establish public schools in Virginia, "My hopes however are kept in check by the *ordinary character* of our state legislatures, the members of which do not generally possess information enough to perceive the important truths, that knolege is power, that knolege is safety, and that knolege is happiness."[24]

In their protracted struggle for universal, quality schooling, the champions of education confronted one of the deep paradoxes of democracy. While they believed in the people and their judgment, this belief was not a blanket trust that whatever the people decided was bound to be good. The Founders were cautiously hopeful that the people, given education and given a social order that supported their natural decency, would by and large exercise good judgment. But who was to be relied upon to ensure that the people themselves received adequate education? If state legislatures proved intractably short-sighted and eloquent appeals such as Jefferson's 1779 preamble and Webster's several essays were unavailing, what more could be done?

Smith and Knox, in their 1797 prize-winning essays for the American Philosophical Society, looked for ways to take some of the power over education out of the hands of miserly state legislatures and incompetent teachers. Smith, perhaps too readily conceding that the country would never be able to afford brilliant teachers, puts his hopes in a system of prescribed textbooks that might guarantee a high quality of instruction, and he suggests offering large rewards for books that can teach "plain and undeniable truths" while avoiding "prejudices or falsehoods." He proposes, moreover, that a board of literature and science be established, consisting of prominent scholars, to form and oversee a national system of compulsory schooling and a national university. Its duties would include awarding prizes for worthy writings and discoveries, founding libraries, governing the university, and assigning the works to be studied at all levels of education, including the highest. Knox, by contrast, stresses the importance of paying sufficient salaries to attract "instructors of the first reputation," and he prefers to allow university professors the discretion to choose their own textbooks. Nevertheless, he too calls for a uniform system of schools, academies, and colleges with prescribed curricula and texts, as well as a university to be established by federal law and to be overseen by a national board of education.[25]

Such centralization, though it might have circumvented the recalcitrant state legislatures, was impossibly alien to the spirit of American republicanism. Knox himself seems quickly to have realized that his national proposal was unlikely to succeed in the foreseeable future and that the nation was still no more prepared than were the states to impose a plan from above. In hopes of making a start of some kind, he offered his ideas to the legislature of his own state with a preface calling for rewards to local initiative that might spur emulation. Instead of urging the legislature to create a school system over the opposition of the counties, he suggested that it would be better to grant state aid only to those communities that valued education enough to first build their own schools; natural rivalry might then prompt backward counties to catch up with their more progressive neighbors.[26]

James Madison likewise hoped that the American resistance to centralized authority might be turned to the advantage of education, by encouraging a healthy and productive competition between states. He noted with satisfaction the country's "general ardor and emulation . . . in establishing schools and seminaries of every grade for the diffusion of knowledge." He regarded this as a fruit of America's "free and confederate system" and as a proof of the merits of popular government. In championing federalism in the sense of extensive state autonomy, he had no wish to heighten sectional differences, much less disagreements on basic principles. Madison saw the federal system rather as a laboratory that allowed controlled experiments in fields like education, limiting the scope of failures and encouraging friendly rivalry in reaching common goals. Yet despite the opportunity presented by federalism, he was forced to acknowledge to Kentucky's lieutenant governor in 1822 that Virginia itself had little to offer its neighbors by way of example in public education; Madison referred him instead to the New England states as models. Here, however, the well-developed system of schools had been established not on liberal republican principles, but as a key part of a deliberate effort to form Christian communities. Madison was hopeful that decentralization and clear-sighted self-interest alone would lead to excellent education, but experience suggested that something more was needed.[27]

Jefferson, too, saw some benefit to be gained from state competition, although he was less sanguine than Madison. In an 1820 letter to Cabell, he voiced optimism that the excellent example of New York's educational progress under Governor Clinton might finally shame Virginia into taking action on public schooling. Realizing that the people were not sufficiently aware of their need for education, he wanted to combine local control with the visible, inspiring leadership of men such as Clinton and himself. But in the last year of his life, he confessed to Cabell:

> I have been long sensible that, while I was endeavoring to render our country the greatest of all services, that of regenerating the public education, and placing our rising generation on the level of our sister states, which they have proudly held heretofore, I was discharging the odious function of a physician pouring medicine down the throat of a patient insensible of needing it.[28]

In the end, the Founders' argument that the nation's civic health depended on good public schools was simply ineffective in persuading the country to build them; most areas remained without a system of public schools until well into the nineteenth century. Why was this? John Adams pointed to the suspicion or even outright hostility toward education that the love of equality on the one hand and the haughty airs of the learned on the other had engendered in many Americans. "Liberty," he wrote, "has no enemy more dangerous than such a prejudice." Adams himself wondered whether this was not a fatal flaw in democracy. He favored a mixed form of government that would include an aristocratic senate patterned after England's House of Lords, and he argued that without such a senate, composed of learned men who respected education, "it is a serious question, whether there is one people upon earth so generally generous and intelligent, as to maintain schools and universities at the public expense."[29]

Jefferson refused to give up hope, but in his correspondence with Adams he suggested another reason for the persistent apathy toward formal schooling—an attitude to which he and Franklin, with their focus on self-reliance, may have inadvertently contributed. "All knolege which is not innate is in contempt, or neglect at least. Every folly must run its round; and so, I suppose, must that of self-learning, and self-sufficiency; of rejecting the knolege acquired in past ages, and starting on the new ground of intuition." A spirit of independence and suspicion of authority also tended to be accompanied by popular resistance to taxes of any kind. Even the federal government, which at the outset placed little burden on the people and subsisted mainly on small import duties and the sale of lands, was considered extravagant by many. School taxes were doubly unpopular among the wealthy, who would pay a disproportionate share, even though they sent their children to private schools. This was what thwarted Jefferson's original school bill when it was finally passed in 1796: The legislature left it to the court of each county to decide when the act should be implemented, and the justices, being wealthy men, took no action.[30]

An even more insuperable problem was simply the sparseness of the population throughout most of rural America, which by itself would have defeated Jefferson's goal of building an elementary school for every hundred families that would be within all the children's daily reach. The pressures of farm life also made it hard for schools to keep children in attendance during much of the year. Ironically, as Clarence Karier has pointed out, the very agrarian economy that Jefferson valued as a foundation for a virtuous republic may have thus been a major reason for the rejection of his educational plans. Later, with the onset of the urbanization and social class tensions that Jefferson had feared as the harbinger of corruption, public school systems proliferated, as Americans increasingly felt the need for workers with new skills, for some suitable occupation for children and adolescents, and for a common education to promote unity and economic mobility in an increasingly immigrant society.[31]

Absent strong religious or economic motives, the need for well-informed citizens did not in itself prove a sufficiently compelling reason to create schools. Jefferson's excellent political arguments for the ward system could not reproduce in Virginia the vigorous civic life that had been set in motion by religious conviction in the townships of New England. But education for citizenship remained a gnawing concern for thoughtful Americans. Through the work of Horace Mann and others, beginning in the 1830s, a version of the Founders' dreams of universal education gradually materialized. In the schools that were created, though true liberal education was often not achieved or understood, civics would long hold an honored place.[32] Meanwhile, until such time as Americans were ready for their ideas, the best the Founders could do was to keep setting an example by their own advocacy and patronage. Most tireless among them was, as always, Jefferson. In his final years he turned his attention to founding the University of Virginia, so that Virginia and its neighboring states might feel the solid benefits of learning, and so that learning itself might win wider respect.

8 · Higher Education

The history of American higher education begins remarkably early, with the founding of Harvard College in 1636 to train Puritan ministers and civic leaders for the fledgling settlement of Massachusetts Bay. After Harvard, except for the establishment of William and Mary by Anglicans in 1693 and of Yale by Congregationalists in 1701, there were no colleges begun in the colonies until the middle of the eighteenth century. Then, commencing with the College of New Jersey (later Princeton) in 1746, a rapid succession of foundings left the infant country in 1788 with some eighteen degree-granting institutions. All, save the University of Georgia, were created under denominational auspices, though some, notably New Jersey and King's College (later Columbia), were more or less interdenominational in spirit. Even the College of New Jersey had as its chief motive the training of clergymen. But from the outset, as is evident in the Harvard Charter of 1650, the promotion of literature and the education of Christian gentlemen were important secondary goals of American higher education.[1]

The proliferation of colleges beginning in midcentury was accompanied by modifications of the traditional course of study, which had integrated theological studies into a largely classical liberal arts program that consisted of grammar, rhetoric, logic, ethics, metaphysics, mathematics, physics, and astronomy, stressing the understanding of ancient texts in the original languages. Most prominent among the leaders of change was John Witherspoon, who devoted a substantial part of his curriculum at Princeton to the Scottish common-sense philosophy of Reid and Hutcheson, to history, and to the writings of political theorists such as Grotius, Pufendorf, Hobbes, Harrington, Locke, Sidney, and Montesquieu. His graduates, as noted earlier, included a distinguished group of early American statesmen, led by James Madison. In nearby Philadelphia, William Smith helped to develop Franklin's academy into the College of Philadelphia (later the University of Pennsylvania). The relation between Smith's educational vision and that of Franklin remains ambiguous, however. It was Smith who, against Franklin's design, limited the program of the English branch of the academy to English and mathematics and subordinated it to the Latin school, which became the preparatory school for the college. On the other hand, he did bring into the college curriculum many of the practical and scientific subjects whose study Franklin had championed. His capacious, three-year course of study ranged from Plato's *Laws* to the works of Bacon, Newton, Locke, and Hutcheson, and included navigation and architecture. Yet, in another departure from Franklin's principles, Smith made the entire program compulsory, for he continued to subscribe to the traditional ideal of turning out liberally educated gentlemen who could be useful to society in any calling.[2]

Indeed, it was the prescribed, compulsory curriculum, weighted heavily in favor of classical works, that remained the rule in postrevolutionary America. Even teachers were often expected to cultivate a gentlemanly well-roundedness rather than expertise in a specialized field, and they typically tutored one class at a time through the entire undergraduate program. This "tutorial" system was supplemented at Harvard by several endowed professorships, most notably one created in 1727 in mathematics and natural philosophy, which brought a higher level of scientific learning to the college. In 1767 Harvard abandoned the practice of assigning each tutor to one class, but at Yale and many other colleges it persisted well into the next century. Even where instructors specialized, students' choices of studies were few, and their opportunities to master the modern sciences and foreign languages were particularly limited.[3] Until late in the nineteenth century, American faculties and libraries were small compared with those of the leading European universities, and the colleges remained too poor and provincial either to attract professors of the first rank from Europe or to prevent large numbers of American youth from traveling abroad for what they and their parents judged a better education. The lure of foreign universities only added to the worries many of the Founders already felt about the civic education of future American statesmen.

Washington's Project of a National University

Thus it was that several of the prominent Founders, especially George Washington, set their sights on a nonsectarian national university that might, with the support of the whole country, attain a preeminence that America's regional colleges had been unable to reach. They hoped that a national university would turn out leaders for the nation in every field but especially in politics, by providing a thorough training in American political principles and law. Benjamin Rush seems to have been the first to call for such an institution, in his "Address to the People of the United States" in the January 1787 inaugural issue of the *American Museum*—a magazine that counted Washington, Jefferson, Madison, Hamilton, Franklin, and numerous other illustrious Founders among its subscribers. The federal university Rush proposes would accept as students only those who had earned degrees in colleges of their respective states. Rush sketches a relatively broad curriculum, stressing "everything connected with government," which embraced not only history and law but agriculture, manufactures, commerce, "and everything connected with defensive and offensive war." In a somewhat more elaborate "Plan of a Federal University" first published in the *Federal Gazette* on 29 October 1788, Rush adds modern languages and the most practical elements of mathematics and science. But his departure from the traditional liberal arts university program is radical, even disdainful.

> While the business of education in Europe consists in lectures upon the ruins of Palmyra and the antiquities of Herculaneum, or in disputes about Hebrew points, Greek particles, or the accent and quantity of the Roman language, the youth of America will be employed in acquiring those branches of knowledge which increase the conveniences of life, lessen human misery, improve our country, promote population, exalt the human understanding, and establish domestic, social, and political happiness.[4]

Rush tacitly excluded religion (along with the classics) from his course of study, and this depite the fact that in these same years Rush was working energetically to found Dickinson College in Pennsylvania as a Presbyterian denominational school. It was for Dickinson College in the first place that Rush wrote his essay on the mode of education proper in a republic, which we discussed in our first chapter. In a letter to a future trustee of the college in 1783, Rush insists that "religion is necessary to correct the effects of learning. Without religion, I believe, learning does real mischief to the morals and principles of mankind." He expresses grave doubts about "people who talk loudly of the increase of liberality and sentiment upon religious subjects since the war": "I suspect that this boasted catholicism arises chiefly from an indifference acquired since the war to religion itself." These last words help explain Rush's silence on religion in the proposed federal university: Rush was convinced that interdenominational religion was the death knell of genuine religious fervor. He criticizes the University of Philadelphia, despite its being ostensibly Presbyterian, precisely for its excessively interdenominational spirit: "From its extreme catholicism, I am sorry to say that as no religion prevails, so no religious principles are inculcated." Since he knew that a federal university could not possibly be denominational, it is understandable that he preferred to leave religion out of the curriculum altogether. The efforts to found Dickinson, and hence inspire other denominations to similar efforts, are consistent with the promotion of a purely secular national university when we give due emphasis to the fact that Rush had in mind a postgraduate institution: students matriculating at the federal university would already have completed a religiously based course of study at a private denominational college in their state.[5]

Rush's overall conception thus implied, whether he fully realized it or not, hostility to the establishment of state universities, either interdenominational or purely secular, and nowhere is the tension between Rush's and Jefferson's educational views more palpable. Moreover, Rush's silence on religion in the plan for a federal university only serves to highlight an underlying dilemma, which may be the deepest reason why the dream of a federal university was never realized: religion is crucial to an education that will support rather than undermine "the morals and principles of mankind"; yet to achieve an education that will foster unity in a nation of many denominations, religion must be kept out of the highest, most unifying, and in the long run most authoritative educational institution. National unity was the chief objective Rush had in mind when he outlined his plan for a national university. He argued that without a common education for the country's leading citizens, the union would be only a rope of sand. With characteristic disregard for what is possible in a democracy, Rush thus recommended that after thirty years, all political offices in the United States should be restricted to persons who had learned federal principles at this school.

At the Constitutional Convention held later in the same year that Rush's "Address to the People" appeared, Charles Pinckney, seconded by Madison, introduced a proposal that Congress be given express authority "to establish an University, in which no preferences or distinctions should be allowed on account of religion." The motion failed, although the only objection to it that Madison reports is the one raised by Gouverneur Morris—that this power was already implied in Congress's exclusive jurisdiction over the Federal City. On the other hand, Roger Sherman later declared in Congress that the convention had voted down the proposal because "it was thought sufficient that this power should be exercised by the States in their separate capacity."[6]

Washington took up the idea of a national university during his presidency. In his First Annual Address to Congress, he made an impassioned appeal to the legislature to give its patronage to "the promotion of Science and Literature," but nothing came of his urgings. By 1795 he was more convinced than ever that the United States needed a central university. Finding no help forthcoming from Congress, he wrote to the commissioners for the District of Columbia, offering a substantial bequest, in the form of fifty shares in the navigation of the Potomac River, once the institution was established on a liberal scale "with a fair prospect of success." But the simple fact was that such a university needed government assistance, and Congress was convinced that its constituents did not wish to be taxed for such a purpose. As David Madsen remarks, when summarizing the debates in Congress in 1796: "At this time, scant opposition to the national university was voiced on purely constitutional grounds. . . . Unquestionably, the most formidable objection to the national university at this time was that it would require large sums of money."[7]

Washington argued that in a well-endowed national university, in contrast to America's existing colleges, "the arts, Sciences, and Belles lettres, could be taught in their *fullest* extent," so that Americans would have in their own country "the means of acquiring the liberal knowledge which is necessary to qualify our citizens for the exigencies of public, as well as private life." The following year, in his Eighth Annual Message to Congress, he reminded his audience of the contribution that a truly eminent university would make to the prosperity and honor of the United States. He regretted the practice of sending American youth overseas for their education, not only because it derogated from the respect that both Americans and foreigners felt for the United States, but more importantly because of its effects on the patriotism of the students who went abroad. Like many of his contemporaries, Washington was concerned about the dissipated habits that young Americans were likely to acquire in Europe, but what he stressed most was the danger to their political principles. In his letter to the federal commissioners, he warns, "Altho' there are doubtless many under these circumstances who escape the danger of contracting principles, unfriendly to republican government; yet we ought to deprecate the hazard attending ardent and susceptible minds, from being too strongly, and too early prepossessed in favor of other political systems, before they are capable of appreciating their own."[8]

Washington appreciated the power of prejudice—or, more positively, the power of direct, personal observation and experience in forming human convictions. He expected that simply living in the United States during their formative years would anchor students' patriotism, as they felt the benefits and watched firsthand the workings of good government. In a letter to Jefferson, Washington explains his choice of the national capital as the location for the institution he has in mind, underscoring the education in politics and law that can be gotten more fully and accurately there than anywhere else. Students with political ambitions will deepen their understanding of both principles and practice if allowed the opportunity to observe Congress and, in the best case, to come to know some of the national leaders personally. A well-designed curriculum for the federal university could add immeasurably to this benefit by making the theoretical defense of republican government, side by side with its practical exposition and experience, a central part of the students' education: "A primary object of such a National Institution should be, the education of our Youth in the science of *Government*. In a Republic, what species of knowledge can be equally important? and what duty, more pressing on its Legislature, than to patronize a plan for communicating it to those, who are to be the future guardians of the liberties of the Country?"[9]

Moreover, there is one crucial lesson that Washington maintains can only be well learned at a school that draws students from the entire country. This is a genuinely national patriotism, without which no amount of knowledge can make a good American statesman. Such love of country, Washington asserts, can only arise when sectional jealousies are overcome—jealousies that he identifies as among the worst threats to the young nation. As he observes to Hamilton, daily intercourse and amity between northerners and southerners is the best antidote for this evil.

> That which would render [the university] of the highest importance, in my opinion, is, that in the Juvenal period of life, when friendships are formed, and habits established that will stick by one; the youth, or young men from different parts of the United States would be assembled together, and would by degrees discover that there was not that cause for those jealousies and prejudices which one part of the Union had imbibed against another part: of course, sentiments of more liberality in the general policy of the Country would result from it. What, but the mixing of people from different parts of the United States during the War rubbed off these impressions? A century in the ordinary intercourse, would not have accomplished what the Seven years association in Arms did: but that ceasing, prejudices are beginning to revive again, and never will be eradicated so effectually by any other means as the intimate intercourse of characters in early life, who, in all probability, will be at the head of the councils of this country in a more advanced stage of it.

Friendships of this kind, Washington claims in his Eighth Annual Message, will further strengthen national unity by promoting "the assimilation of the principles, opinions, and manners" of Americans.[10]

Yet despite his cogent arguments and substantial personal financial commitment, Washington never found allies to carry out his plan, and being deficient in formal education, he lacked the knowledge as well as the time to do it himself. Although the idea of a national university was repeatedly raised in plans and messages issued by and under every president up to John Quincy Adams, nothing was ever done; and with the accumulation of silt and debt, the Potomac Company went out of business in 1828, its property being acquired by the Chesapeake and Ohio Canal Company. It is a measure of the absence of positive interest on the part of Congress that the precise fate or final worth of the once-valuable shares bequeathed by Washington for the national university remains to this day a mystery, and an investigation in 1905 could not even discover a record in the Treasury of the shares' receipt.[11]

A Military Academy

More fruitful was Washington's campaign for a military academy. As with a national university, he was persuaded that the country needed a military school for precisely the reasons that made it most reluctant to establish one: sectional and state animosities, a stingy short-sightedness regarding education, and a dislike and distrust of military power. As soon as the revolutionary war ended, Washington began urging the creation of an academy to preserve the hard-won lessons of the war. He stressed particularly the need to teach expertise in artillery and engineering, "unless we intend to let the Science become extinct, and to depend entirely upon the Foreigners for their friendly aid, if ever we should again be involved in Hostility."[12]

Washington pressed the issue with congressmen during his presidency and included it in his Eighth Annual Message: "In proportion, as the observance of pacific maxims, might exempt a Nation from the necessity of practicing the rules of the Military Art, ought to be its care in preserving, and transmitting by proper establishments, the knowledge of that Art." Later he regretted that (perhaps especially in a democracy) "the want of many useful Institutions are not seen until they are felt." If Congress did perceive the potential need for military expertise, it was even more impressed by the havoc that elite officer corps had so often wreaked on civilian governments, and hence it proceeded reluctantly. Nevertheless, in December 1799, just two days before his death, Washington was able to convey to Hamilton his delight that plans were finally under way for beginning serious military instruction at the United States Army garrison at West Point, New York.[13]

Yet in response to Hamilton's request for his ideas on the best organization and curriculum for the school, Washington had to confess that he had never given it much thought. Hamilton forwarded to President Adams his own elaborate prospectus for an academy that would give specialized instruction in all branches of the military arts, and this plan became the basis for the one that Adams submitted to Congress in 1800. Ironically, the enabling legislation was only passed under Jefferson, who as Washington's secretary of state had denied that the federal government had constitutional power to create a military academy. In keeping with the Jeffersonian outlook, the new school was far smaller and simpler than Hamilton had envisioned and focused less on the training of officers than on military engineering, which Jefferson hoped would contribute to scientific understanding and peacetime prosperity as well as to defense. That

Jefferson had no opposition to military instruction as such, but only to an elite national corps, is indicated by the later provisions for military training in the curriculum for the University of Virginia. Appealing to the example of the ancients, for whom "gymnastics" centering on military exercises "constituted the principal part of the education of their youth," he called for instruction in arms to be "the frequent exercise of the students, in their hours of recreation."[14]

But so neglected was West Point in its early years that by 1810 President Madison had to appeal to Congress just to provide habitable buildings for the students. Reiterating Washington's concern about American suspicion of a military establishment, he urged that "seminaries where the elementary principles of the art of war can be taught without actual war, and without the expense of extensive and standing armies, have the precious advantage of uniting an essential preparation against external danger with a scrupulous regard to internal safety."[15] Only with the War of 1812 did the country feel its deficiency in military expertise and consequently set West Point on the path to becoming a respected institution of higher education.

Jefferson's Early Efforts on Behalf of Higher Education

Whereas Washington lent his support mainly to educational projects that would strengthen and unify the nation, Jefferson's tireless work to improve American schools and colleges was mostly focused on his home state of Virginia. His first attempt to create an eminent modern university in Virginia came in 1779, with the Bill for Amending the Constitution of the College of William and Mary, which completes the system begun by his Bill for the More General Diffusion of Knowledge of the same year. Jefferson argues that the college, supported with public funds and intended solely for the public benefit, can of right be altered by the legislature when it fails to meet the people's expectations. Indeed, he charges that the legislature has a special duty to improve the college at a time when changes of government and the ongoing war call for "extraordinary abilities both in counsel and field," so that "those who are to be the future guardians of the rights and liberties of their country may be endowed with science and virtue, to watch and preserve that sacred deposit." To this end, he proposes streamlining the administration, making the governing board directly answerable to the legislature, and setting the school on a steadier financial footing.[16]

A more responsive administration, Jefferson believed, would facilitate the reorganization and expansion of the curriculum that William and Mary needed to become truly useful to society. The faculty in 1779 consisted of two professors of divinity; two of philosophy, encompassing rhetoric, logic, ethics, physics, and mathematics; one of Latin and Greek; and one missionary to teach English, arithmetic, and Christianity to the Indians. Later, in the *Notes on the State of Virginia*, Jefferson explains that the school of ancient languages "filled the college with children," discouraging more advanced students from enrolling there and rendering the school of philosophy almost useless. He proposes dropping the two chairs of divinity and broadening the rest of the program to fill eight professorships: moral philosophy, natural philosophy and natural history, ancient languages, modern languages, history, mathematics, medicine, and law. In place of the missionary to teach and convert the Indians, Jefferson thought it would be more fitting to send a scholar to study and record their languages and laws, which he believed could reveal much about the structure of language, the origins and migrations of peoples, and the wise ordering of society. This bill, like its companion school bill, was never enacted. The plan had alienated the Anglicans by threatening to weaken their hold on the college, while failing to assuage the jealousies of dissenting sects that still regarded William and Mary as a bastion of Anglicanism.[17]

After he was elected governor of Virginia and appointed as a visitor of the college in 1779, Jefferson was able to effect some of his proposed changes without legislative action. This restructuring left five professorships, including one of natural philosophy and mathematics, one of moral philosophy, and what were apparently the nation's first professorships of modern languages, medicine, and law. But Jefferson was never satisfied with the limited scope of William and Mary. By 1800 financial losses and the removal of the state capital from Williamsburg to Richmond had caused the college to decline, and Jefferson lamented that it was "just well enough endowed to draw out the miserable existence to which a miserable constitution has doomed it."[18] Increasingly, he sought opportunities to establish a completely new university on a more liberal plan.

One intriguing possibility arose in 1794 when the faculty of the University of Geneva, which Jefferson had long considered one of the world's best, found itself opposed by the revolutionary government there and contemplated removing as a body to a new location. Jefferson leapt at the suggestion of a friend of the college, the Geneva historian M. D'Ivernois, that the faculty might be induced to emigrate to America. Jefferson asked his friend Wilson Cary Nicholas to sound the Virginia legislature on the project. While interested, the members concluded that language barriers and expense made the plan unfeasible, especially given Virginia's still relatively sparse population. Regretfully, Jefferson reported this response to D'Ivernois, adding, "I should have seen with peculiar satisfaction the establishment of such a mass of science in my country, and should probably have been tempted to approach myself to it, by procuring a residence in it's neighborhood, at those seasons of the year at least when the operations of agriculture are less active and interesting."[19]

Without holding out to D'Ivernois the hope that another American sponsor might be found, Jefferson wrote the same month to Washington, urging him to use his James and Potomac river shares to bring the Geneva faculty to the United States as the core of a national university. Washington, however, remained cool toward the idea, countering Jefferson's enthusiastic account of the faculty's intellectual brilliance with moral and political arguments that to him were more compelling. Not only were plans and funds for a national university still too uncertain to justify persuading "an entire college to migrate," he replied, but he doubted the benefits to America of "transplanting the Professors in a *body*," since "they might not be all good characters; nor all sufficiently acquainted with our language." Finally, Washington was concerned with the prejudices and jealousies such a move might excite, turning Americans against an institution whose faculty had been out of favor with the democratic party in its own country and perhaps also precluding "some of the first Professors in other countries from a participation."[20] Jefferson was temporarily frustrated in his desire to secure an assemblage of eminent professors either for Virginia or for a national university, but he continued to look for opportunities along both lines.

During his presidency, Jefferson, like Madison after him,[21] embraced the cause of a national university. Jefferson encouraged both Dupont de Nemours and Joel Barlow to draft plans for a university in Washington; Barlow's was considered by Congress in 1806 but never acted upon. Barlow had first become enthusiastic about the idea of a national university when he read a copy of Washington's last will and testament, which had been sent to him in France in 1800. He wrote to Jefferson and received a warm response, and when he finally returned to America, he drew up a prospectus which was printed and circulated by Samuel Harrison Smith, who also contributed to the writing.[22]

Barlow conceives of the national university as part of a broader "national institution" that will have "two distinct objects, which, in other countries have been kept asunder," but which "may and ought to be united." The envisioned "national institution" will be composed of both a university (or, indeed, a university system, since he raises the possibility of numerous campuses throughout the country) and a scientific institute for research, publication, and archival collection, along the lines of the Royal Society of London and the National Institute of France. As James Woodress says, "His plan, in summary, projected an institution very much like a great modern university where basic research, graduate training, and undergraduate teaching go on simultaneously." Barlow suggests that once the institution is in operation, the Patent Office as well as other government departments ought to be affiliated with or subordinated to it, and the military academy moved from West Point to become a division of the larger national institution. He further proposes a press that will publish textbooks to be used throughout the country. This last feature underlines what Barlow calls "the leading principle" of his plan: overcoming sectional diversity through the "assimilation of civil regulations, political principles, and modes of education," in order to secure throughout the country "good morals and every republican virtue."[23]

Indeed, so centralized and overwhelming is to be the authority of the institution that it is somewhat surprising to find Jefferson among its enthusiastic supporters. At this point in his career, however, Jefferson as president was very much preoccupied with the need to strengthen national unity and the energy of the national government. He argued for extensive amendment of the Constitution (he remained a strict constructionist) to permit the federal government to involve itself in or take over the leadership of domestic improvements of all kinds, including preeminently higher education. In his Sixth Annual Message, he suggests that, although the public debt will soon be paid off, import duties on luxuries should be continued to finance this and other projects. He maintains that the patriotism of those who would pay the tax

> would certainly prefer its continuance and application to the great purposes of the public education, roads, rivers, canals, and such other objects of public improvement as it may be thought proper to add to the constitutional enumeration of federal powers. By these operations new channels of communication will be opened between the States, the lines of separation will disappear, their interests will be identified, and their union cemented by new and indissoluble ties. Education is here placed among the articles of public care, not that it would be proposed to take its ordinary branches out of the hands of private enterprise, which manages so much better all the concerns to which it is equal, but a public institution can alone supply those sciences which, though rarely called for, are yet necessary to complete the circle, all the parts of which contribute to the improvement of the country, and some of them to its preservation.[24]

The scope of Barlow's proposal is not its only innovation or remarkable quality. Explicitly appealing to the authority of Francis Bacon, Barlow places the knowledge of science and its technological applications at the heart of the institute's mission. Like Bacon, moreover, he includes "moral and political philosophy" as perhaps the most important branch of modern science. The institute is to focus its energies especially on the study and improvement of the federal and representative forms of government, as crucial to the future not only of the United States but, in exemplary fashion, of freedom throughout the world.[25]

Continuing to be faithful to the rich breadth and depth of the original Baconian vision, Barlow insists that the fine arts ought to occupy a major place in the scheme, despite or precisely because they "have been but little cultivated in America." As the author of the *Columbiad*, an epic poem on the development of America, Barlow recognizes the need to confront the "opinion, entertained by some persons, that the encouragement of the fine arts savors too much of luxury, and is unfavorable to republican principles." He concedes the historical truth that the fine arts "have usually flourished most under despotic governments," but he counters that there has never before been a government formed on truly republican principles. He insists that far from being at odds with republican virtue, the cultivation of the fine arts promotes it. But his key arguments do not succeed in sustaining this thesis.

> The fine arts, both in those who cultivate and those only who admire them, open and expand the mind to great ideas. They inspire liberal feelings, create a harmony of temper, favorable to a sense of justice and a habit of moderation in our social intercourse. By increasing the circle of our pleasures, they moderate the intensity with which pleasures, not dependent on them, would be pursued. In proportion as they multiply our wants, they stimulate our industry, they diversify the objects of our ambition, they furnish new motives for a constant activity of mind and body, highly favorable to the health of both. The encouragement of a taste for elegant luxuries discourages the relish for luxuries that are gross and sensual, debilitating to the body, and demoralising to the mind. The last, it must be acknowledged, are prevailing in our country; they are perhaps the natural growth of domestic affluence and civil liberty.

The last sentence draws our attention to the overwhelming difficulty: while eloquently marshaling moral arguments in favor of the cultivation of the fine arts, Barlow utterly fails to show how such cultivation, and indeed the moral virtues it produces, are in harmony rather than in tension with democracy. The difficulty increases as Barlow goes on to observe that taste in the fine arts is "peculiarly desirable in those parts of our country, at the southward and westward, where the earth yields her rich productions with little labor, and leaves to the cultivator considerable vacancies of time and superfluities of wealth."[26] Do not the fine arts, cultivated for the sake of the aristocratic virtues Barlow celebrates, require at the least a life of true leisure, historically dependent on slaves or a lower, laboring class? Do they not require as well an inclination "to great ideas," a certain contempt for physical comfort and gratification, and a disdain for or ambition beyond commercial and productive activity—all of which are alien to the deepest spirit of modern democracy? These troubling and far-reaching questions are vividly exposed but never addressed in Barlow's discussion.

The University of Virginia

Jefferson seems to have first conceived the idea for a new state university around 1800, when he wrote to Joseph Priestley of his wish to establish in the central, upper country of Virginia "an University on a plan so broad & liberal & *modern*, as to be worth patronizing with the public support, and be a temptation to the youth of other states to come and drink of the cup of knowledge & fraternize with us."[27] Periodically over the next twenty-six years, and continually for the last decade of his life, Jefferson worked to realize this dream.

His efforts began to take definite form in 1814 when he was elected a trustee of the as-yet-unopened Albemarle Academy in Charlottesville, which he helped to transform into a more ambitious project under the name of Central College. While promoting Central College, he was also seeking legislative passage of his bills to create a school system and a state university. When in 1818 the school bill failed but provisions for a university were approved, Jefferson and his friends moved quickly to have Central College's grounds and endowment adopted as the basis for the new university. Securing a site in Jefferson's own neighborhood was of no small importance to him, since it allowed him to oversee every stage of the planning and construction. He was named rector in 1819 (at age seventy-five), though he shared responsibility with his colleagues on the board of visitors, all of them distinguished men. The others deferred to Jefferson, reasoning with James Madison that "as the scheme was originally Mr. Jefferson's and the chief responsibility for its success or failure would fall on him, it was but fair to let him execute it in his own way."[28]

Jefferson's meticulous involvement ranged from drawing up the curriculum and student regulations, to selecting the professors, to designing the buildings, ordering the bricks, and demonstrating for a stonemason how to chisel an Ionic capital. So pervasive was his influence that Emerson would later describe the University of Virginia as but "the lengthened shadow of one man." Jefferson himself chose a more affectionate term in the epitaph that he wrote for his own tombstone, commemorating his three most cherished achievements.

> Here was buried Thomas Jefferson,
> Author of the Declaration of American Independence,
> Of the Statute of Virginia for Religious Freedom,
> and Father of the University of Virginia.

As the inscription shows, liberty was forever uppermost in Jefferson's mind—liberty from tyrants and superstition, liberty to rule one's life according to a free conscience and an unshackled mind—and so it was as he planned the University of Virginia. The school would foster the individual's liberty to study and think by offering high-level instruction in as many fields as possible, especially in the rapidly advancing modern sciences. It would support political liberty by offering sound political and legal instruction to future leaders. Finally, it would tie these public and private functions together by focusing on the knowledge in every field that was evidently most useful for the business of life and the prosperity of society.[29]

The character and structure of the university followed directly from these purposes. It was to be a state school answerable to the legislature, but with extensive freedom for professors to specialize and for students to study what they wished. In the 1818 Rockfish Gap report, the basic plan according to which the University of Virginia was framed, Jefferson specified that the university "should, in all things, and at all times, be subject to the control of the Legislature." The University of Virginia was not to be the first chartered state university (that honor had gone to the University of Georgia in 1785), yet it quickly became the most successful and influential. The state universities that preceded it in Georgia, North Carolina, and elsewhere tended to fall under the power of sectarian groups within the state legislatures and to differ very little at first from traditional church-sponsored colleges. The University of Virginia was, by contrast, strictly nonsectarian. In the Rockfish Gap report Jefferson explained the absence of a professor of divinity as a necessary consequence of Virginia's dedication to religious freedom, although he included within the purview of the professor of ethics the proofs for the existence of God and the "moral obligations . . . in which all sects agree." In response to charges that the university was hostile to religion, Jefferson would later invite all the denominations to establish their own seminaries "on the confines of the University." There, he suggested, the students might enjoy the university's library and all its other resources—and there, as he wrote privately to Thomas Cooper, "by bringing the sects together, and mixing them with the mass of other students, we shall soften their asperities, liberalize and neutralize their prejudices, and make the general religion a religion of peace, reason, and morality." None of the churches, however, chose to take up this offer.[30]

Jefferson's aim was to found a university "where every branch of science, useful at this day, may be taught in it's highest degree." Funds did not permit him to create a school as expansive as Harvard, with its twenty professors. As he told his colleague Joseph Cabell, however, he was confident that scholars of greater distinction could be acquired and that as the university took root, its faculty would increasingly be able to specialize in their chosen fields. "You know we have all, from the beginning, considered the high qualifications of our professors as the only means by which we could give to our institution splendor and pre-eminence over all its sister seminaries." To this end, he proposed "to draw from Europe the first characters in science" by generous salaries, "which would not need to be repeated after the first generation have prepared fit successors, and given reputation to the institution." Equally essential to assembling a prominent faculty, Jefferson thought, would be the "distinguished scale" and beauty of the university's buildings "and the promise of future eminence which these would hold up, to induce them to commit their reputation to its future fortunes." Although Jefferson was to meet with many frustrations in his efforts to attract scholars of the first rank to the University of Virginia, the school was able to open its doors in 1825 with a respectable faculty of seven.[31]

One of Jefferson's setbacks in his search for professors is particularly revealing, since it shows a tension between his dual goals of public responsiveness and academic excellence or freedom. Jefferson was truly concerned with protecting academic freedom. He promised prospective faculty members that their tenure was "in fact for life," dismissal being possible only on a two-thirds vote of the liberal-minded and distinguished board of visitors. Academic freedom was also to be safeguarded by the equality among the faculty; instead of a potentially authoritarian presidency, Jefferson instituted an annually rotating chairmanship. But although the board did not dismiss any professors during Jefferson's lifetime, it was a board answerable to the state government and not the faculty. When the opening of the university was delayed for lack of funds, the visitors were forced to terminate the contract they had made with Dr. Thomas Cooper to teach science and law. It was public opposition to Cooper's religious heterodoxy, however, that prevented Jefferson from reappointing him in 1824 and that for a time damaged the cause of the university among the Virginia public. Jefferson himself clearly believed that a man's freethinking in no way disqualified him as a teacher.[32]

Jefferson hoped that by assembling a group of fine scholars, he would enable the university "to draw to it the youth of every State, but especially of the south and west." To assure that students received the full benefit of their teachers' wisdom, he stipulated that professors should "follow no other calling," and that their salaries "should be a certain but moderate subsistence," supplemented by "liberal tuition fees, as an excitement to assiduity."[33] He proposed to focus the university's resources on the most useful branches of knowledge, although, like Bacon, he construed utility broadly to include whatever promised to contribute to material well-being, good government, and even the contemplative and artistic pleasures of a cultivated life. Finally, he recommended allowing students a free hand in choosing the courses they thought they would profit most from.

As a devotee of modern science and philosophy, Jefferson was impressed by what he called "the wonderful advances in the sciences and arts" which had been made even within his own lifetime. In his 1800 letter to Priestley, he wrote of the irrelevance of "some branches of science, formerly esteemed," for "an institution meant chiefly for use," and he mentioned "oriental learning" as an example, although he did include the classics in subsequent plans for the university. Other disciplines, especially the natural sciences, he wanted taught more fully than they were in contemporary American colleges. But it was not enough to add more practical studies to the prescribed curriculum or to substitute them for some of the traditional subjects. William Smith's modernized program at the College of Philadelphia had been criticized, not without cause, for being so crowded and diverse that all of the courses risked becoming superficial. To do justice to any field of knowledge, Jefferson was convinced, one must make choices, and those choices were best left to the student himself, in consultation with parents and advisers.

> I am not fully informed of the practices at Harvard, but there is one from which we shall certainly vary, although it has been copied, I believe, by nearly every college and academy in the United States. That is, the holding the students all to one prescribed course of reading, and disallowing exclusive application to those branches only which are to qualify them for the particular vocations to which they are destined. We shall, on the contrary, allow them uncontrolled choice in the lectures they shall choose to attend, and require elementary qualifications only, and sufficient age.[34]

Jefferson thus proposed applying the customary college entrance requirements of Latin and Greek only to those who elected to study in the school of ancient languages. The board of visitors confirmed in their 1824 regulations Jefferson's principle of leaving students free to attend the schools of their preference, although the students were expected to follow a more or less prescribed program in each of the schools they entered. Nevertheless, while the visitors welcomed at the university all who wished to study there, offering diplomas only to the most outstanding, they did bow to tradition in defining the requirements for these diplomas.

> But no diploma shall be given to any one who has not passed such an examination in the Latin language as shall have proved him able to read the highest classics in that language with ease, thorough understanding and just quantity; and if he be also a proficient in the Greek, let that, too, be stated in his diploma. The intention being that the reputation of the University shall not be committed but to those who, to an eminence in some one or more of the sciences taught in it, add a proficiency in these languages which constitute the basis of good education, and are indispensable to fill up the character of a "well-educated man."[35]

"The Academical Village"

As soon as Jefferson's friends had secured for the university a site in his neighborhood at Charlottesville, Jefferson threw himself into the construction of the campus. He had long been persuaded that the usual plan of American colleges, consisting of one large building for all purposes, was "equally unfriendly to health, to study, to manners, morals, and order." He created instead an open quadrangle, surrounded by pavilions for the professors to live and teach in, which were connected by student rooms opening onto covered walkways. Study for Jefferson was at heart a solitary affair, or at most a matter for a few friends to engage in together, with the elder offering the younger friendly guidance. While assembling scholars into what he expected would become a large institution, he wanted to maintain the close, informal teacher-student ties that had been important in his own youth and that he judged most conducive both to learning and to morals. To encourage this, he proposed an arrangement whereby each professor would have a part in choosing the students who would live near his quarters, whom he would then oversee and sit with at the head of their table.[36]

Jefferson's unique design for the University of Virginia campus was the culmination of a lifetime of study in and original contributions to the field of architecture. Jefferson was, as he confessed to Madison, "an enthusiast on the subject of the arts," but he justified the enthusiasm by adding that "it's object is to improve the taste of my countrymen, to increase their reputation, to reconcile to them the respect of the world and procure them it's praise." Architecture was the art most suited to form the taste of a young republic, Jefferson thought, because it was both public and solidly useful, and because simple buildings of noble proportions could be built as inexpensively as ugly ones. While he himself loved painting and especially sculpture, he argued that their cost rendered it "useless therefore and preposterous for us to endeavor to make ourselves connoisseurs in those arts. They are worth seeing but not studying."[37]

Even as a young student Jefferson was collecting architecture books, and at twenty-four he began designing his home at Monticello, using the sixteenth-century Venetian master Andrea Palladio as his guide. On his European travels, architecture was second only to agriculture as an object of his attention. When a new state capitol was to be erected in Richmond, Jefferson seized the opportunity to form American taste by providing a design for it based on the Maison Carré at Nimes, an austere Roman temple that he thought perhaps "the most beautiful and precious morsel of architecture left us by antiquity." He also helped arrange for Jean-Antoine Houdon to create a sculpture of George Washington, life-size and in modern dress, to stand in the capitol where the Roman god had stood in the Maison Carré. With this novel adaptation of ancient temple forms for American public buildings, the classical revival in American architecture was begun.[38]

Jefferson was also intimately involved in planning Washington, D.C. For the Capitol he urged "the adoption of some one of the models of antiquity, which have the approbation of thousands of years," and for the president's house, he hoped that the finest modern structures might serve as examples. To educate the aesthetic judgment of the people and determine the style of the new city, he suggested distributing free engravings from his own plates of some of the most beautiful private buildings in Europe. As in the case of the University of Virginia campus, imposing buildings were to be more than ornaments: they were to overcome the country's provincialism and the low expectations that both Americans and foreigners tended to have for things American. A chaste, graceful style of architecture would lend dignity to the country's republican aspirations, conferring a sense of history and authority on the new nation's untried experiment in self-government.[39]

In the enabling legislation that created the University of Virginia, fine arts was the one category the legislature dropped from the list of subjects recommended in the Rockfish Gap report. Jefferson thereupon saved civil architecture by quietly including it along with navigation and military architecture in the school of mathematics. In fact, he designed the campus with the architecture students especially in mind. Although the whole was to stand with Monticello and the Virginia statehouse as a model for his countrymen, each pavilion was to provide for students a model of a different architectural order. "And these buildings being arranged around three sides of a square," Jefferson explained, "the lecturer, in a circuit, attended by his school, could explain to them successively these samples of the several orders." The University of Virginia campus, with the stately rotunda housing the library as its focal point, has attracted wide admiration, and in 1976 the American Institute of Architecture chose it as the finest architectural achievement in the United States since the signing of the Declaration of Independence.[40]

Student Discipline

One reason for Jefferson's unusual campus design was his desire for closer oversight of the students, both to promote learning and to prevent the insubordination and riots that were endemic among the mostly sixteen- to twenty-year-old youths who attended early American colleges. As Jefferson looked forward to the university's opening, he wrote, "The rock which I most dread is the discipline of the institution," and he consulted the regulations of other colleges and sought advice from George Ticknor at Harvard on how best to govern students. When it came to discipline, Jefferson was somewhat divided himself. On the one hand, he wanted students to have the freedom and responsibility of adults. He believed that if the faculty dispensed with petty rules and humiliating punishments, if they allowed students themselves to handle minor offenses through a board of censors, if they expected mature judgment in matters of conduct as in choices of studies, the majority of students would prove themselves serious scholars and the rest would be influenced by their example. To the extent that he acknowledged a need for professors to govern students, he hoped that honor might be their main appeal.

> It may be well questioned whether fear after a certain age, is a motive to which we should have ordinary recourse. The human character is susceptible of other incitements to correct conduct, more worthy of employ, and of better effect. Pride of character, laudable ambition, and moral dispositions are innate correctives of the indiscretions of that lively age; and when strengthened by habitual appeal and exercise, have a happier effect on future character than the degrading motive of fear. Hardening them to disgrace, to corporal punishments, and servile humiliations cannot be the best process for producing erect character. The affectionate deportment between father and son, offers in truth the best example for that of tutor and pupil.[41]

On the other hand, and in keeping with the idea of fatherly guidance, Jefferson wanted to shelter the students somewhat from the rigors of legal adulthood. In laying plans for Central College, he had advocated giving the school's proctor the powers of a justice of the peace on the college grounds, with authority to punish minor infractions of the law at his own discretion by such means as confining a student to his room. Jefferson explained that this authority would allow him to keep order and at the same time "shield the young and unguarded student from the disgrace of the common prison, except where the case was an aggravated one." This provision was unpopular and was not adopted at the University of Virginia, but the board of visitors did make another careful concession to the immaturity of students. In university inquiries into student misconduct, unlike in cases handled by the civil authorities, the faculty would not compel students to give evidence on oath. Jefferson supported this provision out of consideration for the common belief of schoolboys that it was dishonorable for them to bear witness against one another, even though he called such compunctions unfounded; he preferred to overcome sincere scruples by reason and not by force.[42]

In the event, the regulations adopted by the visitors in 1824 fell short of the principles Jefferson had enunciated. Whether he suffered a loss of confidence or was prevailed upon by his colleagues to change his mind, Jefferson approved a body of rules that was in many ways typical of the time. The university, for example, required parents to be notified of all their sons' absences from class, forbade students to hold or to attend "festive entertainments" except with the permission of their professors, and threatened for minor infractions such punishments as "a seat of degradation" in the schoolroom, "removal to a lower class," and "imposition of a task." Perhaps in response to these regulations—perhaps simply because, as Honeywell says, the bulk of students were not serious-minded scholars but the "undisciplined heirs to slave plantations"—disorder erupted on the night of 1 October 1825. Fourteen masked and intoxicated students rioted on the lawn, insulting and throwing brickbats at the professors who tried to quell the disturbance. The board of student censors, which might have helped identify the perpetrators, was not functioning. To the contrary, a majority of the other students signed a petition supporting the rioters. Finally, on 4 October, the visitors called the entire student body before them in the Rotunda. On the board sat two former presidents of the United States, Jefferson and Madison, and a number of Virginia's leading statesmen and jurists. Jefferson, aged and ill, attempted to address the students but was overcome with emotion. A colleague, Chapman Johnson, thereupon appealed so powerfully to the consciences of the offenders that all fourteen came forward to give themselves up. One of the ringleaders turned out to be a great-nephew of Jefferson himself. The board expelled him and two others, turning one over to the civil authorities, suspended eleven more, and allowed their supporters to retract their petition.[43]

Shortly after this incident, the rules were changed. The visitors gave the faculty more power, tightening the restrictions on student conduct in some respects but also dropping some of the more humiliating punishments. Most notably, they determined that prompt recourse to the law was the best means of keeping order for the future. In a letter to his granddaughter, Jefferson sums up his revised views on the place of fear and legal coercion in a college. He expresses satisfaction that the board's vigorous exercise of authority and its referral of one student's case to a grand jury has "struck a terror" into the minority of students who are inclined to make trouble.

> A perfect subordination has succeeded, entire respect toward the professors, and industry, order, and quiet the most exemplary has prevailed ever since. . . . We have no further fear of anything of the kind from the present set, but as at the next term their numbers will be more than doubled by the accession of an additional band, as unbroken as these were, we mean to be prepared and to ask of the legislature a power to call in the civil authorities in the first instant of disorder, and to quell it on the spot by imprisonment and the same legal coercions provided against disorder generally committed by other citizens, from whom, at their age, they have no right to distinction.[44]

Although he was forced to retreat from his vision of the university as an affectionate family, Jefferson's final position was more consistent with his desire to treat students as responsible adults, capable of making use of the learning available to them and answerable, as all citizens, if they overstep the law. Jefferson's hope that students might exercise self-government by taking a share in enforcing the rules on campus was not immediately realized, but some years after his death an honor system was established at the University of Virginia, which proved successful and was imitated elsewhere.

The University Curriculum

In the Rockfish Gap report, Jefferson proposed that the university begin with ten professors. Their fields were to be: (1) ancient languages (Latin, Greek, Hebrew); (2) modern languages (French, Spanish, Italian, German, Anglo-Saxon); (3) pure mathematics (algebra, calculus, geometry of straight lines and curved, including "projectiles, a leading branch of the military art," military and naval architecture); (4) "physico-mathematics" (physics, astronomy, geography); (5) "physics, or natural philosophy" (chemistry, including "the theory of agriculture" and mineralogy); (6) botany and zoology; (7) anatomy and medicine; (8) government, political economy, the law of nature and nations, and history, "being interwoven with Politics and Law"; (9) civil law; (10) "ideology" or philosophy of mind, grammar, ethics, rhetoric, belles-lettres, and the fine arts.

As heavily loaded as some of these professorships were, Jefferson managed to preserve almost the entire curriculum when in 1824 the shortage of funds forced him to reorganize the subjects to fit eight schools, each to be staffed at the outset by a single teacher. Natural philosophy, botany, and zoology were combined into one school, and government and law into another, with history divided between the schools of ancient and modern languages. The fine arts were dropped, and the professor who would originally have taught them had his program further lightened by the removal of rhetoric and belles-lettres to the school of ancient languages. Jefferson's curriculum thus provided for both a college and two professional schools utilizing only eight professors. Taken as a whole it was a massively ambitious project, designed more for the future than for the constraints of the present.[45]

The Natural Sciences

Perhaps the most distinctive feature of the curriculum was its emphasis on the natural sciences. Both as originally planned and as finally enacted, mathematics and science composed fully half of the university offerings. In a letter which Jefferson asked to have circulated among the faculty, he sketched the program that he thought would best suit the majority of students. Since he believed that languages and mathematics provided superior intellectual training for boys in grammar school, he hoped most students would matriculate with a good foundation in these subjects. Classics could be continued and given a "last polish" in the first year of university. Mathematics could also be studied then and the following year, at which time students might begin to focus increasingly on physics, chemistry, and the rest of natural history.[46]

Even in advice that he offered to young men preparing independently for the bar, Jefferson recommended beginning with mathematics, astronomy, geography, and natural philosophy, in order to strengthen the powers of their minds. His letters to young friends and relations enrolled at university often stress these same subjects as the most valuable courses they can take. Thus he counsels his future son-in-law, Thomas Mann Randolph, to attend lectures at Edinburgh in astronomy, physics, natural history, anatomy, botany, and chemistry, but not to waste time attending a professor of history, for "it is to be acquired from books" in the hours of relaxation from more demanding studies. He likewise advises a grandson at South Carolina College to study all the science that he can but to omit Blair's *Rhetoric*, Watts's *Logic*, Kames's *Elements of Criticism*, Paley's *Moral Philosophy*, Butler's *Analogy of Religion*, etc., "which you can read in your closet after leaving College as well as at it." To furnish students with the kind of scientific learning that cannot be easily obtained from books, he advises the creation of a botanical garden, stocked with trees of "distinguished usefulness," an observatory or at least a model of the solar system, a chemical laboratory, and a dispensary for the medical school.[47]

Chemistry was the one science that Jefferson considered most useful, especially for its applications to agriculture. In a revealing letter to John Emmett, the overburdened, discouraged young professor of chemistry, mineralogy, geology, rural economy, botany, and zoology, Jefferson urges him not to worry about turning out accomplished scientists but simply to start students on their way in each of the sciences and above all in chemistry, so that they might be prepared to attain eminence on their own. At other times, however, he suggests that the real goal is not to produce scientists at all but rather solid husbandmen.

In every college and university a professorship of Agriculture, & the class of it's students, might be honored as the first. Young men, closing their academical education with this as the crown of all other sciences, fascinated with it's solid charms, & at a time when they are to chuse an occupation . . . would return to the farms of their fathers . . . & replenish and invigorate a calling, now languishing under contempt & oppression.[48]

Government and Law

Of all the departments of the university, the school of law, government, and political economy was the one Jefferson planned for most carefully and the one
that he found hardest to staff with a suitable professor. In the Rockfish Gap report, he set down as the first aim of the university "to form the statesmen, legislators, and judges, on whom public prosperity and individual happiness are so
much to depend." Since the courses in government and law were, like all those
at the university, wholly voluntary, they would provide mainly a professional
training for the few rather than a civic education for the students at large. Yet
Jefferson did not assume that students would arrive at the university with a firm
grounding in the liberal principles of the American regime, as is evidenced by
the basic texts he expected them to study. Hence it was all the more essential for
Jefferson that the professor be both a United States citizen and a learned lawyer
who held strictly to the spirit and letter of the Constitution. Because the university's salaries could not compete with lawyers' fees, and because so many lawyers
were Federalists or, as Jefferson thought, advocates of "consolidation," someone
meeting Jefferson's criteria was doubly hard to find. When his first choice, Francis Walker Gilmer, was forced by ill health to resign, Jefferson decided to ensure
the teaching of correct principles in the government courses by dictating the
books to be used.

> In most public seminaries, textbooks are prescribed to each of the several
> schools . . . and this is generally done by authority of the trustees. I should
> not propose this generally in our University, because, I believe none of us
> are so much at the heights of science in the several branches as to under-
> take this; and therefore that it will be better left to the professors, until oc-
> casion of interference shall be given. But there is one branch in which we
> are the best judges, in which heresies may be taught, of so interesting a
> character to our own State, and to the United States, as to make it a duty
> in us to lay down the principles which shall be taught. It is that of govern-
> ment. Mr. Gilmer being withdrawn, we know not who his successor may
> be. He may be a Richmond lawyer, or one of that school of quondam feder-
> alism, now consolidation. It is our duty to guard against the dissemination
> of such principles among our youth, and the diffusion of that poison, by a
> previous prescription of the texts to be followed in their discourses.

The visitors believed that the selection of the law professor required special care,
both because they were certain that they understood the true principles to be
taught and because they saw grave threats to these truths from the errors or selfishness of political partisanship.[49]

Jefferson accordingly drew up a list of prescribed books for the course in government and sent it to Madison for his suggestions. While Madison proposed adding Washington's Farewell Address as one of the selections, he was wary of mandating texts at all and hoped that the board could find a politically sound professor who could be trusted to choose his own books. He and his colleagues nevertheless approved Jefferson's recommendations, in a report that underscores their responsibilities as a public university.

It is the duty of this Board to the Government under which it lives and especially to that of which this University is the immediate creation, to pay especial attention to the principles of government which shall be inculcated therein, and to provide that none shall be inculcated which are incompatible with those on which the constitutions of this State and of the United States were genuinely based, in the common opinion.

The report then lists as appropriate texts Locke's *Essay Concerning the True Original, Extent and End of Civil Government*, Sidney's *Discourses on Government*, the Declaration of Independence, the *Federalist Papers*, the 1799 Virginia Resolutions on the Alien and Sedition Acts, and Washington's Farewell Address.[50]

For studying the law, Jefferson thought students should begin with Coke on Littleton.

You will recollect that before the Revolution, Coke on Littleton was the universal elementary book of law students, and a sounder Whig never wrote, nor of profounder learning in the orthodox doctrines of the British constitution, or in what were called English liberties. You remember also that our lawyers were all Whigs. But when his black-letter text, and uncouth but cunning learning got out of fashion, and the honeyed Mansfield-ism of Blackstone became the students' hornbook, from that moment, that profession (the nursery of our Congress) began to slide into toryism, and nearly all the young brood of lawyers now are of that hue. They suppose themselves, indeed, to be Whigs, because they no longer know what Whigism or republicanism means. It is in our seminary that that vestal flame is to be kept alive; it is thence it is to spread anew over our own and the sister States. If we are true and vigilant in our trust, within a dozen or twenty years a majority of our own legislature will be from one school, and many disciples will have carried its doctrines home with them to their several States, and will have leavened thus the whole mass.[51]

How could such prescriptions of books be justified in one who was such a champion of the freedom of the mind? Jefferson's conservatism in politics after the Revolution is especially remarkable given his confidence that free inquiry would bring advancement in other fields, such as science. Indeed, as we have seen, he elsewhere indicated that he expected and welcomed ongoing progress in politics also, even periodic revolutions. After Shays's Rebellion in Massachusetts, which filled so many of his countrymen with gloomy forebodings, Jefferson wrote from Paris that "the tree of liberty must be refreshed from time to time with the blood of patriots and tyrants. It is its natural manure." Jefferson valued such rebellions more for restoring lost liberty—or warning the rulers that the people were willing to fight to restore it—than for introducing new truths. But he also argued often that "the earth belongs to the living," that they and they alone must choose what government is right for them. On this theme, he wrote to Samuel Kercheval in 1816:

> Some men look at constitutions with sanctimonious reverence, and deem them like the ark of the covenant, too sacred to be touched. They ascribe to the men of the preceding age a wisdom more than human, and suppose what they did to be beyond amendment. I knew that age well; I belonged to it, and labored with it. It deserved well of its country. It was very like the present, but without the experience of the present; and forty years of experience in government is worth a century of book-reading; and this they would say themselves, were they to rise from the dead. I am certainly not an advocate for frequent and untried changes in laws and constitutions. I think moderate imperfections had better be borne with; because, when once known, we accommodate ourselves to them, and find practical means of correcting their ill effects. But I know also, that laws and institutions must go hand in hand with the progress of the human mind. As that becomes more developed, more enlightened, as new discoveries are made, new truths disclosed, and manners and opinions change with the change of circumstances, institutions must advance also, and keep pace with the times. . . . Let us, as our sister States have done, avail ourselves of our reason and experience, to correct the crude essays of our first and unexperienced, although wise, virtuous, and well-meaning councils. And lastly, let us provide in our Constitution for its revision at stated periods. . . . Each generation is as independent of the one preceding, as that was of all which had gone before. It has then, like them, a right to choose for itself the form of government it believes most promotive of its own happiness.[52]

But how radical were these advances that Jefferson anticipated in political understanding? In the letter to Kercheval he seems to be speaking more of the prudent application of principles than of basic principles themselves. Moreover, if he believed that experience would make future generations politically wiser, he also feared that the passage of time would inevitably make them more corrupt. Paradoxically, then, while he defends his call for a new Virginia constitution on the grounds that each generation has a right to decide for itself, he later explains it to Kercheval as his wish to avail future generations of the virtue of the present (which is bound not to last), "to put into a chaste and secure form, the government to be handed down to them." The same tension or qualification appears in Jefferson's 1779 Bill for Establishing Religious Freedom. He concludes the bill with an explicit concession that "this assembly . . . have no power to restrain the acts of succeeding Assemblies," yet he declares nevertheless that any revocation or abridgement of the rights therein established "will be an infringement of natural right." Despite his sometimes ardent statements about progress, Jefferson was confident that his generation had already grasped most or all of the fundamental truths about human rights and just government.[53]

At the university, Jefferson was prepared to require the teaching of these truths because he saw the university not as an end in itself but as a teaching institution designed to serve the country's needs. His statement that the visitors should allow most professors to choose their own texts "until occasion of interference shall be given" shows that Jefferson did not consider academic freedom in any field to be an intrinsic right of professors or of universities, but only a prudent rule to be followed as much as possible. Although he wanted the professors, once hired, to be reasonably secure from dismissal because of unpopular opinions, he still expected them to teach what the community decided it was best for the youth to learn. And Jefferson shared the common-sense understanding of his countrymen that America's freedom is only safe if the mass of citizens agree on fundamental principles, committing themselves to respect one another's basic rights and to submit to the rule of the majority, remaining loyal even in opposition. Jefferson saw that an undiscriminating openness to the critics of liberal democracy could easily lead to a rejection of those very principles of natural rights that justify intellectual freedom in the first place. Jefferson was confident that republican principles could withstand the harshest scrutiny when submitted to a reasoned and sober inquiry, but he was well aware that forces other than reason all too often sway the minds of youths, and that most people keep in adulthood whatever principles they have imbibed when young. Hence his advice to a young nephew on what histories to study: "Omit Clarendon as too seducing for a young republican. By and by read him."[54]

Whereas Jefferson thought of the other professors mainly as teachers but also as scholars who might advance knowledge by freely questioning all the received opinions in their fields, the task of the professor of law and government was at once more serious and less exciting: to prepare young men for positions of leadership and trust, by teaching faithfully the principles of the Revolution. But just as Jefferson himself felt more enthusiasm for the burgeoning sciences than for law, could one not expect many of the most talented and ambitious youths to gravitate away from government to fields such as science and business, which still promised to reward bold innovation with riches and prestige?

Aside from his attempts to bring dignity to American public life with fine buildings and to invigorate *local* politics through the wards, Jefferson gave insufficient thought to the problem of drawing good people into public service. We have already seen his own views on the "splendid torments" of government.[55] What is troubling is that his own policies did little to make political life less of a torment while they drained it of much of its splendor. Jefferson was from his youth a vigorous proponent of the idea that leaders were but servants of the people, to be summarily dismissed when they proved unfaithful. He worked hard to remove from government the vestiges of traditional monarchy or aristocracy, and with them went much of the honor that would have attracted high-minded, ambitious youths into government. His principles tended to end government's character as a club for gentlemen, opening it to talent from all classes and so bringing in men of little culture and uncouth manners. He advocated an extensive franchise, so that no one could corrupt the electorate with money, but that policy exposed leaders to the attacks and vicissitudes of the masses. Finally, he fought for the freedom of the press, which subjected leaders to the even more violent attacks of the newspapers. While these measures were essential to liberty as Jefferson understood it, he suggested no special honors to replace those that had formerly been accorded to statesmen.

Jefferson wanted citizens to serve their country out of love for the nation and a desire to make themselves useful. These were surely the passions that motivated Jefferson himself to continue in the nation's service for so long despite his distaste for public life: he found deep satisfaction in guiding the country successfully through troubled times, in laying a firm foundation for an infant polity, in doing what perhaps no one else was capable of. But was it not infinitely easier to acquire a satisfying sense of achievement when the slate had been swept clean, when the nation was casting about for a constitution and the states for new codes of law? Jefferson was encouraged in his labors on the country's behalf by the thought that history would judge him fairly even if his contemporaries did not and by the confidence that he would indeed be remembered as one of the greatest founders of a great nation. But what aspiring statesman could ever again hope for so much?

A decade after Jefferson's death, Abraham Lincoln was to wonder whether the passing of that Founding generation of heroes did not leave the most ambitious spirits with nothing to do but destroy an edifice that they could not improve upon. Although Lincoln suggested that men of intense political ambition would always arise, this expectation by no means implies a confidence that the most patriotic or principled Americans would continue to go into government.

Indeed, he was troubled by what he saw as a general decline in dedication to the Constitution and laws. A reverence for the Founding principles, Lincoln said, had hitherto been kept burning by the living history of the revolutionary patriots' struggle. As the voices of those patriots one by one fell silent, however, liberty could only be upheld if stirring memories were replaced with "other pillars, hewn from the solid quarry of sober reason." Sober reason itself dictates an appeal to passions supportive of reasonable institutions, as is seen by Lincoln's subsequent appeal to the hearts of his hearers.

> Let us have, above all, *a reverence for the constitution* and laws: and, that we improved to the last; that we remained free to the last; that we revered his name to the last; that, during his long sleep, we permitted no hostile foot to pass over or desecrate his resting place: shall be that which to learn the last trump shall awaken our WASHINGTON.

One cannot help a comparison with Jefferson's breezy assertion that "the earth belongs to the living." To say the least, it is not clear that Jefferson's education furnishes the materials for Lincoln's "pillars" of reasoned reverence.[56]

Part of the problem with Jefferson's curriculum was that he was concerned to teach not only the principles that had united the Constitution's Framers but the specific interpretation of the Constitution that defined his Republican party—and southern Republicans especially—over against the Federalists. This partisan concern led him to design a course of study that was too narrow and defensive to give the best grounding in political science. Whereas in 1800 Jefferson had hoped to draw students from the whole country, by 1820 the controversy over Missouri's admission to the union had riveted his attention on the sectional struggle. Thereafter, though he never ceased to abhor slavery, Jefferson saw the university as primarily a school for southern students and hence a bulwark of the South in its assertion of states' rights. In 1821 he wrote that the university was intended for students "who desire the highest degree of instruction for which they now go to Harvard, Princeton, New York, and Philadelphia. These seminaries are no longer proper for Southern or Western students. The signs of the times admonish us to call them home. If knowledge is power we should look to its advancement at home where our resource of power will be unwanting."[57] Jefferson accordingly included in the reading list the 1799 Virginia Resolutions, without giving a fair hearing to the writings of great and intellectually rich political opponents such as his fellow Virginian John Marshall.

The same failure to examine both sides of a controversy appears in Jefferson's exclusion from the program of any premodern or even pre-Lockean political theory. To appreciate fully the strength of the principles their country is built on, students must examine not only the philosophers who articulated those principles but the opponents against whose teachings they argued. In order for leaders to know the deepest limitations of their regime, so as to be able to moderate its most dangerous vices or compensate for its weaknesses, they must acquire a perspective outside it. Such a perspective is best gained through a sympathetic if critical study of alien, competing regimes or ways of life, especially those of the ancients. Basic questions about the nature of man, of freedom, and of just government were open and alive in Jefferson's day; he thought them through for himself and hence had a deep appreciation for his country's fundamental principles. But his proposed curriculum transmits to posterity the answers without the questions; it runs the risk of turning burning issues into dead dogma and leaving students with beliefs that are mere opinions. Jefferson was right to put civic education first in the school of government; he was right that a professor of government ought first and last to make the case for his own country's principles. But by making civic education too partisan and curtailing the liberal education that comes with studying fundamental alternatives, he left his students rooted in thin soil. There is indeed a tension between civic education and liberal education, but there is also a mutual dependence: civic and liberal education need each other if scholars are to possess the moral seriousness without which philosophy becomes an academic game, and if civic leaders are to be inspirited with a patriotism that is reasoned and moderate.[58]

This fundamental deficiency of Jefferson's conception of higher education in politics and law is illuminated by a contrast with the conception outlined by James Wilson in his 1790 lecture course inaugurating the nation's first law school, at the College of Philadelphia. Wilson shared with Jefferson a deep uneasiness at the prospect of American judges, lawyers, and civic leaders being educated through the study of texts and legal precedents that were mainly English and hence unrepublican. Like Jefferson, Wilson deplored in particular the virtual monopoly over legal education exercised by William Blackstone's *Commentaries*. Wilson felt, as strongly as did Jefferson, that a new, distinctly American, and thoroughly republican legal curriculum had to be designed. He was convinced that at the core of the curriculum there had to be Lockean political philosophy—especially those revolutionary, republican, and individualistic elements of Locke that had been questioned or rejected by Blackstone and Hume. Despite the burden of his duties as an associate justice of the Supreme Court, Wilson accepted with enthusiasm the challenge of initiating a formal law school lectureship, convinced that it was through the law school and its lectures that Americans might self-consciously strike out to forge a new, homegrown outlook in legal theory and education. But he saw this great effort as anchored in a dialogue or debate with the greatest pre- or anti-Lockean theorists.

After summarizing his basic disagreement with Blackstone and quoting and rebutting a crucial passage from the *Commentaries* in which Blackstone criticizes and rejects Locke's doctrine of the right to revolution, Wilson draws back to consider the place Blackstone ought to occupy in the education of young American law students.

> As author of the Commentaries, he possessed uncommon merit. His manner is clear and methodical; his sentiments—I speak of them generally—are judicious and solid; his language is elegant and pure. In publick law, however, he should be consulted with a cautious prudence. But, even in publick law, his principles, when they are not proper objects of imitation, will furnish excellent materials of contrast. On every account, therefore, he should be read and studied. He deserves to be much admired; but he ought not to be implicitly followed.

Wilson then applies these educational reflections to the history of political theory generally. This admonition, he says, "should not be confined to William Blackstone: it ought to be extended to all political writers." "The cause of liberty," Wilson explains, and the cause of "the rights of men" require that "in a subject essential to that cause and to those rights, errour should be exposed, in order to be avoided." Illustrating and continuing this pedagogy, Wilson turns to a critical examination of Grotius's theory of sovereignty in its opposition to Lockean theory; and in his second lecture, Wilson extends his critical engagement to arguments with Aristotle, Hobbes, Pufendorf, Barbeyrac, and even the great Locke, insofar as Lockean writings (unintentionally, Wilson believes) "facilitated the progress, and have given strength to the effects of scepticism" in religion.[59]

One may take issue with Wilson's intepretations of and arguments against the classic texts in political philosophy. One may accuse him of having too blithe a confidence in the superiority of Lockean political theory and of moving too superficially and in too harmonizing a spirit through the complex quarrels that divide and animate the history of political philosophy. But it is impossible to deny that his lectures breathe, and in all likelihood conveyed to students, a zest for intellectual debate and a consequent joy in learning and reading that surpass anything comparable to be found in the educational reflections of Jefferson. Rare among the Founders, Wilson proved in action that he knew what it means to deliver before students a memorable, erudite, controversial, and hence thought-provoking lecture on the theoretical principles of the American Constitution.

Languages, History, and Philosophy

Jefferson did of course make some provision for a classical liberal education in the schools of ancient and modern languages and moral philosophy. It was this portion of the university, however, that Edward Everett found most inadequate in his unsigned critique of the Rockfish Gap report, published in 1820. As actually established, the school of ancient languages included advanced Latin and Greek, Hebrew, rhetoric, belles-lettres, and ancient history and geography. Jefferson ensured that Greek and Latin would be studied on a high level by setting minimal qualifications for this school and by specifying that the university was the place where students' "classical learning might be critically completed, by a study of the authors of highest degree." He expected this completion to require the first year for most of the students who chose it. They would then, with a gentlemanly grounding in classical literature and history, proceed to more practical studies that would fit them for an active life.[60]

Everett's objection to this plan is that it will allow neither professor nor students sufficient time for a proper classical program. Even in its original form in the Rockfish Gap report, where the school of ancient languages is assigned simply the Greek, Latin, and Hebrew languages, Everett argues that the duties are too extensive for any one man to discharge with distinction. He compares the university's provisions for the classics unfavorably with "the most ill-provided" grammar schools, suggesting that in its rush to teach everything, the university will sacrifice thorough instruction in the highest classical authors. He goes on to compare the American universities with those on the European continent, which, he explains,

> are properly speaking professional schools; places to which young men who have carried their classical studies to a high degree of perfection, at gymnasia or high schools, resort for the study of their profession, of law, physic or divinity. It is here too, that they prepare themselves for another profession, scarcely known with us, viz. the Classical. All who look forward to places of instruction at the universities or the academies, who propose to get their living as professors or school-masters, together with the students of theology, to which class in fact the other for the most part belongs, these all make philology in its widest sense a great and constant study.[61]

The school of modern languages included French, Spanish, Italian, German, Anglo-Saxon, and modern history and geography. Of these languages, Jefferson in the Rockfish Gap report describes French as the most valuable, both as "the language of general intercourse among nations, and as a depository of human science." Spanish he recommends for its importance in communicating with the other countries in the hemisphere and for reading early histories of America. He praises the many superior works written in Italian for their subject matter and especially for their fine style and composition, and German books for their erudition and scientific value. Anglo-Saxon was a favorite pastime for Jefferson. In

1798 he wrote an essay on it with a view to facilitating its instruction. He believed, as he put it in the Rockfish Gap report, that a few weeks' study of this language would give students a deeper knowledge of English and a "full understanding of our ancient common law." This comment prompted the following response from Everett:

> We were a little grieved, if we may say so without disrespect toward the distinguished name at the head of this report, to hear of "the *few weeks* of attention, which would alone be requisite for the attainment of the Anglo-Saxon." . . . We know not which most to wonder at, the good nature with which discreet people suffer pretenders to confound learning a language, with learning something of it; or the hardihood with which the experience of the world is still set at gross and open defiance, and itinerant sages are imagined to have a magic key, to unlock that chain, by which the gods have bound labour and acquisition together.

While Jefferson himself mastered many languages, he may here again have overestimated his students' capacity for mature, serious application.[62]

Literature and especially modern literature received short shrift in the early University of Virginia curriculum, as in the reading lists that Jefferson drew up for young relations and friends. Summing up Jefferson's attitude toward English literature and education in English, Philip Bruce has observed:

> It is remarkable how slightly he depended for recreation on the variety and beauty of the literature of his own language. He seems to have been indebted to it only for the clarity and precision of his flexible style. Unlike many of his contemporaries, he had no familiar knowledge of Shakespeare. . . . The profound impression which he made on the character of the University of Virginia is revealed in no particular more plainly than in the history of its school of languages. His interest in the ancient tongues caused him to employ the ablest scholars for those professorships who could be procured from Europe; but the nearest approach to an English chair was a barren school of Anglo-Saxon.[63]

Partly based on a principle of economy but partly reflecting Jefferson's low opinion of most literature, he provided in the final plan that the language of each country should be taught mainly through reading its history in the original sources. For Jefferson agreed with Locke that history, in contrast to poetry, was a subject that "a Gentleman should not barely touch at, but constantly dwell upon, and never have done with." Jefferson himself loved historical readings, and all the more as he grew old. As he mused to Nathanial Macon in 1819: "I feel a much greater interest in knowing what has passed two or three thousand years ago, than in what is now passing. I read nothing, therefore, but the heroes of Troy, of the wars of Lacedaemon and Athens, of Pompey and Caesar, and of Augustus too, the Bonepart and parricide of that day. . . . I slumber without fear, and review in my dreams the visions of antiquity." To Anne Randolph Bankhead in 1808 he wrote: "Tacitus I consider as the first writer in the world without a single exception. His book is a compound of history and morality of which we have no other example." Jefferson made it clear, however, that he regarded history as a subject that could as easily be studied independently as with a professor.[64]

The school of moral philosophy was to comprise "mental science generally," including ideology (by which Jefferson meant the science of ideas), grammar, logic, and ethics. Jefferson's estimation of ancient philosophy was unorthodox and mixed. He identified himself as an Epicurean and accorded the highest praise to the writings of Epicurus, his ancient disciple Lucretius, and his modern disciple Gassendi. Although he showed respect for Socrates as presented by Xenophon, he looked with considerable skepticism on the Stoics, dismissed Aristotle's *Politics* as irrelevant to modern conditions, and regarded Plato as worse than useless. As he put it in a letter responding sympathetically to John Adams's expression of disgust with Plato:

> Fashion and authority apart, and bringing Plato to the test of reason, take from him his sophisms, futilities, and incomprehensibilities, and what remains? In truth, he is one of the race of genuine Sophists, who has escaped the oblivion of his brethren, first by the elegance of his diction, but chiefly by the adoption and incorporation of his whimsies into the body of artificial Christianity. His foggy mind, is forever presenting the semblances of objects which, half seen thro' a mist, can be defined neither in form or dimension. Yet this which should have consigned him to early oblivion really procured him immortality of fame and reverence.

Later he observed to William Short: "I consider the genuine (not imputed) doctrines of Epicurus as containing everything rational in moral philosophy which Greece and Rome have left us. Epictetus, indeed, has given us what was good of the Stoics, all beyond, of their dogmas, being hypocrisy and grimace." To law students he recommended the study of Seneca and "the Stoic Cicero's" *De Officiis*, but little else in ancient philosophy.[65]

Jefferson had considerable respect for modern moral philosophy, especially its Epicurean aspects, but his own study of ethics had persuaded him that it would be superfluous for a student to attend lectures in this subject, since nature has provided man with a moral sense sufficient to guide him. In a similar spirit, he wrote to Dr. Thomas Cooper regarding his grandson, "It would be lost time for him to attend professors of ethics, metaphysics, logic. The first of these may be as well acquired in the closet as from living lecture; and supposing the two last to mean the science of the mind, the simple reading of Locke, [Destutt de] Tracy, and [Dugald] Stewart will give him as much in that branch as is real science." This remark helps explain Jefferson's original willingness to put mental and moral philosophy together with grammar, rhetoric, belles-lettres, and the fine arts in the hands of one professor, combining subjects that, as Everett points out, usually comprise at least four great departments of themselves.[66]

Jefferson's belief that history and philosophy did not really need to be studied in the classroom is more an indication of his own immense capacity for independent learning than a sign of disregard for these subjects: his library had numerous volumes of philosophy and especially history, including all the Greek and Latin classics that were available in printed editions in his day. Some of his judgments, notably on the high merit of Xenophon's portrait of Socrates, were far superior to the judgments of the greatest German classical scholars of his time, such as B. G. Niebuhr—scholars to whom Everett tended to look with uncritical admiration. Jefferson's keen grasp of politics prevented his reading of the classical historians from ever becoming so naively enthusiastic as that of such modern commentators as Hannah Arendt or J. G. A. Pocock. Nevertheless, particularly in the case of the philosophers, if not also the historians, one gets the impression that Jefferson too easily mined the ancient writers for his own uses, a bit like the medieval Romans mined the ancient monuments for marble; he seems rarely to confront an ancient work as a whole that commands respect, as a worthy and instructive opponent. Jefferson perhaps rightly felt more kinship with Pericles and Cicero than with the politicians who swarmed the United States capital, yet he also declared that the ancient historians had little to teach us about government. For all his love of classical learning, Jefferson in the end recommended it mainly as an ornament; he never made the case that there was anything compelling in Greek and Latin books that could not be gotten from another source. As a result, he damned the study of classics by faint praise, and to the extent that he was influential, he contributed to making liberal education in the United States less open to the challenge of the classics and hence less truly liberating.[67]

The Influence of the University of Virginia

In improving the level of teaching and learning in southern schools and colleges, the University of Virginia had a considerable impact. When the university opened, its students tended to be poorly prepared because of the uneven quality of grammar schools in the region. As Jefferson had hoped, many of the university's graduates went on to found new schools and colleges, and University of Virginia graduates were particularly prominent in the establishment of the University of Texas. But in other respects, the university did not have the influence that its rapid rise to prominence would have led one to expect.[68]

Although the most successful state university, Virginia was founded in an era that witnessed the resurgence of religiosity and a renewed interest in sectarian rather than state-sponsored colleges. In the words of the leading historian of this aspect of American higher education:

> Although the secular patterns of eighteenth century European thought received a considerable welcome in certain circles in American life during the revolutionary and post-revolutionary eras, and were reflected in the establishment of a few collegiate institutions during the latter part of the eighteenth century, the forces of orthodox religion, after a temporary setback during the Revolution, regained their ascendancy over the cultural life of this country at the turn of the century through a complex of circumstances. . . .

> It still remained to be seen, however, whether the American people were to choose to establish state universities, and thus give their main support to the centralized forms of state education so strongly advocated during the revolutionary era, or to prefer in the next half-century to provide for themselves small denominational colleges, widely scattered over the country, and closely fashioned after local and particular desires and aspirations. . . . The reasons that led the people of this land to choose, in the main, at that time the latter alternative can be understood only in the light of the religious developments that took place during the early decades of the nineteenth century. . . .

> The "denominational era" of our history was ushered in with a series of revivals that spread from the settled communities of the East to the pioneer settlements on the frontier. There took place a veritable "Second Awakening" throughout the land. In the early decades of the century, the older colleges in the east became the centers of a deep and fervid religious life, and the newer colleges on the frontier exhibited signs of true evangelical zeal.[69]

The turning point was the landmark Dartmouth College case, decided by the Supreme Court in 1819. "Until the time of the Dartmouth decision," Donald Tewksbury writes, "the future of denominational colleges, and private colleges in general, was in the balance." The contest was a largely partisan one, between the Federalist and Congregational defenders of the original college charter on the one hand, and the Republicans who asserted the people's right to transform

Dartmouth into a state university on the other. Here, as in the case of William and Mary, Jefferson defended the government's right to alter corporations chartered and partially endowed by it for public purposes. The claim of the college to the sanctity of its charter was championed by Dartmouth alumnus Daniel Webster and upheld in a celebrated opinion written by Chief Justice John Marshall. Chancellor Kent later argued that this case was crucial in protecting the autonomy of American charitable, religious, educational, and commercial institutions. The immediate effect in education was to bolster the movement toward church-sponsored colleges, thus delaying the creation of other great state universities until after the Civil War.[70]

It thus was Benjamin Rush's, rather than Jefferson's, vision of state higher education that predominated. Rush, it will be recalled, had argued strongly for denominational colleges. He had done so because he was convinced, contrary to Jefferson, that denominational protestant religion was the moral backbone of the country and that the various sects should be entrenched and strengthened through their shared, decentralized control over higher education. As he explains in his "Hints for Establishing a College at Carlisle in Cumberland County, Pennsylvania":

Every religious society should endeavor to preserve a representation of itself in government. The Presbyterians suffered greatly under the old government from the want of this representation. At present they hold an undue share in the power of Pennsylvania. . . . To secure a moderate and just share in the power of the state it becomes them to retire a little from offices and to invite other societies to partake of them with them. To prevent the effect of these combinations against them reducing them to their ancient state of oppression and insignificance it becomes them above all things to entrench themselves in schools of learning. These are the true Nurseries of power and influence. They improve talents and virtue and these by begetting wealth form the ingredients that constitute power in all countries.

But if American colleges were overwhelmingly denominational, they were not for that reason narrowly or intolerantly sectarian. One must bear in mind what Frederick Rudolph calls "the paradox that while most colleges of the period were founded by denominations, they were also forbidden either by charter or public opinion to indulge in religious tests for faculty or students."[71]

Jefferson's curricular ideas, like his organizational theories, were of limited influence, at least in the next two generations. The elective curriculum at the University of Virginia attracted considerable attention. George Ticknor of Harvard and Francis Wayland of Brown both visited to see it in operation. Ticknor had been, with Edward Everett, one of the first American students to attend a German university for advanced studies. Soon after returning to take up a new chair of modern languages at Harvard, he proposed a major restructuring of the college. He called for opening courses to nondegree students who wanted to gain specialized knowledge, organizing the college into departments, classing the students in each subject by proficiency and not by year, and allowing some choices of study for degree students. His proposals were briefly implemented in 1823 but never fairly tried. Only in his own department of modern languages were they continued, much to the satisfaction of teacher and students alike.[72]

But it was neither Virginia nor Harvard that was to set the curricular tone for American higher education in the early nineteenth century. Princeton and above all Yale were producing an abundant stream of graduates who set out to found new colleges in the South and West, and these men, more pious and more traditional than their colleagues from Cambridge and Charlottesville, were firmly committed to the classical, prescribed curriculum. They found a credo in the 1828 Yale report, a document written by Yale president Jeremiah Day, classics professor James Kingsley, and a committee of the Yale Corporation, in response to a rising tide of questioning of the old collegiate ways. With its cogent arguments, this paper effectively settled the issue in favor of the classical curriculum until after the Civil War.

"The two great points to be gained in intellectual culture," President Day argues, "are the *discipline* and the *furniture* of the mind; expanding its powers, and storing it with knowledge. The former of these is, perhaps, the more important of the two." The report then defends Yale's comprehensive, prescribed curriculum in general and the classical portion of that program in particular, mainly for their capacity to train the mind. A narrow education can produce skilled specialists, but a combination of such subjects as mathematics, science, ancient and modern literature, logic, and mental philosophy is needed to produce a balanced intellect that can approach any problem with discrimination and judgment. In response to the question of Jefferson and others—"Why should a student waste his time upon studies which have no immediate connection with his future profession?"—Day observes that "every thing throws light on every thing." The man who is both eminent in his profession and generally knowledgeable "has an elevation and dignity of character, which gives him a commanding influence in society, and a widely extended sphere of usefulness." Precisely in a self-governing republic, citizens need a breadth of understanding and a capacity to speak persuasively. Precisely in a practical, active, enterprising nation, it is "highly important, that this bustle and energy should be directed by sound intelligence, the result of deep thought and early discipline."[73]

The Yale report continues with Professor Kingsley's argument that, far from being irrelevant to modern life, a study of the classics "forms the most effectual discipline of the mental faculties. . . . not only the memory, judgment, and reasoning powers, but the taste and fancy are occupied and improved." He speaks of the power of Greek and Roman writers to give a taste for what is "elevated, chaste, and simple." Finally, the report states that classical literature is valuable for providing models of patriotism and noble action, wise precepts, "the knowledge of a most extraordinary and unexampled people," and deeper understanding of human nature. One argument that is not made in the Yale report is that ancient texts offer an alternative vision of human excellence that needs to be confronted by Americans, including in particular a rare glimpse of the truly philosophic life.[74]

Clearly the Yale faculty revered the classics, and their preference for the classically based curriculum rested on considered reasons. What is less clear is that the teachers succeeded in conveying these reasons to students. According to Julian Sturtevant, a Yale graduate from that period, instruction was conducted mainly by tutors in daily recitations whose chief effect was to demonstrate whether students knew their lessons. "The tutors were good drill-masters, but they often lacked culture and the true literary spirit." He recounts that Professor Kingsley, who occasionally instructed their class, once "astonished us by closing a series of readings of Tacitus' *Agricola*, by saying, 'Young gentlemen, you have been reading one of the noblest productions of the human mind without knowing it.' We might justly have retorted to these severe and perhaps deserved rebukes, 'Whose fault is it?' "[75] The educational system at Yale, bolstered by the Yale Report, prevailed almost universally for the next generation. But by relying so heavily on drill rather than discussion, by stressing in their report the intellectual training of students more than the ideas they would encounter in the classics, Kingsley and his colleagues left themselves open to the criticism that subjects such as the natural sciences could develop the intellect equally well, while providing more useful knowledge.

It was President Charles Eliot of Harvard who took up this argument and led the transformation of America's best colleges into world-class universities. Eliot, who was inaugurated in 1869 and held office for forty momentous years, gradually abolished the prescribed curriculum and gave students complete freedom to choose among a rapidly expanding number of specialized courses, taught by a faculty that was increasingly involved in original research. Recitations were dropped in favor of laboratories, lectures, and discussions, and the library was expanded and made more accessible. Like Jefferson, Eliot wanted the students' education to proceed as much as possible on the basis of their own internal direction rather than external compulsion. The growth of the sciences and social sciences in the nineteenth century had increased the pressure for an elective system. America's commitment to utilitarian education was manifested in the Morrill Act of 1862, which established land-grant colleges to teach practical sciences, and this trend ensured that the Harvard elective system promulgated by Eliot would be widely copied.

Eliot did go further than Jefferson in two crucial respects, however, which Harvard historian Samuel Eliot Morison has judged unfortunate. Instead of allowing students to choose the schools in which to study, leaving it to the professors to devise a coherent program within each subject, as Jefferson had, Eliot let them elect any combination of individual courses they wished, subject to a few prerequisites. More significant in the long run was the fact that Eliot dropped not only Latin and Greek requirements for undergraduates but Latin as an entrance requirement for science students and—over the strenuous protest of other university presidents—Greek as an entrance requirement for all students. The classical education that Jefferson himself had cherished and that, through the rigorous gymnasium or high school, provided a foundation for the German universities Eliot admired ceased to be the rule for educated Americans. But if he destroyed the old gentleman's education, Eliot did set a standard among American universities for teaching all of the sciences in the highest degree, thus bringing finally to fruition one of Jefferson's greatest aspirations.[76]

Part Three
Institutions beyond the School

9 · Religion

Most of the Founders' ambitions for American schooling were, at least within their lifetimes, doomed to frustration. Franklin's academy clung to traditional ways; in place of Jefferson's expansive multitiered system, only a university and a few charity schools were built; and the national university, on which Washington pinned such high hopes, was never to materialize. The United States did manage to give most of its citizens the rudiments of literacy, as well as vocational and some civic training, through scattered schools, apprenticeships, and other less formal arrangements; and a college education was available to the small minority who sought and could afford it. What these educational institutions were not sufficiently able to do, however, was to imbue the bulk of the population with the moral and political principles and habits that a flourishing republic requires.

To supplement public schools, or to make up for the absence of progress in establishing them, the Founders looked to a wide range of possible sources of civic and moral education. They sought to create or sustain the religious, economic, and political institutions and practices that they were persuaded were most conducive to good morals and civic spirit. They debated the question of how a free press and voluntary associations might contribute to popular education. Finally, as we shall see in part 4, several of the leading Founders made deliberate efforts to educate by their personal examples, both by serving as models of effective informal education for their families and friends and by living—and skillfully presenting—lives worthy of emulation.

Madison and the Disestablishment of Religion

The cynosure for any consideration of the Founders' diverse views on the educational role of religious beliefs and institutions is the First Amendment: "Congress shall make no law respecting an establishment of religion, or prohibiting the free exercise thereof." The meaning of these lapidary words, especially as regards the "establishment" clause, has been, and properly is, controversial. For the words reflect an uneasy compromise among a range of respectable, intelligent, and well-argued viewpoints represented in the country and voiced in the congressional debates at the time of the drafting of the First Amendment. To a large extent, the controversy grew out of, and has continued to be nourished by, competing conceptions of the scope and importance of religion as a source of civic and moral education.

At the time, a rather extreme opinion (which in the twentieth century has become for the Supreme Court the most authoritative, though never uncontested, opinion) was articulated by James Madison. The occasion was a 1785 bill proposed in the Virginia legislature that would have allocated state funds to support "Teachers of the Christian Religion." This bill was a very modest attempt at nonsectarian Christian establishment. It was proposed in response to the perceived vacuum in governmental support for religion that had arisen in the years since 1776, when the Tory-sympathizing Anglican church was disestablished. Many of the most important advocates of the 1785 bill, led by Patrick Henry and including George Washington and John Marshall, were moved less by theological fervor than by the worry that the loss of governmental support for religion was contributing to the decay of civic spirit and public morality. Madison, backed by George Mason, Thomas Jefferson, and others, spearheaded the opposition. He penned a now-famous "Memorial and Remonstrance" that was widely circulated and was a prime factor in the defeat of the bill. That defeat was accompanied by the enactment instead of the bill for religious liberty that Jefferson had drafted and first submitted in 1779 (now adopted with slight but significant differences).

Madison's case against the bill "establishing a provision for Teachers of the Christian Religion" consists in part, though only secondarily, of sensible arguments referring to the *imprudence* of any religious establishment in republics in general and, more particularly, in the republic of Virginia, given the state's peculiar recent history and likely future development. Speaking to the question of the wisdom of establishing religion in republics generally, Madison invokes a "prudent jealousy" regarding any governmental "experiment on our liberties"; this jealousy he declares to be "the first duty of citizens." He warns, with perhaps some rhetorical exaggeration, that "the same authority which can establish Christianity, in exclusion of all other Religions, may establish with the same ease any particular sect of Christians, in exclusion of all other Sects"; that "the same authority which can force a citizen to contribute three pence only of his property for the support of any one establishment, may force him to conform to any other establishment in all cases whatsoever" (sec. 3).[1]

Regarding the particular situation of Virginia, Madison appeals in the first place to the state's past policy of "offering asylum to the persecuted and oppressed of every Nation and Religion," a policy that "promised a lustre to our country, and an accession to the number of its citizens." The proposed establishment is not only "a departure from that generous policy"; "it is itself a signal of persecution." For it "degrades from the equal rank of Citizens all those whose opinions in religion do not bend." Madison goes so far as to decry the proposal as the first step down a path that will lead to the reenactment of the Spanish Inquisition. If passed, the legislation will act like a "Beacon on our Coast," warning the sufferer of religious harassment "to seek some other haven" (sec. 9). The present population will thin, as citizens depart under the threatened scourge of persecution for religious nonconformity (sec. 10). Worst of all, the proposed establishment "will destroy that moderation and harmony which the forbearance of our laws to intermeddle with religion has produced among its several sects," fanning into life the fires of religious warfare with its "torrents of blood" (sec. 11). Madison warns in addition of the disastrous effects on law and fraternity that will follow from even a mild reestablishment of religion in the face of the outlook and temper of the Virginia citizenry. "Attempts to enforce by legal sanctions, acts obnoxious to so great a proportion of Citizens, tend to enervate the laws in general, and to slacken the bands of Society" (sec. 13). A "measure of such singular magnitude and delicacy ought not to be imposed, without the clearest evidence that it is called for by a majority of citizens: and no satisfactory method is yet proposed by which the voice of the majority in this case may be determined, or its influence secured" (sec. 14).

These arguments are of very considerable weight. They do not, however, form the primary or principal line of remonstrance. In attacking the bill, Madison seizes the opportunity to state a sweeping case against any governmental support, at any time and place, for any religion whatsoever, and in doing so he does not confine himself to sensible prudential arguments. He rests his case chiefly on an appeal to natural rights—an appeal so absolute and uncompromising as to find few parallels in the history of modern natural rights doctrine. The argument is not only uncharacteristically doctrinaire; it is one of the least satisfactory from the perspective of theoretical or even logical coherence that Madison ever allowed himself to state in public.

Madison made the remarkable decision to try to deduce the illegitimacy of any and all governmental support for religion from the right of the free exercise of religion. Now a moment's reflection indicates the difficulty: why should government support for the salaries of religious teachers from a broad range of denominations necessarily prevent anyone from exercising one's religion—or lack of religion? As Richard Henry Lee, president of the Continental Congress and later to become a leading Anti-Federalist, wrote to Madison in 1784:

Refiners may weave as fine a web of reason as they please, but the experience of all times shews Religion to be the guardian of morals—And he must be a very inattentive observer in our Country, who does not see that avarice is accomplishing the destruction of religion, for want of a legal obligation to contribute something to its support. The [Virginia] declaration of Rights, it seems to me, rather contends against forcing modes of faith and forms of worship, than against compelling contribution for the support of religion in general. I fully agree with the presbyterians, that true freedom embraces the Mahomitan and the Gentoo as well as the Xn religion and upon this liberal ground I hope our Assembly will conduct themselves.[2]

In fact, nowhere in the "Memorial and Remonstrance" does Madison successfully demonstrate that freedom of conscience entails prohibiting government from "compelling contribution for the support of religion in general." But his failure to make his case is less troubling than the surprisingly extreme interpretation he gives to the right of free exercise of religion or conscience, as he tries to build a kind of momentum behind his rhetorical enthymeme.

Madison claims that the right of free exercise of conscience is "a gift of nature" (sec. 15), derived from a prior "duty towards the Creator," "unalienable," and "precedent both in order of time and degree of obligation, to the claims of Civil Society"—all perfectly routine natural rights doctrine, found in Locke and others. But then he leaps from this received doctrine to the claim that the right cannot be "abridged by the institution of Civil Society" and stresses that he means by this "that religion is *wholly exempt* from its cognizance" (sec. 1; italics added) and that "religion is *exempt* from the authority of the Society at large" (sec. 2; italics added). Further, he says that no abuse of this freedom "to embrace, to profess and to observe the Religion which we believe to be of divine origin" can ever be considered an offense against society or even mankind or natural rights: "If this freedom be abused, it is an offence against God, not against man: To God, therefore, not to men, must an account of it be rendered" (sec. 4).

Why was Madison led to adopt so absolutist a natural rights argument? Madison was peculiarly, passionately exercised over the issue of religious disestablishment, not only in 1785 but throughout his life; this may have tinged his thought on this issue with an uncharacteristic moral dogmatism. But perhaps considerations of rhetorical strategy played a role; perhaps Madison feared that if he once drew attention to the substantial limits or qualifications necessarily imposed on the free-exercise right (e.g., no more human sacrifices, even of consenting adults), he would have to enter such complicated reasonings that he could no longer so easily or conclusively contend that modest governmental support for multidenominational Christianity inescapably involves an infringement on the right of free exercise. His argument would then have had to rest on more prudential reasonings, which are almost always somewhat inconclusive. Perhaps Madison feared a slippery slope leading from debates among reasonable men over the appropriate degree of separation of church and state, to internecine religious conflict among fanatic sectarian partisans hoping to win state power to the support of their cherished religious beliefs.

Certainly Madison seems to reach out to his evangelical religious allies, such as John Leland.[3] Leaving behind contentions moored in prudence or nature and natural rights, Madison builds on the premise of supernatural revelation or divine right. On this basis, and in a spirit that reflects or anticipates the outlook of some of the evangelical Protestant movements that arose in the years after the Founding, he asserts that governmental support for religion "contradicts" the Christian revelation in particular, since "every page of it disavows a dependence on the powers of this world" (sec. 6). He adds supplementary arguments based on faith illuminated by the historical "fact" that the Christian religion "flourished, not only without the support of human laws, but in spite of every opposition from them." It follows, Madison contends, not only that the Christian religion in particular is in no need of any governmental aid, but that, in addition, to offer the support of human laws is to "weaken in those who profess this Religion a pious confidence in its innate excellence, and the patronage of its Author," while strengthening the "suspicions" of "those who still reject it" (sec. 6). Besides, experience has shown "that ecclesiastical establishments, instead of maintaining the purity and efficacy of religion, have had a contrary operation" (sec. 7).

These arguments based on faith, whatever might be their merits, speak only to the effects of establishment on *religious* fervor and education; but what of the effects on civic and moral education—the concern perhaps uppermost in the minds of the most distinguished supporters of the bill? Here we encounter again the uniqueness and extremism of Madison's position. For he contends, first, that it is impious for government to try to use religion to support civic spirit and, second, that religion is likely, if funded by government, to poison rather than to sustain republican spirit. The notion that government "may employ Religion as an engine of Civil Society" is damned by Madison as "an unhallowed perversion of the means of salvation" (sec. 5); and he claims that religious establishments have historically "in no instance" been "seen the guardians of the liberties of the people" (sec. 8).

Madison never ceased to insist on what he called, in a retrospective letter written to Edward Livingston late in life, "a perfect separation between ecclesiastical and civil matters"—though he severely tempered his earlier, public remonstrance by stating that his principle of "the immunity of Religion from civil jurisdiction" had always been intended with the far-reaching and open-ended proviso, "*where it does not trespass on private rights or the public peace*" (italics added). But Madison never softened his rejection of religion as an instrument available to government for civic education. In the same letter just quoted, he castigates as unconstitutional the appointment of congressional chaplains, to be paid out of public coffers, and regrets being forced as president to proclaim fasts or festivals of thanksgiving (such as for the end of the War of 1812), "so far, at least, as they [the presidential proclamations] have spoken the language of *injunction*" and were not "merely recommendatory." During his presidency, Madison vetoed as unconstitutional a bill that, in granting land, reserved a parcel for a church. Similarly, he vetoed a bill incorporating the Episcopal church in the District of Columbia partly because the bill provided that the church be given the authority to educate poor children. In private, Madison eventually voiced opposition to tax exemption for churches, even under state law, and to the appointment of chaplains for the armed forces.[4]

Though Madison was the most radical of the major Founders in his view that the president utterly lacks authority in religion, he was by no means alone in this outlook. Alexander Hamilton, arguably the leading expert among the Founders on the office and powers of the chief executive, insisted that under the Constitution, prior to and without any dependence on the First Amendment (which Hamilton opposed as unnecessary), the president "has no particle of spiritual jurisdiction." Jefferson when president refused, on constitutional grounds, to declare religious holidays; yet, in contrast to Madison, he admitted that the state governments do have such power. On the other side, however, stands the weighty authority of George Washington. One of his early acts, in response to a request from both houses of Congress, was the proclamation of a National Thanksgiving, 3 October 1789, with the words, "It is the duty of all nations to acknowledge the providence of Almighty God, to obey His will, to be grateful for his benefits, and humbly to implore His protection and favor." The president set aside this day "to be devoted by the people of these States to the service of that great and glorious Being . . . [and to] beseech Him to pardon our national and other transgressions."[5]

Jefferson and the Attempted Transformation of Christianity into a Civil Religion

While Jefferson never went to the extremes of Madison, he also never expressed reservations against any of the arguments in Madison's "Memorial and Remonstrance." Jefferson refers in a famous presidential letter to the need for a "wall of separation between Church and State," though with the large qualification that religious "actions" as opposed to "opinions" are indeed subject to legislation. As he puts it in his Bill for Establishing Religious Freedom, "It is time enough for the rightful purposes of civil government for its officers to interfere when principles break out into overt acts against peace and good order." Most important for the purposes of this study is Jefferson's assertion in the same bill that "our civil rights have no dependence on our religious opinions, any more than on our opinions in physicks or geometry." By assimilating religious opinion to mathematical opinion in this context, Jefferson seems to suggest the Madisonian view that religious convictions have no positive role to play in republican civic education. But the original version of the Bill for Establishing Religious Freedom goes even further, to the radical pronouncement that "the opinions of men are not the object of civil government." This assertion, if taken strictly, would outlaw all governmental concern with moral and civic education. It is no wonder the statement was dropped from the version of the bill that was enacted into law in 1785.[6]

After all, in the same Bill for Establishing Religious Freedom, Jefferson maintains that each citizen must be allowed to choose the minister whose "morals he would make his pattern, and whose powers he feels most persuasive to righteousness"; he then argues that one crucial reason why ministers ought to be paid by their own parishioners on a voluntary basis is that this will hold out to the ministers "those temporal rewards which, proceeding from an approbation of their personal conduct, are an additional incitement to earnest and unremitting labour for the instruction of mankind." In other words, the bill endorses an educative civil function for the clergy and clearly shows that the government that makes this bill law does most certainly have as one chief object the molding of the opinions of its citizens. What is more, in his *Notes on the State of Virginia*, to which he appended in the 1787 edition the Act for Establishing Religious Freedom, Jefferson further undercuts his suggestion, in the bill itself, of the irrelevance of religious opinion to civic health. Spelling out the consequences of the moral disease of black slavery, Jefferson asks, "Can the liberties of a nation be thought secure when we have removed their *only firm basis*, a conviction in the minds of the people that these liberties are of the gift of God? That they are not to be violated but with his wrath?" (italics added). If belief in a just and punitive God is so critical to liberty, it becomes difficult to conceive why government may establish schools to teach the principles of liberty but must avoid providing any support for the teaching of this most fundamental principle of liberty.[7]

As we shall see in detail in chapter 13, Jefferson struggled to establish morality on a purely natural and humanistic basis; but he could never satisfy himself that morality or civic spirit in the population at large could dispense with religious faith, institutional religious guidance, and a belief in supernatural divine sanctions. To what extent Jefferson's hesitation to abjure divine sanctions arose from genuine religious conviction, and to what extent it resulted from a conviction of the political necessity of religious belief in the populace, must remain an open question. Jefferson is notable for the circumspection with which he guarded, even from his own family and closest friends and correspondents, his ultimate religious views: "My religion," he wrote to someone seeking information for a biographical sketch, "is known to my god and myself alone." Certainly there is the ring of truth in the contrast Perry Miller draws between the zeal for religious liberty of the Puritan Roger Williams and the superficially similar zeal of Jefferson: Williams "was a libertarian because he contemned the world, and he wanted to separate church and state so that the church would not be contaminated by the state; Thomas Jefferson loved the world and was dubious about the spirit, and he sought to separate church and state so that the state would not be contaminated by the church."[8]

Jefferson wished to cultivate religious sentiments and preachings that would overcome religious sources of disunity and provide educative support and guidance for good citizenship. To that end he argued and worked for the reform of his fellow Americans' religious beliefs in a specific direction: away from divisive theological disputation and the demands of ascetic moralism, and toward a deistic or unitarian secular ethical humanism. With this end in view—and inspired partly by Joseph Priestley's *History of the Corruptions of Christianity* (1793) and *Socrates and Jesus Compared* (1803) and later encouraged by John Adams's letters—Jefferson undertook a thorough revision of the Scriptures. He expunged what he claimed were the false accretions, including Jesus' claims to divinity, miraculous healing, and inspiration by divine grace, as well as most of his and others' references to sin, atonement, redemption, and the resurrection. Although this remarkable work of theological and historical revision was not (for reasons of political prudence) published in his lifetime, Jefferson urged others—most notably Joseph Priestley—to carry forward and into the public eye the work of "purification" of the Christian Scripture. In his later days, Jefferson repeatedly expressed in private letters his hope and expectation that the United States would within the next couple of generations become almost entirely Unitarian in its religious outlook.[9]

Yet there remained one cardinal tenet of traditional Christianity that marked, for Jefferson, religion's unique and irreplaceable contribution to civic education: the belief in an afterlife, in which a just God would mete out condign reward and punishment.[10] Whether Jefferson himself truly believed in a life after death—and if so, how he squared this belief with his adamant materialism, or denial of the existence of the incorporeal soul—is another open and perplexing question.[11]

The Anti-Federalists and Protestant Establishment

Other leading Founders, and a large proportion of the populace, felt much more strongly than Jefferson the need for some degree of governmental establishment of religion, especially in the various states. An anonymous "Proposal for Reviving Christian Conviction," published in the *Virginia Independent Chronicle* on 31 October 1787, gives perhaps the best succinct summation of the underlying reasoning.

> Whatever influence speculative vanity may ascribe to the indefinite principle termed honor, or political refinement, to an artful collusion of interests, sound reason as well as experience proves that a due sense of responsibility to the deity, as the author of those moral laws, an observance of which constitutes the happiness and welfare of societies as well as individuals, is the mean most likely to give a right direction to the conduct of mankind. The man who carries his prospects forward to futurity, and considers himself a candidate for the favor of omnipotence, will be actuated, in the general tenor of his life, by motives that elevate him above the little interests and passions which disturb the peace of society, and will discharge the relative duties of his station, unawed by the fear of man, with a consistence and steadiness correspondent to the principle from which he acts. It has been the misfortune of our infant legislature that in the multiplicity of business which has come before them, they have not had leisure to attend sufficiently to the importance of religious concerns to the welfare of the state.[12]

The charge that the proposed constitution would weaken, or at any rate was insufficiently attentive to supporting, the religious belief essential to a reliable republican citizenry was a frequent Anti-Federalist criticism. This judgment did not reflect a fundamental disagreement with the Federalists over the ends of government, or a desire to return to Puritan or authentically classical conceptions of the purposes of society and education. Even the most religious of the Anti-Federalist writers, a writer who took the significant and unusually unclassical pen name "David," declared that "it is agreed on all hands, that the business of government is to secure the subjects in the enjoyment of their lives, liberty, and property." But in their estimation of the best way to prosecute this business, the Anti-Federalists generally put less faith than did the Federalists in the competition of factions orchestrated by shrewd constitutional arrangements and saw more need, as "David" says, of "prepossessing the people in favour of virtue by affording publick protection to religion."[13]

Anti-Federalists criticized the Constitution both for failing to guarantee freedom of conscience and for failing to establish Protestant Christianity. In calling for religious freedom, they usually had in mind the positive freedom to believe and worship as one saw fit, not the negative freedom from religion or from all governmental involvement in religion. Accordingly, as Herbert Storing sums up their views, "they saw no inconsistency between liberty of conscience and the public support of the religious, and generally Protestant, community as the basis of public and private morality." Nevertheless, there was a certain division apparent among the Anti-Federalists who spoke to the religious question. For some, the primary target of criticism was the lack of security for religious freedom—a criticism often accompanied by strongly expressed opposition to any *national* establishment of religion. For others, the chief concern was the decline in the public acknowledgment and support of Protestant Christianity.[14]

In the first category are those like Patrick Henry and "An Old Whig," who expound the classic Lockean argument in favor of religious freedom and often go well beyond Locke, making no exception of "papists and atheists." Henry warns that without an explicit bill of rights including freedom of conscience, religion "will be prostituted to the lowest purposes of human policy." Henry thus seems to echo, if only dimly, some of Madison's worry about the effects of religious establishment, though there is no sign Henry had changed his mind about the need for nonsectarian governmental support for religion. The "Old Whig" in Pennsylvania "hoped and trusted" that "there are few persons at present hardy enough to entertain thoughts of creating any religious establishment for this country"—though the context suggests that he means a national church, with specific articles of faith, of the sort found in England. Indeed, it seems fair to say that the Anti-Federalists who agitated for a bill of rights guaranteeing freedom of conscience did not intend that such a guarantee would or could be used to outlaw the mild and multidenominational religious establishments that then existed in many of the states and state constitutions. As Storing says, their position on religion was essentially conservative.

> The Anti-Federalist position was not so much that government ought to foster religion as that the consolidating Constitution threatened the healthy religious situation as it then existed. The religious diversity of the whole United States seemed so great as to strain to breaking point any publicly useful religious foundation for the nation as a whole. Consolidation would require, then, substituting for religion some other foundation of political morality—which the Anti-Federalists foresaw would be an aggregate of selfish interests held together by force.[15]

Prominent among those who focus their criticisms primarily on the difficulty of maintaining adequate government support for religion under the proposed constitution is "Agrippa" (probably James Winthrop), who protests against uniting Massachusetts with the morally and religiously inferior South.

> The unequal distribution of property, the toleration of slavery, the ignorance and poverty of the lower classes, the softness of the climate, and dissoluteness of manners, mark their character. Among us, the care that is

taken of education, small and nearly equal estates, equality of rights, and the severity of the climate, renders the people active, industrious and sober. Attention to religion and good morals is a distinguishing trait in our character. It is plain, therefore, that we require for our regulation laws, which will not suit the circumstances of our southern brethren, and the laws made for them will not apply to us.

A Portland, Maine, "Customer" voices the opinion that the new constitution is part of a tide in the country that is drawing Americans to "employ our time, that heretofore has been employed in politicks and religion, to the pursuit of wealth, to enable us to pay our debts, and support the dependants on government in the style of the great men of the east." The bitingly satirical "praise" of the proposed constitution by the Pennsylvanian who wrote under the name "Aristocrotis" stresses that the new government will be historically without precedent in its entire liberation from any clerical or religious restraint on its use and abuse of power.[16]

"Aristocrotis" also points out that the Constitution's prohibition on religious tests for office lays "the axe to the root of the tree" of religion in general and Christianity in particular: the Constitution deliberately seeks to "extirpate" the Christian religion from America. The Bostonian who significantly took the pen name "Samuel" passionately attacks the prohibition on religious tests for office, by which "all religion is expressly rejected, from the Constitution. Was there ever any State or kingdom, that could subsist, without adopting some form of religion?" The New Hampshire "Friend to the Rights of the People" (probably Thomas Cogswell) perceives, in the Constitution's "discarding of all religious tests," the alarming consequence that religion is "all swept off at one stroke totally contrary to our state plans. . . . It may be said the meaning is not to discard it, but only to shew that there is no need of it in public officers; they may be as faithful without as with—this is a mistake—when a man has no regard to God and his laws nor any belief of a future state; he will have less regard to the laws of men." Cogswell continues, "I think therefore that so much deference ought to be paid" religion, "as to acknowledge it in our civil establishment; and that no man is fit to be a ruler of protestants, without he can honestly profess to be of the protestant religion."[17]

If there was to be a consolidated national government, then it had to lend some moral support to religion in general and to the state establishments in particular. Thus Charles Turner, who admonished the Massachusetts ratifying convention that "without the prevalence of *Christian piety, and morals*, the best republican Constitution can never save us from slavery and ruin," and who voted finally and with reluctance to ratify the new constitution, decried a general moral deterioration already afoot, which would be accelerated under the new system. "Nor have I," Turner avowed, "an expectation" of a "greater prevalence of Christian moral principles,"

> unless some superiour mode of *education* shall be adopted. It is EDUCA-
> TION which almost entirely forms the character, the freedom or slavery,
> the happiness or misery of the world. And if this Constitution shall be
> adopted, I hope the Continental Legislature will have the *singular honour*,
> the *indelible glory*, of making it one of their *first* acts, in their *first* session,
> most *earnestly* to recommend to the several States in the Union, the institu-
> tion of such means of education, as shall be *adequate* to the *divine, patriotick*
> *purpose* of training up the children and youth at large, in that solid learn-
> ing, and in those pious and moral principles, which are the *support*, the *life*
> and SOUL of the republican government and liberty. . . . May *religion*,
> with sanctity of morals prevail and *increase*.[18]

A Virginian writing under the name "Denatus," who like Turner reluctantly opted in the end for adoption, though with massive amendments, goes unusu-ally far, arguing that

> the first, or second article of the said constitution, ought to contain some-
> thing to this effect—That as soon as possible, academies shall be estab-
> lished at every proper place throughout the United States for the educa-
> tion of youth in morality; the principles of the christian religion without
> regard to any sect, but pure and unadulterated as left by its divine author
> and his apostles: The principles of natural, civil, and common law, and of
> our constitution: And the art of defending and conquering nations in bat-
> tle, either by land or sea—These academies to be regulated from time to
> time by Congress, and their establishment to be perpetual.[19]

A much milder sort of governmental support for religion, and one that was widely commended, was the Northwest Ordinance, passed by Congress under the Articles of Confederation on 13 July 1787. Article 1 of the "compact, be-tween the original States and the people and States in the said territory," de-clared that "no person, demeaning himself in a peaceable and orderly manner, shall ever be molested on account of his mode of worship, or religious senti-ments"; while Article 3 declared that "religion, morality, and knowledge being necessary to good government and the happiness of mankind, schools and the means of education shall forever be encouraged." The fact that the ordinance was reapproved without alteration by the same Congress that drew up, under Madison's floor management, the Bill of Rights would seem to suggest that no one at the time thought that state-sponsored education aimed at cultivating religious faith was contrary in spirit or letter to freedom of conscience or the First Amendment.[20]

The Intentions of the Authors of the Establishment Clause

The concern to protect and even encourage the establishment of multi-denominational Protestant Christianity in the states was shared by many and repeatedly voiced in the state legislative and federal congressional discussions that issued in the framing of the First Amendment. A number of state ratifications had been accompanied by requests for amendments, chiefly amendments that would constitute a bill of rights. Virginia and North Carolina pressed for the adoption of a provision about religion that would have included the words, "No particular religious sect or society ought to be favored or established by law in preference to others"; New York urged a similar stipulation. Madison, in weaving together a proposed bill of rights from the many suggestions, formulated this statement: "The Civil Rights of none shall be abridged on account of religious belief or worship, nor shall any national religion be established, nor shall the full and equal rights of conscience be in any manner, nor on any pretext infringed." (He also added what no state had suggested, a provision protecting individuals from *state* violations of the equal rights of conscience.) A select committee revised the proposed limitation on congressional action to read, "No religion shall be established by law, nor shall the equal rights of conscience be infringed." This proposal, as Michael Malbin says, "was debated by the First Congress at greater length than almost any other item in the Bill of Rights"; the speeches "concentrated on the establishment question."[21]

Peter Sylvester from New York opened the debate by voicing the fear that the wording "might be thought to have a tendency to abolish religion altogether." As Malbin observes, Sylvester's misgiving seems incomprehensible unless one assumes his premise was that "some form of governmental assistance to religion was essential to religion's survival." Supporting Sylvester, Elbridge Gerry from Massachusetts "said it would read better if it was, that no religious *doctrine* shall be established by law." Madison claimed that this was essentially what the words were intended to mean: "He apprehended the meaning of the words to be, that Congress should not establish a religion, and enforce the legal observation of it by law." To this Benjamin Huntington replied warily that "he feared, with the gentleman first up on this subject, that the words might be taken in such latitude as to be extremely hurtful to the cause of religion. He understood the amendment to mean what had been expressed by the gentleman from Virginia [Madison]; but others might find it convenient to put another construction upon it." Huntington worried that someone arrested for failing to pay the required contributions to ministers' salaries or church buildings might go before a federal court to find release from his obligations under state law.[22]

Madison then replied that he "thought, if the word national was inserted before religion, it would satisfy the minds of honorable gentlemen." What he understood the people feared and sought to avert, Madison explained, was not federal governmental support for religion generally, but that "one sect might obtain a pre-eminence, or two combine together, and establish a religion to which they would compel others to conform. He thought if the word national was introduced, it would point the amendment directly to the object it was intended to prevent." But Elbridge Gerry, a former leader of the Anti-Federalists, protested any use of the word "national" as implying that the government was a consolidated union rather than a federation. The House ultimately sent to the Senate the wording offered by Fisher Ames: "Congress shall make no law establishing religion." The Senate, after much back-and-forth debate of alternative wordings, finally returned to the House a much narrower and more precise version: "Congress shall make no law establishing articles of faith or a mode of worship." The House refused this suggestion, and in conference between representatives of both houses, the current version was devised: "Congress shall make no law respecting an establishment of religion." As Malbin argues, the crucial innovation of the word "respecting" is best understood as intending to prevent *both* a specific religious establishment on the federal level *and* any federal interference in the religious establishments in place in the states. Madison compromised his own views rather considerably, although one cannot rule out the possibility that he hoped that future interpretation would steadily erode the scope of state powers of establishment.[23]

It does appear in fact that the state establishments waned partly because of the spread of Madisonian and Jeffersonian principles in the popular consciousness. However, the chief reasons for the decline of state legislation supporting religion were, initially, a general trend toward secularism; then weariness at the endless bickering among competing denominations over their shares of whatever financial support was forthcoming from the state governments; and finally the rise of evangelical sects, with their libertarian rebellion against all traditional forms of authority in religious matters.

The view of the relation between religion and government that predominated among the most generous and thoughtful of the Founders is perhaps best stated by Tench Coxe.

> Almost every sect and form of Christianity is known here—as also the Hebrew church. All are admitted, aided by mutual charity and concord, and supported and cherished by the laws. . . . Mere toleration is a doctrine exploded by our general condition; instead of which have been substituted an

unqualified admission, and assertion, "that their own modes of worship and of faith equally belong to all the worshippers of God, of whatever church, sect, or denomination."[24]

The link, in the Founders' minds, between civic education and the cherishing of religion is expressed most lucidly and effectively in Washington's Farewell Address.

Of all the dispositions and habits which lead to political prosperity, religion and morality are indispensable supports. In vain would that man claim the tribute of Patriotism, who should labour to subvert these great Pillars of human happiness, these firmest props of the duties of Men and citizens. The mere Politician, equally with the pious man ought to respect and to cherish them. A volume could not trace all their connections with private and public felicity. Let it simply be asked where is the security for property, for reputation, for life, if the sense of religious obligation *desert* the oaths, which are the instruments of investigation in Courts of Justice? And let us with caution indulge the supposition, that morality can be maintained without religion. Whatever may be conceded to the influence of refined education on minds of peculiar structure, reason and experience both forbid us to expect that National morality can prevail in exclusion of religious principle.[25]

10 · Economic and Political Life as Sources of Moral Education

The Yeomanry Backbone of the Citizenry

A leading and abiding concern shared by most Americans of the Founding era was the preservation of the independent, agrarian way of life that they saw as the womb of virtue. At the time of the Revolution, the Americans' growing consciousness of themselves as a separate people was rooted in the perception that, unlike the Europeans, they were mainly a nation of yeoman farmers; and it was to this that they attributed, in large measure, their unusual capacity for self-rule. In Jefferson's oft-cited words:

> Those who labour in the earth are the chosen people of God, if ever he had a chosen people, whose breasts he has made his peculiar deposit for substantial and genuine virtue. It is the focus in which he keeps alive that sacred fire, which otherwise might escape from the face of the earth. Corruption of morals in the mass of cultivators is a phenomenon of which no age nor nation has furnished an example. It is the mark set on those, who not looking up to heaven, to their own soil and industry, as does the husbandman, for their subsistance, depend for it on the casualties and caprice of customers. Dependance begets subservience and venality, suffocates the germ of virtue, and prepares fit tools for the designs of ambition.[1]

As Franklin puts it, a life of independent farming breeds the "country habits" of temperance, frugality, and industry. By contrast, cities harbor extremes of opulence and poverty, and create the greatest opportunities for idleness, dissipation, and luxury.[2]

Americans were especially horrified by the exploitation and misery they saw in large British factories, and most were determined to avoid industrialization as long as possible. Cottage industry, on the other hand, they welcomed, especially if it employed idle hands in the production of solid necessities and added to a family's self-sufficiency. Indeed, the varied modes of production on a well-run farm were part of what was thought to make the farmer a superior citizen. "Where people live principally by agriculture, as in America," Noah Webster explains,

> every man is in some measure an artist—he makes a variety of utensils, rough indeed, but such as will answer his purpose—he is a husbandman in summer and a mechanic in winter—he travels about the country—he converses with a variety of professions—he reads public papers—he has access to a parish library and thus becomes acquainted with history and politics, and every man in New England is a theologian. . . . Knowledge is diffused and genius roused by the very situation of America.[3]

Nevertheless, there were tensions and complexities in the American view of country simplicity. The Anti-Federalists tended to outdo the Federalists in praising the virtues of small, austere, agrarian republics. Yet, despite reservations about the civic character of merchants, they did not and could not advocate anything but a *commercial* agrarian republic. Not only were they deeply attached to the gain, comfort, and convenience that commerce brings, but they discerned an intimate link between commercialism and individual liberty. "Commerce is the hand-maid of liberty," said the Anti-Federalist "Centinel" (probably Samuel Bryan), thus foreshadowing Jefferson's First Inaugural Address. Moreover, they detected in commerce, moderately regulated, a foundation for civic solidarity or fraternity. A leading Anti-Federalist series of letters by "Agrippa" proclaimed that the spirit of commerce

> is the great bond of union among citizens. This furnishes employment for their activity, supplies their mutual wants, defends the rights of property, and producing reciprocal dependencies, renders the whole system harmonious and energetic. Our great object therefore ought to be to encourage this spirit. . . .
> . . . A diversity of produce, wants and interests, produces commerce, and commerce, where there is a common, equal and moderate authority to preside, produces friendship.

A Maryland "Farmer" (probably John Francis Mercer) and "A Newport Man" (the sole Anti-Federalist writer to rely on Rousseau) could cite with praise the example of San Marino ("a little bee-hive of free citizens, who have made a delicious garden of the top of a bleak barren mountain"). Yet as the Federalist John Adams tellingly observes, using just this example:

A handful of poor people, living in the simplest manner, by hard labor, upon the produce of a few cows, sheep, goats, swine, poultry, and pigeons, on a piece of rocky, snowy ground, protected from every enemy by their situation, their superstition, and even their poverty, having no commerce nor luxury, can be no example for the commonwealth of Pennsylvania, Georgia, or Vermont, in one of which there are possibly half a million of people, and in each of the others at least thirty thousand, scattered over a large territory.[4]

In the Americans' rejection of the austerity of San Marino or Sparta or Xenophon's Persia lies one of the sharpest contrasts between the ancient and the modern republican concepts of virtue. Franklin, who expresses the new outlook with unrivaled clarity, identifies virtue not with self-sacrifice but with the industry and prudence that lead to prosperity. He sees a danger in loving wealth too much—loving it to the exclusion of everything else—but unlike the classical republicans, he recognizes no natural limit to the amount of wealth that can be useful or desirable. Indeed, he also sees a danger in loving wealth too little: "Is not the Hope of one day being able to purchase and enjoy Luxuries a great Spur to Labour and Industry? May not Luxury, therefore, produce more than it consumes, if without such a Spur People would be, as they are naturally enough inclined to be, lazy and indolent?" For the frontier farmer this was a special temptation, since without commercial intercourse he could all too easily lapse into a life of isolated, savage subsistence with few ties to civilization and little concern for his country. Following this logic, Franklin and Jefferson sought a middle course between the overly austere constraints of the precommercial republic and the dangerous inequalities of a fully developed manufacturing, urbanized economy. If the arrival of the latter was ultimately inevitable, it could be postponed by promoting frontier settlement, and the industry of the settlers could be assured by providing access to markets. Hence opening the Mississippi and securing direct trade with the West Indies and France became major objectives in the early republic, especially for Jefferson. Since, according to this vision, a healthy republic should rest on agriculture with "commerce as its handmaid," westward expansion and free trade became the core of the Jeffersonians' policy.[5]

But this balance, however attractive, was unstable. Virtually all previous agrarian societies have been aristocracies, with the ruling class tied to the land by family pride and tradition, and the laborers by necessity. Such had been the colonial structure of Tidewater Virginia. Yet this model of agrarian society Jefferson consciously and decisively rejected. As Frederick Jackson Turner observes, Jefferson's ground-breaking legislation to abolish entail and primogeniture, his opposition to slavery and to the established Anglican church, his advocacy of universal education, and his untiring encouragement of agricultural societies

and scientific farming all worked to break the power of the plantation aristocrats and to promote a new type of farmer—independent, educated, hardworking,
and prosperous—who would in many ways bear closer resemblance to a small
businessman than a traditional country aristocrat. This new model of country
life proved immensely attractive to Americans, as long as there was free land.
Attempts to stem the flow of settlement were invariably unsuccessful; but it was
precisely the popularity of something like the Jeffersonian vision of the rural
businessman and democrat that led rather soon to its demise. The "many centuries" of free land Jefferson had anticipated proved to be only one, and in 1893
Turner issued his famous declaration that the American frontier had closed.[6]

Almost from the outset the forces that Jefferson helped set in motion began
to erode his agrarian ideal. As farming became a business, it became subject to
the pressures of business—the efficiencies of scale, the mechanization that leads
to fewer employees, the alacrity with which workers leave one business when another promises greater profits. As young people became better educated, they
became more sophisticated and eager to leave the farm for the glitter and luxury
of the city. And as American agriculture grew ever more productive, it generated
a growing demand for manufactured goods, and thus an impetus to further urbanization. Alexander Hamilton, seeing the tendency of a free economy to lead
in this direction, openly welcomed manufacturing in the United States, and
even cheerfully accepted the prospect of women and children working in factories, insofar as such labor promoted their prosperity and the nation's strength.
Hamilton was more consistent than his Jeffersonian opponents in not depend-
ing for continued freedom on a permanent agrarian order that his liberal principles undermined. But Jefferson and the Anti-Federalists, for all their ambivalence, were concerned with problems of civic spirit that Hamilton never
addressed.[7]

Law and the Governmental Process as Vehicles of Education

While looking to the agrarian way of life to provide basic support for honesty,
industry, and self-reliance, Jefferson, along with the Anti-Federalists, emphasizes
the importance of other institutions that might give a more directly political education to the American people. One of the Anti-Federalists' central criticisms
of the Constitution is that it pays insufficient attention to this problem of ensuring the right spirit and principles in the citizenry. According to Melancton
Smith: "Government operates upon the spirit of the people, as well as the spirit
of the people operates upon it—and if they are not conformable to each other,
the one or the other will prevail. . . . Our duty is to frame a government friendly

to liberty and the rights of mankind, which will tend to cherish and cultivate a love of liberty among our citizens."[8]

The Anti-Federalists call again and again for a bill of rights, not only to prevent usurpation but to educate the people in their nation's fundamental principles. As one of the minor writers puts it, the enumeration of rights, "in head of the new constitution, can inspire and conserve the affection for the native country; they will be the first lesson of the young citizens becoming men, to sustain the dignity of their being." The "Federal Farmer" (thought to be Richard Henry Lee) lays out clearly the arguments for enumerating and reaffirming rights.

> We do not by declarations change the nature of things, or create new truths, but we give existence, or at least establish in the minds of the people truths and principles which they might never otherwise have thought of, or soon forgot. If a nation means its systems, religious or political, shall have duration, it ought to recognize the leading principles of them in the front page of every family book.

"Natural and inalienable rights," the Federal Farmer observes, belong to everyone always, but they do not by themselves make men free. The difference between nations that cherish and enjoy natural rights and those that allow them to be violated is one of education. The English correctly insisted on recording their rights in the Magna Carta, and yet even this

> wise men saw was not sufficient; and therefore, that the people might not forget these rights, and gradually become prepared for arbitrary government, their discerning and honest leaders caused this instrument to be confirmed near forty times, and to be read twice yearly in public places, not that it would lose its validity without such confirmations, but to fix the contents of it in the minds of the people, as they successively come upon the stage.

The Federal Farmer likewise praises the American revolutionaries' wisdom in "constantly keeping in view, in addresses, bills of rights, in news-papers, etc. the particular principles on which our freedom must always depend."[9]

In a similar way, the Anti-Federalists were especially alarmed because they felt the proposed constitution did not sufficiently protect the right to trial by jury. They valued trial by jury not only as a safeguard for the rights of the accused in criminal cases but as a means of preventing encroachments in all types of cases and keeping the people educated and informed about public matters. Again, the Federal Farmer makes this concern most explicit.

> By holding the jury's right to return a general verdict in all cases sacred, we secure to the people at large, their just and rightful controul in the judicial

department. . . . Nor is it merely this controul alone we are to attend to: the jury trial brings with it an open and public discussion of all causes, and excludes secret and arbitrary proceedings. This, and the democratic branch in the legislature . . . are the means by which the people are let into the knowledge of public affairs—are enabled to stand as the guardians of each others rights, and to restrain, by regular and legal measures, those who otherwise might infringe upon them.

What is more, juries can educate the citizens by keeping them practiced in moral reasoning. The Maryland Farmer, answering the charge that "the Commons" are too ignorant or irrational to be entrusted with legal decisions, concedes that their judgment is often poor, because they are too seldom called upon to exercise it: "Men no longer cultivate, what is no longer useful,—should every opportunity be taken away, of exercising their reason, you will reduce them to that state of mental baseness, in which they appear in nine-tenths of this globe—distinguished from brutes, only by form and the articulation of sound—*Give them power and they will find understanding to use it.*"[10]

To a lesser extent this kind of solicitude was present among the Federalists also. James Wilson in particular took a broad view of the educative function that law, juries, and judges could and should perform in a free country. In his inaugural lecture as the College of Philadelphia's first law professor, addressing his audience with a subtle blend of praise mixed with exhortation to make itself worthy of praise, he characterizes the virtues of the best republican citizens.

Illustrious examples are displayed to our view, that we may imitate as well as admire. Before we can be distinguished by the same honors, we must be distinguished by the same virtues.

What are those virtues? They are chiefly the same virtues, which we have already seen to be descriptive of the American character—the love of liberty, and the love of law. But law and liberty cannot rationally become the objects of our love, unless they first become the objects of our knowledge.[11]

One means that Wilson and other members of the federal judiciary found to educate citizens in the law was through the instructions they gave to grand juries. A prime example is Wilson's charge to a Virginia grand jury in 1791, which presents a clear and concise summary of the entire criminal law of the United States. But Wilson's goal is to do more than simply inform. Intending to kindle in the jurors a pride and reverence for their country's laws, he argues for the superior effectiveness, humanity, and simplicity of American law, compared even with such a widely admired legal system as that of England. And once again, his praise and reverence are mingled with exhortation. By showing the crucial role of a good criminal code in attaching citizens both to the law and to the principle of lawful self-restraint, he encourages the jurors to care about having the best laws possible and to actively look for improvements to recommend.[12]

Wilson took issue with the cultlike practice of wrapping the law in layers of abstruse language, intelligible only to the learned few: "The knowledge of those rational principles on which the law is founded, ought, especially in a free government, to be diffused over the whole community." Consequently, he devoted his last years to preparing a digest of the laws of Pennsylvania that would reduce them all to plain English.

> By the first assembly of Pennsylvania an act was made "for teaching the laws in the schools." This noble regulation is countenanced by the authority and example of the most enlightened nations and men. Cicero informs us, that when he was a boy, the laws of the twelve tables were learned . . . as a piece of composition at once necessary and entertaining. The celebrated legislator of the Cretans used all the precautions, which human prudence could suggest, to inspire the youth with the greatest respect and attachment to the maxims and customs of the state. This was what Plato found most admirable in the laws of Minos.
>
> If youth should be educated in the knowledge and love of the laws: it follows, that the laws should be proper objects of their attachment, and proper subjects of their study. Can this be said concerning a statute book drawn up in the usual style and form? Would any one select such a composition to form the taste of his son, or to inspire him with a relish for literary accomplishments?[13]

Jefferson shared Wilson's distaste for mystifying legal jargon, as well as the conviction that law should go beyond cataloging rules and sanctions to give an account of the principles we live by. Hence he attached preambles to his most important bills, with memorably worded statements of first principles. But if Jefferson and Wilson wanted the nation's youth to know and love their country's laws, it was in a very different spirit from that of the ancient republics. There, reverence for the laws was intertwined with reverence for what was old, for ancestral custom, and for the gods who were said to have inspired the lawgivers. The American Founders boldly sought to ground reverence on an entirely different basis—on reason and the adherence to self-evident principles. Wilson, in his charge to the Virginia grand jury cited earlier, reveals the tightrope walk that such a project entails: inspiring a reverence that must not tip over into unthinking complacency; inspiring a zeal for reform that must not turn into arrogant disregard for the Founding principles and a blind pursuit of pet projects or of self-interest. Jefferson, as noted in chapter 6, was less conscious of the problem.

In retrospect, one cannot help but feel that this effort to teach a popular knowledge of and reverence for the law was a losing battle almost from the start—not simply because of the dry and impenetrable language that seems endemic among lawyers, but above all because of the public attitudes that have allowed law to become the province of technical specialists in the first place. Citizens of ancient republics were much more inclined than Americans to see law as constitutive, as an honored guide and not a necessary evil, as a defender and supporter of what is noble. Paradoxically, where citizens' knowledge of and involvement in legal and political matters is less essential, as in the United States, the lesser but still necessary degree of interest can be even harder to sustain.[14]

How can a free country of unprecedented extent and diversity keep its citizens interested in and informed about the workings of its government, and how can a distant government retain their confidence and affection? The Anti-Federalists, for whom these questions were so vivid, focused on the legislature as the most important point of contact between the people and their government. As the Federal Farmer writes, it is "in the representative branch" of the legislature that "we must expect chiefly to collect the confidence of the people, and in it to find almost entirely the force of persuasion." And as "Brutus" (perhaps Robert Yates) argues, the confidence of the people in government requires not only that they choose the legislators but that they know them personally; the representatives ought to "be viewed by the people as part of themselves," with the same interests and feelings. Hence the number of representatives needed to be increased, the Anti-Federalists thought, to the point where ordinary men and not just the learned and wealthy few could expect to win election. This would have the further advantage of allowing the people's honest virtues to be reflected in the government. For, as Melancton Smith puts it in a familiar argument, those in "middling circumstances" face less temptation because they are less able to gratify their passions and are more obliged to develop steady, industrious habits; hence they are "more temperate, of better morals, and less ambitious than the great." Where confidence in government is lost and the laws are not upheld by persuasion and the patriotic attachment of the people, they must be maintained by military force, at which point even the semblance of liberty will be lost.[15]

The Anti-Federalists contended that the smaller republics of the states were better suited to provide an adequate representation in their legislatures and to hold the affection of the people; thus they sought to preserve as much as possible the sovereignty of the states. A few went further. The Maryland Farmer argued for a return to a modified form of direct democracy, as it was then practiced in some of the Swiss cantons.

Every Swiss farmer is by birth a legislator, and he becomes a voluntary soldier to defend his power and his property. . . . A free Swiss acquires from his infancy, a knowledge of the fundamental laws of his country, and the leading principles of their national policy are handed down by tradition from father to son—the first of these is never to trust power to representatives, or a national government. . . .

The love of the Switzers for their country is altogether romantic and surpasses the bounds of credibility. . . . The same amor-patriae, the same divine love of their country, universally pervades the bosom of every citizen, who in right of his birth, legislates for himself.

In keeping with this classical tone, the Maryland Farmer calls for sumptuary laws to "guard the public manners" and a council of censors to punish offenses against morality. As the capstone of his system, he proposes that

Seminaries of useful learning, with professorships of political and domestic oeconomy might be established in every county; discarding the philosophy of the moon and skies, we might descend to teach our citizens what is useful in this world—the principles of free government, illustrated by the history of mankind—the sciences of morality, agriculture, commerce, the management of farms and household affairs—The light would then penetrate, where mental darkness now reigns.—Do these things, and in a very few years, the people instead of abusing, would wade up to their knees in blood, to defend their governments.[16]

Such views are, however, at an extreme even in the spectrum of Anti-Federalist thought. Yet in its very radicalism, the Maryland Farmer's contribution to the ratification debate illustrates how deeply American society would have needed to change in order to acquire the sense of community and the high degree of personal involvement of a classical republic.

Occasionally, other Anti-Federalists speak of the moral education that a small, representative democracy can provide by encouraging the political aspirations of numerous citizens: "A well digested democracy has this advantage over all others," writes "Cato" (perhaps George Clinton), in that

it affords to many the opportunity to be advanced to the supreme command, and the honors they thereby enjoy fill them with a desire of rendering themselves worthy of them; hence this desire becomes part of their education, is matured in manhood, and produces an ardent affection for their country, and it is the opinion of the great Sidney, and Montesquieu that this is in a great measure produced by annual election of magistrates.

But more typical is the protective tone of the Anti-Federalists' preference for smallness that is evidenced in Cato's quotation of a frequently cited passage from Montesquieu.

> It is natural to a republic to have only a small territory, otherwise it cannot long subsist: in a large one, there are men of large fortunes, and consequently of less moderation; there are too great deposits to intrust in the hands of a single subject, an ambitious person soon becomes sensible that he may be happy, great, and glorious by oppressing his fellow citizens, and that he might raise himself to grandeur, on the ruins of his country. In large republics, the public good is sacrificed to a thousand views; in a small one the interest of the public is easily perceived, better understood, and more within the reach of every citizen; abuses have a less extent, and of course are less protected.[17]

For most of the Anti-Federalists, the modified small republic of the American states is indeed an important teacher, but the education for which it is valued is of a decidedly conservative stamp. Rather than inspiring Americans to acts of heroism and self-sacrifice, they seek to preserve the sound and sober morals they believe Americans already possess. Rather than emphasizing the potential of political participation to elevate and enrich citizens' lives, they stress the need to keep a lid on dangerous ambition by limiting temptations or opportunities to amass great wealth and power. The Anti-Federalists thus show particular concern about the potential for corruption in the projected federal capital city, which the Maryland Farmer calls "a lure to the enterprizing ambitious" and which Cato predicts will breed all the vices of courts—the idleness, pride, flattery, intrigue, and "above all, the perpetual ridicule of virtue." Likewise, they feared a standing army—typical of large countries and not forbidden by the Constitution—for its habits of indolence and violence: "When a standing army is kept up, virtue never thrives." Finally, the Anti-Federalists' conservatism shows itself in their discussions of religion, which include few positive proposals for fostering religion and instead reveal a concern with shielding the diversity of mild religious establishments that then existed in the states.[18]

What is striking in the Anti-Federalists' praise of the small republic is the education they do *not* generally expect it to provide—a direct education in justice and courage and self-control, an education in austere devotion to the common good. For them, politics, and especially political ambition, are cast in largely negative terms. Centinel expresses this spirit of wariness when he asks, "What is the primary object of government, but to check and control the ambitious and designing?" Seen in this light, government is indeed, as Patrick Henry puts it, only a necessary evil. But this outlook, in turn, makes the Anti-Federalists' celebration of the small republic ring rather hollow. Part of the charm of a small republic is that it needs its citizens, but why should they pour out their time and talents for it if there is little inherent reward or fulfillment in doing so?[19]

This is perhaps the most troubling unanswered question that haunted Jefferson's ward system. Jefferson amassed compelling arguments to demonstrate that it is prudent for communities to handle their own affairs as much as possible, and that many matters will be more safely, economically, and effectively managed if left to those most immediately affected. What he could never quite bring himself to say is that it is good for *individuals* to spend their time serving on local committees and running for local office, that individuals will be happier sacrificing their private economic and familial concerns for public concerns. It is not surprising that Jefferson's ward system and the Anti-Federalists' small republic remained unrealized dreams: their theories were simply unable to breathe the fire into local political life that would allow it to hold men's hearts.[20] Talk about the dignity of collective self-reliance fudges and fails to meet the issue. History suggests that it is only the danger and excitement of disaster and warfare, the resistance to or drive for imperial expansion, and the threat from challenging competitors at every level that evoke the sort of passionate political commitment which must be resuscitated from time to time to keep vital even the smallest and most mundane communal life. Can any substitute be found in pacific, just, commercial, day-to-day existence?

This fundamental problem receives, not its definitive answer, but its most profound and suggestive treatment in the somewhat melancholy study of democracy in America written in the 1840s by the great French liberal theorist Alexis de Tocqueville. What Tocqueville praises in American civic life is not precisely the practice in ruling and being ruled, as Aristotle characterizes republican political life in his *Politics*, but rather the cooperative efforts of people who feel their need for one another and join spontaneously in projects for mutual benefit. Whereas Aristotle focuses in his *Ethics* on the difficult virtues that can be elicited and honed by political competition and rule, Tocqueville's interest is in something at once gentler and more rudimentary: forging a sense of connectedness and drawing men out of themselves. It is especially critical for citizens in a democracy to form a habit of entering into political and civil associations, Tocqueville argues, because the unprecedented "individualistic" spirit inextricably embedded in modern democracy tends relentlessly toward a narrowing isolation. "Sentiments and ideas are revitalized, the heart is enlarged, and the human mind is developed only by the reciprocal action of men upon one another," Tocqueville observes; and "this action is almost null in democratic countries. It must therefore be artificially created. And this can only be accomplished by associations." Although the common life that modern democratic man needs is not exclusively political, Tocqueville asserts that it must be rooted in politics.

The political arena is the first and most obvious place where individuals realize that they must combine to attain their ends. But in doing so, they cannot help learning lessons about conducting meetings and working together on large projects; success in political associations encourages them to combine for other purposes, including bold entrepreneurial ones. "Political associations may therefore be considered as large free schools, where all the citizens go to learn the general theory of association." Freedom at the local level is crucial for nurturing this process because it is at this level that people feel most keenly the effects of public policy upon their lives and their own ability to act and make a difference.[21]

On the other hand, Tocqueville recognizes that state and national politics have a different power to draw people out of their narrow private lives: the excitement of great issues and great contests, especially party contests. "Whatever natural repugnance may restrain men from acting in concert, they will always be ready to combine for the sake of a party." The Founders looked with unease at factionalism, as they called it, and made no plans for a party system; but Tocqueville, feeling more strongly the dangers of apathy and reclusive individualism in society, and seeing more clearly how the political spirit that divides men can also lead them ultimately into a vast web of social and economic associations that knit them together, cautiously welcomes it. Tocqueville, viewing America from the perspective of the Old World, is able to grasp perhaps more deeply than did the Founders the educative value of the political system they established. Through the rich opportunities this system offers for political and other associations, we learn perhaps the central lesson of our moral education: that we are not isolated beings but part of a larger whole, and that in turning from ourselves to cherish the connections with our fellows, we may make ourselves better and even happier.[22]

11 · Education through the Free Exchange of Ideas

Proclamations, the jury trial, local political life, and a close relationship between the people and their legislators are all useful means of fostering civic virtue; yet each depends on a further agency of education, perhaps more important than all the rest: a free and flourishing press. Jefferson sums up the benefits of a free press in a letter written at the end of his life.

> This formidable censor of the public functionaries, by arraigning them at the tribunal of public opinion, produces reform peaceably, which must otherwise be done by revolution. It is also the best instrument for enlightening the mind of man, and improving him as a rational, moral, and social being.[1]

Tocqueville also underlines the tremendous importance of a free press in America, and he adds precision to Jefferson's remarks about the role of the press in the people's moral education. He argues that local freedom, associations, and newspapers are all interdependent and that the press is indispensable for keeping men informed about their common concerns in a world where traditional bonds of family, class, and birthplace are severed and individual isolation and political apathy are a growing danger.

> A newspaper is an adviser that does not require to be sought, but that comes of its own accord and talks to you briefly every day of the common weal, without distracting you from your private affairs.
>
> Newspapers therefore become more necessary in proportion as men become more equal and individualism more to be feared. To suppose that they only serve to protect freedom would be to diminish their importance: they maintain civilization.[2]

Justification for the Freedom of the Press

The Founders also defend the freedoms of speech and of the press as fundamental rights, but their practical arguments, tying a free press to the essential needs of a self-governing community, show how different these freedoms are from another that is closely related: the freedom of religion. Jefferson could claim an *absolute* freedom of religion on the grounds that just government simply has no purview over religious truths and falsehoods: "The legitimate powers of government extend to such acts only as are injurious to others. But it does me no injury for my neighbor to say there are twenty gods, or no god. It neither picks my pocket nor breaks my leg."[3] But a free press *can* injure individuals by depriving them of their reputation; a free press can threaten the public peace by disseminating malicious lies about the government or by attacking the principles of the regime itself. Precisely because they valued the press as the educator of a free people, the Founders were concerned to keep it from betraying their trust and abusing its powers.

It was during the Revolution that the people's freedom had been most in danger; this had led to obvious violations of the loyalists' rights, but it had also induced a keen awareness of how problematic the freedoms of speech and press can be in times of fundamental disagreement. Francis Hopkinson, a member of the Continental Congress and signer of the Declaration of Independence, explains that while he cherishes the liberty of the press,

> when this privilege is manifestly abused, and the press becomes an engine for sowing the most dangerous dissensions, for spreading false alarms, and undermining the very foundations of government, ought not that government upon the plain principles of self-preservation to silence by its own authority, such a daring violator of its peace, and tear from its bosom the serpent that would sting it to death?[4]

After the crisis had passed, Franklin in particular remained anxious about the potentially tyrannical power of an unregulated press. In a wry exposition, he calls it "the supremest court of judicature in Pennsylvania," able to "judge, sentence, and condemn to infamy, not only private individuals, but public bodies, etc., with or without inquiry or hearing, *at the court's discretion*." One possible remedy, he suggests, is to join the liberty of the press with the "liberty of the cudgel" to punish private libels, and, when the public is affronted, "*as it ought to be*, with the conduct of such writers . . . we should in moderation content ourselves with tarring and feathering, and tossing in a blanket." But in case his fellow citizens should find this remedy inappropriate, he humbly proposes that they pass a law to mark explicitly the limits of the press's freedom and to secure citizens from assaults to their reputations as well as their persons. Even Jefferson, who hoped for so much from the free press, despaired when he saw newspapers turn into dishonest party rags: "Suppression of the press could not more compleatly deprive the nation of it's benefits, than is done by it's abandoned prostitution to falsehood."[5]

Now if religious freedom is considered a right because it concerns only the private conscience, over which government has no legitimate authority, on what basis can one claim a right to criticize and so perhaps undermine one's government? Leonard Levy, the leading historian on the subject, seems to derive this right from the claim that no opinion may be justly suppressed because the truth of all opinions—including those underlying any particular regime—is "relative rather than absolute."[6] But if Levy is correct, and all truth is relative, then why isn't his own opinion opposing restriction on freedom of speech and press just as relative or subjective, just as defensible or indefensible, as that of the most willful and capricious opponent of freedom? An examination of the sources of the Founders' understanding of free speech suggests a far more coherent and morally sophisticated (i.e., nonrelativistic), understanding of the freedom of the press. It was precisely the conviction that their political system rested on universally valid truths that led the Founders to uphold the freedoms of speech and of the press as objective rights—and that governed the application and defined the limits of those rights.

We have already examined one important source of the Founders' thinking on this subject: Milton's *Areopagitica*. Milton did not, to modern eyes, carry the argument for freedom of the press very far, but he carried it as far as it could go without a new, liberal conception of politics. Only when the purpose of government was held to be the preservation of men's rights and not the salvation of their souls—only when the authority of government was held to rest upon popular consent—could the freedoms of speech and of the press come to be regarded as *natural* rights. In practical terms, this growing liberalism had the effect of extending to the public at large the freedom first claimed by the British Parliament for itself. By 1689 Parliament had secured from the king the right to speak freely and critically, but in England and in early colonial America, legislatures still punished private persons for a "breach of parliamentary privilege" if they printed the proceedings of the government without permission. Published reports that reflected badly upon the government were prosecuted in court as seditious libels, because of their presumed tendency to cause a breach of the peace. On this view, as Levy notes, the truth of one's statements does not excuse and can even be said to aggravate the crime, since true charges may provoke greater disaffection and turmoil than false charges.[7]

In the eighteenth century, building on Locke's teachings about the source of political authority, a broader view of free speech emerged—a view expressed with striking boldness and clarity in Trenchard and Gordon's popular series of essays, *Cato's Letters*.

> That men ought to speak well of their Governors, is true, while their Governors deserve to be well spoken of; but to do publick Mischief, without hearing of it, is only the Prerogative and Felicity of Tyranny: A free People will be shewing that they are so, by their Freedom of Speech.
>
> The Administration of Government, is nothing else but the Attendance of the Trustees of the People upon the Interest and Affairs of the People: And as it is the Part and Business of the People, for whose Sake alone all publick Matters are or ought to be transacted, to see whether they be well or ill transacted; so it is the Interest, and ought to be the Ambition, of all honest Magistrates, to have their Deeds openly examined, and publickly scanned: Only the wicked Governors of Men dread what is said of them.[8]

These arguments were eventually elaborated by the American Founders. Madison, in his otherwise controversial 1800 "Report on the Virginia Resolutions," sums up the American consensus on this point. Because the people have a right to a government of their own choosing, because they cannot choose well without information, and because the right to vote is useless without a full discussion of the merits and demerits of all candidates, the freedoms of speech and of the press are essential rights of citizens in a republic and "the only effectual guardian of every other right." And if republicanism more than other regimes requires for its proper functioning that the truth be generally known, Madison writes, republicanism is also the regime that has least to fear from the truth:

> The nature of governments elective, limited, and responsible, in all their branches, may well be supposed to require a greater freedom of animadversion than might be tolerated by the genius of such a government as that of Great Britain. In the latter it is a maxim that the King, an hereditary, not a responsible magistrate, can do no wrong, and that the Legislature, which in two-thirds of its composition is also hereditary, not responsible, can do what it pleases. . . . Is it not natural and necessary, under such different circumstances, that a different degree of freedom in the use of the press should be contemplated?[9]

Not only is republicanism safe with free inquiry because bad administrations can be peacefully voted out of office, but it is safe, the Founders believed, because it rests upon a foundation of self-evident truths, which they were confident free inquiry would only strengthen. Today we live with the paradox that while elite opinion has come to reject these "self-evident truths" as culture-bound and hopelessly naive, many of the peoples now emerging from totalitarianism are confirming by their choices that democratic governments devoted to the protection of individual rights do indeed answer to deep and abiding needs in human nature. Be this as it may, what becomes clear from the Founders' statements is that for them, the freedoms of speech and of the press were rights intrinsically linked to a certain kind of government. If this government is justified in part by its dedication to leaving the individual mind and conscience unshackled, a free press is in turn justified, in part, by its responsibility to ferret out and publicize the truth about political affairs.

Limits on Press Freedoms

Therefore it comes as no surprise that when the Founders came to revise the old common law governing press freedoms, they did so with a special regard for the role of the truth. The history of American prosecutions for seditious libel reveals a progress that was uneven and, in the heat of party conflicts, too often fraught with hypocrisy. But the policy that the nation groped toward and ultimately reached consensus upon was the one articulated by Alexander Hamilton as counsel for the defense in the influential 1804 New York case, *People v. Croswell.* Croswell had been convicted of libeling Thomas Jefferson. The trial judge denied him the opportunity to prove the truth of his statements and charged the jury to determine only the fact of publication and the truth of the innuendoes, i.e., whether the meaning given the words by the prosecution was accurate. In the appeal, with arguments reminiscent of the famous *Zenger* case seventy years before, Hamilton said that the jury should have been allowed to judge Croswell's intent, and that the veracity of his statements had a direct bearing on the question of intent. As the court record summarizes his argument:

> The liberty of the press consisted in publishing with impunity, truth with good motives, and for justifiable ends, whether it related to men or to measures. . . . If this right was not permitted to exist in vigor and in exercise, good men would become silent; corruption and tyranny would go on, step by step, in usurpation, until at last, nothing that was worth speaking, or writing, or acting for, would be left in our country.
>
> But he did not mean to be understood as being the advocate of a press wholly without control. He reprobated the novel, the visionary, the pestilential doctrine of an unchecked press. . . . It would encourage vice, compel the virtuous to retire, destroy confidence, and confound the innocent with the guilty.

And indeed, "in determining the character of a libel . . . the truth may not always be decisive; but being abused may still admit of a malicious and mischievous intent, which may constitute a libel."[10]

Thus the rule of public discourse was to be "the truth with good motives, and for justifiable ends." The people would be badly served if the press did not keep watch on the rulers and expose their errors, but they would be equally ill-served if citizens of character avoided public office for fear of being gratuitously dragged through the mud. Partly because the press of their day was so intemperate, the Founders were more than a little troubled by the tone of public discourse they saw emerging around them. It is true that the painful "torrent of slander" that Jefferson decried did not stop him or Washington or any of their colleagues from serving in office; but their standing as gentlemen, as men of learning, and as revolutionary heroes allowed them to treat the newspapers' attacks with a certain contempt that later politicians were less likely to muster.[11]

On the other hand, while there came to be broad agreement on Hamilton's formulation, dissenters remained. One was James Madison, whose "Report on the Virginia Resolutions" defended his state's resistance to the 1798 federal Sedition Act. This defiance had arisen even though the act incorporated the principles of jury trial and truth as a defense, which were adopted in most state laws only after *Croswell*. Although the crux of the Republicans' resistance was their belief that the regulation of the press belonged of right to the states and not to the federal government, Madison also made arguments that called the fairness of *any* seditious libel prosecution into question. He noted that malicious intent was too often simply inferred from the publication of words tending to bring the government into contempt, even though that contempt might be deserved. He stressed the difficulty at times of proving the truth of remarks that may in fact be correct, and the difficulty at all times of proving the truth of opinions. And with this last argument, we come to a troublesome question. How much scope should a free government allow for the expression of political opinions—opinions that it may consider not only false but subversive of its very foundations? Does Madison's argument imply that all opinion should be tolerated, and that if as a consequence a government loses the people's support, that government is ipso facto illegitimate? This was the view of Oliver Wendell Holmes, who wrote in his famous *Abrams* dissent:

> When men have realized that time has upset many fighting faiths, they may come to believe even more than they believe the very foundations of their own conduct that the ultimate good desired is better reached by free trade in ideas,—that the best test of truth is the power of the thought to get itself accepted in the competition of the market; and that truth is the only ground upon which their wishes safely can be carried out. That, at any rate, is the theory of our Constitution.[12]

But as Walter Berns has contended, there is something absurd in carrying free speech to such lengths that we allow it to destroy freedom itself.[13] Holmes wrote in the salad days before the emergence of fascism and communism as mass movements of frightening popularity and viciousness. The Founders, far less naïve, took much less for granted. They were not impressed by whatever "fighting faiths" might win over a majority of public opinion, as is seen from Publius's comments about mobs and the Federalists' horror at the excesses of the French Revolution. To the Founders, the American regime was legitimate not only because it had the people's consent but above all because it rested on true principles; and if the Framers were hopeful that the regime would continue to hold the people's consent, they were too deeply aware of the power of passion and prejudice to be complacent. That is why they gave so much thought to education, and why Jefferson opposed the free immigration of monarchists, who "will bring with them the principles of the governments they leave, imbibed in their early youth."[14]

Although Holmes's relativism is a far cry from the spirit of the Founders, they nevertheless came to agree that it was best, *as a matter of policy*, to allow a very broad freedom for dissenting opinion in politics as in all fields. The Founders never said with Levy that a free government cannot be libeled or that words alone cannot be criminal.[15] What they did come to believe was that in a free and stable society, prosecution for seditious libel was unnecessary, and that as a dangerous and potentially oppressive tool, it should be dispensed with. To say that a free government *cannot* be libeled suggests that the government is merely the people's servant, to be given orders, examined, and dismissed at will whenever the people so choose. The Founders had a more classical understanding of the importance of reverence for political institutions and authorities. They believed, however, that government can best keep this respect by open rebuttals of charges rather than by prosecuting its critics. As Jefferson said in his First Inaugural Address:

> Every difference of opinion is not a difference of principle. . . . If there be any among us who would wish to dissolve this Union or to change its republican form, let them stand undisturbed as monuments of the safety with which error of opinion may be tolerated where reason is left free to combat it.

When Jefferson spoke these words, the nation had just come through a political convulsion in which each party feared that the other would prove the undoing of the entire republican experiment and the idea of a loyal opposition was still in its wobbling infancy. Four years later, the nation's unity was more solid, and an experiment with extreme freedom of the press had persuaded Jefferson that an honorable government could not be "written down by falsehood and defamation." He concluded that since truth and reason have maintained their ground against false opinion in league with false facts, the press, confined to truth, needs no other legal restraint; the public judgment will correct false reasonings and opinions, on a full hearing of all parties, and no other definite line can be drawn between the inestimable liberty of the press and its demoralizing licentiousness.[16]

The Founders were content to let trials for seditious libel fall out of use, but they never proposed dispensing with libel proceedings altogether, even on behalf of public figures. If the immediate goal of these lawsuits was to protect the reputations of the individuals in question, a much broader public purpose was also to be served, in holding the press's factual reporting to a standard of truth and in maintaining a tone of respect in public discourse.

Journalists as Educators

Yet even the threat of lawsuits did not ensure that the newspapers would, as Jefferson hoped, make their readers more rational or moral human beings. Fisher Ames, a leading Federalist and member of the House of Representatives during Washington's administration, contended that in fact newspapers were having precisely the opposite effect. He charged the partisan press of his day with inflaming readers' fears, hatreds, and prejudices, while doing nothing to encourage moderation and reasoned debate.

The press . . . has left the understanding of the mass of men just where it found it; but by supplying an endless stimulus to their imagination and passions, it has rendered their temper and habits infinitely worse. . . .

By the help of the press we see invisible things; we forsee evils in their embryo, and accumulate on the present moment all that is bitter in the past or terrible in the future. A whole people are made sick with the diseases of the imagination. They see a monarch in Washington, and conspirators in their patriots.[17]

And when the press is not fanning the flames of party hatreds, he writes, too often it is indulging other unhealthy proclivities. In an address to printers, Ames castigates them for filling their columns with "murders, suicides, prodigies, [and] monstrous births." Such sensationalism is worse than useless; stories of crime inspire imitators, while a stream of shocking accounts loses, in time, its ability to shock, and leaves the mind vacant and unable to attend to serious matters that require real reflection. Ames never questions the idea of a party newspaper, but he would have his party's leading paper set a new standard of responsibility, eschewing all abuse of public figures, never lying even for a good cause, explaining the Federalist position, but avoiding disputation.[18]

Taking the Founders' arguments for the freedom of the press together with Ames's critique of its irresponsibility, it is apparent that something both less and more than extensive government regulation is needed to make the press useful to a republic. A number of early editors joined Ames in his criticisms, challenging their colleagues to shoulder more squarely their obligations as civic educators. John Ward Fenno of the Federalist *Gazette of the United States* called for educational and professional standards for editors, "qualifications and pledges from men on whom the nation depends for all the information and much of the instruction that it received," and he hoped that well-regulated colleges would fill this need.[19] Nathan Hale, nephew of the revolutionary hero, upbraided the readers of his *Boston Daily Advertiser* for grasping at rumors, being unwilling to wait for full and accurate accounts, and expecting editors to condense news to the point that "it may be comprehended at a single glance . . . a luxury with which we have strenuously refused to indulge the readers of this paper."[20] But it is Noah Webster, in the opening issue of his *Minerva*, who gives perhaps the best exposition of the significance and responsibility of newspaper editors in a democracy.

> Most of the Citizens of America are not only acquainted with letters and able to read their native language; but they have a strong inclination to acquire, and property to purchase, the means of knowledge. Of all these means of knowledge, Newspapers are the most eagerly sought after, and the most generally diffused. In no other country on earth, not even in Great-Britain, are Newspapers so generally circulated. . . . But Newspapers are not only the vehicles of what is called news; they are the common instruments of what is called social intercourse, by which the citizens of this vast Republic constantly discourse and debate with each other on subjects of public concern. It is by means of these, that in times of danger, either from open hostility or insidious intrigue, an alarm is instantly conveyed and an unanimity of opinion is formed, from Maine to Georgia. . . . The foundation of all free governments, seems to be, a general diffusion of knowledge. People . . . must have just ideas of their own rights, and learn to distinguish them from the rights of others, before they can form any rational system of government, or be capable of maintaining it. To know that we have rights, is very easy; to know how to preserve those rights, to adjust contending claims, and to prescribe the limits of each; here lies the difficulty.

A chief function of the papers, then, should be to foster the practical wisdom that comes through studying the application of general principles to concrete cases. Such wisdom, in turn, is the only sure protection against corruption and abuse of power. Therefore, Webster argues, government should take care to encourage newspapers: "Like schools, they should be considered as the auxiliaries of government, and placed on a respectable footing; they should be the heralds of truth, the protectors of peace and good order."[21]

Over time, these hopes for a professional, accurate, and reasonably nonpartisan press have been abundantly realized. Whereas the first American newspapers, run by poorly educated printers, reprinted essays and whatever scraps of news came to hand, and the partisan press of the late eighteenth century loaded its pages with much political controversy and little reliable information, since that time the mainstream press has improved immeasurably in tone and in accurate reporting. But while much has been gained, something also has been lost: the sense of mission Franklin had in mind when he suggested that in the scattered but literate republic of the United States, journalism might fill the same function as public oratory in the classical republics. Today the very idea of rhetoric has come into disrepute, assuming connotations of dishonest arguments, slick public relations, or demagogues playing on the passions of a crowd. But responsible rhetoric has a different purpose. By it, what is publicly useful in the abstruse thought of the learned is made available, and made appealing, to those who lack the leisure or the understanding to plumb that thought itself. For American newspapers, this mission would mean devoting more attention to educating the minds and tastes of readers with lively but thoughtful pieces on political and moral subjects. As Franklin wrote in his *Autobiography*:

> I consider'd my Newspaper also as another Means of Communicating Instruction, and in that View frequently reprinted in it Extracts from the Spectator and other moral Writers, and sometimes publish'd little Pieces of my own which had been first composed for Reading in our Junto. Of these are a Socratic Dialogue tending to prove, that, whatever might be his Parts and Abilities, a vicious Man could not properly be called a Man of Sense. And a Discourse on Self denial, showing that Virtue was not secure, till its Practice became a Habitude, and was free from the Opposition of contrary Inclinations.[22]

In undertaking to write serious essays for a popular audience, Franklin was joined by many of the best minds of his day. These included John Dickinson, whose "Letters from a Farmer" were perhaps the most thoughtful political writings in prerevolutionary America; Samuel and John Adams; and Madison, Hamilton, and Jay with their classic *Federalist Papers*, to say nothing of the less famous but often equally trenchant arguments on both sides of the constitutional debate, all of which were printed in newspapers. While contemporary opinion pieces rarely descend to the depths of scurrility and blatant falsehood that was common in the nation's early papers, they also rarely reach the heights of these finer works. What is lacking today are essays that confront the most fundamental questions of politics and morality—what true virtue is, or what the sources of rights are, for example—in a way that is informed by genuine philosophy.

In a provocative essay, Gordon Wood has argued that the Founders were themselves responsible for the decline in the level of public discourse that has occurred since their day. These leaders, he says, addressed themselves chiefly to other "gentlemen," while at the same time unleashing democratic forces that would ultimately bring "a decline in the intellectual quality of American political life and an eventual separation of ideas and power." The Founders did indeed address one another, expressing many of their thoughts in private letters and filling their published essays with learned citations and historical allusions. But Wood misses or blurs the crucial point when he concludes from this that they were elitist, "essentially engaged, despite their occasional condescension towards a larger public, in either amusing men like themselves or in educating men to be or think like themselves."[23] Surely they were kept from elitism by precisely this last commitment: by their intent to educate through their writings, to reach the intellectually able at all social levels, and to inspire the intellectually ordinary with a greater share of sound reasoning.

Wood argues that in vying for power, revolutionary leaders were led to express more democratic sentiments than they felt. Once they had roused the people, they found that politics was no longer an exclusively gentlemanly affair, and they were forced to yield ground to the egalitarian ideology of the Revolution. There is surely some truth in this. But Wood understates the extent to which the Founders *were* cautiously optimistic about popular government, when hedged and channeled by all the new improvements in the science of politics that Hamilton and Madison celebrate in the *Federalist Papers*. The Founders were taking a great gamble, hoping that by challenging the entrenched aristocracy they might establish a new, more open and fluid aristocracy of talents and merit. If their experiment ended by bringing political life and public discourse down to the level of the masses rather than bringing the people up to their level, they are not altogether to blame. Responsibility lies also with the American people, who failed to rise to the challenge, as well as with the subsequent generations of American journalists and intellectuals. The fact that the Founders' hope has been so imperfectly realized points to a certain paradox of modern writing. While journalists and intellectuals are careful not to talk down to their readers and are afraid of seeming to preach, both fail to take the public quite seriously enough to consider the education of the people the noblest goal of a lifetime of high-quality writing.

Libraries, Philosophic Societies, and Almanacs

However much the Founders looked to journalists as educators, they realized that newspapers would generally cater to, rather than change, the tastes and interests of their readers. Newspapers were simply too dependent on the public to keep them in business. Hence it was essential to cultivate in the citizens a habit of reading good books, and the best way to do this was to make serious literature freely available through public libraries. Franklin and Jefferson shared a keen interest in libraries, perhaps because they each combined a warm sympathy for the common people with a thirst for knowledge and a gift for self-instruction. Jefferson, always a connoisseur of libraries, laid the foundation for the great Library of Congress in 1814 with the sale of his own collection of six thousand books. As early as 1779, he had drafted a bill for a public library in Richmond, to be dedicated to the "learned and curious," which he describes in his autobiography as an integral part of his plan for education in Virginia.[24] This bill, like many others, ran aground on the Virginia legislature's flinty stinginess. Franklin had succeeded in a similar venture by carrying the idea of self-help one step further and raising funds from the library's future users. The effort prospered even better when he presented the plan as originating with this group of readers, rather than putting himself forward as the author of his own project. But this bit of strategic modesty did not prevent him from boasting about the library's success years later.

> The Institution soon manifested its Utility, was imitated by other Towns and in other Provinces; the Librarys were augmented by Donations, Reading became fashionable, and our People having no publick Amusements to divert their Attention from Study became better acquainted with Books, and in a few Years were observ'd by Strangers to be better instructed and more intelligent than People of the same Rank generally are in other Countries.

There had been other lending libraries in America before Franklin established his in 1731, but most were religious both in origin and in the bulk of their holdings. Franklin's was the first subscription library, and its initial collection was perhaps unique in containing a mixture of classics and practical works, with no volumes of theology at all.[25]

Similar in motive were Franklin's exertions to form the American Philosophical Society. Entitling his 1743 plan "A Proposal for Promoting Useful Knowledge among the British Plantations in America," he explains that the drudgery of settling new colonies is essentially over and that there is time now for leisure and speculation. Yet the leisured activities he especially wishes to cultivate are the making and promoting of useful discoveries. Thus his compendious list of topics for inquiry contains, together with mathematics, geology, and chemistry, such items as the discovery of useful plants, cider making, medicine, distillation, brewing, assaying of ores, labor-saving devices, trades, manufactures, surveying, animal husbandry, gardening, "and all philosophical experiments that let light into the nature of things, tend to increase the power of man over matter, and multiply the conveniences or pleasures of life." The society was to be a focus for correspondence, publish regular reports and transactions, and communicate with the Royal Society of London and the Dublin Society. Though the original organization soon faltered and was revived only in 1767, it was significant as one of a growing number of societies—scientific, agricultural, medical, and commercial—that sprang up in the years before and after independence and that embodied the spirit of self-help most clearly exemplified by Franklin himself.[26]

Self-help was also the theme of Franklin's educational efforts at the other end of the intellectual scale. With *Poor Richard's Almanac*, he found an admirable means of reaching the many Americans who were barely literate (and in the process, he admits cheerfully, turning a tidy profit for himself). Almanacs were the one volume besides the Bible that virtually every farm family owned, and Franklin's was an instant and enduring success during the quarter-century that he published it. As he explains:

> I consider'd it as a proper Vehicle for conveying Instruction among the common People, who bought scarce any other Books. I therefore filled all the little Spaces that occurr'd between the Remarkable Days in the Calendar, with Proverbial Sentences, chiefly such as inculcated Industry and Frugality, as the Means of procuring Wealth and thereby securing Virtue, it being more difficult for a Man in Want to act always honestly, as (to use here one of those proverbs) *it is hard for an empty Sack to stand upright*.[27]

The sayings that filled the almanac came, as he acknowledges, from many other writers, but Franklin gave them their memorable phrasing and selected them to illuminate his characteristic refrain of virtue as the surest path to happiness. Here, more than in the *Autobiography*, Franklin addresses himself to the common person of modest talents and modest means, and his sayings are well adapted to this audience. Together the aphorisms constitute a running attack on idleness, vanity, and foolish pride, an encouragement never to envy the great and glorious, and a call to the solid and attainable respectability that rests on self-knowledge, self-reliance, industry, and thrift. There is a subtle balance between his praise of contentment with one's lot and his praise of hard work, as there is between the hope of prosperity he holds out and his gentle denigrating of mere wealth unaccompanied by justice and generosity. Because of their fragmentary and occasionally contradictory nature, these sayings lead one to wonder whether there is a deeper organizing principle to Franklin's moral world. In particular, they raise the question of the relation of means to ends. If industry and frugality are "the means of procuring wealth and thereby securing virtue," what is this ultimate virtue at which prudence aims? Does it point beyond self-interest to something higher, or is it simply self-interest in a richer and more expansive form? This question will be a central theme of the next three chapters.

Part Four
Education through Emulation

12 · George Washington and the Principle of Honor

Although the Founders cast a wide net in their search for institutions that could help educate republican citizens, they believed that in the critical work of cultivating virtue, schools and other institutions could at best only supplement the moral education that must come from attentive parents and inspiring personal examples. A successful training in virtue must begin in infancy and proceed on the basis of close observation of the individual character and passions of the child. The parent or mentor must love as well as know the child. Perhaps more important than the quality of interaction, however, is the ideal of human excellence that parent and child are steering toward. This goal, to be compelling, must be embodied not so much in maxims as in intimately known—or vividly portrayed—human models.

For parents and communities wrestling with this irreducibly personal core of moral education, the Founders offer two types of guidance. The family letters of several Founders, especially Thomas Jefferson, provide a paradigm (to some extent self-conscious, given Jefferson's peculiarly intense awareness of the written record he was leaving) of thoughtful education, showing the kind of advice and inspiration that these men believed would best produce honorable citizens.[1] Second, leaders of the Revolution and of the Founding generation understood that their own lives could and should serve as examples for young Americans to follow. This attempt to become a worthy exemplar was most seriously sustained in the man who would also become the preeminent leader of his time, George Washington. And for Benjamin Franklin, private guidance and public example are combined in the classic autobiography that he addresses to his son, in which he tells his life as he wishes to have it remembered and helps the reader draw the appropriate conclusions from the story. In the process of writing to their families and presenting their lives as objects of emulation, Washington, Jefferson, and Franklin reveal many of their deepest reflections on the nature of human virtue and the perplexing problem of how it may be taught.

Gentlemanly Generosity and Paternal Guidance

We begin with George Washington, a pivotal figure who embodies more than any other Founder the virtues celebrated by classical republicanism, while simultaneously pointing forward to a distinctly modern American conception of virtue. In his contributions to the education of those around him, Washington was distinguished first of all by his generosity. He was a well-known patron of schools and colleges, and a discreet, sometimes anonymous source of tuition for numerous young relatives and promising sons of deceased or indigent friends. As he followed the progress of these boys through their studies, Washington's letters to some of them show the kind of stern moral guidance he thought necessary in early life. His letters portray youth as a perilous time, requiring deference to the wisdom of elders and constant vigilance in the choice of one's activities and friends. "You must be employed, and if it is not in pursuit of those things which are profitable, it must be in pursuit of those which are destructive." For Washington, virtue is easy to recognize but hard to attain, resting more on habituation than on careful reasoning. Rather than encouraging speculation on moral questions, he calls for unremitting efforts to establish habits of industry, justice, and a dignified self-control. "Idleness and vice," he warns in a typical passage, "will approach like a thief, working your passions, encouraged, perhaps, by bad examples, the propensity to which will increase in proportion to . . . your yielding."[2]

At the very least, the character formation Washington has in mind is meant to lay the foundation for prosperity. But the man who is useful to himself is also in a position to be useful to others. As Washington writes to one young charge concerning his studies, "It is you yourself who is to derive immediate benefit from these. Your country may do it hereafter." Washington generally links happiness with being "a useful member of society." Through the discipline of school, he insists, one can learn not only valuable information but important virtues that one needs to become a productive citizen.

> The first and great object with you at present is to acquire, by industry and application, such knowledge as your situation enables you to obtain, as will be useful to you in life. In doing this two other important advantages will be gained besides the acquisition of knowledge: namely, a habit of industry, and a disrelish of that profusion of money and dissipation of time which are ever attendant upon idleness.[3]

The Relation between Moral and Intellectual Virtue

At times this focus on utility led Washington to appear to denigrate a life of study for its own sake. Washington certainly valued learning itself chiefly for the contribution it could make to a useful and moral life. To his stepson's tutor he wrote, "Not that I think his becoming a mere scholar is a desirable education for a gentleman; but I conceive a knowledge of books is the basis upon which other knowledge is to be built." Still, Washington saw knowledge as beneficial because it gives one the means to live nobly as well as comfortably. This keen sense of the noble is what caused him ultimately to respect or even revere the life of the mind. Thus he expresses his appreciation for a mathematical work that is largely beyond his grasp:

> The science of figures, to a certain degree, is not only indispensably requisite in every walk of civilised life, but the investigation of mathematical truths accustoms the mind to method and correctness in reasoning, and is an employment peculiarly worthy of rational beings. In a clouded state of existence, where so many things appear precarious to the bewildered researcher, it is here that the rational faculties find a firm foundation to rest upon. From the high ground of mathematical and philosophical demonstration, we are insensibly led to far nobler speculations and sublimer meditations.[4]

Washington's ambivalence about the scholarly life calls to mind that of certain somewhat sophisticated gentlemen who appear in Plato's dialogues, such as Nicias and Cephalus. While in some way looking up to philosophy and willing to have their sons study it, they would be distressed to see their grown heirs give up the prosperous, dignified life of independent farming and civic action in order to walk about, barefoot and always talking, like Socrates. Washington had great respect for learning, and he was deeply disappointed when his father's early death deprived him of the opportunity of pursuing a liberal education abroad. But like the more enlightened among Plato's gentlemen, he cherished a confidence that in the best cases, speculation would illuminate and equip a life of moral and purposeful activity, supporting rather than undermining his own prior, and most serious, concerns. Although Washington was himself, as Jefferson said, not a "bookish" man, his high regard for learning and consequent intellectual modesty nevertheless added to his stature and authority, by helping to keep him out of divisive disputes that could sap his influence, and perhaps also by channeling his energies more vigorously into the areas in which he excelled.[5]

The Gentleman as Exemplar

For after all, Washington's greatest contribution to American education lay not in his efforts on behalf of schools and schoolboys but in the example he set by his whole life, a life in which educational activity played but a small part. That he chose to teach more by example than by precept is seen in a comment made at the end of his life: "With me, it has always been a maxim, rather to let my designs appear from my works than by my expressions." If Washington did not from the first contrive to be emulated, he did care deeply throughout his life about being worthy of emulation, and about his image as well as the substance of his accomplishments. This concern is evident in his love of military regalia, in his much-remarked noble bearing, in the fine style of Mount Vernon, and in his unwillingness to entertain guests there—or to do anything else—in a "niggardly" fashion. More important, it is apparent in his attempt to act, and to encourage others to act, in a manner worthy of their new republic: in his endeavors during the revolutionary war to inspire his officers with discipline and a sense of honor, for example, or in his struggle as president to invest his new office with dignity, to rise above factions, and to set a precedent for orderly transitions of power with his resignation. Even in international relations Washington expressed faith in the persuasive power of good examples. In a famous passage of his Farewell Address, he argued that America's best gift to the world would be realized not through intervention abroad but through providing an exemplar for others to follow.[6]

Washington succeeded, in every way, in becoming an influential model. As early as 1759, his officers in the Virginia defensive force had written of his ability to educate and inspire those who served under him.

> In our earliest infancy, you took us under your tuition, trained us in the practice of that discipline which alone can constitute good troops. . . . Your steady adherence to impartial justice, your quick discernment and invariable regard to merit—wisely intended to inculcate those genuine sentiments of true honor and passion for glory, from which the greatest military achievements have been derived—first heightened our natural emulation, and our desire to excel.[7]

Washington was an object of awe for all of the Founders (if also a source of envy for some), and he served as a mentor for Alexander Hamilton in particular, as well as for Lafayette. During the Constitutional Convention, his moral authority helped discourage the delegates' pettiness and stubbornness, and afterwards his well-known advocacy of the Constitution was one of the most important factors tipping the scales in favor of ratification. Above all, Washington became a model for future presidents. Since the drafters of the Constitution, partly out of their trust in him, had only sketched with a broad brush the duties of the office they expected him to fill, his precedent determined in large measure the powers and customs that would define the American presidency.

Washington's friends and admirers, especially John Marshall, expanded the usefulness of the example he set by writing biographies of his life. Marshall's was explicitly intended to be educational and was recast into a shorter version for use in schools. While glowing, this work still adheres to standards of scholarly accuracy. But others, led by Mason Locke Weems, abandoned all historical scruples in their attempt to forge out of Washington the perfect American hero. The result of this fictionalizing was a collection of pious stories, including the famous cherry tree incident, which were engraved in the nation's consciousness through the *McGuffey Readers*. These stories left us with a Washington at once moralistic and monumentally lifeless. Such sanitized heroes are less useful than their more earthy originals: they stand as irresistible targets for the leveling popguns of resentful debunkers, who use them to insinuate to students that *all* greatness is a myth. And what serious child could even wish to pattern himself after a man who never showed a shred of selfishness or unruly passion, who appears as a kind of cross between an angel and "an impossible prig"?[8]

What is the Love of Honor?

To restore Washington to the place that he and his contemporaries intended him to have in the nation's education, one would have to begin with a frank and fresh examination of his character. One would need to help students identify not only his virtues but his struggles and his motives in order to make him again the human and appealing model he sought to be for the young.

Modern scholarship has cast these motives in a rather questionable light. Recent commentators tend to concede to Charles Beard that the Founders, like all men, were moved mainly by selfish passions, although some scholars have tried to restore a place for a kind of public-spiritedness by including in their analysis other forms of self-interestedness besides the economic one. Thus Douglass Adair has argued that the desire for fame allowed Washington and his fellow Founders to serve themselves through serving their country. By keeping a long view and looking to the approbation of enlightened opinion and of posterity, they rose above the common run of politicians to become true benefactors of the nation. The theory that fame was the chief spur that impelled the Founders to make their great efforts and sacrifices is given weight by Alexander Hamilton's pregnant remark in the *Federalist Papers* that the love of fame is "the ruling passion of the noblest minds."[9]

There is surely no question that Washington felt both a tremendous thirst for glory and a sometimes painful sensitivity about his reputation. But precisely because he knew firsthand and thought much about the love of grand honor, he understood—perhaps better than any scholar can—how problematic a passion it is. Washington was penetrated by the awareness of this conundrum: if one's real motive for acting is only a desire to be honored, and not a desire to be honorable, then the honor one receives is not deserved. Ordinary people honor a leader for what they perceive to be his devotion to their good and the exertions he makes to attain it, or for his devotion to justice and the sacrifices he makes to uphold it, not for his skill at winning applause—even the applause of posterity. This view is in accord with the depiction of the true gentleman in Aristotle's *Ethics*. Such a man does value honor, but as a confirmation of his virtue; he does not regard his virtue as a means to win acclaim.[10]

Washington wrestled with the tension between his desire to win honor and his desire to act honorably in a pair of letters written the same day in 1775, as he considered returning to the frustrating task of leading Virginia's defensive forces. To a friend he complained, "No man can gain any Honour by conducting our Forces at this time, but rather lose in his reputation." Thus he expected to forfeit "what at present constitutes the chief part of my happiness; i.e., the esteem and notice the country has been pleased to honour me with." But writing to his mother, he pondered the other side: if the country pressed him to accept the command again, "it would reflect eternal dishonour upon me to refuse it."[11] We may surmise that he spoke more frankly to his friend and more loftily (and defensively) to his mother, who always wanted him at home. Yet the fact remains that he accepted the command. He would always speak proudly about his sense of honor, but increasingly as he grew older, he struggled both to conceal and to overcome his love of mere reputation. The contortions that this struggle occasionally put him through are fascinating and instructive.

When, for example, the Virginia legislature awarded him shares in the James and Potomac river companies for his service in the revolutionary war, he was distressed that the gift would deprive him of the honor of having served his country entirely without remuneration; yet he feared to decline it lest he seem ungrateful or ostentatious.[12] When elected to the presidency, he worried that people might charge him with "levity and inconsistency," if not "rashness and ambition," since he had promised, on resigning as commander in chief, to give up public life forever. His willingness to resume public service did indicate a remarkable change of heart. In a letter to Lafayette at the end of the revolutionary war, he had said:

> At length my dear Marquis I am become a private citizen on the banks of the Potomac, and under the shadow of my own Vine and my own Fig-Tree, free from the bustle of a camp and the busy scenes of public life, I am solacing myself with those tranquil enjoyments, of which the soldier who is ever in pursuit of fame, the Statesman whose watchful days and sleepless nights are spent in devising schemes to promote the welfare of his own, perhaps

the ruin of other countries, as if this globe was insufficient for us all, and the Courtier who is always watching the countenance of his Prince, in hopes of catching a gracious smile, can have very little conception. I am not only retired from all public employments, but I am retiring within myself; and shall be able to view the solitary walk, and tread the paths of private life with heartfelt satisfaction. Envious of none, I am determined to be pleased with all; and this my dear friend being the order for my march, I will move gently down the stream of life, until I sleep with my Fathers.

When he again wrote to Lafayette in 1789, he explained his reluctant change of heart by America's great need at this critical juncture and by his belief that he saw "a path, as clear and as direct as a ray of light," by which the country could be made prosperous and happy. But he still worried about being thought inconsistent and ambitious. "Nay further," he went on, in unfolding his dilemma to Henry Lee,

would there not even be some apparent foundation for the two former charges? Now justice to myself and tranquillity of conscience require that I should act a part, if not above imputation, at least capable of vindication. Nor will you conceive me to be too solicitous for reputation. Though I prize, as I ought, the good opinion of my fellow citizens; yet, if I know myself, I would not seek or retain popularity at the expense of one social duty or moral virtue.

Indeed, Washington need not have worried about deserving the charge of ambition at this moment. His own desire for fame prompted him rather to decline the presidency, which could hardly be expected to enhance, and might well jeopardize, his already glorious reputation. But this fear also he made up his mind to resist: "Whensoever I shall be convinced the good of my country requires my reputation to be put in risque, regard for my own fame will not come in competition with an object of so much magnitude."[13]

To take into account sentiments such as these, Forrest McDonald, following Adair, stresses the importance of patriotism as well as the love of fame among the passions that govern men.[14] But is this sufficient to explain Washington's motives? Especially in 1776, the notion of patriotism was itself deeply ambiguous: was one to be loyal to the mother country or to the new country, which existed only in thought? On what grounds should a person choose? How should one determine the true good of the country one sought to serve except by looking from passions to something higher, such as principles of justice?

We would suggest that the very attempt to explain a man like Washington by his passions alone is beset by difficulties. Washington was, to be sure, a deeply passionate man, especially in his youth. As an adolescent, he was in love with love, and as a young man he showed himself intensely ambitious for honor and often prone to great fury. But part of the interest in his life lies in his steady and successful efforts to master these passions. His marriage was a triumph of sensible prudence over romantic (and adulterous) longings; his struggles with fame we have seen; and as for his indignation, Jefferson, from whom Washington died estranged, could not but acknowledge that although "his temper was naturally irritable and high toned . . . reflection and resolution had obtained a firm and habitual ascendancy over it." Even Washington's feelings of patriotism were informed by the belief that his country represented a higher principle, beyond itself. As he put it, "The preservation of the sacred fire of liberty and the destiny of the republican model of government are justly considered as *deeply*, perhaps as *finally*, staked in the experiment entrusted to the hands of the American people." By Washington's own account, it was precisely a sense of what was right and honorable that moved him to risk his own reputation and his tranquillity for such a cause. If we are to take seriously his account of himself, as well as the assessment of his contemporaries, we must at least begin with the presumption that in the important choices of his life, he acted not from passion but from principle, not from a desire to win honor but from a desire to be worthy of the greatest honor.[15]

Addison's Cato *as a Clue to the Meaning of Honor*

If Washington was right about himself, how can we understand the motives behind such a sense of honor? Forrest McDonald has shed valuable light on Washington's understanding of honor by calling attention to the importance of Joseph Addison's play *Cato* as an inspiration for him and, through him, for his troops. Washington saw the play a number of times, quoted lines from it throughout his life, and encouraged his men to perform it at Valley Forge to rally their spirits. The American colonists loved the play even before the Revolution for its noble sentiments and moral teachings, but as the dispute with England heated up, it became their most popular drama, staged with increasing frequency to inspire courage in the fight for liberty. As Fredric Litto has pointed out, Patrick Henry and Nathan Hale adapted their most famous lines from the play, and many others quoted it freely.[16] After the war, *Cato* remained for the Founders a prime example of didactic poetry. Thus Noah Webster included extracts from it in his reader, which educated a whole generation of citizens, there being seventy-seven editions in the half-century after 1785. Although its language is too stilted and its moralizing too overt for the play to have remained popular into the twentieth century, only the most jaded reader comes away wholly untouched by the charm that honor holds for its leading characters. Conveying a taste for this charm is central to the drama's educative aim. *Cato* thus provides not only a clue to what Washington admired and emulated but an example of what the Founders understood to be the proper use of poetry in shaping the morals and passions of their young countrymen.

Set in the waning days of the Roman Republic, the play tells the story of Cato the Younger, who has withdrawn to Utica to rally what is left of Rome's republican Senate against the encroaching power of Caesar. His followers are split into two camps, one preparing to mutiny in the face of near-certain defeat, the other fiercely loyal. The various characters show the whole range of possible views on honor.

First there is the Numidian general Syphax, who prefers the simple life of hunting to Rome's refinements and sees in honor only a foolish pride. His co-conspirator, Sempronius, is a Roman senator who appreciates only too well the honors of public life: he is willing to stoop to any treachery or deceit to attain them. He sees Cato's "ruined cause" as a bar to his ambition, and he hopes that "Caesar's favor / That showers down greatness on his friends, will raise me / To Rome's first honours."[17] We could not have a clearer example of the man who is guided simply by the love of fame, and as the plot unfolds, Sempronius becomes more and more of a scoundrel.

In direct contrast is the Numidian prince, Juba, more Roman than the Roman senator, who would rather "die ten thousand deaths / Than wound my honour." As he describes it:

> Honour's a sacred tie, the law of kings,
> The noble mind's distinguishing perfection,
> That aids and strengthens virtue where it meets her,
> And imitates her actions, where she is not.

This sense of honor makes him independent of the opinions of all but a few worthy judges—among whom Cato stands preeminent: "I'd rather have that man / Approve my deeds," says Juba, "than worlds for my admirers."[18] But Juba is *not* the play's prototype of a mature man of honor: He worries about Cato's opinion because he is still young, unsure of himself, and in love with Cato's daughter.

For Cato, however, the judgment that matters is almost entirely within himself. In the famous scene where he faces down the mutineers and shames them into submission, Cato shows the combination of passions and principles that an honorable man would be guided by.

> Perfidious men! and will you thus dishonour
> Your past exploits, and sully all your wars?

> Do you confess 'twas not a zeal for Rome,
> Nor love of liberty, nor thirst of honour,
> Drew you thus far; but hopes to share the spoil
> Of conquered towns and plundered provinces?[19]

Cato, like Washington, loves glory, but he subordinates it to his love of Rome and of liberty—and his sense of justice. Without justice, glory becomes a monstrous species of selfishness.

> Are not the lives of those who draw the sword
> In Rome's defence intrusted to our care?
> Should we thus lead them to a field of slaughter,
> Might not the impartial world with reason say
> We lavished at our deaths the blood of thousands,
> To grace our fall, and make our ruin glorious?

In the end Cato defends his decision to fight on by arguing that there is still hope. But in his explanation, we see a subtle shift: his concern for the life of his subjects gives way to his love of the noble action that they may share in.

> 'Twill never be too late
> To sue for chains and own a conqueror.
> Why should Rome fall a moment ere her time?
> No, let us draw her term of freedom out
> In its full length, and spin it to the last,
> So shall we gain still one day's liberty;
> And let me perish, but in Cato's judgment,
> A day, an hour, of virtuous liberty
> Is worth a whole eternity in bondage.[20]

Cato may be judged an ascetic of a sort, and his asceticism, a bit like that of St. Francis, is fueled by an almost erotic passion for virtue. His love of virtue makes all other cares pale by comparison. It enables him not only to scorn the opinions of all who do not understand him but to scorn as well "what the world calls misfortune and affliction." To him "these are not ills," because they befall "the best of men." They are only occasions to exercise and display one's virtue. It is this reasoning that Cato's son seems to have adopted when he says, "'Tis not in mortals to command success, / But we'll do more, Sempronius; we'll deserve it." This outlook even allows Cato to receive with equanimity the brave death of his other son. But it does not leave him quite so independent of fortune as he thinks. Although he is able nobly to commit suicide rather than submit to Caesar, Caesar has the power to make life unlivable for him. Cato is unable to retire to private life when public life holds no possibility for honorable action. For he is, in both Addison's and Plutarch's accounts, a thoroughly political man who needs the good fortune of living in a free country in order for his virtues to find any significant expression or even for his life to have meaning. To this extent, Cato's spirit is not as independent as that of his modern-day follower, George Washington.[21]

Addison sheds additional light on the meaning of honor for men such as his hero Cato in an essay written for the *Guardian*.

> True honour, though it be a different principle from religion, is that which produces the same effects. . . . Religion embraces virtue, as it is enjoined by the laws of God; honour, as it is graceful and ornamental to human nature. The religious man *fears*, the man of honour *scorns* to do an ill action. The one considers vice as something that is beneath him, the other as something that is offensive to the Divine Being; the one as what is unbecoming, the other as what is forbidden. Thus Seneca speaks in the natural and genuine language of a man of honour, when he declares, that, were there no God, to see or punish vice, he would not commit it, because it is of so mean, so base, and so vile a nature.

By this interpretation, the true honor that looks to what is beautiful and fitting is an even more autonomous principle than religion, which involves a fear of punishment. True honor's charm is the charm of the noble and beautiful; the passion that impels one to honorable action is not vanity but a thirst to excel in the most important endeavors of human life. We would have to say, then, that while a defective form of honor imitates the action of virtue "where she is not," the true honor of Cato and Juba is a kind of crowning virtue that provides a spur to all the others.[22]

McDonald, however, after discussing Addison's play and essay, surprisingly comes back to the dogmatic position that all honor is a concern for the opinions of others. He even maintains that according to *Cato*, Shakespeare's dictum "to thine own self be true" is foolish, and that one should seek rather to be true to others.[23] McDonald goes on to argue that while a modern, acquisitive republic cannot regulate itself by classical republican virtue, honor, so understood, is a promising substitute. Yet what McDonald describes seems closer to the honor that is the principle of monarchic regimes, as Montesquieu portrays that principle, than to the honor depicted in Addison's play. But how relevant has this monarchic honor been to American life, and how well can it take the place of virtue?

Monarchic as Opposed to Classical Republican Honor

As Montesquieu explains, and as we noted in the opening chapter, the honor that forms the animating passion of modern monarchies does serve as the chief bulwark of liberty in those societies.[24] For despotism in its essence is the political system run by terror, where all power is concentrated in one or a very few hands without any reliable check or balance and all the individuals feel themselves weak and isolated. Honor, by contrast, while giving the members of every class or group an acute sensitivity to their rank and place in society, also gives vigor and cohesiveness to those groups. Monarchic society is kept in motion by the profound disagreements between members of the court, the country nobility of diverse regions, the clergy, and the urban bourgeoisie. These deeply rooted and more or less permanent groupings—of family, profession, locale, and religion— protect their individual members and lend them communal strength, not only to compete against rival alliances but also to resist centralized authority. More- over, these groupings encourage in their members that pride, and that shame at appearing cowardly or base, which together constitute one of the most powerful counterweights to fear and hence to attempts to rule by intimidation. And fi- nally, the honorable quest for prestige is a sharp spur to political action, inspir- ing members of the privileged classes to look for great causes to champion and leading the people to long for the honor of serving under such champions.

Yet Montesquieu also teaches that these moral and political strengths of mon- archic honor are clouded by severe blemishes and costs. The principle of noblesse oblige cannot hide the basic unfairness of the class structure, or the fundamental lack of sympathy between the ruling elites and the often exploited masses. Even the exquisite politeness that is cultivated among the aristocrats must not deceive us into thinking that honor gives rise to a genuinely humane desire to please or com- fort one's fellow man. Speaking of his native France, Montesquieu writes, "we are polite out of pride: we feel ourselves flattered by having manners that prove that we are not lower-class, and that we haven't lived among *that* sort of people." *Politesse* has its real home at the royal court and among the courtiers, and we have seen the constellation of vices that both Montesquieu and eighteenth-century Americans found at the royal courts. Above all, monarchic honor is rooted in and conduces to a warlike temper. War, in fact, "is the distinguished profession, because its risks, its successes, and even its reverses, lead to grandeur." This zeal for the test of manly combat tends to go hand in hand with a disdain for productive labor and com- merce; honor inclines men to regard peace less as a time for productivity than as a time for indulging in fanatic duelling, along with imaginative luxuries and gallant love affairs.[25]

Moreover, the education of noblemen in monarchies breeds a certain "con- tempt for the honesty of the lower classes," because that ordinary honesty is grounded in a naive love of truthfulness, whereas the aristocratic virtue of frankness is grounded less in love of truth for its own sake and more in love of demonstrating one's independence and strength by a refusal to hide or to deceive. Accordingly, education through honor "permits deceit when it is joined to the idea of grandeur of spirit or greatness of affairs, as in politics."[26]

In this connection it is worth noting a less obtrusive but ultimately more decisive Montesquieuian criticism of the monarchic principle of honor. Montesquieu points out that the posture toward truth produced by this sense of honor is opposed not only to the un-self-conscious honesty of ordinary folk but also to the genuine and fully self-conscious love of truth that characterizes philosophy, or the highest form of education. The love of and pride in self that moves the typical European aristocrat is a love of and pride in, not one's true self, but one's self as viewed or regarded by others. Montesquieu thus anticipates to some extent the fundamental distinction on which Rousseau bases his searing critique of monarchic or aristocratic honor: the distinction between *amour propre*, or the self-love that can be almost identified with vanity, and *amour de soi*, or the genuine and independent love of and respect for oneself. In his very first thematic discussion of the principle of monarchy, Montesquieu puts the point with his inimitable ironic grace.

> It is true that, philosophically speaking, this is a false honor which moves all the parts of the State; but this false honor is as useful to the public, as the true would be to those individuals who might have the capacity to possess it. And isn't this quite an achievement—to oblige men to perform all the difficult actions, actions requiring force, without any other recompense except the noise those actions make?

In monarchy at its best, romance and heroism may flourish and the fine arts may scale splendid heights, but at a high price to the security, prosperity, and even the virtue of the populace at large.[27]

By and large, the Founders believed and hoped that some version of a gentlemanly sense of honor would continue to be one of the mainstays of leadership and public life in the new republic. But the monarchic honor that focused so heavily on distinction and prestige was largely alien and even galling to the American spirit. Much more appealing and valuable for the new nation was the independent-spirited republicanism of men like Cato, whose honor was not a substitute for virtue but an integral part of that virtue. Washington's example would indicate that a classical sense of honor could still take root, though rarely, in American soil. Let us examine more closely what specific form his sense of honor took, given that soil and given the principles of equality that he espoused.

Washington's Distinctive Republican Sense of Honor

In the first place, as we have seen, Washington's sense of honor did not depend upon his being active in politics. His freedom from the need for political involvement and power was connected to his American origins, to the fact that he was educated to respect the simple pleasures and simple dignity of owning one's own land and managing one's own affairs well. In the years before the outbreak of hostilities with England, Washington worked to give more substance to the independence of Virginia landowners by showing how they could diversify their crops and produce simple necessities by cottage industry, thereby breaking free of the perpetual debt to British agents to which most tobacco farmers fell prey. If these concerns seem mundane next to the heroism of the Roman Republic, it was, on the other hand, the very intensity of political life and political competition in Rome that helped make the advent of a Caesar almost inevitable. Washington, in lending dignity to the "tranquil enjoyments" of private life, demonstrated an independence that his humblest fellow citizen could emulate, and so strengthened the liberty of the country.

But given the momentous drama unfolding about him, Washington's sense of honor did require that he play a part in politics. As he and the other Founders agreed, the greatest question of the age concerned the fate of liberty or self-government. James Madison spoke proudly of "that honourable determination which animates every votary of freedom to rest all our political experiments on the capacity of mankind for self-government."[28] The cause was noble because it promised to bring honor to human nature, but the nature of the cause also made Washington's political task especially difficult. Not only did he need to accomplish great things in the revolutionary war and the presidency; he needed to achieve them in such a way that the people's honorable determination to rule would be supported. In leading a modern, commercial republic dedicated to the equal rights of its citizens, Washington could not live as the gentlemen of an aristocracy did. He had to give less attention to the splendor of his own life and to the cultivated artistic and scholarly pursuits of leisure, and more to the practical needs of the people. The very dedication to republican principles in which he took such pride set limits on his ambition: he satisfied the demands of his honor by resigning his military title when the war was won and by resigning from what could have become an elective monarchy for life so that his fellow citizens could compete regularly for the nation's highest office.

In conducting the war and disbanding the army at its close, Washington's republican code of honor dictated a strict adherence to lawfulness, even when this meant suffering great deprivations and military disadvantages. Convinced that liberty depended on the military's strict subordination to civil authorities, he resigned himself to accepting Congress's nearly worthless currency and accommo-

dated as best he could Congress's delinquencies in supplying the army and paying the troops. He resorted to forced requisitions only with great reluctance and
under strong pressure from the people's representatives themselves, preferring to
win the country's loyalty with his self-restraint while the British reaped hatred
through their disrespect for private property. Both his devotion to lawfulness
and his appreciation of the importance of public opinion led Washington to
take a similarly gentle position toward Tories and Tory property.[29]

The critical test of his willingness to uphold civilian authority came in the famous near-mutiny of officers at Newburg in 1783. Alexander Hamilton and the
top American financiers were secretly encouraging officers in Washington's
army to refuse to disband, and even threaten a revolt, unless Congress was allowed to impose a tax to pay the federal debts to the soldiers and creditors. Seeking to strengthen the central government, they thus risked destroying the nation. Washington, drawing upon his political skill as well as the influence he had
with the army, first condemned the irregular meeting of officers that had been
ominously proposed to consider new courses of redress and then called a meeting of his own, which he implied he would not attend. Catching the leaders off
guard, he appeared unexpectedly and addressed the officers. He castigated the
mutinous suggestions in anonymous letters that had been circulating in the
camp and gave an impassioned appeal to reason and moderation, to the men's
duty, their patriotism, and their honor. Sensing that the officers' smoldering resentment was still unquenched, he produced a reassuring letter from a congress-
man. He began to read it, stumbled, paused, and pulled out a pair of spectacles.
"I have grown gray in the service of my country," he said, "and now it seems I
am going blind." His officers wept, and the uprising crumbled. As Jefferson later
observed, "The moderation and virtue of a single character probably prevented
this Revolution from being closed, as most others have been, by a subversion of
the liberty it was intended to establish." No one knew better than Washington
the terrible defects of Congress under the Articles of Confederation, but he was
convinced that the only true solution to a free government's errors was to persuade and educate that government or the people themselves, thus honoring
the public's right and ability to make its own choices. Washington showed the
same spirit during the debate over the Constitution. After he had become a
staunch advocate of ratification, he protested a new post-office regulation that
impeded the free circulation of newspapers, for "the friends of the Constitution," he wrote, wished "the Public to be possessed of every thing, that might be
printed on both sides of the question."[30]

But if Washington's sense of honor impelled him to limit his personal ambitions and otherwise exercise self-restraint for the sake of the free government he
believed in, his honor also brought to his generalship and his presidency a high
tone and a stern dignity. In the army, severity was absolutely essential for com-

bating the disorder and insubordination of his democratically minded troops. Soon after he joined the Continental army in Boston, one observer remarked: "There is great overturning in the camp, as to order and regularity. New lords, new laws. . . . The strictest government is taking place, and great distinction is made between officers and soldiers. Every one is made to know his place and keep in it, or be tied up and receive thirty or forty lashes according to his crime."[31]

Washington understood that authority required coercion and punishment, but he believed that for force to be justified and truly effective, the men needed officers they judged worthy of respect, while the officers needed careful support for their personal sense of honor. Warning that officer and soldier ought not be put "too nearly on a level," he advised the governor of Virginia, Patrick Henry, that

> the person commanded yields but a reluctant obedience to those, he conceives, are undeservedly made his Superiors. The degrees of rank are frequently transferred from Civil life into . . . the Army. The true Criterion to judge by . . . is, to consider whether the Candidate for Office has a just pretention to the Character of a Gentleman, a proper sense of Honour, and some reputation to loose.[32]

In a thoughtful discussion on the role of honor and interest in the motives of ordinary men, Washington wrote:

> When men are irritated, and the Passions inflamed, they fly hastely to Arms; but after the first emotions are over, to expect, among such People, as compose the bulk of an Army, that they are influenced by any other principles than those of Interest, is to look for what never did, and I fear never will happen. . . . The few therefore, who act upon Principles of disinterestedness, are, comparatively speaking, no more than a drop in the Ocean. . . . As this Contest is not likely to be the Work of a day . . . you must have good Officers[;] there are, in my Judgment, no other possible means to obtain them but by establishing your Army upon a permanent footing; and giving your Officers good pay; this will induce Gentlemen, and Men of Character to engage; and till the bulk of your Officers are composed of such persons as are actuated by Principles of Honour, and a spirit of enterprize, you have little to expect from them. . . . They ought to have such allowances as will enable them to live like, and support the Characters of Gentlemen. . . . There is nothing that gives a Man Consequence, and renders him fit for Command, like a support that renders him Independent of Everybody but the State he Serves.[33]

Washington saw clearly that honor alone could not be counted on to make Americans serve the republic against their interests, but he saw equally clearly that without it the cause was lost. Though by itself too fragile a reed to build upon, the desire to act honorably can be supported and reinforced with the aid of outward honors. Among these money is especially important, but so too is the prospect of engaging in a respectable enterprise with the hope for regular advancement, which could be provided by "establishing the army on a permanent footing."

Washington seems to have had these same concerns in mind when he tried in a quiet way (too quietly for John Adams and some of the Federalists) to invest the presidency with "the dignity and respect that was due to the first Magistrate"—not only deploying his own great personal reserve, but arranging such ceremonies as formal levees and tea parties. He brought to the presidency his lifelong love of simple elegance, or as he put it, his taste for "everything which can tend to support propriety of character without partaking of the follies of luxury and ostentation." On the other hand, when we hear that Washington's preferred title for the president was "His High Mightiness, the President of the United States and Protector of their Liberties," we are likely to reflect that since simple elegance was not always his taste, it is well that more modest counsel prevailed. Less obtrusive, less monarchic, and less controversial—at least until the Jacksonians—was the stress laid, by Jeffersonians as well as Federalists, on the need for gentlemanly character and breeding in the federal civil service.[34]

Washington's great dignity was also useful to him in allowing him to remain somewhat above the political fray. This was important in the early days of his presidency, when his fairness, his diligence in making appointments strictly on merit, and his generally dignified conduct helped dissolve all opposition to the new Constitution.[35] It was equally useful to him at the end, as he resisted the terrible public clamor over the Jay Treaty and made the unpopular decision to ratify it, which was almost certainly best for the nation in the long run. A sense of honor of the kind Washington intended to cultivate helps a leader resist the worst traits of democracy—the adulation that can tempt popular leaders into tyranny, the insubordination that can destroy discipline, and the instability of passions that can lead to reckless and erratic courses of action. Eventually the young republic matured in some ways and the threat of monarchy, at least, receded. Yet such a sense of honor is still needed, if dauntingly difficult to attain. It takes a deeply rooted self-respect to withstand the pressures of angry public opinion, and great self-restraint to resist pleasing the people in ways that are not good for them. If we are right that Washington did indeed exercise these difficult virtues, it may be objected that the picture again begins to look somewhat incredible. How can a man give so much and take for himself so little?

Let us look once more at Cato. He also seems, in a sense, too noble to be credible. Yet in another sense, we may say that Cato is a man who takes all the nobility for himself, who commands his son to retreat to an "obscurely good" private life while he chooses the noble death of a martyr to liberty. Even in his willingness *not* to lavish his followers' blood in order to make his own end more glorious, he chooses for himself the higher nobility of being generous. Such sublime motives have little in common with what we usually regard as selfishness, yet we must not lose sight of the fact that what Cato acts upon *is* self-love. For the deepest self-love is not a love of pleasure, money, long life, or even reputation, but a love of one's soul which one longs to make as fine and as splendid as possible, by claiming for oneself the most worthy actions.[36]

Washington's case is of course complicated by the fact that he did not seem to love or need political action in the way that Cato did. If his alacrity in resigning power and his professed reluctance to assume it made him all the more trusted by the people, it also makes his motives harder to understand. Yet Cato, too, was cool to *most* of what charmed other men about politics. And for all of his talk of duty and sacrifice, it was also Washington who said, "There is no truth more thoroughly established, than that there exists in the economy and course of nature, an indissoluble union between virtue and happiness."[37] In the end, given the choices he found himself facing, Washington clearly felt that only a life of continued public service was truly worthy of him and his talents—that though such a life's frustrations were many, and its pleasures somewhat rare or rarified, it could be deemed ultimately the life most noble and most worth having. To this extent Washington, like Cato, reveals a deeply enlightened self-interest. By failing to take seriously virtue or true honor as a motive, most modern scholars fail to see the rich form of self-love present even here. Such men as Washington are not truly "disinterested," but neither can they be called selfish. Indeed, by providing an example of what it looks like to care for oneself in the deepest possible way, they gave their countries perhaps their greatest gift.

We have devoted considerable space to Washington's life because we believe that the kind of example he offers is what is most needed in the civic education of any republic, and especially that of contemporary America. The monarchies of Montesquieu's Europe could keep even shallow and thoughtless men living up to a code of honor by appealing to their concerns for appearance, and they could elicit impressive sacrifices from those most ambitious for fame. But a country that is free of rigid class structures is also left without the clear-cut expectations and public censure that restrains most members of monarchic society. Appealing to the love of fame today is as likely to evoke dreams of becoming a rock star or even a powerful drug dealer as to encourage hopes of serving in politics. We need an education that explores frankly and insistently not the question of what will make us shine but the question of what is genuinely good for us as human beings: what kind of life will bring the deepest and most lasting happiness, the richest friendships, and the most challenging and satisfying work. There is of course more than one kind of life that can claim to provide these things. But a strong case can be made that each claimant must include integrity and a measure of service to others, and that the pursuit of fame is hollow unless we begin and end with the question of what we ourselves truly respect and would be proud to become. This question will be answered badly if teachers and students try, as too often they do, to examine their desires and aspirations in the abstract. The inquiry can be fruitful, however, if conducted in the light of a life like Washington's, and if Washington himself is presented in all his struggling humanity and his true greatness.

13 · Thomas Jefferson and the Natural Basis of Moral Education

Washington is a daunting model. For a bold few he may provide a pattern to emulate directly, but for most of us he serves best as a kind of pole star—a reminder of much of what is highest in human nature and of potentialities within ourselves that should be encouraged. Just as Washington's rather distant respect for learning made him a deeper and more dignified man, though he never became a scholar, so ordinary citizens who have none of his capacity for leadership may become more serious individuals by studying, reflecting upon, and honoring men like Washington. Less forbidding, and in his account of virtue more encouraging, was Thomas Jefferson. Whereas the dignity that made Washington inspiring to the whole nation kept him somewhat aloof from even his closest aides and protégés, Jefferson cultivated unusually warm and lasting ties with a large number of young relations and students. His rich correspondence with some of these individuals provides a model of the fatherly guidance that he thought was most effective, especially in moral education. And through his letters, Jefferson elaborates an understanding of virtue that fits with his trust in the common man.

The Moral "Sense" and the Clarity of Virtue

Like Washington, Jefferson presents morality as primarily a simple matter, requiring no special training or subtle reasoning. Indeed, the clarity and accessibility of morality is part of Jefferson's fundamental creed.

> He who made us would have been a pitiful bungler if he had made the rules of moral conduct a matter of science. For one man of science, there are thousands who are not. What would have become of them? . . . State a moral case to a ploughman and a professor. The former will decide it as

well, and often better than the latter, because he has not been led astray by artificial rules."[1]

Whereas Washington emphasizes the great self-overcoming needed to live according to what we know to be right, Jefferson stresses the natural foundation of virtue, in what he calls the "moral instinct."

What exactly does Jefferson mean by the moral instinct, or sense, and how far does he suggest it is to be trusted? For Jefferson, morality comprises those principles of action that are necessary in order for human beings to live happily together in society. As he explains to his nephew Peter Carr in the same letter just quoted: "Man was destined for society. His morality therefore was to be formed to this object. He was endowed with a sense of right and wrong merely relative to this." In a famous 1814 letter to Thomas Law, Jefferson gives his fullest analysis of the motives that impel men to follow the principles of morality or virtue.[2] People do not do what is right out of respect for the truth (the truth, for instance, that the money one is tempted to steal does not belong to one), or out of a sense of the noble or beautiful—this, he argues, only governs matters of taste, not morals. Nor is the ultimate cause of virtue a love of God, for then "whence arises the morality of the atheist?" And neither, finally, is self-love the spur to morality. Jefferson concedes that we naturally take pleasure in being useful to others, especially when they are suffering. But he refuses to conclude that we perform moral acts for the sake of the pleasure that they bring us, for then we would really be acting selfishly. The key question, he argues, is *why* do good acts give us pleasure? The reason is, "because nature hath implanted in our breasts a love of others, a sense of duty to them, a moral instinct, in short, which prompts us irresistibly to feel and to succor their distresses."

In other words, man is a being who chooses to act not only to secure his own welfare and happiness but also to promote the welfare and happiness of others. A love for our fellows, or a sense of duty to them (which is not quite the same thing), is what allows us to go beyond the dictates of narrow self-interest, extending ourselves and even sacrificing ourselves in order to comfort, assist, and defend the rights of others. Jefferson maintains that the capacity to feel a bond with one's fellows, and an instinctive knowledge of how they should be treated, is, like sight or hearing, naturally present in all men and in men of all races, with the exception of a misshapen few. He indicates that motives to virtue beyond the moral sense, including calculations of self-interest, a desire for love, and the fear of punishment in this world or in the next, are all incidental supports, which become essential only where the moral sense is absent or truncated. At the same time, he observes that the moral instinct, like the arm or the leg, can be strengthened through exercise or atrophied through disuse: hence the importance of a moral education that will support and exercise it.

Utility as the Guide of the Moral Sense

While he does not confront the difficulty involved in defining the moral sense as simultaneously both love or inclination and duty, Jefferson does go on, in the letter to Law, to address another far-reaching problem. Why, it may be objected, should a natural moral sense have produced such varied codes of conduct that "the same actions are deemed virtuous in one country and vicious in another"? Jefferson gives no examples, but presumably he has in mind such well-known oddities as the Spartans' rewarding young boys for theft if they get away uncaught. In reply Jefferson writes, "Nature has constituted *utility* to man the standard and test of virtue." Nature does not teach individuals to perform specific acts, but to love and promote the happiness of those around them. In a society dedicated to ceaseless warfare, stealth and cunning make one valuable to one's fellows. Jefferson thus recognizes a kernel of goodness at the core of even the strangest moral rules, and to this extent he makes allowance for cultural differences. But his understanding is that the differences among moral codes result in part from hard necessities—like the need to be always fighting, or the oppressions of a tyrannical government—and in part from fundamental disagreements about what constitutes human happiness—disagreements, for example, between those who see happiness as the salvation of the soul through repentance and those who identify it with the cultivation of a proud martial valor. Now on disputes about the nature of happiness, Jefferson is far from neutral. He therefore could never agree with the modern dictum that all cultures, and all cultures' moralities, are equal.

In particular, Jefferson excoriates the social and moral effects of an absolute monarchy like that of France, where, as he puts it in a letter to an American lady, "the people here are ground to powder by the vices of the form of government." This judgment does not prevent Jefferson from delighting in the smoothness and grace of French aristocratic manners, and he grants in the same letter that perhaps "their manners may be the best calculated for happiness to a people in their situation." Even if their "pursuits of happiness" are ultimately "fallacious," focusing as they do, not on virtuous independence, but on luxury, vanity, and sexual intrigue, yet "they seem on the whole to furnish the most effectual abstraction from a contemplation of the hardness of their government." Thus while French manners and morals are arguably the best that they can be under the circumstances, they are far from being the best simply: "Every step we take towards the adoption of their manners is a step to perfect misery." In monarchic France the moral sense might lead one to sooth the vanity of one's friends and to divert them from contemplating the oppression of a government they cannot change, but what may be relatively useful in a corrupt society is not what will be most truly useful for people living as they were intended to live and can live under the best form of government.[3]

Jefferson's allowance for cultural differences, however, casts into question his claim that virtue is clear and simple. For if virtue means promoting the true happiness of others, and if nations have differed radically in their account of this happiness, then true virtue requires a deep probing into the nature of man and human happiness; or, at the least, the good fortune to chance upon teachers who possess a correct understanding of these deep matters. Accordingly, Jefferson lived and wrote as though the young did not know the nature of true happiness, but needed to be taught it.

The Problematic Relation Between the Moral Sense and Virtue Conceived as Self-Sufficiency

In a revealing statement of the function of the elementary schools, after discussing the importance of teaching history—and denying the appropriateness of Bible study—Jefferson continues:

> The first elements of morality too may be instilled into their minds; such as, when further developed as their judgments advance in strength, may teach them how to work out their own greatest happiness, by shewing them that it does not depend on the condition of life in which chance has placed them, but is always the result of good conscience, good health, occupation, and freedom in all just pursuits.[4]

Paradoxically, although the moral sense knits society together and makes people care about each others' happiness, correct judgment would seem to teach that happiness is largely the result of self-sufficiency. Truly being of service to others would thus involve guiding them to live in a clear-sighted way, to rely on themselves, to cherish liberty as the greatest of goods, and not to be tempted to injustice by failing to see that the power to be happy lies within. Jefferson of course thought of utility largely in material terms and believed that an important means of promoting America's happiness lay in making the country more prosperous. He even once wrote, with characteristic hyperbole, that "the greatest service which can be rendered any country is to add a useful plant to its culture."[5] Yet even here, the essential utility consists not so much in feeding mouths as in helping people of modest means to become more successfully self-reliant.

What are the practical consequences for moral education of Jefferson's association of virtue with self-sufficiency? In the training that he in fact helps provide for his young charges, the main thrust of his efforts appears to be aimed less at impressing them with a sense of duty, than at instilling in them a certain view of happiness and—despite his denial that morality involves taste—cultivating a relish or an inclination for the life of independence and industry. "The whole art of being happy consists in the art of finding employment," Jefferson writes to his daughter Martha. "I know of none so interesting, and which crowd upon us as much, as those of a domestic nature." Or, as he warns her in another typical passage:

> It is your future happiness which interests me, and nothing can contribute more to it (moral rectitude always excepted) than the contracting a habit of industry and activity. Of all the cankers of human happiness, none corrodes it with so silent, yet so baneful a tooth as indolence. . . . If at any moment you catch yourself in idleness, my dear, start from it as you would from the precipice of a gulph.[6]

An idle person is dependent on others both for the comforts and necessities of life and for relief from ennui, Jefferson goes on to explain. But if his daughter learns industry and resourcefulness, she will be well prepared for life in America, where, remote from all other aid, "we are obliged to invent and to execute; to find means within ourselves, and not to lean on others." More important, she will be thereby prepared for a greater happiness: the solid happiness and self-esteem of one who has learned to amuse herself through music and drawing, learned to enjoy and profit from books, invention, and exercise, and above all learned the rewards of managing her household effectively and living harmoniously in her domestic circle. In seeking to make his children and grandchildren capable and industrious, Jefferson fills his letters with friendly cajoling—to work at everything from Latin to needlepoint, to control their tempers, to read Cervantes, to make puddings and to observe closely when the whippoorwills and peas first appear in spring. "It is wonderful how much may be done," he writes, "if we are always doing."[7]

What is the precise relationship between the moral sense and the self-reliant happiness that is always the goal of Jefferson's moral instruction? Happiness, as Jefferson presents it, is close to Locke's understanding, which involves living in a rational, dignified way, being master of oneself, and enjoying the blessings of liberty and the free exercise of one's rights. But in Locke's philosophy, men's obligations to one another are defined by their rights; there is no teaching about a moral sense. Jefferson, following Shaftesbury and the Scottish enlightenment thinkers Shaftesbury influenced, apparently felt that in Locke's account there was something missing. On the one hand, Locke's philosophy did not seem to do justice to what Jefferson saw as the genuine benevolence that binds humanity together and that goes beyond calculations of mutual advantage. On the other hand, Locke's system, despite its carefully worked-out education in virtue, may not adequately explain why people should make difficult sacrifices for one another, as every society at times requires them to do. Jefferson thus supplements a fundamentally Lockean view of human nature with the idea of the moral sense, which may help to bridge the gap between the good of the individual and that of society.

Still, it is not clear that in Jefferson's understanding the moral sense will ever obligate people to forfeit their true good for that of others. Jefferson gives many reasons why moral action is good for the man who performs it: he will enjoy the pleasure that one naturally feels in exercising virtue and will win for himself love and gratitude, which are intrinsically precious to beings created to be social. Jefferson also insists that it is always most prudent in the long run to hold oneself to "truth, justice, and plain dealing." Following his argument, clear-sighted individuals will see that their own interests are served by promoting the liberty and prosperity of their nation and even of other nations.[8]

Yet in Jefferson's most comprehensive and theoretical account of virtue—the letter to Law—he emphasizes that morality is directly opposed to selfishness. He maintains that for the person whose moral sense is not defective, virtuous action is first and foremost for the sake of others, rather than oneself, and only secondarily for the sake of the pleasure one derives from benefiting others.

Nevertheless, in writing to his young relations, Jefferson consistently extols virtue as the best means to their *own* happiness. One may wonder if Jefferson ever entirely made up his mind as to whether virtue is altogether for others, or really for oneself, or felicitously and almost miraculously for both at the same time.

Protecting and Cultivating the Moral Sense

This much is clear: in Jefferson's view, preserving and strengthening the moral sense in its natural purity is essential to living well, not only because of the joys of human fellowship but above all because moral corruption leads men to pursue an illusory happiness. Jefferson finds in the simplicity and ruggedness of life in the American countryside a great support for purity of morals as well as for self-reliant independence. Consequently, he argues for keeping American youths away from the vices of European cities. There, as he describes it, they will learn to be fascinated with the privileges of aristocracy, with luxury, and with sexual intrigue, and they will return home ignorant and contemptuous of the simple manners, the practical arts, the language, and the people that they need to know and respect in order to make their way.[9]

This same concern not to corrupt the simple and therefore healthy taste of young Americans is seen in Jefferson's desire—paradoxical in such a champion of enlightenment—to restrict his daughter's reading of certain kinds of books, particularly novels.

> A great obstacle to good education is the inordinate passion prevalent for novels, and the time lost in that reading which should be instructively employed. When this poison infects the mind, it destroys its tone and revolts it against wholesome reading. Reason and fact, plain and unadorned, are rejected. Nothing can engage attention unless dressed in all the figments of fancy, and nothing so bedecked comes amiss. The result is a bloated imagination, sickly judgment, and disgust towards all the real business of life.[10]

According to Jefferson, the moral sense is a faculty that needs to be nurtured and exercised as well as shielded from corruption. Thus he instructs Peter Carr to "read good books, because they will encourage, as well as direct your feelings. The writings of Sterne, particularly, form the best course of morality that ever was written." Laurence Sterne apparently wins such a high recommendation from Jefferson mainly on the strength of his published sermons. A popular and engaging but morally serious writer, Laurence Sterne portrays throughout his sermons the charms of virtue and the ugliness of vice. He puts charity or compassion at the very core of virtue, describing the pleasure of doing a charitable act as the greatest of pleasures, and the rewards of social intercourse as that which makes life worth living. Like Jefferson, he believes that an all-wise Creator "has implanted in mankind such appetites and inclinations . . . as would naturally lead him to the love of society and friendship." Sterne is intent on vindicating human nature against those who would malign it by calling all people selfish, for "surely, 'tis one step towards acting well, to think worthily of our nature."[11]

Reading these sermons would remind the young person to respect and cherish that which Jefferson and Sterne agree is best in human nature and which Jefferson calls the moral sense. But Stern interlaces this cheerful and encouraging view of mankind with expressions of the more ominous side of Christianity: reminders of the judgment day to come and admonitions that life on earth is fleeting and full of vanity and sorrow. While Sterne does appeal to the moral inclinations, then, suggesting at times that the virtuous will be happy, he elsewhere relies heavily upon hopes of divine reward and fears of divine punishment, and implies that little else matters. But Jefferson, in the same letter in which he recommends Sterne, urges the young Peter Carr to be fearless in questioning religion, arguing that he will find sufficient incentives to virtue "in the comfort and pleasantness you feel in it's exercise, and the love of others which it will procure you." Jefferson's referral to such a course of sermons, however, raises some question as to how clear he was in his own mind about jettisoning the support of faith altogether.

Jefferson also engages in his own exhortation to strengthen the moral sense. He calls on his daughter Martha to listen always to her conscience, to "lose no opportunity of exercising your heart in benevolence," and to perform the good offices of teaching her small sister to be truthful, never angry, and constantly industrious. But in praising virtue and kindness to his daughters, he, like Sterne, invariably draws in other motives beyond the pure feelings of benevolence. Later, urging a now-married Martha not to desert her sister-in-law who has been accused of adultery, he appeals to her compassion: "Never throw off the best affections of nature in the moment when they become most precious to their object; nor fear to extend your hand to save another, lest you should sink yourself." But right away he adds, "Your kindness will help her and count in your own favor also." The tone of all his advice is summed up in this counsel to twelve-year-old Mary: "Be good my dear, as I have always found you, never be angry with any body, nor speak harm of them, try to let every body's faults be forgotten, as you would wish yours to be; take more pleasure in giving what is best to another than in having it yourself, and then all the world will love you, and I more than all the world."[12] Here and elsewhere, Jefferson unabashedly holds out his love not only as a reward but as a crucial incentive for good behavior.

The Power of Examples

Jefferson urged his young charges to strengthen their moral sense through exercise, until they had acquired established habits of doing what is right. Yet his opportunities to oversee even his own children's practice of virtue were limited, since his political duties allowed for intermittent contact at best. From a distance, he cajoled and demanded that the youngsters provide frequent accounts of themselves. He hoped that giving Martha the duty of instructing her younger sister in virtue would make Martha more careful about her own behavior. But ultimately Jefferson believed that the strongest influence on one's habits lay in the examples one found to emulate.

Pointing youths who were far from home toward good models was a special concern for Jefferson. In a fatherly letter to his sixteen-year-old grandson, away at school for the first time, he holds up his own youth to the boy to illustrate the use that one should make of others' examples.

When I recollect that at fourteen years of age, the whole care & direction of myself was thrown on myself entirely, without a relation or a friend qualified to advise or guide me, and recollect the various sorts of bad company with which I associated from time to time, I am astonished I did not turn off with some of them, & become as worthless to society as they were. I had the good fortune to become acquainted very early with some characters of very high standing, and to feel the incessant wish that I could ever become what they were. Under temptations & difficulties, I would ask myself what would Dr. Small, Mr. Wythe, Peyton Randolph do in this situation? What course in it will insure me their approbation? I am certain that this mode of deciding on my conduct tended more to its correctness than any reasoning powers I possessed.[13]

Jefferson goes on to describe the many types of men that he was occasionally captivated by as a boy, from horse-racers to clever lawyers to great statesmen, and he recounts how in moments of excitement he would regain perspective by asking himself which kind of reputation he would ultimately prefer. He urges the wisdom of "these little returns into ourselves," in which one takes time to envision a picture of the life that seems most admirable and uses this picture to inspire and steady oneself in pursuing the goal, particularly at moments when passions run high and threaten to subvert reason. In asking, "What would Wythe do?" or in considering his future reputation, then, Jefferson was not simply relying on others' opinions for moral guidance, nor was he appealing to his own vanity to the exclusion of his moral instinct. For without independent good judgment, he never could have singled out the most virtuous mentors or recognized the superior merit in being known as—and being—"the honest advocate of my country's rights." At the same time, Jefferson's letter shows that personal models are so powerful precisely because they do appeal to more than one motive. The image of a fine life captivates us and makes us want to be like the one we admire, but the knowledge that such a life would captivate others, bringing us a fine reputation, is itself a part of that life's charm.

Jefferson understood that inspiring exemplars are far more persuasive to the young than cold reasoning, an insight that has been shared by thoughtful individuals in every civilization: this is why storytelling and not philosophical argument has always been at the core of effective moral education. But Jefferson himself did not carry this awareness as far as he might have. Although in the letter to Law he calls the moral instinct "the brightest gem with which the human character is studded" and considers "the want of it as more degrading than the most hideous of the bodily deformities," he never stresses the connection between beauty or the arts and morality; as his remarks on novels attest, he is ambivalent about enlisting the imagination as an ally in moral education. Jefferson himself was able as a young man to win the friendship of leading Virginians, and he could recommend to Martha the company of David Rittenhouse, one of the country's greatest living scientists, as a model of the "rational life." Yet ordinary citizens, lacking these personal contacts, may find their best inspiration in colorful stories about outstanding characters—stories that will capture the imagination at the same time that they lend support to living rationally. It is this crucial role of popular literature that Jefferson seems not to have sufficiently appreciated.[14]

The Difficulty in Jefferson's Moral Sense Teaching

Jefferson's use of a variety of motives in moral education leaves us wondering whether the moral sense alone is ever adequate to fill the function that he assigns to it. Does the moral sense in fact carry within it sufficient incentives to make men treat one another justly and generously? In the rather theoretical letter to Law, Jefferson suggests that motives beyond the love of others, and the natural inclination to be good to them, are really only needed in the worst cases. He implies that the main work of moral education will be to preserve, encourage, and exercise the child's natural benevolence. But his more practical family letters show a recognition that consistent appeals to further motives are indeed necessary. While Jefferson may find Locke's conception of morality too narrow, he never dispenses with the external sanctions Locke recommends, and in fact he follows Locke's educational advice rather closely. Both Jefferson and Locke seek to avoid the use of coercion, fear, and public humiliation. Both minimize the role of religion (or "superstition") in education, delaying the introduction of Bible study and keeping religious instruction as simple and rational as possible. Both rely heavily on the young person's desire to be loved and on the sense of shame that makes him crave the good opinion of those that matter to him. We are reminded again of Jefferson's call for moderation in governing students at the University of Virginia.

> Pride of character, laudable ambition, and moral dispositions are innate correctives to the indiscretions of that lively age; and when strengthened by habitual appeal and exercise, have a happier effect on future character than the degrading motive of fear. Hardening them to disgrace, to corporal punishments, and servile humiliations cannot be the best process for producing erect character. The affectionate deportment between father and son, offers in truth the best example for that of tutor and pupil.[15]

Pride and ambition, not themselves moral dispositions, are needed to impel students to seek excellence and also to buttress their natural benevolence. Exhortation can provide a "habitual appeal" to the moral sense and to pride, honor, and other motives as well. But these techniques are unlikely to build a sterling char-

acter without something more: the affectionate bond between a youth and a father or fatherly friend whom he can admire and copy and whose love and respect he hungers for. We are reminded again of the young Juba in Addison's
Cato. Moral education is difficult or impossible without love.

Why does virtue require so much reinforcement if the moral sense is natural?
Is it only because the passions of youth cloud one's vision? Are the incentives of
winning love and reputation needed only by those who are immature and have
not yet acquired habitual ascendancy over their impulses? Jefferson seems to indicate that virtue can stand on its own once self-control becomes habitual, for
then the individual will find confirmation for the claim that honoring one's natural love for others will make one happy and fulfilled. Yet there remains in Jefferson's writing a shadow lingering over this sunny portrayal. The problem is that
the convergence of virtue and happiness is *not* altogether clear. Although Jefferson criticizes the ancient philosophers' coldness in failing to teach peace, charity, and love for all humanity, he elsewhere calls himself an Epicurean and summarizes Epicurus's moral teachings as follows:

> Happiness the aim of life.
> Virtue the foundation of happiness.
> Utility the test of virtue.
> Pleasure active and In-do-lent.
> Indolence is the absence of pain, the true felicity.
> Active, consists in agreeable motion; it is not happiness, but the means
> to produce it.
> The *summum bonum* is to be not pained in body, nor troubled in mind.[16]

The tension between the moral sense that prompts a person to generous
action and the philosophy that counsels tranquil detachment is recalled in Jefferson's famous dialogue between the head and the heart. Addressing a married
lady with whom he has fallen in love, Jefferson voices alternately the part of
himself that reproaches his reckless proclivity for sentimental attachments and
the part that finds in love and friendship the joy of life. The head declaims:

> The most effectual means of being secure against pain is to retire within
> ourselves, and to suffice for our own happiness. Those, which depend
> on ourselves, are the only pleasures a wise man will count on; for nothing is
> ours which another may deprive us of. Hence the inestimable value of in-
> tellectual pleasures. Friendship is but another name for an alliance with the
> follies and the misfortunes of others.

But the heart has the last word. Scorning the idea of self-sufficiency in a world
so full of "want and accident," the heart knows the need for friends and reflects

that "nobody will care for him, who cares for nobody." But further, "Friendship is precious, not only in the shade, but in the sunshine of life." The heart closes by asserting its title to rule in the moral realm and by commanding the head to confine its claims of preeminence to matters of science.[17]

Throughout his life Jefferson lived with the tension that he here describes as a dichotomy between head and heart. At nearly every important juncture, he chose to act according to the "heart" and its social urgings, surrounding himself with company and devoting himself to public service. Yet again and again, he spoke and wrote in a way that denigrated public life. Not only does he characterize politics as a burden, and political honors as "splendid torments," but he portrays the highest as well as the happiest life as one of quiet contemplation. In a remarkable letter to David Rittenhouse, he concedes the "obligation those are under" who are able to conduct government, but he puts Rittenhouse above this obligation: "Are those powers then, which being intended for the erudition of the world, like air and light, the world's common property, to be taken from their proper pursuit to do the commonplace drudgery of governing a single state, a work which may be executed by men of an ordinary stature, such as are always and everywhere to be found?"[18] Presumably Rittenhouse escapes political duty only because he contributes something more valuable to the world; and to that extent, the letter does not simply support Jefferson's Epicurean side. But by depicting the contemplative life so brightly and public life so darkly, Jefferson renders problematic his claims about political duty. Whence arises the "obligation" to "drudgery" in people of moderate talents? Jefferson does not explain this, and clearly if his heart teaches him that he has such an obligation, it does not teach him to enjoy fulfilling it.

After all, the teaching of the heart is deeply ambiguous. The heart is selfish as well as generous; that is why people must be *commanded* to love one another. As Jefferson puts it, self-love is "the antagonist of virtue." Even when self-love is kept in check, the social instincts of the heart may lead only to close ties with a few and not to universal benevolence, service, or even minimal justice. Again addressing one of his daughters, he writes: "The circle of our nearest connections is the only one in which faithful and lasting affection can be found, one which will adhere to us under all changes and chances. It is therefore the only soil on which it is worth while to bestow much culture."[19]

None of this is to deny that a child's selfish urges may be countered by a concerted effort to encourage his or her benevolence, compassion, sensitivity to others' feelings, and desire to win love. But constant reliance on such motives may well reduce the child's moral impulse to a general obligingness that is not anchored in firm and clearly articulated principles and that therefore falls short of true virtue. For the problem is that virtuous action is at times neither comfortable nor pleasant nor useful to us nor endearing to those around us. Jefferson's guidelines offer little support for one whose conscience tells one to take a lonely and unpopular stand, to remain honest when cheating would seem immune to discovery and harmful to no one, to shoulder responsibility for one's own actions even if great damage might result and a convenient scapegoat is ready at hand, or indeed to die for one's country. Considerations of reputation may help in the last case, but on the other hand, if one's country is fighting an unpopular war, they may not. By stressing the social nature and social rewards of virtue, Jefferson's system runs the risk of leaving people at the mercy of public opinion and their sense of shame, both of which may steer them amiss. And by emphasizing the utility of virtue, Jefferson may increase the temptation to see morality as a tool that may be set aside when its contribution to one's own happiness looks doubtful.

The Original, Aristotelian Teaching on the Moral "Sense"

At those moments when virtue is most difficult, the argument that it always promotes one's personal happiness, made in the way that Jefferson makes it, begins to ring hollow. But there is another way of understanding the connection between virtue and happiness that more successfully meets this problem. This understanding finds its clearest expression in Aristotle's *Nicomachean Ethics*, the work that is in fact the fountainhead of the idea of the moral "sense" (*aisthēsis*).[20] Aristotle argues that virtue is, at root, not only a proper stance toward other people, as Jefferson claims, but even more a proper stance toward oneself. The moral sense of the truly virtuous man leads him to choose to be courageous and just, not primarily because of the benefits that will accrue to others, or because of the gains he may expect for himself in security or reputation or love, but above all because courageous and just deeds are in themselves noble, and because in performing them, he makes himself a nobler man. What characterizes virtue for Aristotle is its inherent beauty or nobility; the Greek word, *to kalon*, serves equally for both.

Aristotle contends that virtue brings happiness because it is the excellence or proper fulfillment of human nature—and not just of one instinct in human nature that is opposed by other instincts, as Jefferson seems to suggest. Long experience in life, or an upbringing by parents and civic leaders who have such experience, gives individuals a "perception" or "sense" of the moral and of the specific virtues that belong to it. These virtues must be applied with careful thought to circumstances, but in Aristotle's account, they have a validity that does not depend upon consistently useful outcomes and still less on the approbation of shifting public opinion. Aristotle thus provides moral strength in those situations where shame and considerations of utility can encourage moral weakness. Aristotle goes so far as to deny that shame is compatible with a fully developed moral sense. Shame is appropriate for the young, not the mature moral person. Yet while Aristotle's system supports friendship and justice, it does not teach the universal benevolence that Christianity does. Indeed, in encouraging its followers to view virtue chiefly as a duty to themselves, it can leave them somewhat cold in its exercise, at times treating other men less as brothers to be loved than as objects upon which virtue may exercise and display itself. One may wonder whether Aristotle resolves, or only brings out and forces one to confront, the fundamental tension in moral life between duty to others and concern for the health of one's own soul.

The Uneasy Jeffersonian Compromise

Jefferson does occasionally speak of virtue in terms reminiscent of Aristotle. In an early letter to Peter Carr, he describes virtue as the greatest of goods and the source of "the most sublime comforts" throughout life. Although he never explains why virtue produces the highest or greatest comforts, it seems likely that he sees in a good conscience the core of self-respect. Given his deep concern with fostering independence and dignity in the individual, he might well have put more emphasis on self-respect as a motive to virtue, but at least it is implicit in this letter. Jefferson goes on to make the familiar argument that honesty is the best policy. He buttresses it, however, with reflections on how mean, pitiable, and contemptible the inveterate liar is, and how a habit of dishonesty corrupts the heart "and in time depraves it of all its good dispositions." To his fifteen-year-old nephew, then, Jefferson commends virtue as a fine thing in itself—good not only for the fortunes, but for the soul of the one who possesses it.[21]

Yet this characterization is rather at odds with Jefferson's argument that virtue is a social duty, performed for the sake of others. And the problem with Jefferson's rather easygoing eclecticism is that he rarely confronts and tries to resolve the tensions between the many threads of his thought. We are left with two predominant strands in his moral reasoning, which pull ultimately in different directions and which exhibit two dangerous proclivities. On the one hand, Jefferson's account of happiness focuses on independence, self-reliance, and the quiet but solid enjoyments of study and domestic life. Especially when there is little stress laid upon cultivating the excellence of a noble or beautiful soul, a pursuit of such happiness can degenerate into what Tocqueville describes as "individualism," a failure to care about anything beyond oneself and one's small circle of intimates. The other strand in Jefferson's thought is his teaching about the moral sense. This teaching is designed to promote harmony and respect for the feelings and opinions of others in a community of ordinary men, and hence (unlike Aristotle's aristocratic and rather competitive virtue), it is suited to a democracy. Yet for the same reason, this conception of virtue tends to undermine that very spirit of personal independence that Jefferson cherishes and considers a bulwark of freedom. Tocqueville identifies this danger also, as one aspect of the "tyranny of the majority." And Tocqueville further reveals the connection between the two problems: The more individuals withdraw into themselves, the more isolated and insignificant they become, and the more easily they are overawed by the opinions of the mass of their fellows. Jefferson's community-oriented virtue is of course useful in checking the ambitions of dangerous leaders. But by encouraging individuals to be swayed by the crowd, it works to prevent the rise of the "great-souled man" whom Aristotle praises, the proud and independent spirit like Winston Churchill, who alone can steer a nation safely through its gravest crises.

14 · Benjamin Franklin and the Art of Virtue

Of all the Founders, the one who set himself up most deliberately as a model for moral education was Benjamin Franklin. Franklin did not cherish the role of personal mentor to the extent that Jefferson did, and his relations with his own family were often somewhat distant. Yet in his chief contribution to American education, the intimate if carefully edited self-portrait that he provides in his *Autobiography*, Franklin virtually takes the whole country into his confidence. The work is frankly didactic, and its lessons are all in one sense or another moral lessons. Drawing over his immodest ambitions the decorous but in no way obscuring veil of two friends' letters, Franklin reveals at the beginning of part 2 of the *Autobiography* the hopes for this book that have inspired him to resume his narrative. The work is meant to form future great leaders and promote the happiness of everyone, by teaching wisdom, prudence, industry, frugality, temperance, pacific manners, good humor, self-education, the resolution to do good and the means to carry it out, freedom from shame at one's low origins, patience, the art of enjoying life, disinterestedness, and, of course, modesty. Moreover, Franklin expects the book to serve as the best advertisement for America that anyone could devise. Through it, he hopes to further international understanding, give crucial historical information on a great and rising people, and prove that he, "the author" of the Revolution, has been influenced by virtuous principles—thereby demonstrating that human nature is essentially good as well as capable of continuing improvement. Finally, the *Autobiography* will teach a fine style of writing, and give innocent pleasure "not only to a few, but to millions."[1]

How Franklin could be at once so didactic, so ingenuously presuming, and so irresistibly charming is one question that this chapter will take up. Our more central concern will be to explore a further, less explicit, but equally audacious ambition of the *Autobiography*: Franklin's endeavor to change the whole way we look at virtue. For Franklin undertakes to prove that properly understood, there truly is no tension between virtue and self-interest, or between the good of oneself and the good of others. In his efforts to overcome this problem that lurks unresolved in Jefferson's moral thought and that renders puzzling Aristotle's moral philosophy, Franklin is remarkably if not wholly successful.

Industry and Humanity

The lessons of the *Autobiography* come mainly by example. There are many stories with many characters and morals here, but always in the midst of them is the young Franklin, who enters Philadelphia at seventeen as a runaway apprentice, hungry and exhausted, with no friends, no credentials, a few odd coins, and presently two large rolls to stuff in the pockets of his dirty clothes (75–76). Franklin dwells on these details to excite the hope and quiet the shame of any reader who might be borne down by his own low circumstances. (Franklin of course has no objections if the tale of these "unlikely Beginnings" also adds glory to his own later achievements.) More important, Franklin teaches those whose expectations he has whetted what they must do to succeed. Countless anecdotes urge the merits of honesty, frugality, resolution, and especially industry. For Franklin it is a fundamental tenet that "one man of tolerable Abilities may work great Changes, and accomplish great Affairs among Mankind, if he first forms a good Plan, and, cutting off all Amusements or other Employments that would divert his Attention, makes the Execution of that same Plan his sole Study and Business" (163).

Franklin illustrates the rich rewards of prudent industry through his own bright, energetic, Yankee example, but no less through the shadowy tales of those self-indulgent or improvident acquaintances who fail and drift off to the West Indies, there presumably to sink into an alcoholic stupor or to languish of some tropical disease.[2] The material gains from industry are not, however, its only or even its greatest rewards. Franklin tells the story of how he led a small force to the frontier to build fortifications and of the rapid progress that they made on fair days, interrupted by days of hard rain.

> This gave me occasion to observe, that when Men are employ'd they are best contented. For on the Days they work'd they were good-natur'd and chearful; and with the consciousness of having done a good Days work they spent the Evenings jollily; but on the idle Days they were mutinous and quarrelsome, finding fault with their Pork, the Bread, &c. and in continual ill-humour. (234)

Franklin is convinced that nothing is so indispensable for human happiness as self-respect and that the habit of working diligently and well is the bedrock on which an unassailable self-respect may be built. With this teaching he holds out hope to men and women of all capacities and in all circumstances in life. Writing in a very different time and place, Alexander Solzhenitsyn confirms the truth of this lesson even for a prisoner in the Soviet gulag: the mason Shukhov is an abused prisoner most of the time, but when he is building a wall with energy and skill, he is in his heart a free man.[3] Industry, so understood, is perhaps the archetypical virtue for Franklin. Industry is praiseworthy because it involves self-mastery under the direction of reason, and not because it exacts any self-sacrifice. Indeed, what is perhaps most admirable in the industrious man is his success in providing for his own happiness.

A further lesson that the *Autobiography* offers to those seeking to make their way is the benefit of recognizing people's need for one another and their power to advance one another's fortunes. Franklin conveys this teaching in a negative way with the story of his misguided insistence on a minor point of justice in the London printing house where he worked and of his eventual discovery that it is "Folly" to be "on ill terms with those one is to live with continually" (100). The same lesson appears more positively in the many small pieces of help and advice that come to him from individuals he has managed to impress or oblige, such as the Quaker matron who warns him away from two thieving strumpets (84): whether he is relieved to avoid an involvement with them because of their bad morals, their threat to his property, or the danger to his reputation he leaves us to speculate. As a young man alone in the world, Franklin must trust to his own efforts and good sense, but almost instinctively he turns many of those efforts toward drawing his fellows together for their common advantage. This spirit of reciprocity appears in the Junto that he organizes for the self-education and advancement of young tradesmen in Philadelphia and in countless other projects—from volunteer fire companies and militias to the American Philosophical Society—in which citizens join to promote their own welfare more effectively than they ever could do alone. At the same time, these joiners begin discovering a capacity to provide for themselves many of the benefits of civilization that hitherto have been the unreliable gifts bestowed by kings, nobles, and clerics.

Even Franklin's manner of conversation eventually comes to be governed by this habit of seeking mutual benefits. Though a "disputacious" youth, he ultimately decides that the triumph of winning arguments is hollow compared with the friendships that can flourish when men and women speak only with a view to pleasing, enlightening, and benefiting one another—and perhaps themselves (60, 65, 213). This self-made American, who openly and cheerfully pursues for himself what is good in life, becomes an inveterate bridge-builder as well, not only because he sees that he cannot prosper without help, but even more because a life of lonely success does not seem to him worth pursuing at all.[4]

The Pleasures of Public Spirit

Franklin never falls prey, then, to the absurdity of narrow capitalism, the outlook that sees friends and virtues primarily as a means to wealth and wealth as a means to more wealth, or an end in itself. Although Max Weber interprets Franklin this way, he does so only by ignoring the generous friendship, the philanthropy, the wide-ranging curiosity, and the spirited defense of political principles that infuse almost every page of the *Autobiography*.[5] Even the "Poor Richard" of Franklin's almanac, who focuses much more narrowly on the means to prosperity than the *Autobiography* does, says, "Drive thy business; let not that drive thee." And Franklin himself, for all his talent in business, loved science far more, and seems to have enjoyed business chiefly for the opportunity it offered to exercise his wits, to advance useful projects and ideas through his newspaper and pamphlets, and to acquire the dignity and ease of an independent fortune. Once he made this fortune he retired from business forever. He was even willing to risk all that he had accumulated for the defense of the colonies in General Braddock's ill-fated campaign.[6]

The early Franklin's enthusiastic pursuit of wealth never consumed his whole energy. To the extent that he did consider business his duty and felt at times a twinge of uneasiness (if also irony about his own uneasiness) at being "debauch'd" from his work by a book, this only reflects his sense that first things must come first (126). In the prefaces to his proposals for an academy and for the American Philosophical Society, he shows the same sense of order in describing the natural development of a new society, from the "first Drudgery" of providing the mere necessities of life to the more refined pursuits that leisure makes possible.[7] Likewise for an individual, just as "it is hard for an empty sack to stand upright" (164), so learning to take proper care of oneself is the solid flooring that Franklin believed should undergird a life devoted to philanthropy, to politics, or to speculation. He himself, having laid his foundation well, went on to enjoy and excel at all three.

Now of course there is a real danger that those who follow Franklin's model and build thriving businesses will fall in love with their own creations, and will always tell themselves that there will be time enough tomorrow for the higher things in life, when the press of business is less urgent. But if Franklin makes Americans want to imitate his industry and frugality, he also portrays in attractive colors the allure of a more extensive kind of virtue—the public-spiritedness that pervades his life. Here is a do-gooder without a whiff of sanctimonious stuffiness, who would rather inspire a little constructive envy than a flood of guilty or grudging gratitude. His message throughout the *Autobiography* is that leading projects for the common good is really great fun. Franklin tells with relish his boyhood adventure of building a wharf with stolen blocks, even while he concedes his father's point that "nothing was useful which was not honest" (54). As a young man, he gives himself the lively competition and good fellowship of the Junto and, later, the amusement of being able to influence public opinion through a number of subordinate clubs, each of which is ignorant of the others' existence. He derives pleasure from good books and the pride of seeing reading become fashionable through his library, and finds mischievous delight in using crafty stratagems to beat out his rival newspapermen and almanac-makers, while using his own publications to benefit the public. He enjoys the fellowship and security, but also the excitement and dramatic successes of a fire company, and he seizes the worrisome but nonetheless amusing challenge of getting a Quaker-dominated assembly to vote funds for the common defense. He has the distinction of founding the city's first academy and the satisfaction of watching its students go on to make their mark in society. Finally, he savors the sweet triumph of maneuvering both people and legislature into generously endowing a hospital, by inventing the device of a government grant of matching funds. Through it all, Franklin gratifies his vanity by coming to be known as the prime mover of useful projects in Philadelphia.

The Congruence of Duty and Happiness

Franklin is at no pains to hide his triumphs or his flattered vanity, because he has never believed that one's motives must be purely selfless in order to be good. As Ralph Lerner has pointed out, "The mixed motives of man are a leading theme of the book."[8] Franklin accepts and even delights in revealing these mixed motives, persuaded that, just as virtue is beneficial to its possessor, so a clear-sighted pursuit of one's own good inevitably supports both what is right and what is good for others. The virtue of modesty is a perfect example of how what would seem to be self-denial turns out not to be so. Franklin reports that modesty in discussion has paradoxically caused him to prevail more often over his interlocutors and also spared him the mortification of having his proud assertions refuted (159). Moreover, by humbly concealing his own authorship of the projects he wishes to advance, he meets with less resistance. Perhaps most delightfully of all:

> The present little Sacrifice of your Vanity will afterwards be amply repaid. If it remains a while uncertain to whom the Merit belongs, some one more vain than yourself will be encourag'd to claim it, and then even Envy will be dispos'd to do you Justice, by plucking those assum'd Feathers, and restoring them to their right Owner. (143)

Again and again Franklin makes a point of showing that his virtue has not prejudiced his interest, but he does so without simply reducing virtue to self-interest. In arguing that newspapers should not be made a vehicle for "Libelling and Personal Abuse," or for scurrilous attacks on friendly governments, Franklin adds, "These Things I mention as a Caution to young Printers, and that they may be encouraged not to pollute their Presses and disgrace their Profession by such infamous Practices, but refuse steadily; as they may see by my Example, that such a Course of Conduct will not on the whole be injurious to their Interests" (165–66). This passage helps to put Franklin's teachings about the source of moral obligation in perspective. For in explaining how his various virtues have benefited him, Franklin often gives the impression that all virtue comes down to the thoughtful and disciplined pursuit of what is good for oneself. Indeed, more than once he claims that "vicious actions are not hurtful because they are forbidden, but forbidden because they are hurtful" (158, cf. 115). Still, we must ask, hurtful to whom? Even though Franklin plainly asserts that all vice is detrimental to the vicious man himself, does the warning to printers not also imply that people have an independent duty to avoid hurting others? Franklin could easily have argued that printers should maintain high professional standards in order to enhance their reputations, but he chooses not to. What he seems to trust most, what he tries most to encourage, is the person who will act both from principle and from calculation and will see clearly the beautiful convergence between the two.

What would be the source of one's obligation to behave in a principled way, if it is not ultimately self-interest? Although he does not often speak of it, Franklin himself seems to have carried through life a certain sense of duty to transcend (though not forsake) his own good for the good of mankind, a sense of duty nourished by his gratitude for the goods he has already received in life. In explaining his decision not to take out a patent on his wood stove, he writes: "I declin'd it from a Principle which has ever weigh'd with me on such Occasions, viz. *That as we enjoy great Advantages from the Inventions of others, we should be glad of an Opportunity to serve others by any Invention of ours, and this we should do freely and generously*" (192). It is perhaps this grateful and generous spirit that Franklin is thinking of when he speaks of the "beauty" as well as the "usefulness" of virtue. It is surely what he has in mind when he defines "True Merit" as "consisting in an *Inclination* join'd with an *Ability* to serve Mankind, one's country, Friends, and Family."[9]

How does it happen, then, that this service to humanity should dovetail with the good of the individual so perfectly that it is always "our Interest to be compleatly virtuous" (148)? In the end we must say that Franklin exaggerates the harmony here, if only because he, the peace-loving civilian, with his boundless hope in the power of reason to settle disputes, never wholly faces up to the problem of a soldier who must die bravely or flee in cowardice. At certain extreme moments in life virtue and self-interest do not coincide, and these moments may be more revealing about the true nature of virtue than Franklin assumes. But in limiting himself to the ordinary business of life, Franklin paints a compelling picture of how an unusually just and generous man can also be unusually happy, because he is naturally sociable and because the good things in life are not scarce and need not be fought over. In little organizations like the Junto, knowledge is gained by being shared, and friendships are multiplied and nurtured. In the capitalistic society of the United States, wealth is acquired not by conquest but by enterprise that benefits everyone.

But what about honor and power, the goods that, together with wealth, inspire the most injustice? Franklin never denies the pleasure he has gotten from "standing before kings," but he holds out some hope that diligence may bring us equal honors (144). More seriously, he turns our thoughts to the ways we may acquire *self*-respect, and he shows the honest workman that he will be esteemed if he esteems his own calling and even learns to take pride in pushing his own wheelbarrow (126). As for power, Franklin leads us to focus on the pleasures of doing good. Rather than seeking to dominate others by force or fear, he demonstrates how we may channel our ambition into attacking practical problems whose solutions can benefit everyone, and how we may enjoy spreading our influence through the power of gentle (if sometimes devious) persuasion.

Now if virtue is such a fine and useful thing, we may ask, why is it hard, and why does it need so many advertisements? Franklin is certain that much of the difficulty is simply that people have misunderstood virtue, but he is aware that the problem also lies in the dismayingly frequent *divergence* between our inclinations and our true good. Despite all his own astonishing energy, Franklin sees with unusual clarity the prodigious mass of laziness that most people must fight their way out from under in order even to start making themselves happy.[10] He himself is surprised at how difficult it is to follow his virtuous resolutions; bad habits have a stubborn inertia all their own, as he discovers in trying to overcome his tendency to disorder. Yet on the whole, Franklin sees his life as an example of how closely one may approach perfect virtue, even though one may never quite attain it. In the *Autobiography* he records only five actions that he truly regrets, and these he significantly terms "errata," or printing errors. They include taking advantage of his brother's troubles with the authorities to escape his apprenticeship (70); spending money that had been entrusted to him (86); forgetting his engagement to Deborah Read (96); printing a certain metaphysical pamphlet (96); and making improper advances to a woman who had turned to him in distress (99). Behind these errata lie various passions but also a great deal of simple thoughtlessness about the effects of his actions on others. From none except perhaps the first did Franklin gain anything, but neither did they do him much harm. What seems to have troubled Franklin most about these actions is the breaches he created in the web of human relations and the unnecessary suf-

fering that he caused for others. Most revealing is the erratum that is quite liter-
ally a printing error: Franklin's publishing at age nineteen his *Dissertation on Liberty and Necessity, Pleasure and Pain.*[11] Examining this essay and his later
comments about it will help illuminate Franklin's understanding of human virtue, its motivations, and what he concluded people need to believe about virtue
in order to be good.

The Nature of God and the Foundations
of Human Responsibility

An acquaintance with the practical, flexible Franklin of the *Autobiography* leaves
us unprepared for this early essay, with its tightly logical arguments that in
places defy all common sense. Franklin takes as his premise the existence of an
all-good, all-wise, and all-powerful God, since he finds nearly universal agreement about such a deity. From these attributes of God he argues that evil cannot exist, because nothing bad can happen against the will of a God who possesses both the inclination and the power to prevent it. In response to the
contemporary moralist William Wollaston, who distinguishes between good and
evil with the argument that virtue means living according to the truth and vice
always involves some lie or denial of the truth, Franklin maintains that everyone always lives according to the truth—the truth of one's own nature, which
may make one a thief, and perhaps even the truth that man "has not power
over his own actions." After reaching this dangerous conclusion, Franklin adds,
a bit defensively:

> I would not be understood by this to encourage or defend Theft; 'tis only
> for the sake of the Argument, and will certainly have no *ill Effect*. The Or-
> der and Course of Things will not be affected by Reasoning of this Kind;
> and 'tis as just and necessary, and as much according to Truth, for *B* to dis-
> like and punish the Theft of his Horse, as it is for *A* to steal him.[12]

As further grounds for his claim that human beings are not morally free
agents, Franklin reasons that an all-wise Providence would never leave us "blun-
dering about in the dark," when in our ignorance of unforeseen consequences,
"we have but as one Chance to ten thousand, to hit on the right Action;" thus
God must direct the will of every creature. Moral freedom would in fact be as ridiculous in this well-governed universe as wheels with their own spontaneous
motion would be in a carefully designed clock. But if there is no free will, there
can be no merit or demerit. All creatures must be equally esteemed and approved by the Creator; and all must then be equally happy. Franklin proceeds in

the second half of the essay, with more ingenuity than sense, to explain why all human beings in fact *are* equally happy, despite appearances.

It is little wonder that Franklin later comes to regret the pernicious tendency of such a performance, which not only takes away moral responsibility, and rewards and punishments as motives to virtue, but undermines compassion as a motive to benevolence. Franklin also recognizes the assailability of his reasoning on logical grounds. In another piece, now lost, he proves for argument's sake that all things must not be destined by God, because if they were, God would also have ordained prayer. Yet since "it can produce no change in things that are ordained," prayer must be "useless and an absurdity." Franklin does not say that these unsatisfactory and conflicting conclusions led him to doubt his premise, the existence of a perfect and benevolent God. Instead he writes, "The great uncertainty I found in metaphysical reasonings disgusted me, and I quitted that kind of reading and study for others more satisfactory."[13] But neither does he ever quite disavow the fatalism of his first essay. As he puts it in the *Autobiography*, the misbehavior of those he has converted to deism, and some of his own lapses from good conduct, have persuaded him that "this Doctrine, though it might be true, was not very useful." The *Dissertation on Liberty and Necessity* now seems less clever to him, and he suspects that *perhaps* it is infected with some unperceived error (114). In all of this Franklin is a little too cagey to be charged with simply believing whatever is most useful. But what *does* the mature Franklin believe about his early fatalism, and why does he not disown it?

Clearly Franklin's experience in life has taught him that parts of what he asserted in the essay are simply wrong. If observation of others and his own misfortunes have convinced him that "*Truth, Sincerity, and Integrity* in Dealings between Man and Man" are of "the utmost Importance to the Felicity of Life," then virtue and vice cannot be "empty Distinctions," whatever their true source might be (114). Franklin has also learned from experience that human beings *can* "hit on the right action" most of the time, if they govern their lives by reason, and that the happiness available to one in life can be vastly augmented by prudence and foresight. What remains from the essay, which Franklin may not have rejected, is the idea that God is a designer but not a moral judge who rewards and punishes. It also leaves the idea that there is no "free will" in the Christian sense of a free choice between good and evil, since all men are compelled to act as they do by their natures and by what seems good to them. The only meaningful liberty would then be the freedom from external constraints, or the freedom from blind compulsion that comes with self-knowledge and a judicious self-command. Franklin's modified fatalism would still allow room for a natural benevolence in human beings that could be praised as beautiful, but it would not justify either moral indignation or the view that actions in this life call for an afterlife of bliss or suffering.

Does Franklin, then, permanently reject the conventional understanding of moral responsibility? Is he convinced that, since it is in their interest to be virtuous, individuals are as good as their natures and their understanding allow them to be, so that the proper response to evil is not anger but pity? His statements about religion, including as they do a "just" God who avenges evil, suggest the contrary. But how far are these statements to be trusted? Franklin tells us openly that his radical deism, which denied moral responsibility, had bad results and hence ought not to be promoted. Although the religious statements that he makes after this strategic decision also contain tenets of deism, this is deism of a more salutary kind. His 1731 statement of beliefs, like the 1784 summary in the *Autobiography*, includes the concept of a benevolent Creator who should be worshiped, who is best served by serving mankind, and who rewards and punishes men according to their deserts.[14] Yet the first of these creeds is significantly entitled "Doct. to be Prea[che]d," and the latter is part of a frankly didactic project, in which Franklin defines the virtue of sincerity as using "no hurtful deceit" (150).

One other exposition of Franklin's beliefs seems on the surface equally clear about providence, heaven, and hell, and on closer inspection equally ambiguous: his 1790 letter to Ezra Stiles.[15] Franklin begins with a lie: this is the "first time I have been questioned" about religion. Then he proceeds in the course of three paragraphs to contradict himself completely: the soul "will be treated with Justice in another Life," but "I have no doubt" of God's continuing benevolence in the afterlife, "though without the smallest Conceit of meriting such Goodness." Is this just a lapse of Franklin's normally incisive mind? Or is he not somewhat playfully refusing (yet again) to reveal his deepest thoughts on religion? As for the kind providence that Franklin has always experienced and expects to continue experiencing, the *Autobiography* offers a clue to its meaning. Telling the story of the establishment of an academy in Philadelphia, Franklin writes that "Providence" threw into the founders' way a fine building for the school, but a page later we learn that this providence consists in the fact that Franklin was a trustee for both the academy and the building and was able to negotiate a deal (193–95). Life has undeniably been good to Franklin, but is that because providence has been benevolent, or simply because Franklin himself has learned to make the best of it?

Although his overtly religious statements do not decisively answer the question of whether Franklin believed in a judging God and hence in the kind of moral virtue and vice that would merit heaven and hell, we may find more reliable evidence of his true understanding in his actions. Like Socrates, whom he admired, Franklin showed a remarkable freedom from indignation. He could dine amicably with his staunchest political opponents, able to see their personal virtues and the way they were constrained by their instructions from the Pennsylvania proprietors. He is usually as gentle with the faults of others as he is with his own; as Lerner has remarked, he exhibits striking restraint in assessing the character of Governor Keith, who sent Franklin to England at age eighteen with the promise of setting him up in business and instead left him stranded and penniless.[16] As he concludes: "But what shall we think of a Governor's playing such pitiful Tricks, and imposing so grossly on a poor ignorant boy! It was a Habit he had acquired. He wish'd to please every body; and having little to give, he gave Expectations. He was otherwise an ingenious sensible Man, a pretty good Writer, and a good Governor for the People" (95). And as Verner Crane puts it in his biography, when Franklin found himself in a personal feud with a colleague in the diplomatic service, he "characteristically" paid it little heed. This is not to imply that Franklin was utterly free of anger. The *Autobiography* minimizes the bitterness of political and other contests he engaged in, and its silence about his own children covers a grim rupture between himself and his loyalist son, William.[17] But his usual equanimity and his efforts to moderate resentment when it did arise fit well with a belief that indignation is unreasonable and that vice results from ignorance of what is good for oneself or ignorance of how to achieve it.

Further indications about Franklin's beliefs comes, of course, from the peculiar way in which he honors and values religion. He never looks to God for relief from the torment of guilt, in contrast to his Puritan contemporary Jonathan Edwards. He always has trouble finding any time to go to church, and when the magnetic George Whitefield comes to town with his harangues about sin and guilt, Franklin finds himself suddenly fascinated with an experiment in acoustics that will carry him out of the range of the preacher's booming voice (175–79). As a young man Franklin does design a program for personal worship, believing that religious devotion can make him more virtuous.[18] But he has to posit a demigod of the solar system who might care about human beings and their worship, since he is certain that the creator of the universe would be above such concerns. This little experiment in trying to believe what seems convenient to believe apparently fails; the demigod disappears from his statements about religion, and presumably all worship along with this deity. The mature Franklin is then quite happy to leave *others* undisturbed in their faith and goes so far as to contribute to all of their churches, but he himself shows no interest in religion beyond its usefulness in promoting the virtue of believers. Like Jefferson, he is persuaded that nonbelievers can do perfectly well without it; he even quotes Jesus' statement, "I am not come to call the righteous, but sinners," as rebuttal to his Christian critics.[19] This strictly utilitarian approach to religion may seem shallow and thoughtless when taken by itself, but if it is in fact a long reflection on virtue that has convinced Franklin that the moral assumptions of Christianity are false, then it is somewhat more understandable that he should not trouble himself further with theological questions. Without disrupting his fellow Americans' faith, Franklin sets out in the *Autobiography* to make that faith less necessary, by teaching a new understanding of virtue and a method that will make virtue accessible to everyone.

The Project of Moral Perfection

Franklin tells us that he developed this method when, as a young man, "I conceived the bold and arduous Project of arriving at moral Perfection." There is in his report of this undertaking a characteristic breezy confidence about fundamental questions: Franklin sees little difficulty in knowing what virtue is, and views the disagreements between moral writers as merely the result of different methods of cataloguing the virtues. (But as always, we cannot be certain that the Franklin presented here is the same as the Franklin who is writing the book. "I knew, or thought I knew, what was right and wrong," he explains, hinting cryptically that he may ultimately have come to see more difficulty in knowing what is right than this summary implies [148].) In his catalogue he includes thirteen virtues, ordered so that the mastery of the first may make easier the acquisition of the latter. The virtues are temperance, silence, order, resolution, frugality, industry, sincerity, justice, moderation, cleanliness, tranquillity, chastity, and humility. Altogether it is a much more self-regarding, rudimentary, and attainable array of virtues than, for example, the classic list of eleven virtues presented in Aristotle's *Ethics*. The most significant of Franklin's omissions is courage, the first virtue that every society must demand of its citizens in order to survive and a test of the individual's willingness to sacrifice himself for the good of his country. But neither does Franklin include generosity, magnificence, the proper posture toward honor, greatness of soul, or the social virtues of friendliness and wittiness that figure prominently in Aristotle's account of the perfect gentleman. This is not to say that Franklin himself altogether lacks these qualities. Indeed, a man whose character was adequately summed up in the thirteen virtues of Franklin's list would be a far narrower and duller creature than the Benjamin Franklin who lived. Rather, in his program for moral perfection we see Franklin pruning away obvious faults without trying to cultivate at once all the qualities that make one admirable. He demands of himself only what seems most essential, but he goes on to live a life that is eminently spirited, generous, and graceful—yet without ever abandoning his homespun roots.

Franklin helps make virtue attainable not only by his careful selection and ordering of moral goals, but also by the method he devises to shepherd himself toward those goals. And since he sees the impediments to virtue as only bad habits and not a willfully evil heart, becoming virtuous for him is *only* a matter of finding the right method. Franklin characteristically minimizes the importance of nature in determining one's disposition, even though his own accomplishments rest on a truly rare combination of natural energy and endowments. But his method can enable anyone to progress toward virtue. The key to this approach is patient, consistent attention to one small problem at a time, until gradually a series of new habits is built up. Again, the contrast with Jonathan Edwards is instructive. Franklin and Edwards, despite all their differences, shared an unusually serious lifelong concern with improving themselves. Next to the ruthless soul-searching revealed in Edwards's *Personal Narrative*, Franklin looks complacent, to say the least.[20] But although Edwards aches and yearns to become pure like God, and although he writes of the growth of his faith through grace, he is not able to report progress in virtue. Contemplating himself is always painful for Edwards because of the evil that he finds within; were he to see there a laudable improvement, he would judge himself guilty of pride, the worst of sins.

Franklin, however, makes friends with his pride as he does with his vanity. Not only does he realize that pride is simply impossible to uproot—"even if I could conceive that I had compleatly overcome it, I should probably be proud of my Humility"—but he discovers that most of the advantages of humility can be gained equally from the appearance of humility (159–60). Above all, Franklin appreciates the ineradicable human need for the moderate pride of a justified self-respect. This insight into the value of self-esteem has become a platitude in modern education, so much so that we sometimes forget the importance of a true if unflattering appraisal of oneself, and the subsequent need for self-overcoming. But Franklin is a master at finding a balance between self-overcoming and self-acceptance, the balance that is arguably most fair as well as demonstrably most productive of steady change. His cheerful acceptance of his limitations does mean that Franklin is simply closed to the possibility that Edwards represents, the possibility that there is evil at man's core and that the true human condition is grim and incapable of amelioration without divine assistance. On the other hand, Franklin's success in gently and patiently taking himself in hand is testimony for his claim that ordinary people, at least, are not incorrigibly evil, but only mired in bad habits that they have not learned to escape.

Franklin's method, with a week assigned to each virtue and four courses of thirteen weeks in each year, was so successful that he planned to expound it in a book.

> I purposed writing a little Comment on each Virtue, in which I would have shown the Advantages of possessing it, and the Mischiefs attending its opposite Vice; and I should have called my Book the ART *of Virtue*, because it would have shown the *Means* and *Manner* of obtaining Virtue, which

would have distinguish'd it from the mere Exhortation to be good, that does not instruct and indicate the Means; but is like the Apostle's Man of verbal Charity, who only, without showing to the Naked and the Hungry *how* or where they might get Cloaths or Victuals, exhorted them to be fed and clothed. *James* II, 15, 16. (157–58)

Franklin never got around to writing this volume, which in his later years came to seem a rather daunting project. Perhaps the plan was a bit too dry and abstract, or even too orderly, and Franklin chose to indulge his love of recollection and storytelling by composing the *Autobiography* instead. But surely he also realized along the way that the *Autobiography* would be a much more powerful instructor in virtue. Although a treatise would provide reasons why virtue is good and a method for attaining it, still more is needed—and Franklin knew well the limits of reason's power to persuade the heart. After years of praising virtue in his almanac through epigrams that were both witty and memorable, he collected many of his best sayings into a speech that he put into the mouth of one "Father Abraham." This little piece was wildly popular and was reprinted in hundreds of editions and translated into a number of foreign languages. But while Franklin would fully enjoy the fame that this work was to bring him, he quietly reveals at its end his true estimate of the difference it will really make: "The People heard it, and approved the Doctrine, and immediately practised the contrary, just as if it had been a common Sermon." As he writes in his essay "A Man of Sense," everyone pays lip service to virtue, but those who declare that virtue is in men's interest and yet do not practice it speak "only by rote"; their hearts have not been reached and changed by a genuine conviction of what they say.[21] How is such a conviction to be instilled? Franklin knows that he will succeed only if he appeals to the taste as well as the reason of his readers, only if he persuades them to delight in what he delights in and to see through his eyes. And this is an education that only a story can provide.

Franklin, the Contested Genius of American Moral Education

How is it, then, that Franklin made his stories so compelling that they have captured the imaginations of generations of readers? He was a master at the art of teaching by example and not just by precept, although his book does both. Interspersed among his stories are reflections on what makes for effective communication, and all of these lessons are applied in the *Autobiography* itself. Franklin praises and uses John Bunyan's technique of mixing narrative and dialogue, "a Method of Writing very engaging to the Reader, who in the most interesting Parts finds himself as it were brought into the Company, and present at the Discourse" (72).[22] He faults a polemical style for its tendency to anger rather than to win over an audience (60, 213), and in his book he adopts instead a gentle irony toward those whose example he would not have us follow. He tells us that "the chief Ends of Conversation are to *inform*, . . . to *please* or to *persuade*" (65), and he himself does all of these, with stories that are agreeably brief and witty and always richly insightful. Indeed, they are more enjoyable because of their peppery observations, and more instructive because they are so pleasant.

Despite Franklin's thoroughly didactic intent, he writes with a disarming informality which suggests that he does not need to persuade us, but that he only wants us to gratify an old man by listening to a tale or two. Even the vanity implicit in this request is charming, because Franklin is so open about it and so untroubled by it.

> Most people dislike Vanity in others whatever Share they have of it themselves, but I give it fair Quarter wherever I meet with it, being persuaded that it is often productive of Good to the Possessor and to others that are within his Sphere of Action: And therefore in many Cases it would not be quite absurd if a Man were to thank God for his Vanity among the other Comforts of Life. (44)

In contrast to the prickliness of John Adams, Franklin's is not a disappointed vanity, nor is he disagreeably conceited: in recounting his life he shares his often bemused affection for his subject, and he mingles accounts of his triumphs with invitations to join him in laughing at himself.[23] And since Franklin is so willing to give fair quarter to his own vanity, he more readily does the same for ours. Humor is but one means that he finds to soothe the envy of his democratic audience, and thus to teach without becoming overbearing. He also makes his accomplishments seem attainable, by focusing on his low beginnings and his early business and civic pursuits while shifting to the background the scientific discoveries and diplomacy that required his rare genius. He pointedly defends those low but solid projects—such as arranging for the cleaning and paving of the city streets—that are within the capacity of any enterprising citizen. "Human Felicity is produc'd not so much by great Pieces of good Fortune that seldom happen, as by little Advantages that occur every Day" (207). Yet if Franklin is a hero within reach, he is also a hero who makes us reach. He allows glimpses into the many facets of his life and of his subtle thought, and with all of them he challenges us to think for ourselves and to try to make a mark on the world, as he has.

Franklin's story is of course engaging and convincing for another reason, and that is its fascinating central figure. Franklin has the perfect personality to illustrate the lessons about virtue that he wants to teach. The gap between virtue and happiness is unusually small in his case, because he is so sociable, so good-natured and generous, so peaceful and accommodating, so resourceful, and so ready to take life as it comes. He may exaggerate these qualities in his *Autobiography*, but they are still his qualities. If true merit consists in serving one's fellows, that is also what comes naturally to Franklin. And because he is so forthrightly pursuing his own happiness even as he pursues a public career, because he has come to terms with the large share of self-interest present in everybody's motives, he is less vulnerable to the pain of ingratitude that Washington and Jefferson both felt at times when public opinion or the press turned against them. But are these traits the result of Franklin's natural disposition, or of deliberately cultivated habits? The stories and lessons of the *Autobiography* are indeed inextricably tied to Franklin's own character. Yet the metaphor of one's life as a book that runs through the work reminds us that books have authors, and clearly Franklin means to suggest that the main author of his life is not a distant providence but Franklin himself. Through the portrayal of his character, as well as the account of his actions, he is inviting us to approach life as he does, to pattern our own souls after his. How far our natures will allow us to go in doing so is still an open question, but the spirit of Franklin's example is undeniably contagious.

There are problems inherent in Franklin's project, however, and if critics are right that his lessons have a pernicious tendency, the charm of his story only makes it more dangerous. In all of his writing, Franklin advises readers to rely on themselves and their own judgment, to measure things by their utility, and to follow the dictates of reason in preference to any established authority. Yet he also teaches the slipperiness of reason. He relates that as a young man he was for some time a vegetarian, believing that killing animals is "a kind of unprovok'd Murder," until one day his companions cooked a meal of freshly caught cod.

> I had formerly been a great Lover of Fish, and when this came hot out of the Frying Pan, it smelt admirably well. I balanc'd some time between Principle and Inclination: till I recollected, that when the Fish were opened, I saw smaller Fish taken out of their Stomachs: Then thought I, if you eat one another, I don't see why we mayn't eat you. . . . So convenient a thing it is to be a *reasonable Creature*, since it enables one to find or make a Reason for every thing one has a mind to do. (88)

Reason, or "something that pretended to be Reason," also suggests to Franklin, when he finds the struggle to become completely virtuous rather too onerous, that "such extream Nicety as I exacted of my self might be a kind of Foppery in Morals," which would be either ridiculous or too provoking of envy.

(Note the contradictory fears.) Thus he surmises that perhaps "a benevolent Man should allow a few Faults in himself, to keep his Friends in Countenance." Franklin very carefully does not quite endorse this conclusion, but he extends his humorous affection to the man who does—the man who wants to make the whole face of his ax as bright as its edge, but who decides after prolonged laborious grinding that "I think I like a speckled Ax best" (156). How is each of Franklin's independent-minded followers to judge for himself how virtuous is virtuous enough? What rule can we apply to distinguish reason from what pretends to be reason? Or is reason itself the culprit? As Jefferson found, reason can only too easily justify a narrow selfishness. Franklin trusts that his portrait of a generous and public-spirited life will convince our hearts that this life is most worth having. But as we have seen, much of the pleasure in Franklin's civic projects lies in conniving and manipulating, albeit in a good cause. In the hands of one who is willing to let reason excuse whatever one desires, such a penchant for subterfuge could have dangerous consequences.

Another, rather different kind of danger is the focus of an attack by D. H. Lawrence, one of Franklin's most vociferous critics. Lawrence is horrified by the way Franklin subjugates his passions to calculating reason and molds his whole character by the sheer force of will. He sees Franklin as a truncated man who has learned to find kinship and harmony with the rest of humanity only at the cost of what is most precious in his soul. He has become "at one with all men, through suppression and elimination of those things which make differences—passions, prides, impulses of the self which cause disparity between one being and another." Lawrence takes special issue with Franklin's plan for moral perfection, which he regards as a systematic repression of the passions for the sake of "the material benefit of mankind." Franklin's dutifulness irks him as much as his materialism: "And how can any man be free without a soul of his own, that he believes in and won't sell at any price? But Benjamin doesn't let me have a soul of my own. He says I am nothing but a servant of mankind—galley-slave I call it—and if I don't get my wages here below . . . why, never mind, I shall get my wages HEREAFTER."[24]

Lawrence sees Franklin as motivated by a combination of smug moralism and calculation that reduces God to little more than a cheap insurance policy. He thus at least recognizes a certain rationality in Franklin—unlike Max Weber, who interprets Franklin's sense of duty as an ethic of pointless cultivation of industry and wealth for their own sakes. But like Weber, Lawrence misses the extent to which Franklin's virtue successfully aims at a rich happiness in this life, sufficient to keep him from having to depend on the hope for an afterlife to compensate for sacrifices made in the present.

What is it that gives man inner independence and integrity, according to Lawrence? Not hard work, but a reverence for the divine within. Lawrence offers his own gloss on Franklin's thirteen virtues, to counter Franklin's confined, "barbed wire" definitions. Two examples will show the contrast in spirit.

> *Temperance.* Franklin: "Eat not to Dulness. Drink not to Elevation." Lawrence: "Eat and carouse with Bacchus, or munch dry bread with Jesus, but don't sit down without one of the gods."
> *Chastity.* Franklin: "Rarely use Venery but for Health or Offspring; Never to Dulness, Weakness, or the Injury of your own or another's Peace or Reputation." Lawrence: "Never 'use' venery at all. Follow your passional impulse, if it be answered in the other being; but never have any motive in mind, neither offspring nor health nor even pleasure, nor even service. Only know that 'venery' is of the great gods. An offering-up of yourself to the very great gods, the dark ones, and nothing else."[25]

This line of attack is echoed by Charles Angoff, who argues that Franklin "makes a religion of Babbitry," of the petty, economically focused self-improvement that knows nothing of poetry, honor, nobility, grandeur of soul, reverence, or mystery.[26] Both of these critics seem to be responding more to Franklin's rather narrow plan for moral improvement than to the complex, full-blooded man of the *Autobiography* as a whole. But even if Franklin was not himself the petty character that they denounce, is it not true that his writings may support such pettiness in others? Franklin's combination of earthy practicality, human sympathy, and a richly cultivated mind saves him from the shallowness that Lawrence charges him with, but is not this combination of qualities precisely what makes him so inimitable? Is not even a public-spirited follower of Franklin likely to be public-spirited in a small-minded way, attending to his country's prosperity and comfort but doing nothing to cultivate reverence for rare virtue, for serious thought, or for what is divine and mysterious in God or man? And if so, must we not conclude that, despite all his superb subtlety and sparkling versatility, Franklin lacks depth—the depth to see the longings of the human spirit that will never be satisfied by well-formed committees and well-paved streets, the longings for something noble to devote oneself to and to anchor oneself by?

Franklin might fairly reply, however, that Lawrence's mystical yearnings are nothing but vague, futile quests for gods that do not exist; that the wise person lives according to what is true and possible, not according to what one wishes, and that making deities out of uncontrolled passions does not give life more richness and dignity, but less. Indeed, Lawrence provides little in the way of a positive alternative to Franklin beyond calling for us to follow our passional impulses, wherever they may lead. His rejection of reason and order, his exhortation to "abide by your own deepest promptings" and "sacrifice the smaller thing to the greater," to "kill when you must, and be killed the same," is chilling, especially in the light of the subsequent cataclysms of the twentieth century in which similar claims of depth and passionate authenticity were used to justify atrocities. Despite Lawrence's talk about the "dark forest" of his soul, he and Franklin turn out to *share* a failure to appreciate the ineradicable and destructive impulses in the human heart.[27]

This failure in Franklin is made manifest in what is surely the most disappointing passage of the *Autobiography*. At the end of his life, Franklin describes with approval a plan that he conceived more than a half-century earlier: to form the "good Men of all Nations" into a "Party for Virtue" that would be distinguished from ordinary political parties in that it would not pursue the members' private interests, or even the party's aggregate interest, but rather the good of mankind (161–63). Leaving aside the contradiction between this idea and Franklin's usual arguments for the harmony between virtue and one's carefully considered self-interest, leaving aside the incongruity between the selfless principles that are to motivate the society's members and the promise that members will promote one another's businesses, we may ask how Franklin expected the virtuous men of the world to find one another without being fooled by imposters and without quarreling about what is good for mankind. Franklin's greatest limitation is that he is simply too sanguine; his sunniness prevents him from taking seriously the disagreements that have divided humanity. He assumes that reasonable people will always be virtuous as he understands virtue, that virtuous people will always be reasonable, and that everyone else is benighted or trapped in bad habits, although never beyond hope if they can be reached by education. As Ormond Seavey has pointed out, Franklin sees no tension in life between competing, powerful visions of the good (or between competing gods); the only choice "is between one's own best interest on the one hand and the variety of short-sighted, destructive possibilities on the other."[28]

Franklin seems not to have reckoned with the strength of the human heart's longings for sources of sublime transcendence, transfiguration, and redemption—from an existence that appears intolerably limited or confined. Without doing justice to such longings, and the purported experiences that satisfy them, how can Franklin suppose he has reasonably disposed of the challenge presented by religious revelation, in its many manifestations? Moreover, even if Franklin is right that reason can shed light on all of life and show us how to live, has he successfully demonstrated that his active, pragmatic life is what reason unequivocally supports? Socrates, Franklin's model in so many ways, argues that the life of philosophy—involving relentless questioning of oneself and one's assumptions, a continuous "quarrel" between philosophy and poetry, and a ceaseless quest for the permanent truth about God and human nature—is the only life that can fulfill man's noblest capacities or satisfy his deepest longings. Has

Franklin given sufficient reflection to the human possibilities and the questions represented by Socrates?

None of this is to suggest that Franklin should be rejected as a model for American education. Franklin's teaching and life provide an example of independence, self-reliance, and a spirited championing of liberty that is inspiring and even noble, and perfectly suited to the American character. Yet a free and serious nation may require something further, not only to lend support to moral integrity but to satisfy the human need for objects of reverence that can give life a more elevated meaning. As Franklin's own generosity to churches suggests, religious faith deserves and requires encouragement as well as critical examination. But when faith has withered, it cannot be manufactured. Then more than ever young people need stories of human heroes, of prudent Franklins but also of stern, great-souled Washingtons, and of the classical republican leaders who inspired Washington. Devotion to these heroes must not be thoughtless, however. We must rise to Franklin's challenge to think for ourselves and to contemplate the most important of all questions: the relationship between virtue and happiness, between what is truly admirable and what is finally best for one's own soul.

Conclusion

Our study has culminated in an exploration of the models offered by three of the greatest Founders, because it is such models that must furnish the goals for any comprehensive and fully humane education. It is clarity precisely about such models and guidance that seems most lacking in the public discussions of our contemporary crisis in education. While Washington, Jefferson, and Franklin all share fundamental political and moral principles, they exhibit the diversity and even the fruitful disagreement that are the natural outcome of the acceptance of those basic principles. The three models invite, as we have tried to demonstrate, probing scrutiny and illuminating controversy. Whether one accepts any or all of these three models, we believe one must acknowledge their power to awaken and direct serious thought about what it means to be a truly educated or well-formed human being. They focus our attention on the most significant questions, the answers to which define what we should be striving toward as educators.

To be sure, the Founders' experience reveals vividly how much more is needed besides clear goals and models. The opposition and indifference the Founders encountered in trying to establish schools is a sobering indication of the depth and rootedness of the tendency of American democracy to neglect education. Beneath the familiar and often justified complaints are deeper problems, problems that Tocqueville suggests are inherent in democracy: the proclivity to undervalue learning and the arts, or to demand that they be productive of other goods; the enfeebled aspiration to excellence; the sway of majoritarian public opinion and the concomitant pressure to conform in matters of the spirit and mind; the diminished respect for or understanding of the radically detached contemplative life; the disregard of obligations to future generations and even to distant fellow citizens. The Founders learned that appeals to the political importance of citizenship education could not produce good schools in the absence of powerfully felt religious motives or vocational needs. We are finding today that

285

no degree of concern over the necessity for competent workers can produce meaningful educational improvements in the absence of a respect for learning— whether biblical, civic, or theoretical—as something good in itself because it is good for the spirit. Education will thrive in the United States only if it is nour- ished from more than one spring, and the spring that we must guard most care- fully, because its waters run at a trickle, is the clear-sighted reverence for what we may become in our souls, as dedicated citizens and as moral and rational be- ings. Washington and Jefferson suggest that the patronage of prominent individ- uals is therefore crucial, and especially the leadership that stresses these aspects of education that the nation is most likely to neglect.

Especially relevant to our situation are the Founders' reflections on civic edu- cation. Jefferson suggests that the training of citizens is best advanced not in a separate "civics" class but in moral and political lessons integrated into the en- tire curriculum. Franklin sketches an academy program that recaptures some- thing of the spirit of ancient republican education. Continual practice in ora- tions, debate, and journalistic writing—all focused on momentous moral and political issues of the day—will give a public-spirited tone to the classroom and, if rightly conducted, a sense of the great responsibility statesmen and journalists ought to feel in undertaking to guide the public discourse. Washington reminds us of the need to aim at a balance between vigilance against government's en- croachments on rights and a veneration for the nation's laws, finest leaders, and guiding principles. The sentiments of men like Patrick Henry, and the example of the early American press, remind us that the perception of government as a dirty affair or a necessary evil is at least as old as America itself, and that venera- tion for democratic authority does not come naturally to the people of a democ- racy. Hence we find Washington bending his chief efforts to instilling a spirit of honor in government rather than a spirit of suspicious vigilance against govern- ment. Recent experience suggests that vigilance itself collapses into apathetic cynicism in the absence of a reasoned respect for the country's political life. Per- haps the time has come for us to start again at the beginning, by giving students what Washington gave his troops—models like Cato, and like Washington him- self, models capable of reigniting enthusiasm for what political life can be at its best.

At the same time, the fate of the national university and national plans for education suggest what Madison more than once proposed: that our strengths will be found not in uniform schemes imposed from a centralized government above, but in local initiative, diversity, and competition, including both the free- dom of students to choose schools and the freedom of schools to experiment. Moreover, we find in both Franklin and Jefferson support for the idea that local initiative should mean above all parental involvement, not only because the schools and students' development require it, but equally because parents need the civic education that comes through collectively formulating and pursuing serious goals.

This balance between vigilant involvement and reverence for the law that we need to regain is akin to another balance that the Founders may have groped unevenly toward in their proposals but exemplified beautifully in their lives. That is the balance between conviction and openness. Should we not strive to encourage in students the same rootedness in fundamental principles, together with the same willingness to explore new ideas and welcome disagreements, that we see in the Founders themselves? Although none of the leading Founders rose to the level of truly philosophic self-questioning, all displayed the mixture of thoughtfulness and conviction that is perhaps the optimum soil for both philosophy and responsible citizenship. In contrast, a dogmatic education, replete with tidy lessons and clean heroes, leaves students unmoved and unprepared to face challenges to what they have been taught. More of a danger today is the opposite extreme: an openness so relativistic, or so persistent a debunking of our own system, as to leave students with no moral grounding and with a contemptuous disbelief in truth that saps the impetus to serious thought.

Of all their inquiries, perhaps the deepest and most instructive for us is the Founders' probing of the relationship between virtue and happiness. In an age when old-fashioned honor is nearly extinct and religious faith cannot be counted on to sustain morality, it is essential for us to explore this question with the young. As the Founders never tired of emphasizing, moral education proceeds best through example. Hence it seems wise that we put at the core of moral education—indeed, at the core of our entire curriculum—the study of rich biographies of individuals who exemplify different or competing visions of human excellence. Through these, we can lead students to ponder Jefferson's questions: Which man or woman would I most like to be? Which one's reputation would I most like to have? Which person's respect seems most worth having, and how could it be won? How do my head and my heart answer the question of what is the best and happiest life? As we have seen, Jefferson recommends that we start with small children, teaching them (perhaps through examples such as Jefferson's own) that happiness "does not depend on the condition of life in which chance has placed them, but is always the result of good conscience, good health, occupation, and freedom in all just pursuits."[1] Of course the latter part of the sentence qualifies the beginning, for if happiness depends on freedom rather than slavery, it depends on *some* circumstances. But what better lesson is there to instill in children? How much more useful is this than much of contemporary moral education, which portrays people as largely the slaves of circumstance? Jefferson might well argue that, though evil circumstances can indeed be found everywhere, to focus on them or their power to determine existence is to promote bitterness, rage, and feelings of victimization and pity, instead of spirited initiative and generosity.

Franklin's *Autobiography*, as we have seen, builds on the same theme. Here we find a story that argues persuasively for the congruence between personal effort and happiness, and between individual happiness and the pursuit of the public good. At the same time, it reminds students (as well as their teachers and parents) of how widely our inclination can diverge from our true good, and hence of the need for constant small steps to form habits of self-mastery. The *Autobiography*'s perspective on human nature and human motivations does more than provide ample food for thought; it encourages affectionate laughter at the foibles of mankind, and patient, constructive action to solve problems, rather than rage or cynicism over human failings.

Nevertheless, as Franklin's most serious critics have argued, a free and serious people may require something further, not only to lend support to moral integrity but to satisfy the human need for objects of reverence that can give life a higher and more compelling purpose. True education must touch the deepest longings of the spirit; it must appeal to eros, to the imagination, and to the love of beauty. It needs, then, to explore some of the sternest and noblest challenges presented by previous ages, with their alien conceptions of happiness and human flourishing. A full education must explore poetry, the Bible, and, ultimately, the challenge of Socratic philosophy. All of this must begin with the right foundations in childhood. For while the longings of the soul that point beyond the prudent lessons of Franklin are natural, they are a slender growth that requires careful cultivation.

Notes

Introduction

1. James Madison, Alexander Hamilton, and John Jay, *The Federalist Papers*, ed. Clinton Rossiter (New York: New American Library, Mentor Books, 1961), no. 9 (pp. 71-72); all references to the *Federalist Papers* will be to paper number and pages of this edition. John Adams seconds these sentiments of Hamilton's, so critical of classical republicanism, and extends them to a detailed critique of contemporary European republics and the Italian republics of the Middle Ages in his *Defence of the Constitutions of Government of the United States of America, against the Attack of M. Turgot, in His Letter to Dr. Price, Dated the Twenty-second Day of March, 1778*, in three volumes—see esp. vol. 1, preface and chap. 1; vol. 2, chaps. 1-10; and vol. 3, conclusion—in *The Works of John Adams, Second President of the United States*, ed. Charles Francis Adams, 10 vols. (Boston: Little, Brown, 1851-1856), vols. 4-6, esp. 4:283-89, 303; 5:181-82, 289-90; and 6:217.

2. For the discussion of John Adams in the paragraphs that follow, see esp. "Thoughts on Government," in *Works* 4:194-200, and *Defence of the Constitutions*, in *Works* 4:448, 462, 526, 556-58, and 6:219. Clearly discernible in Adams's break with classical republican principles is the influence of Machiavelli; see Adams's mixture of criticism and praise for Machiavelli's republican theory in *Works* 5:29-30, 39-40, 44-45, 48-49, 66-67, 82, 88-89 and see 5:289 and 426 for illuminating applications of this discussion of Machiavelli to the United States.

3. Adams, "Thoughts on Government," in *Works* 4:194, 199.

4. Plato, *Laws* 751b-c. Translations from this and all other works not written in English are our own except where otherwise noted. Cf. Eva T. H. Brann, *Paradoxes of Education in a Republic* (Chicago: University of Chicago Press, 1979), 33-34.

5. *The Works of Thomas Jefferson*, ed. Paul L. Ford, 12 vols., Federal Edition (New York: G. P. Putnam's Sons, 1905), 12:6.

6. Adams, *Defence of the Constitutions*, in *Works* 6:219; 4:556-58 and 526.

7. Montesquieu, though in the final analysis a partisan of the Enlightenment rather than of classical republicanism, nevertheless vividly captured and conveyed to his American readers this spirit of classical civic education; see esp. *Spirit of the Laws*, bk. 4, chaps. 5-7; bk. 5, chaps. 2, 7, 19; bk. 7, chaps. 8, 14; bk. 8, chaps. 2, 13.

8. Jefferson to Roger C. Weightman, 24 June 1826, *The Life and Selected Writings of Thomas Jefferson*, ed. Adrienne Koch and William Peden (New York: Random House, Modern Library, 1944), 729-30. Cf. John Adams, *Defence of the Constitutions*, preface, in

Works 4:292–93: "The United States of America have exhibited, perhaps, the first example of governments erected on the simple principles of nature; and if men are now sufficiently enlightened to disabuse themselves of artifice, imposture, hypocrisy, and superstition, they will consider this event as an era in their history. . . . The people were universally too enlightened to be imposed on by artifice; and their leaders, or more properly followers, were men of too much honor to attempt it." See also Adams's "Dissertation on the Canon and the Feudal Law" (1765), in *Works* 3:448–64. For important uses of the term *enlightenment* (in the sense we have indicated) in the *Federalist Papers*, see nos. 26 (p. 168), 29 (p. 187), 37 (p. 227), 47 (p. 301), 60 (p. 367), and 77 (p. 464).

9. In particular, Frederick Rudolph's discussion of the meaning of "enlightenment" in the educational writings of Americans at the time of the Founding suffers from an insufficient awareness of the individualistic, rights-centered, or "state of nature" implications of the term and the notion; see Rudolph's introduction to *Essays on Education in the Early Republic* (Cambridge: Harvard University Press, 1965), esp. xv–xvi. In this regard, there is a remarkable contrast between Rudolph's characterization of the documents in his collection and what one finds in those documents themselves, especially the most theoretical of them, Robert Coram's "Political Inquiries: to Which Is Added, a Plan for the General Establishment of Schools throughout the United States" (1791), with its elaborate discussion of the state of nature and social contractual basis of all society, in ibid., 79–145; see also Samuel Harrison Smith, "Remarks on Education: Illustrating the Close Connection between Virtue and Wisdom" (1798), in ibid., 180, 220–21.

10. For some vivid illustrations, see *The Writings of Samuel Adams*, ed. Harry Alonzo Cushing, 4 vols. (New York: G. P. Putnam's Sons, 1904–1908), 4:340–60, esp. 343, 347, 349, 355–60; see also 4:124–25, 371, 377–79, 401–4; and 2:350–54. Cf. George Washington's Farewell Address, *The Writings of George Washington from the Original Manuscript Sources*, ed. John C. Fitzpatrick, 39 vols. (Washington, D.C.: Government Printing Office, 1931–1940), 35:229–30 (unless otherwise specified, all references to Washington's *Writings* will be to this edition, not to that of Jared Sparks). See, above all, Jefferson's preamble to his Bill for the More General Diffusion of Knowledge, *The Papers of Thomas Jefferson*, ed. Julian P. Boyd et al., 22 vols. to date (Princeton, N.J.: Princeton University Press, 1950–), 2:526–28.

Chapter 1. The Problematic Heritage of European Education

1. Noah Webster, *A Grammatical Institute, of the English Language, Comprising, an Easy, Concise, and Systematic Method of Education, Designed for the Use of English Schools in America. In Three Parts*, pt. 1 (Hartford, Conn.: Hudson and Goodwin, 1783; facsimile reprint, Menston, England: Scolar Press, 1968), 3, 4, 14.

2. Noah Webster, "On the Education of Youth in America" (1790), in Rudolph, *Essays on Education*, 77; cf. 45. For similar sentiments, see Benjamin Rush, "Thoughts upon Female Education, Accommodated to the Present State of Society, Manners, and Government in the United States of America" (1787), in ibid., 27–28, 36; and the documents in Edgar W. Knight, *A Documentary History of Education in the South before 1860*, 5 vols. (Chapel Hill: University of North Carolina Press, 1950), vol. 2, chap. 1 (entitled "Opposition to Foreign Education"), esp. Jefferson's letter to J. Banister, Jr., 15 October 1785. See also Lawrence A. Cremin, *Traditions of American Education* (New York: Basic Books, 1977), 41–44.

3. The address is reprinted in Harry G. Goode, *Benjamin Rush and His Services to American Education* (Berne, Ind.: Witness Press, 1918), 198–206; quotation is from 198.

4. See esp. Lawrence A. Cremin, *American Education: The Colonial Experience,*

1607–1783 (New York: Harper and Row, 1970), 475–78 and 564–70; and *American Education: The National Experience, 1783–1876* (New York: Harper and Row, 1980), 1–3; Jon Teaford, "The Transformation of Massachusetts Education, 1670–1780," in B. Edward McClellan and William J. Reese, eds., *The Social History of American Education* (Urbana: University of Illinois Press, 1988), 30–31. Cremin's account, in "Reading, Writing, and Literacy," *Review of Education* 1 (1975): 517–21, indicates that Rudolph exaggerates the illiteracy and lack of education among Americans prior to the Revolution in *Essays on Education*, xvi–xvii.

5. Webster, "On the Education of Youth in America," in Rudolph, *Essays on Education*, 65–66; cf. also 69–70. Webster's appeal to the authority of Montesquieu in this regard is quoted approvingly by Robert Coram in his "Political Inquiries" (in ibid., 125–26). For another striking, direct echo of Montesquieu's analysis, see John Adams to John Penn, January 1776, *Works* 4:204.

6. For our purposes, the most important sections of *The Spirit of the Laws* devoted to education are bk. 3, chaps. 1, 2, 5–8; bk. 4, chaps. 1, 2, 4; and bk. 5, chaps. 9, 19.

7. Carter Braxton, "An Address to the Convention of the Colony and Ancient Dominion of Virginia on the Subject of Government in General, and Recommending a Particular Form to Their Attention" (1776), in Charles S. Hyneman and Donald S. Lutz, eds., *American Political Writing during the Founding Era, 1760–1805*, 2 vols. (Indianapolis: Liberty Press, 1983), 1:330.

8. William Blackstone, *Commentaries on the Laws of England*, 4 vols. (Oxford: Clarendon Press, 1765–1769; facsimile reprint, Chicago: University of Chicago Press, 1979), 1:153 (bk. 1, chap. 2).

9. See the illuminating discussion in David Epstein, *The Political Theory of the Federalist* (Chicago: University of Chicago Press, 1984), 15–16, 20–22, 32–34, 119–25, 145–46, 153, 183–85, 192, 196–97. For the persistence, in the new nation's civil service, of the principle of aristocratic honor, see Leonard White, *The Federalists: A Study in Administrative History 1789–1801* (New York: Macmillan, 1948), chaps. 21, 22, 25; and *The Jeffersonians: A Study in Administrative History 1801–1829* (New York: Macmillan, 1951), 356–68, 547–49.

10. See especially John Adams's essay "On Private Revenge" and his "Dissertation on the Canon and Feudal Law," in *Works* 3:427–32, 438–44, 450–52; see also the opening of David Ramsay's 1778 "Oration on the Advantages of American Independence," in Wilson Smith, ed., *Theories of Education in Early America 1655–1819* (Indianapolis: Bobbs-Merrill, 1973), 223.

11. For the continuing significance of aristocratic (Renaissance) honor in Puritanism, see Michael Walzer, *The Revolution of the Saints: A Study in the Origins of Radical Politics* (New York: Atheneum, 1973), chap. 7 (entitled "Puritanism and the Gentry"), esp. 253–54, 266–67.

12. A. J. P. Taylor, *Bismarck: The Man and the Statesman* (New York: Random House, Vintage Books, 1967), 148–49. For a useful historical survey that brings the literature on the Catholic church's attitude to liberal democracy up to date, see Paul E. Sigmund, "The Catholic Tradition and Modern Democracy," *Review of Politics* 49 (1987): 530–48.

13. John Locke, *A Letter Concerning Toleration: Latin and English Texts Revised*, ed. Mario Montuori (The Hague: Martinus Nijhoff, 1963), 88–93.

14. Samuel Adams, "The Rights of the Colonists," *Writings* 2:352–53. Cf. Montesquieu, *Spirit of the Laws*, bk. 19, chap. 27, p. 580.

15. Worthington C. Ford et al., eds., *Journals of the Continental Congress, 1774–1789*, 34 vols. (Washington, D.C.: Government Printing Office, 1904–1937), 1:83, 87–88.

16. The friendly message the same Continental Congress sent five days later to the inhabitants of Quebec, asking them to join in the resistance to England and assuring them

that "we are too well acquainted with the liberality of sentiment distinguishing your nation, to imagine, that difference of religion will prejudice you against a hearty amity with us" seems to indicate that the protest to the people of Great Britain was a bit rhetorical (see ibid., 105–13).

17. Adams to Jefferson, 19 May 1821, *The Adams-Jefferson Letters,* ed. Lester J. Cappon, 2 vols. (Chapel Hill: University of North Carolina Press, 1959), 2:573; on Roman Catholicism, cf. Adams to Jefferson, 22 June 1815 (pp. 447–51), 6 May 1816 (p. 474), 9 August 1816 (p. 486), 4 November 1816 (p. 494), 28 January 1818 (p. 523), 3 February 1821 (p. 571); Jefferson to Adams, 1 August 1816 (p. 484), 17 May 1818 (p. 524), and 4 September 1823 (p. 596), along with the editor's comment on p. 477. Cf. Jefferson to Roger C. Weightman, 24 June 1826, *Life and Selected Writings,* 729. See also Walter Berns, *Taking the Constitution Seriously* (New York: Simon and Schuster, 1987), 59–60.

18. For the discussion that follows, see *On the Laws of Ecclesiastical Polity,* in *The Works of That Learned and Judicious Divine Mr. Richard Hooker,* ed. J. Keble, 3 vols., 7th ed. (New York: Burt Franklin, 1970), esp. preface; bk. 1, entire; bk. 5, chaps. 1–2, 62, 65, 76; bk. 7, entire; bk. 8, chaps. 1–4, 6, 8. The best analysis of Hooker's thought is Robert K. Faulkner, *Richard Hooker and the Politics of a Christian England* (Berkeley and Los Angeles: University of California Press, 1981); see 141–67 for an account of the practical import of Hooker's conception of an established religion. Hooker's reputation, as a political theorist favorable to popular government and as a theologian who had elaborated the authoritative Anglican interpretation of Christian political doctrine, remained high among some of the American Founders in the eighteenth and early nineteenth centuries: see esp. James Wilson, *Of the Study of Law in the United States* (1790), in *Selected Political Essays of James Wilson,* ed. Randolph G. Adams (New York: Alfred A. Knopf, 1930), 222–23, 239, 254, 290.

19. Locke, *Letter Concerning Toleration,* 14–17 (our translation); see also 42–45.

20. Montesquieu, *Spirit of the Laws,* bk. 20, chap. 8, and bk. 19, chap. 27, pp. 580–81; Blackstone, *Commentaries,* bk. 3, chap. 7; bk. 4, chaps. 4, 8, 28; Hume, *History of England from the Invasion of Julius Caesar to the Revolution in 1688,* 6 vols. (New York: John W. Lovell, n.d.), vol. 3, chap. 29, beginning, pp. 24–27; Hume, *Essays: Moral, Political, and Literary,* ed. Eugene F. Miller (Indianapolis: Liberty Press, 1985), 65–67; Smith, *An Enquiry into the Nature and Causes of the Wealth of Nations,* ed. R. H. Campbell et al., 2 vols. (Indianapolis: Liberty Press, 1981), bk. 5, chap. 1, pt. 3, art. 3, pp. 792–93.

21. Cf. Faulkner, *Richard Hooker and the Politics of a Christian England,* 4: "Burke is far from sharing the priority Hooker gave to faith, theory, Christ, and Aristotle; nor did Hooker have Burke's regard for evolutionary progress, politics, and freedom of enterprise, to say nothing of toleration."

22. Burke, *Reflections on the Revolution in France* (Garden City, N.Y.: Doubleday, 1961), 103–20.

23. For the central meaning and the diverse, broad, and complex connotations of the term *Puritan*—a term that was employed by the enemies rather than the advocates of Calvinist "purification" of the Church of England—see Christopher Hill, *Society and Puritanism in Pre-Revolutionary England,* 2d ed. (New York: Schocken Books, 1972), chap. 1 (entitled "The Definition of a Puritan"), 13–29.

24. On Cromwell, see Ernst Troeltsch, *The Social Teaching of the Christian Churches,* trans. Olive Wyon, 2 vols. (Chicago: University of Chicago Press, 1976), 2:634; Walzer, *Revolution of the Saints,* 139–40, 328; and the lively, sympathetic biography by the liberal statesman John Morley, *Oliver Cromwell* (New York: Century Company, 1900), esp. 237–38, 326–27, 379–92. On Winthrop, see Edmund S. Morgan, *The Puritan Dilemma: The Story of John Winthrop* (Boston: Little, Brown, 1958), esp. chap. 7 (entitled "A Due Form of Government"), 84–100. Cf. the characterization of John Knox's political doctrine in

Walzer, *Revolution of the Saints*, 109: "Revolution could not wait upon majorities; Knox described instead the political privileges of a small minority, a revolutionary elect 'to whom God granteth knowledge.' Political right 'devolved' only to the godly among the people." For Calvin himself, see esp. *The Institutes of the Christian Religion*, trans. John Allen and revised Benjamin B. Warfield (Philadelphia: Westminster Press, 1945), bk. 4, chap. 20.

25. The classic study is Samuel Eliot Morison, *The Intellectual Life of Colonial New England*, 2d ed. (Ithaca, N.Y.: Cornell University Press, 1980), chaps. 1–4. It does seem to us that Morison's treatment is marred by his overcompensatory zeal to correct what he sees as the great mistake of previous scholars: their slighting of the *secular* dimensions of Puritan educational doctrine and practice. Morison himself seems to err in the opposite direction: see esp. 31, 44, 67–69, 90. Contrast Edmund Morgan, *The Puritan Family: Religion and Domestic Relations in Seventeenth-Century New England*, rev. and enl. ed. (New York: Harper and Row, 1966), 88–92, 101.

26. See Perry Miller and Thomas H. Johnson, eds., *The Puritans: A Sourcebook of Their Writings*, rev. ed., 2 vols. (New York: Harper and Row, 1963), introduction, 1:15–19 and 53–54; the latter pages provide an impressively incisive and powerful description of the supra-rational illumination that was understood to accompany the awareness of election or regeneration ("only those who have experienced it will be able to understand aright the law of nature or be able to guide the steps of reason").

27. Troeltsch, *Social Teaching of the Christian Churches* 2:617–20; cf. the kindred, though more hostile, characterization of the New England Puritan educational tradition by John Quincy Adams, in John Quincy Adams and Charles Francis Adams, *John Adams*, 2 vols. (New York: Chelsea House, 1980), 1:18–20.

28. Walzer, *Revolution of the Saints*, 10, 124–25, 255–60, 273–75, 301. For the contrasts between the Huguenots and the Puritans (or their forebears, the Marian exiles) and the latter's departures from or elaborations on Calvin himself, see esp. 64, 66–116, 212. For the similarities in outlook and the intimate links between the radical English Puritans who arose out of the Marian exile and the leaders of the New England settlers (e.g., John Winthrop), see 142–43 and 150–51, where Walzer takes issue with Perry Miller's more "conservative" interpretation of New England Puritan political and educational thought.

29. "Copy of a Letter from Mr. Cotton to Lord Say and Seal in the Year 1636," appendix 3 to Thomas Hutchinson's *History of the Colony and Province of Massachusetts-Bay*, ed. Lawrence Mayo, 3 vols. (Cambridge: Harvard University Press, 1936), 1:415; cf. Miller and Johnson, *The Puritans* 1:208.

30. Winthrop, "A Modell of Christian Charity, Written on Boarde the Arrabella, on the Atlantick Ocean," in Miller and Johnson, *The Puritans* 1:195.

31. Hubbard, "The Happiness of a People in the Wisdome of Their Rulers Directing and in the Obedience of Their Brethren Attending" (1676), in Miller and Johnson, *The Puritans* 1:247–49; see also Morgan, *The Puritan Family*, 11–12, 19–21.

32. Winthrop, Speech to the General Court, 3 July 1645, in Miller and Johnson, *The Puritans* 1:206–7.

33. Barnard, *The Throne Established by Righteousness* (1734), in Miller and Johnson, *The Puritans* 1:276; cf. 270–75. On the Calvinist rejection of representative government and majority rule, see Walzer, *Revolution of the Saints*, 84–85; Hill, *Society and Puritanism*, 241, 439–40, 493–94.

34. Winthrop, Speech to the General Court, 3 July 1645, and "A Modell of Christian Charity," in Miller and Johnson, *The Puritans* 1:207 and 195–96. Winthrop thought that democracy would be "a manifest breach of the Fifth Commandment" (quoted in Hill, *Society and Puritanism*, 459). For the complex, ambivalent Calvinist and Puritan attitude to-

ward patriarchal authority, see Walzer, *Revolution of the Saints*, 32–33, 49, 82, 188–98, which corrects the rather two-dimensional, overly authoritarian picture drawn in Hill, *Society and Puritanism*, 458–65. See also Morgan's *Puritan Family*, 45–48, 59–64.

35. Ward, *The Simple Cobbler of Aggawam in America* (orig. pub. 1647), in Miller and Johnson, *The Puritans* 1:227–32; editors' comments, in ibid. 1:185; cf. introduction, 1:16 ("Cromwell's New England brethren . . . looked upon his policy of toleration as the sole stain upon the otherwise flawless record of the pre-eminent warrior saint of the age"), and Morley, *Oliver Cromwell*, 410–14. What Morgan has called "Puritan tribalism" expressed itself in the requirement that everyone attend church but that membership in church be limited to those already converted, with little attempt to convert the unconverted: see *The Puritan Family*, chap. 7, esp. p. 174.

36. *The Judgement of the Rector and Tutors of Yale College, Concerning Two of the Students Who Were Expelled; Together with the Reasons of It* (1745), in Richard Hofstadter and Wilson Smith, eds., *American Higher Education: A Documentary History*, 2 vols. (Chicago: University of Chicago Press, 1961), 1:79, 81.

37. Miller and Johnson, *The Puritans* 2:385; Walzer, *Revolution of the Saints*, 215; cf. 44, 226, 303–5. See Troeltsch's respectful but far-reaching critique of his teacher Max Weber's thesis concerning the "Protestant ethic and the spirit of capitalism" in Troeltsch, *Social Teaching of the Christian Churches* 2:608–12, 625, 648–49, 915, 987–90. See also Hill, *Society and Puritanism*, chap. 6 (entitled "Discipline"), especially the quotations from Milton and Adam Smith at 225–27.

38. John Milton, *Paradise Lost: A Poem in Twelve Books*, ed. Merritt Y. Hughes (Indianapolis: Bobbs-Merrill, 1975), bk. 2, lines 299–309, 521–70; bk. 5, lines 469–543, 772–end.

39. Winthrop, journal entry of 21 June 1641, in Miller and Johnson, *The Puritans* 1:205; see the editors' discussion at 1:23. For examples of resistance by American Puritans to the introduction of classical republican political ideals, see Richard M. Gummere, *The American Colonial Mind and the Classical Tradition* (Cambridge: Harvard University Press, 1963), 37–38, 40–52. See also Sheldon S. Cohen, *A History of Colonial Education, 1607–1776* (New York: John Wiley and Sons, 1974), 38–39; and, on John Knox's opposition to the classics, Walzer, *Revolution of the Saints*, 101.

40. Rush Welter, *Popular Education and Democratic Thought in America* (New York: Columbia University Press, 1962), 9. Welter's characterization does indeed find some support in the enthusiastic wartime rhetoric of David Ramsay's 1778 "Oration on the Advantages of American Independence": "During the long past night of 150 years, our minds were depressed, and our activity benumbed by the low prospects of subjection" (in Smith, *Theories of Education*, 226).

41. Bernard Bailyn, *Education in the Forming of American Society* (New York: W. W. Norton, 1972), 27–28, and Morison, *Intellectual Life of Colonial New England*, 63, 107–8.

42. Miller and Johnson, *The Puritans* 1:19, 193-94; for the key excerpts from the text of Wise's treatise, see 1:257–69.

43. See the discussion and references in Wilson Carey McWilliams, "Civil Religion in the Age of Reason: Thomas Paine on Liberalism, Redemption, and Revolution," *Social Research* 54 (1987): 448–59, 488–900; see also Steven M. Dworetz, *The Unvarnished Doctrine: Locke, Liberalism, and the American Revolution* (Durham, N.C.: Duke University Press, 1990); John Adams, "A Dissertation on the Canon and Feudal Law," in *Works* 3:451–56; Alice M. Baldwin, *The New England Clergy and the American Revolution* (Durham, N.C.: Duke University Press, 1928); Claude M. Newlin, *Philosophy and Religion in Colonial America* (New York: Philosophical Library, 1962); Cremin, *American Education: The Colonial Experience 1607–1783*, 457–59.

44. Welter, *Popular Education*, 27–28; cf. 36–38.

45. Samuel Adams to John Adams, 4 October 1790, *Writings* 4:343.

46. Samuel Adams to John Adams, 25 November 1790, ibid. 4:347, 349.

47. Benjamin Rush, "A Plan for the Establishment of Public Schools and the Diffusion of Knowledge in Pennsylvania; to Which Are Added, Thoughts upon the Mode of Education, Proper in a Republic," in Hyneman and Lutz, *American Political Writing* 1:675–92; quotation is from 683.

48. "The Bible as a School-Book," in *The Selected Writings of Benjamin Rush*, ed. Dagobert D. Runes (New York: Philosophical Library, 1948), 122, 128–29.

49. Ibid., 122.

Chapter 2. Classical Republican Educational Ideals

1. Rush, "A Plan for the Establishment of Public Schools," in Hyneman and Lutz, *American Political Writing* 1:681, 684–86, 689.

2. Ibid., 685–86, 689.

3. Rush shortened and tempered his essay in subsequent editions of 1789 and 1806, deleting references to instruction in the art of war and paragraphs stressing the need for Spartan discipline in the comportment of teachers and students: see Smith, *Theories of Education*, 242–43. It seems to us that Frederick Rudolph, Linda Kerber, and Gordon Wood have rather exaggerated the degree to which Rush's essay (misdated by Wood to 1798) can be seen as reflecting the thinking of "many" other Americans who spoke out in the Founding period on the need for a new educational program for Americans: see Rudolph, *Essays on Education*, xv; Linda K. Kerber, *Federalists in Dissent: Imagery and Ideology in Jeffersonian America* (Ithaca, N.Y.: Cornell University Press, 1970), 108–9; and Gordon Wood, *The Creation of the American Republic, 1776–1787* (New York: W. W. Norton, 1972), 423–29 (esp. 427) and also 61 and 124. Somewhat more reserved, and certainly more informative about Rush's relation to his contemporaries in this respect, is Cremin, *American Education: The National Experience 1783–1876*, 114–27.

4. Rush, "A Plan for the Establishment of Schools," in Hyneman and Lutz, *American Political Writing* 1:685–90.

5. Samuel Adams to John Scollay, 30 December 1780, *Writings* 4:238; cf. Wood, *Creation of the American Republic*, 117–18. There is a tendency in Wood (and many other scholars who cite Adams's invocation of a "Christian Sparta") to overstate the degree to which Adams's remark was representative of American thinking at the time. Even the intended seriousness in Adams's own mind of this epistolary outburst is unclear: see Wood's subsequent and quite different characterization of Adams's thinking in the early 1780s in ibid., 421. For some of Adams's other explicit, but rather rare and sometimes reluctant appeals to classical republican educational models, see *Writings* 4:212–14, 258, 272, 359.

6. Knox, "An Essay on the Best System of Liberal Education, Adapted to the Genius of the Government of the United States. Comprehending also, an Uniform General Plan for Instituting and Conducting Public Schools, in This Country, on Principles of the Most Extensive Utility. To Which is Prefixed, an Address to the Legislature of Maryland on That Subject" (1799), in Rudolph, *Essays on Education*, 309.

7. *Federalist Papers*, no. 10 (p. 77), no. 51 (p. 322).

8. The term *liberal democracy* seems to have been employed for the first time by John Adams, though not in our contemporary sense. Adams contrasts "contracted aristocracy," in which officeholding is restricted to a minority, to "liberal democracy," in which offices are open to the people: see *Defence of the Constitutions*, in *Works* 4:312–13.

9. Hume, "Of Commerce," in *Essays*, 259–60, 262–63. Hume's assessment is reflected in the *Federalist Papers*, no. 8 (pp. 68–69). See in a similar vein John Adams, *Defence of the*

Constitutions, in *Works* 5:289. Cf. Fisher Ames, "American Literature" and "Hints and Conjectures Concerning the Institutions of Lycurgus," in *The Works of Fisher Ames,* ed. W. B. Allen, 2 vols. (Indianapolis: Liberty Classics, 1983), 1:33–34, 94–115; and Noah Webster, *On the Education of Youth in America,* in Rudolph, *Essays on Education,* 43–44. See Jefferson's firm rejection of Aristotle's political science in his letter to Isaac H. Tiffany of 26 August 1816, *The Writings of Thomas Jefferson,* ed. Andrew A. Lipscomb and Albert E. Bergh, 20 vols. (Washington, D.C.: Thomas Jefferson Memorial Association, 1903), 15:65–66 (unless otherwise specified, all references to Jefferson's *Writings* will be to this edition, not to that of Henry A. Washington). Louis Wright's account of Jefferson's relation to classical thought suffers from an excessive reliance on the fact of Jefferson's wide learning in and citation of the classics and an insufficient reflection on the deep issues over which Jefferson decisively breaks with classical thought: see "Thomas Jefferson and the Classics," in Merrill Peterson, ed., *Thomas Jefferson: A Profile* (New York: Hill and Wang, 1967), 195–217 (especially damaging is Wright's ill-considered belittling of the "battle of the books," or the "quarrel between the ancients and the moderns," 199–200).

10. John Trenchard and Thomas Gordon, *Cato's Letters or, Essays on Liberty, Civil and Religious, and Other Important Subjects,* 3d ed., 4 vols. (New York: Russell and Russell, 1733; facsimile reprint, 1969), esp. letters 31, 33, 40, 62, 67, 68. This work is listed as one of the "Classicks" that should form the core canon of readings for students in Benjamin Franklin's *Proposals Relating to the Education of Youth in Pennsylvania* (1749), in *The Papers of Benjamin Franklin,* ed. Leonard Labaree et al., 28 vols. to date (New Haven, Conn.: Yale University Press, 1959–), 3:405–6.

11. See esp. Locke's *Essay Concerning Human Understanding,* bk. 2, chap. 21.

12. Locke, *A Letter Concerning Toleration,* 44–45 (our translation); "Essay Concerning Toleration" (1667), in Henry R. Fox-Bourne, *The Life of John Locke,* 2 vols. (New York: Harper and Brothers, 1876), 1:174ff. (quotation is from 181). Richard Gummere's account, in *The American Colonial Mind and the Classical Tradition,* of the significance of the natural law tradition in eighteenth-century American political thought drastically underestimates the fundamental shift in meaning and emphasis between Stoic natural law and the doctrine of natural law understood as derived from natural rights in the "state of nature."

13. Plato, *Laws* 650b.

14. For some muted reflections among Americans of the classical republican, as opposed to the liberal or Lockean, conception of popular sovereignty, see the references to James Otis, Thomas Hutchinson, and, above all, John Wise in Gummere, *The American Colonial Mind and the Classical Tradition,* 99–103 and 111. Wise paraphrases Cicero's *Offices,* bk. 2, sec. 44: "Nothing is more suitable to nature than that those who excel in understanding should rule and control those who are less happy in these advantages."

15. Mather, *Corderius Americanus. An Essay Upon the Good Education of Children. And What May Hopefully Be Attempted, for the Hope of the Flock. In a Funeral Sermon upon Mr. Ezekial Cheever. The Ancient and Honourable Master of the Free-School in Boston. Who Left Off, But When Mortality Took Him Off, in August, 1708, the Ninety-Fourth Year of His Age. With an Elegy and an Epitaph Upon Him. By one that was a Scholar to him.,* in Smith, *Theories of Education,* 29–30. See also Paul L. Ford, ed., *The New England Primer: A History of Its Origins and Development, with a Reprint of the Unique Copy of the Earliest Known Edition* (New York: Teachers College, Columbia University, 1962), or the excerpts from the primer in Ellwood P. Cubberly, *Readings in Public Education in the United States* (Boston: Houghton Mifflin, 1934), 49–50, and the discussion by David B. Tyack in *Turning Points in American Educational History* (Waltham, Mass.: Blaisdell, 1967), 2–3. See also Prov. 1:7, 9:10, and Ps. 111:10 ("the fear of the Lord is the beginning of wisdom"), as well as Job 28:28 and Acts 9:31.

16. Witherspoon, *Letters on Education*, letter 5, in Smith, *Theories of Education*, 213, 215–16.

17. Aristotle, *Nicomachean Ethics* 1177a12–1179a33.

18. John Milton, *Areopagitica and Of Education*, ed. George H. Sabine (Northbrook, Ill.: AHM Publishing, Crofts Classics, 1951). For testimony to the significance in America of Milton's educational writings, see Benjamin Franklin's 1749 *Proposals Relating to the Education of Youth in Pennsylvania*, in *Papers* 3:397–421, and Samuel Harrison Smith, "Remarks on Education," in Rudolph, *Essays on Education*, 205.

19. This is perhaps the best place to register our major criticism of Lawrence A. Cremin's often very helpful, monumental, quasi-official history of American education (cosponsored by the American Historical Association and the United States Office of Education). Cremin stresses the impact on the colonists of the classical educational treatises ("libraries in all the colonies proffered images of man via Plato, Aristotle, Plutarch, Seneca, Homer, Virgil, and Ovid"), but he is strangely silent about Xenophon, whom he tends consistently to ignore. Cremin documents the leading role of works such as Plato's *Laws* and Xenophon's *Memorabilia* in eighteenth-century American college curricula; he highlights the impact in eighteenth-century America of Locke's *Essay Concerning Human Understanding* and *Some Thoughts Concerning Education* ("the colonists were thoroughly familiar with the *Essay* and the *Thoughts*, which circulated briskly in all regions and were commonly referred to in letters and periodicals"); and he notes in particular the impact of Locke's educational theory on Franklin and Jefferson. He also spends considerable space discussing and analyzing Thomas More's *Utopia* and Erasmus's educational works, several much less significant Renaissance followers of Plato, and the creators of "mirrors of princes" (for instance, Thomas Elyot) who provide pale imitations of the fountainhead of that great genre, Xenophon's *Education of Cyrus*, yet Cremin fails to discuss or analyze the contents of the classic works themselves—unless we are mistaken, Cremin passes over in silence *The Education of Cyrus*—and he provides rather misleading indications as to the actual contents of Locke's educational writings. As a consequence, the incisive contrasts between these twin peaks of civic educational theory looming over all American thought about education—the Socratic and the Lockean—are barely visible in Cremin's presentation. Even worse, for our purposes, is that crucial contrasts as well as tensions or controversies in American educational thinking in the late colonial and Founding periods are blurred or submerged. See *American Education: The Colonial Experience 1607–1783*, esp. 68, 96, 365, 379–83, 437, 460, 463–64, 470.

20. Xenophon, *Education of Cyrus* bk. 1, chap. 2, secs. 2–3. Cf. Samuel Adams, Governor's Message to the Massachusetts Legislature, 17 January 1794, *Writings* 4:359: "Human laws excite fears and apprehensions, least crimes committed may be detected and punished: But a virtuous education is calculated to reach and influence the heart, and to prevent crimes."

21. Xenophon, *Education of Cyrus* bk. 1, chap. 2, secs. 3–5.

22. Ibid. secs. 6–8 and 11.

23. Milton, *Of Education*, in *Areopagitica and Of Education*, 69–70.

24. Ibid., 70.

25. Ibid., 63, 67–68.

26. Milton, *Areopagitica*, in *Areopagitica and Of Education*, 23.

27. Ibid., 5.

28. Ibid., 24–25; see Plato, *Laws* 788c and 822d.

29. Ibid., 22.

30. Plato, *Republic* 377–78, 598d–608b; *Laws* 660d–664b, 718b–723d, 817a–d; for a fuller discussion see Leo Strauss, *The Rebirth of Classical Political Rationalism: An Introduc-*

tion to the Thought of Leo Strauss, ed. Thomas L. Pangle (Chicago: University of Chicago Press, 1989), 171–83.

31. See, for example, Jefferson's letter to John Brazier of 27 January 1800, *Writings* 10:146–47. See also Noah Webster, "On the Education of Youth in America"; Samuel Harrison Smith, "Remarks on Education"; and Samuel Knox, "An Essay on the Best System of Liberal Education," in Rudolph, *Essays on Education*, 46–48, 64, 195–96, 281–84, 301–3, 338–43, 353.

32. Rollin, *The Method of Teaching and Studying the Belles Lettres; or An Introduction to Languages, Poetry, Rhetorick, History, Moral Philosophy, Physicks, etc., with Reflections on Taste; and Instructions with Regard to the Eloquence of the Pulpit, the Bar, and the Stage. The Whole Illustrated with Passages from the Most Famous Poets and Orators, Ancient and Modern, with Critical Remarks on Them. Designed More Particularly for Students in the Universities*, 7th ed., 4 vols. (London: W. Strahan et al., 1770, orig. pub. 1731).

33. Franklin, *Papers* 3:397–421. Rollin's influential *Ancient History of the Egyptians, Carthaginians, Assyrians, Babylonians, Medes & Persians, Macedonians, and Grecians*, 13 vols. (London: James, John, and Paul Knapton, 1734–1739), and his *Roman History from the Foundation of Rome to the Battle of Actium*, 16 vols. (1739–1750), were also authoritative texts, frequently cited and recommended for the use of upper school education (see, e.g., Franklin, *Papers* 4:105). Especially noteworthy are the discussions of Greek education and the lengthy account of Socrates: bk. 9, chap. 4, and bk. 10, chap. 1, art. 2, sec. 10 of *Ancient History of the Egyptians*. William Gribbin, writing a few years ago at the peak of the fashionable enthusiasm for "classical republican paradigms" in American eighteenth-century political thought, makes claims that we do not think can be sustained for the importance of Rollin and, even more contestable, for the perfect congruity of Rollin's outlook with that of the Americans: "Rollin's Histories and American Republicans," *William and Mary Quarterly*, 3d ser., 29 (1972): 611–22.

34. Rollin, *Method of Teaching* 1:1–2, 8, 22–23.

35. Ibid. 4:248.

Chapter 3. The Lockean Revolution in Educational Theory

1. Preface to Coste's French translation, *De l'education des Enfans* (Amsterdam: Antoine Schelte, 1695), as translated by James Axtell in *The Educational Writings of John Locke: A Critical Edition with Introduction and Notes* (Cambridge: Cambridge University Press, 1968), 52; see also Axtell's remarks on 51–53.

2. *The Educational Writings of John Locke*, 112; Locke's words obviously contradict Axtell's rather preposterous claim that "it simply never occurred to Locke that all children should be educated" (ibid., 51). Further quotations from *Some Thoughts Concerning Education* are cited in the text by section number.

3. See also *Two Treatises of Government*, bk. 1, secs. 90 and 93; bk. 2, secs. 56, 65, 67, 68, 69, 81, 170; and Locke's marginal note to the fifth edition of the treatise on education, quoted in *The Educational Writings of John Locke*, 164 n. 4. Cf. Nathan Tarcov, *Locke's Education for Liberty* (Chicago: University of Chicago Press, 1984), 3–5. We are much indebted to Tarcov's illuminating and thorough interpretation of Locke's treatise on education, and not least to Tarcov's erudite discussion of the education treatise's relation to the rest of Locke's political philosophy.

4. See Locke's rather harsh proposal for poor-law reform in his Report to the Board of Trade, 19 October 1697, in Fox-Bourne, *The Life of John Locke* 2:377–91. It is striking, revealing, and characteristic how little Locke has to say about the *religious* instruction of the children of the poor.

5. Although at the time of the publication of the treatise on education the schools of England had declined from their peak condition in 1660, one must not suppose that in the England known to Locke schools were rare; the Reformation, under both the Elizabethans and the Puritans, had led to a remarkable growth in secondary, though not elementary, schooling: "England in 1660 was better provided with secondary schools, many of them free in part, than at any time prior to the Education Act of 1870; . . . but the restoration of the monarchy in 1660 marks a distinct decline in standards and facilities" (Morison, *Intellectual Life of Colonial New England,* 59, 61; cf. also 86ff.).

6. Plato, *Laws* 942a–d; compare the definition of "liberal education" in bk. 1 of the *Laws* (643e–644a): "The education from childhood in virtue, that makes one desire and love to become a perfect citizen who knows how to rule and be ruled with justice. It is this upbringing alone, it appears to me, that this discussion would wish to isolate and to proclaim as education. As for an upbringing that aims at money, or some sort of strength, or some other sort of wisdom without intelligence and justice, the argument proclaims it to be vulgar, illiberal, and wholly unworthy to be called education."

7. See especially Aristotle, *Nicomachean Ethics* 1179b–end; and *Politics* 1260a10–25.

8. Plato, *Laws* 666–67.

9. See especially ibid. 817e–24a.

10. For the wide impact of this basic thesis of Lockean education theory on the literature read throughout the English-speaking world in the eighteenth century, see Kenneth MacLean, *John Locke and English Literature of the Eighteenth Century* (New York: Russell and Russell, 1962), 32–39. For a full discussion of the philosophic framework of Locke's conception of human nature, see Thomas L. Pangle, *The Spirit of Modern Republicanism: The Moral Vision of the American Founders and the Philosophy of Locke* (Chicago: University of Chicago Press, 1988).

11. Francis Bacon, *The Advancement of Learning and New Atlantis* (London: Oxford University Press, 1974), bk. 1, chap. 5, sec. 11. "Bacon, throughout the seventeenth century, was a name to conjure with in America. . . . In North and South, from the first quarter of the seventeenth century onward, he was regarded as an apostle of the new learning, and his *Advancement of Learning* was read and quoted as an authority by preachers, schoolmasters, and politicians. It was to Bacon that educational theorists looked for wisdom": Louis B. Wright, *The Cultural Life of the American Colonies 1607–1763* (New York: Harper and Brothers, 1957), 135. For striking later instances of the influence of Bacon on the conception of the relation between theory and practice, see Benjamin Franklin's programmatic statement calling for the founding of the American Philosophical Society in 1743, *Papers* 2:380–83; and Samuel Harrison Smith's essay, which shared the prize of the American Philosophical Society in 1797, attacking Rousseau and the ancients in the name of Bacon, in Rudolph, *Essays on Education,* 178–79, 198–99. See also Eugene Miller, "On the American Founders' Defense of Liberal Education in a Republic," *Review of Politics* 46 (1984): 77–79, 85.

12. Obadiah Walker, *Of Education, Especially of Young Gentlemen,* 2d ed. (Oxford: n.p., 1673; facsimile reprint, Menston, England: Scolar Press, 1970).

13. John Witherspoon, *Letters on Education,* in Smith, *Theories of Education,* 186–220 (references will be to letter number and pages of this edition). The letters were first written in 1765 to a Scottish gentleman, while Witherspoon himself was still a resident of Scotland. Witherspoon, born in 1723, arrived in America in 1768, to serve as president of the College of New Jersey, later Princeton University, until his death in 1794. James Madison was his most famous student. Witherspoon served as a member of the Continental Congress, was a signer of the Declaration of Independence, and worked for the ratification of the Constitution. The letters were printed for the first time in 1775, in the *Pennsylvania Magazine,* and reprinted five times thereafter prior to 1822.

14. Tarc v, *Locke's Education for Liberty*, 5.

15. Locke, *Essay Concerning Human Understanding*, bk. 1, chap. 3, secs. 9 and 13. On the mastery of the inclinations, see *Some Thoughts Concerning Education*, secs. 33, 36, 38, 45, 48, 50, 52, 55, 63, 75, 77, 90, 103, 107, 139, 200.

16. Walker, *Of Education*, 25–27, 30–33, 43–44, 48–53, 114–15, 199–201, 206, 214–15, 238, 245. See also Milton, *Areopagitica*, 18: "Assuredly we bring not innocence into the world; we bring impurity much rather: that which purifies us is trial." Cf. also Cotton Mather's 1706 entry in his diary, "Some Special Points, Relating to the Education of My Children," in *The Diary of Cotton Mather*, 2 vols. (New York: Frederick Ungar, 1957), 1:534–37. See also Morgan's *Puritan Family*, 92–97.

17. Witherspoon, letter 1, p. 188, as well as 189–90; letter 3, pp. 201–3.

18. Cremin, *American Education: The Colonial Experience 1607–1783*, 277; cf. also 422, where Cremin assimilates the goals of Locke's educational program—"virtue, wisdom, breeding, and learning"—to those of John Dury's *Reformed School* of 1649—"piety, health, manners, and learning."

19. Robert H. Horwitz and Judith B. Finn, "Locke's Aesop's Fables," *Locke Newsletter* 6 (1975): 71–88; quote is from 83. Contrast the central role of Bible study, and the learning of Hebrew, and also Aramaic, in Milton's "Of Education," 64, 66, 67.

20. For Locke's treatment of religion in *Some Thoughts Concerning Education*, see also secs. 1 (first sentence), 61, 122 (end), 135–40, 157–59, 189–92, 200. Quotation from Juvenal is from *Satires* 10, line 365.

21. Cf. Locke, *Some Thoughts Concerning Education*, secs. 60, 78; contrast Aristotle's *Nicomachean Ethics* 1128b10–35, and St. Thomas Aquinas, *Commentary on the Nicomachean Ethics of Aristotle*, ad loc. Locke's decisive break here with both the classical and the Christian traditions regarding the essence of virtue is echoed by David Hume, *An Enquiry Concerning the Principles of Morals*, sec. 9, pt. 1, in *Enquiries Concerning the Human Understanding and Concerning the Principles of Morals*, ed. L. A. Selby-Bigge (Oxford: Clarendon Press, 1955), 276—a passage in turn echoed by the *Federalist Papers*, no. 72 (p. 437), where Hamilton refers to "the love of fame, the ruling passion of the noblest minds."

22. Witherspoon, letter 5, p. 214.

23. Walker, *Of Education*, 43–44, 206; cf. 48–59 and 205. See also Milton, "Of Education," 63–64.

24. [Plutarch?], "On the Education of Children," 10d–e. See also Quintilian, *Education of the Orator*, bk. 1, prolegomenon, sec. 19 and chap. 10, secs. 1–8.

25. Witherspoon, letter 3, p. 202.

26. Plato, *Laws* bk. 7, 822d–end; Xenophon, *Education of Cyrus* bk. 1, chap. 2, secs. 9–11 (but contrast *Oeconomicus* chaps. 4–5); *On Hunting with Dogs*.

27. See also secs. 6, 37 (where Locke is especially harsh on mothers who consciously or unconsciously teach their daughters "to be *Proud* of their Clothes"), and 70. Locke's treatise on education all too characteristically has not a word to say about the need for husband and wife to come to well-considered agreement regarding education as a necessary preparation for raising children; contrast the first letter on education of the much more patriarchal John Witherspoon. Locke's individualist attack on patriarchy goes together with his silence on the responsibilities of spouses to one another.

28. Locke, *Two Treatises of Government*, bk. 2, sec. 55.

29. Lord Kames, *Loose Hints upon Education, Chiefly Concerning the Culture of the Heart*, as excerpted in Smith, *Theories of Education*, chap. 8; quote is from 135.

30. Contrast Walker, *Of Education*, 32.

31. Cremin, *American Education: The Colonial Experience 1607–1783*, 66.

32. Walker, *Of Education*, pt. 1, chap. 2.

33. Ibid., 214–15 (consider also Walker's altogether un-Lockean insistence that charity is the heart of true civility); Witherspoon, letter 4, pp. 206, 208.

34. Contrast Walker, *Of Education*, 205–6, 229–30.

35. Ibid., 109.

Chapter 4. Benjamin Franklin and the Idea
of a Distinctively American Academy

1. John Clarke, *An Essay Upon the Education of Youth in Grammar-Schools. In Which the Vulgar Method of Teaching Is Examined, and a New One Proposed, for the More Easy and Speedy Training Up of Youth to the Knowledge of the Learned Languages; Together with History, Chronology, Geography, &c.*, 2d ed. (London: Arthur Bettesworth, 1730; orig. pub. 1720); Isaac Watts, *The Improvement of the Mind: With a Discourse on the Education of Children and Youth* (London: T. Nelson, 1849; orig. pub. 1741, 1751). See the excerpts and comments in Smith, *Theories of Education*, 61–126. See also Cremin, *American Education: The Colonial Experience 1607–1783*, 273ff., 367. For a discussion of some lesser intermediaries between Lockean educational doctrine and Americans, see Jacqueline S. Reinier, "Rearing the Republican Child: Attitudes and Practices in Post-Revolutionary Philadelphia," *William and Mary Quarterly*, 3d ser., 39 (1982): 150–63.

2. Franklin, *Proposals*, in *Papers* 3:397–421; "Idea of the English School," in ibid. 4:401–8; "Observations," in *The Works of Benjamin Franklin*, ed. Jared Sparks, 10 vols. (London: B. F. Stevens, 1882), 2:133–59. Franklin prefaces his *Proposals* with a section on "Authors Quoted in this Paper." In the paper, he refers to or quotes Locke eleven times, sometimes at great length; Milton's *Of Education* eight times; David Fordyce's *Dialogues Concerning Education* (which Franklin erroneously supposes to be written by Francis Hutcheson) four times; Obadiah Walker's treatise twice; Rollin's treatise seven times; and George Turnbull's *Observations upon Liberal Education* thirteen times. David Tyack has suggested that Franklin's set of references to previous writers was perhaps a "hoax," added to adorn his new notions with the veil of august authority while preserving as much as possible his accustomed sly self-effacement in launching "projects": "To sanctify his Proposals he swamped his own prose in interminable footnotes" (*Turning Points in American Educational History*, 52). Tyack therefore prints the bare text of Franklin's *Proposals*, shorn of the voluminous citations. But these citations, even if part of a rhetorical strategy, show the authorities to whom Franklin knew his audience bowed and are therefore revealing of the temper of Americans at the time. Moreover, while it is indeed likely that politic calculations played a role in Franklin's Socratic rhetoric—in this as in all cases—and while it is also true that the roguish Franklin's wit cannot be underestimated, it seems to us that the citations represent a substantial part of Franklin's argument and help flesh out his sketch. He himself indicates as much by the fact that, when he returns in 1789 to the proposal and quotes from it, he quotes the footnote citations of Locke as if they were an integral part of the proposals. On the other hand, what is more significant, as we shall see, and what Tyack does not observe, is the way in which the benevolently duplicitous Franklin doctors the quotations, sometimes in plain contradiction of his claimed "authority" (e.g., Milton).

3. Smith, *Theories of Education*, 176; for a good brief survey of the history of the academies, whose predominance peaked around 1820, see David L. Madsen, *Early National Education, 1776–1830* (New York: John Wiley and Sons, 1974), 107–13. See also Cremin, *American Education: The Colonial Experience 1697–1783*, 403–4.

4. "But there was no obligation on the part of parents to send children to school at any time in the colonial period" (Morison, *Intellectual Life of Colonial New England*, 76).

For the text of the laws and other pertinent documents, see Cubberly, *Readings in Public Education*, 16–20.

5. For the character of the Quaker schools in Philadelphia and their influence on Franklin, see Carl Bridenbaugh and Jessica Bridenbaugh, *Rebels and Gentlemen: Philadelphia in the Age of Franklin* (New York: Oxford University Press, 1962), 30–34, 41.

6. George Whitefield to Franklin, 26 February 1750, in Franklin, *Papers* 3:467–69; Franklin, *Proposals*, in *Papers* 3:413.

7. Franklin to Samuel Johnson, 24 December 1751, *Papers* 4:222.

8. Franklin, *Papers* 3:419; Milton, *Of Education*, 59, italics added. See also Cremin, *American Education: The Colonial Experience 1607–1783*, 302.

9. The character and importance of these private "writing schools" has been clarified recently: see Jon Teaford, "The Transformation of Massachusetts Education, 1670–1780," in McClellan and Reese, *Social History of American Education*, 31–35. Robert Middlekauf's account would now seem to require some revision ("A Persistent Tradition: The Classical Curriculum in Eighteenth-Century New England," *William and Mary Quarterly*, 3d ser., 18 [1961]: 54–67); but the picture of stubborn persistence in the academies of the older classical studies, predominating over the new Franklin vision, still seems largely valid. For the day and evening English schools, for girls as well as boys, that had sprung up in Philadelphia prior to Franklin's proposals, and for the influence they had on Franklin, see Bridenbaugh and Bridenbaugh, *Rebels and Gentlemen*, 35–41, 49–50; and Cremin, *American Education: The Colonial Experience 1607–1783*, 400–402.

10. Franklin, *Papers* 4:108.

11. Franklin, *Proposals*, in *Papers* 3:404–5, quoting secs. 161 and 210 of Locke's *Some Thoughts Concerning Education*. It is notable that Locke puts this advice about accounting almost at the end of his treatise, and at the end of his discussion of learning, while Franklin moves it to the very beginning.

12. Franklin, "Idea of the English School," in *Papers* 4:102–8; *Proposals*, in ibid. 3:405–6, quoting sec. 168 of Locke's *Some Thoughts Concerning Education*, with slight variations.

13. Milton, *Of Education*, 63–4; Franklin, *Papers* 4:106; see similarly 3:408.

14. Bernard Bailyn's influential essay, "An Interpretation," in his *Education in the Forming of American Society*, 3–49, is marred by an insufficient appreciation of the impact of politics on the early history of American schooling. He neglects both political theory and political action, and above all the Revolution, which in his account had little impact (see 48–49). Nowhere is this flaw more evident than in Bailyn's treatment of the educational thought of Franklin (see esp. 33–36). In Bailyn's presentation, Franklin's educational thought is reduced to a concern with the vocational, and he makes only the barest reference to the moral and civic aims underlying Franklin's discussion of the vocational aspects of education. Bailyn goes so far as to claim that Franklin "stated his *whole* philosophy of education in the single sentence with which he concluded his 'Idea of the English School': 'Thus instructed youth will come out of this school fitted for learning any business, calling, or profession' " (35, italics added).

15. Ramsay, "Oration on the Advantages of American Independence," in Smith, *Theories of Education*, 224–25.

16. Franklin, "Idea of the English School," in *Papers* 4:104; *Proposals*, in *Papers* 3:413–15; see also Samuel Knox, "An Essay on the Best System of Liberal Education," in Rudolph, *Essays on Education*, 345. It is striking to note that on this capital point, Franklin appeals to and takes the side of Obadiah Walker against Locke—the former having praised, the latter having condemned, the tradition of scholastic disputation. See pt. 1, chap. 10, p. 117 of Walker's *Of Education*; contrast sec. 189 of Locke's *Some Thoughts Concerning Education*. Later, however, in his *Autobiography*, Franklin seems to withdraw his support of debating: see *Autobiography*, 60, 65, 212–13. John Quincy Adams eloquently championed the study of rhetoric in his lectures as Boyleston Professor at Harvard: see Kerber, *Federalists in Dissent*, 127–29.

17. Franklin, *Proposals*, in *Papers* 3:410–11; Locke, *Some Thoughts Concerning Education*, secs. 184, 164, 177.

18. Franklin, *Papers* 3:415.

19. Ibid., 413.

20. Locke, *Some Thoughts Concerning Education*, sec. 192.

21. Franklin, *Papers* 3:416–17, 4:105, 3:417–18.

22. See esp. Montesquieu, *Spirit of the Laws*, bk. 21; Franklin, *Proposals*, in *Papers* 3:418–19; Bacon, *New Organon*, bk. 1, aphorism 118 (cf. aphorism 81); and Locke, *Essay Concerning Human Understanding*, bk. 4, chap. 12, secs. 10–12.

23. Franklin, *Papers* 3:385–88. The letter is no. 13 of bk. 4 of Pliny's *Letters*; the translation Franklin uses is William Melmoth's. Pliny was one of the most famous students of Quintilian, whose *Education of the Orator* opens with perhaps the best-known classical argument for an academy education.

24. Franklin, *Papers* 3:400–401; the first paragraph of the quoted passage is reproduced with insignificant variations in "Constitutions of the Publick Academy in the City of Philadelphia," in ibid., 427.

25. Franklin, "Observations," in *Works* 2:133–34, 140–42, 144, 148, 153, 156.

26. Franklin, "Constitutions of the Publick Academy," in *Papers* 3:422–28; "Observations," in *Works* 2:140–41.

27. See Clarence J. Karier, *The Individual, Society, and Education: A History of American Educational Ideas*, 2d ed. (Urbana: University of Illinois Press, 1986), 69–71. Karier traces the history of the "ancients vs. moderns" struggle through the nineteenth century, observing that the decisive decline of education in the classical languages comes with the introduction of the elective system and new entrance requirements at Harvard by President Eliot. The universities, colleges, and public high schools seem to have been more classically oriented than the private academies, in part because of the link that was perceived between classical learning and the religious tradition (see esp. 74–76 and 80–81 in Karier). For the "battle of the books" in the early years of the nineteenth century, see Kerber's *Federalists in Dissent*, chap. 4 (entitled "Salvaging the Classical Tradition") esp. 114–31. Kerber elucidates the controversy surrounding Benjamin Rush's "Enquiry into the Utility of a Knowledge of the Latin and Greek Languages, as a Branch of Liberal Education, with Hints of a Plan of Liberal Instruction without Them," published anonymously in *American Museum* 5 (June 1789): 525–35.

28. Franklin, *Proposals*, in *Papers* 3:405–8, quoting sec. 168 of Locke's *Some Thoughts Concerning Education*, and bk. 3, no. 3 of Pliny's *Letters*.

29. "The Greek and Roman authors," Noah Webster wrote near the end of the century, "will ever be held in the highest estimation both for style and sentiment, but the most valuable of them have English translations, which, if they do not contain all the elegance, communicate all the idea of the originals." In an accompanying footnote, however, Webster admitted his Greek and Latin were not good enough, and he lacked the leisure anyway, to read much classical literature and hence to know how accurate the translations really were: "On the Education of Youth in America," in Rudolph, *Essays on Education*, 44–48; cf. Benjamin Rush, "Thoughts upon the Mode of Education," in Hyneman and Lutz, *American Political Writing* 1:688.

Chapter 5. The American Insistence on Public Schooling as Essential to Democracy

1. George Washington to William A. Washington, 27 February 1798, *Writings* 36:172.

2. Samuel Harrison Smith, "Remarks on Education," in Rudolph, *Essays on Education*,

205; Amable-Louis-Rose de Lafitte du Courteil, "Proposal to Demonstrate the Necessity of a National Institution in the United States of America, for the Education of Children of Both Sexes" (1797), in ibid., 244–45; Samuel Knox, "An Essay on the Best System of Liberal Education," in ibid., 307; see also Franklin, "Idea of the English School," in *Papers* 4:102, 105, 107.

3. Knox, "An Essay on the Best System of Liberal Education," in Rudolph, *Essays on Education*, 306, 311; Lafitte du Courteil, "Proposal to Demonstrate the Necessity of a National Institution," in ibid., 243; Franklin, "On the Need for an Academy," in *Papers* 3:386.

4. Smith, "Remarks on Education," in Rudolph, *Essays on Education*, 205–9; Webster, "On the Education of Youth in America," in ibid., 52–53; cf. Knox, "An Essay on the Best System of Liberal Education," in ibid., 358–59.

5. Rush, "Thoughts upon the Mode of Education," in Hyneman and Lutz, *American Political Writing* 1:686–87; Webster, "On the Education of Youth in America," in Rudolph, *Essays on Education*, 52–54. On 31 July 1750, Franklin presented a "Paper on the Academy" to the Common Council of the city of Philadelphia as part of an effort to gain financial support from the city; in it he listed as the first of the "Benefits expected from this Institution" that "the Youth of Pennsylvania may have an opportunity of receiving a good Education at home, and be under no Necessity of going abroad for it; whereby not only a considerable Expence may be saved to the Country, but a stricter Eye may be had over their Morals by their Friends and Relations" (*Papers* 4:35–36). See also Rush, "Thoughts on Female Education," in Rudolph, *Essays on Education*, 38–39.

6. Adams, "Twenty-six Letters upon Interesting Subjects Respecting the Revolution of America, Written to Holland, in the Year 1780," letter 7, in *Works* 7:283. Compare the characterization of the educational situation in Vermont, something of a backwater, in Samuel Williams's 1794 *Natural and Civil History of Vermont*, chap. 13: "Among the customs which are universal among the people, in all parts of the state, one that seems worthy of remark, is, the attention that is paid to the education of children. . . . All the children . . . are accustomed from their earliest years to read the Holy Scriptures, the periodical publications, newspapers, and political pamphlets; to form some general acquaintance with the laws of their country, the proceedings of the courts of justice, of the general assembly of the state, and of the Congress, &c. Such a kind of education is common and universal in every part of the state. . . . This custom was derived from the people of New-england; and has acquired greater force in the new settlements, where the people are apprehensive their children will have less advantages, and of consequence, not appear equal to the children in the older towns" (reprinted in Hyneman and Lutz, *American Political Writing* 2:951–52).

7. See the documents and testimonies collected in Knight, *Documentary History of Education in the South before 1860*, vol. 1, chap. 14 (entitled "Tutorial Practices"), 571–664. Cf. the quotation from John Adams in Cremin, *American Education: The Colonial Experience 1607–1783*, 520.

8. David Rice, "Slavery Inconsistent with Justice and Good Policy" (the text was printed and circulated three months before the convention and reprinted subsequently as well), in Hyneman and Lutz, *American Political Writing* 2:881–82; see also Lowell H. Harrison, *The Antislavery Movement in Kentucky* (Lexington: University Press of Kentucky, 1978), chap. 2 (entitled "The Early Opposition"), 18–37; Robert McColley, *Slavery and Jeffersonian Virginia*, 2d ed. (Urbana: University of Illinois Press, 1973), chap. 6, (entitled "Gentlemen's Opinions on Race and Freedom"), 114–40, and epilogue, 182–89; quote is from 120. For a survey of some major statements in the debate over slavery and the status of blacks in the early years of the republic, see Kerber's *Federalists in Dissent*, chap. 2 (entitled "Against Virginia and Antislavery"), 23–66; see also G. C. Woodson,

The Education of the Negro prior to 1861 (New York: Arno Press, 1968), and Abraham Blinderman, *American Writers on Education before 1865* (Boston: Twayne Publishers, 1975), 34–36, 55. One of the most radical antislavery essays, which argues for racial equality and builds explicitly on Montesquieu, is Rush's 1773 "Address to the Inhabitants of the British Settlements in America upon Slave-Keeping," in Hyneman and Lutz, *American Political Writing* 1:217–30.

9. Adams, *Defence of the Constitutions*, in *Works* 6:168, 197; letter to John Jebb, 10 September 1785, *Works* 9:540. The passage from Aristotle that Adams quotes is from *Politics* 1310a12ff.; Aristotle goes on to say: "If lack of self-control exists in a single person, it also exists in a city. And to be educated relative to the regime is not to do the things that oligarchs or those who want democracy enjoy. . . . in those democracies that are held to be most especially democratic, what has become established is the opposite of what is beneficial. The cause of this is that they define freedom badly. . . . in democracies of this sort everyone lives as he wants and 'toward whatever end he happens to crave,' as Euripides says. But this is contemptible."

10. Adams, *Works* 4:199; Franklin, *Papers* 3:427, 435; 4:35, 325; Jefferson, *Notes on the State of Virginia*, ed. William Peden (New York: W. W. Norton, 1972), query 14, p. 148; Webster, "On the Education of Youth in America," in Rudolph, *Essays on Education*, 66–67; Knox, "An Essay on the Best System of Liberal Education," in ibid., 333; cf. 309.

11. Franklin to Cadwallader Colden, 13 February 1750, *Papers* 3:462; *Proposals*, in *Papers* 3:399; "Paper on the Academy," in *Papers* 4:36. Franklin was deeply worried that the influx of German-speaking immigrants would swamp the English-speaking population and fundamentally alter the character of Pennsylvania; he looked to English school education as a key measure for dealing with this local problem: see Theodore Thayer, *Pennsylvania Politics and the Growth of Democracy 1740–1776* (Harrisburg: Pennsylvania Historical and Museum Commission, 1953), 35–36.

12. Joel Barlow, *A Letter to the National Convention of France on the Defects in the Constitution of 1791, and the Extent of the Amendments Which Ought to Be Applied* (London: J. Johnson, 1792), 58–59; and *Two Letters to the Citizens of the United States and One to General Washington, Written from Paris in the Year 1799, on Our Political and Commercial Relations* (New Haven: Sidney's Press, 1806), letter 2, 79–80 (facsimiles reproduced from the Yale University Library in *The Works of Joel Barlow*, 2 vols. [Gainesville, Fla.: Scholars' Facsimiles and Reprints, 1970], 78–79 and 437–38). See in a similar vein Samuel Harrison Smith, "Remarks on Education," in Rudolph, *Essays on Education*, 198–99.

13. Robert Coram, "Political Inquiries," in Rudolph, *Essays on Education*, 112–13. Coram characteristically does not say a word about the all-important role of the private tutor in Rousseau's masterpiece, *Emile; or, On Education*; like so many "followers" of Rousseau, Coram fails to take into sufficient account those aspects of his master's complex system with which he disagrees. It may be noted, by the way, that a perusal of Locke's proposed poor-law reform shows that Locke's conception of the government's coercive role in guiding the lives of the poor, and especially the children of the poor, is if anything even more intrusive than Coram's: see Henry Fox-Bourne's *Life of John Locke* 2:377–91.

14. Aristotle, *Nichomachean Ethics* 1125a11–12.

15. Simeon Doggett, "A Discourse on Education, Delivered at the Dedication and Opening of Bristol Academy, the 18th Day of July, A.D. 1796," in Rudolph, *Essays on Education*, 158–59.

16. Noah Webster, "On the Education of Youth in America," in Rudolph, *Essays on Education*, 68–69; Benjamin Rush, "Thoughts upon Female Education," in ibid., 28.

17. Webster, "On the Education of Youth in America," in ibid., 69–70; cf. Simeon Doggett, "A Discourse on Education," in ibid., 159. Thomas Paine's *Age of Reason*

(1794–1796), exemplifying the most radically anti-Christian strain of the Enlightenment, sounded an alarm at women's control over early education, on account of the female tendency to support biblical faith and, perhaps worse, biblical morals rooted in love rather than justice, feeling rather than reason, and infantilist longings for security rather than mature individual independence and acceptance of the natural world: see McWilliams's "Civil Religion in the Age of Reason," 472–83.

18. Benjamin Rush, "Thoughts upon Female Education," in Rudolph, *Essays on Education,* 27–32; cf. Linda K. Kerber, "Daughters of Columbia: Educating Women for the Republic 1787–1805," in Stanley Elkins and Eric McKitrick, eds., *The Hofstadter Aegis: A Memorial* (New York: Alfred A. Knopf, 1974), 36–59; and also Kerber, *Women of the Republic* (Chapel Hill: University of North Carolina Press, 1980), 265–88. On the need for practical studies for women as future wives or widows, see *The Autobiography of Benjamin Franklin,* ed. Leonard W. Labaree (New Haven, Conn.: Yale University Press, 1964), 166. Franklin's proposals on the academic education of youth do not refer to school education for women, although on other occasions he indicated its importance and in 1732 he embarked on an essay on the education of women; that essay was never finished, and no trace of it has thus far been found (see *Papers* 1:254–55). On women and reading, see also Jefferson to Nathaniel Burwell, 14 March 1818, *Works* 12:91.

19. See Anne Firor Scott, "The Ever-Widening Circle: The Diffusion of Feminist Values from the Troy Female Seminary, 1822–1872," in McClellan and Reese, eds., *Social History of American Education,* 137–59.

20. Noah Webster, "On the Education of Youth in America," in Rudolph, *Essays on Education,* 57 and 59 (consider the context); cf. Simeon Doggett's "Discourse on Education," in ibid., 160. For a survey of unflattering descriptions of teachers in American literature in the years after the Founding period, see Blinderman's *American Writers on Education before 1865,* 9–10, 25–26. As Clarence Karier has pointed out, the establishment of separate institutions for teacher training was to bring its own problems, providing technical expertise in teaching methods but denying students an intellectually rigorous education, and so perpetuating the status of teachers as something less than true professionals. This problem persists today, even though schools of education have moved into the university (*The Individual, Society, and Education,* 62–63).

Chapter 6. Thomas Jefferson on the Education of Citizens and Leaders

1. Jefferson to Madison, 20 December 1787, *Papers* 12:442. There is no satisfactory and complete critical edition of Jefferson's writings; the Boyd edition (*Papers*) will be such if and when completed, but after forty years of editorial labor it now reaches only to 1791 and is not rapidly nearing completion. For a good brief account of the merits and demerits of the various printed collections, see Frank Shuffelton, "Bibliographic Essay," in Merrill D. Peterson, ed., *Thomas Jefferson: A Reference Biography* (New York: Charles Scribner's Sons, 1986), 453–56. The least reliable edition is that of Henry Washington (*Writings,* 1853–1854) and we have used it as sparingly as possible.

2. Jefferson, *Papers* 2:526–27. In a letter of 13 August 1786 to his fellow committeeman George Wythe, Jefferson calls this proposal "by far the most important bill in our code" (*Papers* 10:244).

3. Jefferson to Joseph Cabell, 14 February 1826, *Early History of the University of Virginia as Contained in the Letters of Thomas Jefferson and Joseph C. Cabell,* ed. Nathaniel Francis Cabell (Richmond, Va.: J. W. Randolph, 1856), 373.

4. Jefferson to John Tyler, 26 May 1810, *Life and Selected Writings,* 604.

5. See John Locke, *Second Treatise of Government*, chaps. 10 and 19.

6. Jefferson to John Adams, 28 October 1813, *Adams-Jefferson Letters* 2:388.

7. Jefferson to Roger Weightman, 24 June 1826, *Life and Selected Writings*, 729–30. Cf. Jefferson's First Inaugural: "Sometimes it is said that man cannot be trusted with the government of himself. Can he, then, be trusted with the government of others? Or have we found angels in the forms of kings to govern him?" (ibid., 323); A Bill for the More General Diffusion of Knowledge, *Papers* 2:527; Jefferson to James Monroe, 20 May 1782, *Life and Selected Writings*, 364–65. On his assessment of public versus private life, see Jefferson's letters to James Madison (9 June 1793), to John Adams (25 April 1794), to Francois D'Ivernois (6 February 1795), and to William Short (6 October 1819), ibid., 522–25, 527–28, 530, 693–97.

8. See chapter 13 below; the most important statements of Jefferson's view of the moral sense are his letter to Thomas Law of 13 June 1814, *Life and Selected Writings*, 636–40, and his letter to Peter Carr of 10 August 1787, ibid., 430–31.

9. Jefferson to Edward Carrington, 16 January 1787, *Life and Selected Writings*, 411–12.

10. Aristotle, *Politics* 1318b1–1319a6.

11. *Federalist Papers*, no. 49 (p. 314); Jefferson to Madison, 6 September 1789, *Life and Selected Writings*, 488–93; Madison to Jefferson, 4 February 1790, *Papers* 16:146–54; see also Jefferson to John Cartwright, 5 June 1824, *The Complete Jefferson*, ed. Saul Padover (New York: Duell, Sloan, and Pearce, 1943), 296. Contrast, however, Jefferson to Samuel Kercheval, 12 July 1816, *Works* 12:11–14: "I am certainly not an advocate for frequent and continued changes in laws and constitutions"; and *Notes on the State of Virginia*, query 17, p. 161.

12. Hamilton to John Jay, 26 November 1775, *The Papers of Alexander Hamilton*, ed. Harold C. Syrett et al., 27 vols. (New York: Columbia University Press, 1961–1987), 1:176–77.

13. Washington, First Annual Message, 8 January 1790, *Writings* 30:493.

14. Jefferson to Joseph Cabell, 13 January 1823, Jefferson and Cabell, *Early History of the University of Virginia*, 267–68. It seems to us that Joseph Kett, in his generally very helpful essay "Education" (in Peterson, *Thomas Jefferson*, 243) is mistaken in asserting that for Jefferson after 1816 "primary and higher education were no longer conjunctive ideals in his mind" but were rather "competing alternatives, and in the competition his preference was clearly for higher education." Kett, like a number of other scholars, seems to have been misled by Roy Honeywell, *The Educational Work of Thomas Jefferson* (Cambridge: Harvard University Press, 1931), 13–22, and Charles Flinn Arrowood, *Thomas Jefferson and Education in a Republic* (New York: McGraw-Hill, 1931), 33–36, who claim that Jefferson opposed, and his friends led by Cabell in the legislature defeated, an 1817 plan by the Federalist Charles Fenton Mercer to establish first elementary schools, then academies, colleges, and a university, out of state funds. In fact, Cabell voted for the bill, and Jefferson seems to have had nothing to do with the opposition to it. It is true that once the construction of the University of Virginia was in fact under way, Jefferson wanted to use all the available state money for it, postponing another effort on the part of primary education until the university was launched; but this was simply prudent allocation of resources. See Philip Alexander Bruce, *History of the University of Virginia 1819–1919: The Lengthened Shadow of One Man*, 5 vols. (New York: Macmillan, 1920–22), 1:81; Jefferson to General James Breckenridge, 15 February 1821, *Writings* 15:314–18; Dumas Malone, *Jefferson and His Time*, 6 vols. (Boston: Little, Brown, 1948–1981), vol. 6, *The Sage of Monticello*, 252–53 and 271 n. 16; see also 234, 237, 245, 248, 251, 267–69.

15. Jefferson, A Bill for the More General Diffusion of Knowledge (1779), *Papers* 2:528; An Act for Establishing Elementary Schools (1817), *Complete Jefferson*, 1075; ibid., 1074–75n; see also Jefferson to Chevalier De Onis, 1814, *The Writings of Thomas Jefferson*,

ed. Henry A. Washington, 9 vols. (New York: Riker, Thorne, 1853–1854), 6:342, and Jefferson to Dupont de Nemours, 24 April 1816, *Writings* (ed. Lipscomb and Bergh), 14:491–92.

16. Jefferson, *Notes on the State of Virginia*, query 14, p. 147; Prov. 22:6. See, e.g., Cotton Mather's comment on catechizing children: "And what though the Younger little Things may not fully apprehend the import of what they *Repeat?* We must not call this a *Taking of God's Name in Vain*, albeit they have not such Reverent Apprehension of God, as the Elder people have. The *Repetition* which they make of Divine Things is an *Introduction* and a *Preparation* to the further Acknowledgments of God, which they will one Day make with more of *Reverence*" (*Cares about the Nurseries*, in Smith, *Theories of Education*, 16). Locke, *Some Thoughts Concerning Education*, sec. 159; Jefferson, "Syllabus of an Estimate of the Merit of the Doctrines of Jesus, Compared with Those of Others," and An Act for Establishing Elementary Schools, *Complete Jefferson*, 949, 1072, 1076; Jefferson to John Adams, 12 October 1813, *Adams-Jefferson Letters* 2:383–84; Jefferson to Peter Carr, 10 August 1787, *Papers* 12:15.

17. Jefferson, A Bill for the More General Diffusion of Knowledge, *Papers* 2:528; *Notes on the State of Virginia*, query 14, p. 148.

18. On Jefferson's response to Marshall's biography, see Albert Beveridge, *The Life of John Marshall*, 4 vols. (Boston: Houghton Mifflin, 1916–1919), 3:228–29 and 265–69. On Hume and the unreliability of history in general, see Jefferson's letter of 25 October 1825 to an unnamed member of the University of Virginia faculty, *Complete Jefferson*, 1096, and his letter of 29 August 1787 to the editor of the *Journal de Paris*, ibid., 74.

19. Report of the Commissioners Appointed to Fix the Site of the University of Virginia (the Rockfish Gap report), *Complete Jefferson*, 1097–98.

20. See especially Jefferson to Adams, 28 October 1813, *Adams-Jefferson Letters* 2:391.

21. Colonel Coles, Jefferson's private secretary, to Cabell, 17 July 1807, in Jefferson and Cabell, *Early History of the University of Virginia*, 18n; Jefferson to Cabell, 2 February 1816, *Life and Selected Writings*, 660–62; on the New England townships, see Jefferson to Governor Tyler, 26 May 1810, *Writings of Jefferson*, ed. Washington, 5:525–26; on Anglo-Saxon self-government, see Jefferson to John Cartwright, 5 June 1824, *Complete Jefferson*, 293–95; on wards as essential for self-government, see Jefferson to Cabell, 31 January 1814, *Works* 11:382. Part of Jefferson's opposition to Hume stemmed from Hume's lack of respect for Anglo-Saxon England and its rude, simple farmers: see Jefferson to an unnamed member of the University of Virginia faculty, 25 October 1825, *Complete Jefferson*, 1095–96.

22. Jefferson to Cabell, 2 February 1816, in Honeywell, *Educational Work*, 229.

23. Jefferson to Governor Wilson C. Nicholas, 2 April 1816, *Writings* (ed. Lipscomb and Bergh), 14:454; Jefferson to Cabell, 2 February 1816, in Honeywell, *Educational Work*, 228. According to Bruce (*University of Virginia* 1:79) quoting an unpublished letter by Jefferson to Cabell, 28 November 1820, "there was an additional reason now,—and a highly characteristic one, too,—why Jefferson advocated the ward school: it would keep elementary education out of the hands of fanatical preachers, 'who, in the county elections,' he said, 'would be universally chosen, and the predominant sect of the county would possess itself of all its schools.'"

24. "Kentucky Resolutions," *Complete Jefferson*, 128–34; Jefferson to Thomas Jefferson Smith, 21 February 1825, ibid., 1038.

25. Rockfish Gap report, *Complete Jefferson*, 1098; Jefferson to Governor Nicholas, 2 April 1816, *Writings* 14:452.

26. Jefferson to Adams, 28 October 1813, *Adams-Jefferson Letters* 2:388–90; Jefferson to Cabell, 14 January 1818, *Works* 12:85–86.

27. A Bill for the More General Diffusion of Knowledge, *Papers* 2:532; *Notes on the*

State of Virginia, query 14, p. 146; Bill for the Establishment of District Colleges and a University (1817), *Complete Jefferson*, 1080. By Honeywell's calculation, Jefferson's 1779 plan would have resulted in 153 annual scholarships, as against 18 in his 1817 plan (*Educational Work*, 30). Although neither the grammar schools nor the scholarship competition was open to girls, Jefferson did provide for his own daughters a modified classical education using modern translations, and he sent them to a convent school when they were in France. Even his 1779 proposal for coeducational elementary schools was somewhat ahead of its time, coming ten years before Boston opened its public schools to girls (ibid., 22–23). Mercer's defeated educational bill of 1817 made provision for academies for girls: see Malone, *Jefferson and His Time*, vol. 6, *The Sage of Monticello*, 252.

28. Jefferson, *Notes on the State of Virginia*, query 14, pp. 147–48; Jefferson to John Brazier, 24 August 1819, *Complete Jefferson*, 1087; Jefferson to Joseph Priestley, 27 January 1800, *Works* 9:103.

29. Jefferson to Adams, 5 July 1814, *Adams-Jefferson Letters* 2:434.

30. Jefferson to Peter Carr, 7 September 1814, in Honeywell, *Educational Work*, 222–27; ibid., 42–43.

31. History is not listed as a separate course of study for the academies in Jefferson's 1779 school bill, or in his 1817 Bill for the Establishment of District Colleges and a University, or in the Rockfish Gap report, although he does mention it as part of the curriculum in a letter of 25 November 1817 in which he describes his plans to George Ticknor (*Works* 12:78).

32. Jefferson to Cabell, 13 January 1823, Jefferson and Cabell, *Early History of the University of Virginia*, 267.

Chapter 7. The Unfulfilled Visions for
a System of Public Schooling

1. Harry R. Warfel, *Noah Webster: Schoolmaster to America* (New York: Macmillan, 1936), 42; Webster, "An Examination into the Leading Principles of the Federal Constitution Proposed by the Late Convention Held at Philadelphia. With Answers to the Principal Objections that Have Been Raised against the System," in Paul L. Ford, ed., *Pamphlets on the Constitution of the United States Published during Its Discussion by the People, 1787–1788* (Brooklyn, N.Y.: n.p., 1888), 57–58; Webster, "On the Education of Youth in America," originally published 1787–1788, revised 1790, and reprinted in Rudolph, *Essays on Education*, 45.

2. Webster, "On the Education of Youth in America," in Rudolph, *Essays on Education*, 46–48.

3. Ibid., 49–52, 54; Warfel, *Noah Webster*, 37–39.

4. Webster, "On the Education of Youth in America," in Rudolph, *Essays on Education*, 55–57.

5. "A Letter to the Author, with Remarks," in Webster, *A Collection of Essays and Fugitiv Writings* (Boston: Thomas Andrews, 1790), 248.

6. Samuel Knox, "An Essay on the Best System of Liberal Education," in Rudolph, *Essays on Education*, 371.

7. Knox, ibid., 312–14.

8. Webster, "On the Education of Youth in America," in ibid., 64, and "Examination into the Leading Principles of the Federal Constitution," in Ford, ed., *Pamphlets on the Constitution*, 59–61; Montesquieu, *Spirit of the Laws*, bk. 4, chap. 5.

9. Samuel Harrison Smith, "Remarks on Education," in Rudolph, *Essays on Education*, 180, 220–21.

10. Webster, *Grammatical Institute*, pt. 1, 14. For various estimates of the cumulative sales of the speller, see Warfel, *Noah Webster*, 70–71; Richard Rollins, *The Long Journey of Noah Webster* (Philadelphia: University of Pennsylvania Press, 1980), 34–35; and E. Jennifer Monaghan, *A Common Heritage: Noah Webster's Blue-Back Speller* (Hamden, Conn.: Archon Press, 1983), 11–12, 31.

11. Webster to William Webster, 9 November 1835, as quoted in Monaghan, *A Common Heritage*, 207; *Grammatical Institute*, pt. 1, 5–6; Warfel, *Noah Webster*, 128–29.

12. Webster, *A Grammatical Institute, of the English Language, Comprising, an Easy, Concise, and Systematic Method of Education, Designed for the Use of English Schools in America. In Three Parts*, pt. 2 (Hartford, Conn.: Hudson and Goodwin, 1784; facsimile reprint, Menston, England: Scolar Press, 1968), 3–6; Warfel, *Noah Webster*, 79–81, 126–29, 136, 140–41.

13. Webster, *Grammatical Institute*, pt. 1, 12; Warfel, *Noah Webster*, 86; cf. Webster, "On the Education of Youth in America," in Rudolph, *Essays on Education*, 49–50, and Benjamin Rush, "The Bible as a School Book," in Runes, *Selected Writings of Benjamin Rush*; on Webster's edition of the Bible, see Monaghan, *A Common Heritage*, 158, and Warfel, *Noah Webster*, chap. 18.

14. See Ford, ed., *The New England Primer*.

15. Webster, *Grammatical Institute*, pt. 1, 113–18, 110, 111, and 112. Richard Rollins presents Webster's early speller as advocating "youthful rebellion" and "antiauthoritarianism" (*The Long Journey of Noah Webster*, 36). Although Webster does explicitly call for Americans to break free of the shackles of a corrupt Europe, a look at his discussions of children and parents in his first speller shows how carefully qualified Webster's rejection of authority was even in his youth. Rather than attend to such subtleties, Rollins imposes psychological stereotyping on a rather complex man. The change from the young, more republican and hopeful Webster to the old, disillusioned and authoritarian Webster is not as stark as Rollins's book suggests.

16. "A Moral Catechism," in Webster, *The American Spelling Book* (Boston: Isaiah Thomas and Ebenezer T. Andrews, 1794), 145–53; *Noah Webster's Elementary Spelling Book, with a Facsimile of the 1831 Edition*, ed. Henry Steele Commager (New York: Teachers College, Columbia University, 1958), 124. For a comparison of *The Elementary Spelling Book* with Webster's earlier spellers, see Monaghan, *A Common Heritage*, 129–30, 202–4.

17. Webster, *American Spelling Book*, 154ff.; *The Little Reader's Assistant* (Hartford, Conn.: Babcock, 1790), 1–2 of appendix.

18. Webster, *An American Selection of Lessons in Reading and Speaking* (Philadelphia: David Hogan, 1810); aphorism is from 19. Webster's dictionary definition of "education" is quoted from Rollins, *The Long Journey of Noah Webster*, 137.

19. Warfel, *Noah Webster*, 92–93; Webster, "On the Education of Youth in America," in Rudolph, *Essays on Education*, 64–65.

20. Webster, *American Selection of Lessons in Reading and Speaking*, 214ff.; Warfel, *Noah Webster*, 184.

21. Webster, "On the Education of Youth in America," 72–77; Adams to John Jebb, 10 September 1785, *Works* 9:540.

22. Milton, *On Education*, 63–64. Cf. the thoughtful and thought-provoking reflections of Brann, in *Paradoxes of Education*, 42–43, 53–54, 101–2.

23. Webster, "On the Education of Youth in America," in Rudolph, *Essays on Education*, 47; Smith, "Remarks on Education," in ibid., 178–79, 176, 175, 185, 189.

24. Jefferson to George Ticknor, 25 November 1817, *Works* 11:78, emphasis added; cf. Jefferson to Adams, 27 May 1795, *Adams-Jefferson Letters* 1:258.

25. Smith, "Remarks on Education," in Rudolph, *Essays on Education*, 194, 212–16; Knox, "An Essay on the Best System of Liberal Education," in ibid., 291, 317–25.

26. Knox, ibid., 291–94.

27. Madison to Richard Rush, 22 July 1823, to George Ticknor, 6 April 1825, and to W. T. Barry, 4 August 1822, *Letters and Other Writings of James Madison*, 4 vols. (Philadelphia: J. B. Lippincott, 1865), 3:332, 486, and 276–81. For a good brief survey of the depressing lack of support for education in all the states, including New England, in the decades after the Founding, see David Madsen, *Early National Education 1776–1830*, 88–92.

28. Jefferson to Joseph Cabell, 28 November 1820, *Works* 12:170; presumably Jefferson is referring to DeWitt Clinton, who became governor in 1817. Jefferson to Cabell, 4 February 1826, quoted in Bruce, *University of Virginia* 1:82.

29. Adams to J. D. Sergeant, 21 July 1776, and to Joseph Hawley, 25 August 1776, *Works* 9:425–26, 434; *Defence of the Constitutions*, in ibid. 6:198; cf. letter to Samuel Adams, 18 October 1790, ibid. 416.

30. Jefferson to Adams, 5 July 1814, *Adams-Jefferson Letters* 2:434; Jefferson to Cabell, 24 January 1816, Jefferson and Cabell, *Early History of the University of Virginia*, 48.

31. Clarence J. Karier, *The Individual, Society, and Education*, 32–33, 45–46; Michael B. Katz, *Reconstructing American Education* (Cambridge: Harvard University Press, 1987), chap. 1; Tyack, *Turning Points in American Educational History*, 92, 121–25, 130–33. Tyack elsewhere argues that a public-spirited religiosity, rooted in evangelism and Victorian moralism, seems to have been an important part of the impetus behind the nineteenth-century public school movement: "The Spread of Public Schooling in Victorian America: In Search of a Reinterpretation," *History of Education* 7 (1978): 173–82.

32. See especially Edward Everett's "Importance of Education in a Republic" (1839), in *Orations and Speeches on Various Occasions*, 2 vols. (Boston: Little, Brown, 1878), 2:316–21. Everett stresses in particular the need for education to prepare citizens to participate in elections, to serve in the military and on juries, and to act as competent local magistrates; but Everett also, characteristically, makes mention of the cultivated use of leisure.

Chapter 8. Higher Education

1. For a detailed chronology of college foundings, with denominational affiliations, see Donald G. Tewksbury, *The Founding of American Colleges and Universities before the Civil War: With Particular Reference to the Religious Influences Bearing upon the College Movement* (New York: Teachers College, Columbia University, 1932), table 4, pp. 32–35; for the training of ministers as the chief purpose of almost all the colleges founded before the University of Virginia, see the discussion and documentary evidence assembled at ibid., 58–62 and 78–82. The Harvard charter, along with other early charters and accounts of purpose, in particular of the College of New Jersey and of King's College, may be found in Hofstadter and Smith, *American Higher Education*, vol. 1, pts. 1 and 2; see esp. 1:10, 81, 92–94, 99–111, 114–15, 145.

2. For a discussion of the traditional liberal arts curriculum that the American colonies inherited from Europe, see Morison, *Intellectual Life of Colonial New England*, chap. 2; R. Freeman Butts, *The College Charts Its Course: Historical Conceptions and Current Proposals* (New York: McGraw-Hill, 1939), chaps. 2–3; Cremin, *American Education: The Colonial Experience, 1607–1783*, 213–15. See the curricular descriptions in the documents collected in Hofstadter and Smith, *American Higher Education*, vol. 1, esp. Statutes of Harvard (pp. 8–10), Cotton Mather's History of Harvard (pp. 17–18), Charter and Statutes of William and Mary (pp. 34, 44), and Yale Laws (p. 56). For the curricular innovations, see ibid., Laws and Orders of King's College (p. 120), Charter of Rhode Island

College (p. 136), and Witherspoon's account of his curriculum (p. 141); Cremin, *American Education: The Colonial Experience, 1607–1783*, 378–384 and 462–66; Butts, *The College Charts Its Course*, chap. 4, esp. 70–72.

3. Butts, ibid., 61–63, 65; Samuel Eliot Morison, *Three Centuries of Harvard: 1636–1936* (Cambridge: Harvard University Press, 1965), 58, 66–67, 79, 90.

4. Benjamin Rush, "Address to the People of the United States," in Goode, *Benjamin Rush and His Services to American Education*, 202–3; "Plan of a Federal University," in *Selected Writings*, 101, 105; see also Rush to Richard Price, 25 May 1786, *Letters of Benjamin Rush*, ed. L. H. Butterfield, 2 vols. (Princeton, N.J.: Princeton University Press, 1951), 1:388.

5. Rush to General John Armstrong, 19 March 1783, quoted from the Rush Archives, Ridgway Library, Philadelphia, vol. 41, p. 20, in Goode, *Benjamin Rush and his Services to American Education*, 110–11; on the relation of Dickinson College to the essay on the mode of education proper for a republic, see Rush to John Montgomery, 15 November 1783, Rush Archives, vol. 41, p. 49, in ibid., 123.

6. Records of 29 May, 18 August, and 14 September, in Max Farrand, ed., *The Records of the Federal Convention of 1787*, 4 vols. (New Haven, Conn.: Yale University Press, 1966), 2:321, 325, 616, 620; 3:122, 362, 609.

7. David L. Madsen, *The National University: Enduring Dream of the USA* (Detroit, Mich.: Wayne State University Press, 1966), 36–37. Washington's shares in the navigation of the Potomac River, together with 100 shares in the navigation of the James River, had been awarded him in gratitude by the Virginia legislature at the close of the revolutionary war. It had been Washington's settled policy to refuse remuneration for his wartime services. Nevertheless, in order to avoid giving offense by spurning a generous gift, he had accepted the shares, with the understanding that he might dedicate them to some public purpose. His preference at this time was to give the shares in both companies for a university in the capital, but in deference to the wishes of the Virginia legislature, he bequeathed the James River shares to Liberty Hall Academy in his home state, later to evolve into Washington and Lee University. The Potomac shares he left in his will for the still-cherished project of a federal university, reiterating there the arguments he had made repeatedly for its importance: Washington, First Annual Address, 8 January 1790, *Writings* 30:493; letter to the Commissioners of the District of Columbia, 28 January 1795, ibid. 34:107; Last Will and Testament, 9 July 1799, ibid. 37:279–81.

8. Washington to Commissioners, 28 January 1795, ibid. 34:106; Eighth Annual Message, 7 December 1796, ibid. 35:316; Washington to Commissioners, 28 January 1795, ibid. 34:106.

9. Washington, Eighth Annual Message, 7 December 1796, ibid. 35:317; Washington to Jefferson, 15 March 1795, ibid. 34:147; see also Washington to Hamilton, 1 September 1796, ibid. 35:199.

10. Washington to Hamilton, 1 September 1796, ibid. 35:199–200; Eighth Annual Message, ibid. 35:316.

11. Washington, Last Will and Testament, ibid. 37:280–81 and 281 n. 15; Madsen, *National University*, 33–34.

12. Washington, Sentiments on a Peace Establishment, 2 May 1783, *Writings* 26:397. Henry Knox, Washington's chief of artillery and later secretary of war, had been, with John Adams, the first to call for a military academy. See Stephen E. Ambrose, *Duty, Honor, Country: A History of West Point* (Baltimore: Johns Hopkins University Press, 1966), 7–9; John Adams, *Works* 3:85; 9:384–85.

13. Washington, Eighth Annual Message, 7 December 1796, *Writings* 35:317; Washington to Alice Delancey Izard, 20 July 1798, ibid. 36:355; Washington to Hamilton, 12 December 1799, ibid. 37:473.

14. Report of the Secretary of War to Congress, 13 January 1800, in Walter Lowrie and Matthew Clark, eds., *American State Papers: Documents, Legislative and Executive, of the Congress of the United States,* Military Affairs, 2 vols. (Washington, D.C.: Gales and Seaton, 1832), 1:133–35; see also Report of the Secretary of War to Congress, 31 January 1800, in ibid. 1:142–44. Jefferson, memo of 23 November 1793, *Works* 1:330–31; Malone, *Jefferson and His Time,* vol. 5, *Jefferson the President, Second Term,* 510–11; White, *The Jeffersonians,* chap. 18; Rockfish Gap report, in Honeywell, *Educational Work,* 256; Resolutions of the Board of Visitors of the University of Virginia, 4 October 1824, in Jefferson, *Writings* 19:450–51.

15. Madison, Second Annual Message, 5 December 1810, *The Writings of James Madison,* ed. Gaillard Hunt, 9 vols. (New York: G. P. Putnam's Sons, 1908), 8:129.

16. Jefferson, A Bill for Amending the Constitution of the College of William and Mary, and Substituting More Certain Revenues for Its Support, *Papers* 2:538–39.

17. Ibid., 539–40; *Notes on the State of Virginia,* query 15, pp. 150–51. For Jefferson's own account of the failure of the college bill, see his *Autobiography,* in *Works* 1:75–76. See also Bruce, *University of Virginia* 1:71, 96–97.

18. Jefferson to Joseph Priestley, 18 January 1800, *Works* 9:96. Still later, Jefferson sought to liquidate William and Mary and use its funds either for the University of Virginia or to establish his long-planned grammar schools; see Jefferson to Joseph Cabell, 16 May and 22 December 1824, and 22 January 1825, Jefferson and Cabell, *Early History of the University of Virginia,* 308–12, 320–23, 335; Honeywell, *Educational Work,* 49–52.

19. Jefferson to D'Ivernois, 6 February 1795, *Works* 8:164–65. For Jefferson's assessment of the University of Geneva, see his letters to John Banister, Jr., 15 October 1785, *Papers* 8:635–37, and to Archibald McCalester, 22 December 1791, ibid. 22:429–30.

20. Jefferson to Washington, 23 February 1795, *Writings* 19:108–14; Washington to Jefferson, 15 March 1795, *Writings* (of Washington), 34:147–48; cf. Washington to Jefferson, 15 November 1794, ibid. 34:22–23.

21. Madison, Second Annual Message, 5 December 1810, *Writings* 8:127; Seventh Annual Message, 5 December 1815, ibid., 342–43; Eighth Annual Message, 3 December 1816, ibid., 379.

22. Jefferson to Joel Barlow, 24 February 1806, *Works* 10:232–33; James Woodress, *A Yankee's Odyssey: The Life of Joel Barlow* (Philadelphia: J. B. Lippincott, 1958), 241; Charles Burr Todd, *The Life and Letters of Joel Barlow* (New York: G. P. Putnam's Sons, 1886), 208; Madsen, *National University,* 46, 49. For a summary of the Du Pont de Nemours plan, see Bruce, *University of Virginia* 1:63–64.

23. Barlow, *Prospectus of a National Institution to Be Established in the United States* (Washington, D.C.: Samuel H. Smith, 1806; facsimile reprint in vol. 2 of *The Works of Joel Barlow*), 3–4, 5, 6, 35, 36; Woodress, *A Yankee's Odyssey,* 242.

24. Jefferson, Sixth Annual Message, 2 December 1806, *Works* 10:317–18; Honeywell, *Educational Work,* 61–64.

25. Barlow, *Prospectus of a National Institution,* 10, 12–17.

26. Ibid., 17–20; it is worth recalling in this connection that Bacon's political philosophy is emphatically unrepublican (see *The New Atlantis*). Consider Rousseau's ambiguous and complex praise of Bacon, "perhaps the greatest of the philosophers," and of scientific institutes established under monarchs, in the concluding paragraphs of his *Discourse on the Arts and Sciences.* Rousseau addresses profoundly and comprehensively the problems of which Barlow is only very dimly aware.

27. Jefferson to Joseph Priestley, 18 January 1800, *Works* 9:96–97.

28. Madison's comment is paraphrased in Honeywell, *Educational Work,* 68; for Madison's unwavering support for Jefferson regarding the University of Virginia and the efforts he continued to make after Jefferson's death, see Adrienne Koch, *Jefferson and Mad-*

ison: The Great Collaboration (New York: Oxford University Press, 1964), 261–83, and Drew McCoy, *The Last of the Fathers: James Madison and the Republican Legacy* (Cambridge: Cambridge University Press, 1989), 198–202.

29. Emerson as quoted in Honeywell, *Educational Work*, 67; epitaph in *Works* 12:483; cf. Bruce's discussion of the epitaph, *University of Virginia* 1:2–3.

30. Rockfish Gap report, in Honeywell, *Educational Work*, 258, 256; Report of the Board of Visitors, 7 October 1822, in Jefferson, *Writings* 19:413–16; Jefferson to Thomas Cooper, 2 November 1822, *Works* 12:272.

31. Jefferson to Adams, 5 July 1814, *Adams-Jefferson Letters* 2:434; Jefferson to Joseph Cabell, 3 February 1824, *Writings* 16:6; Jefferson to Joseph Priestley, 18 January 1800, *Works* 9:98; Jefferson to Joseph Cabell, 28 December 1822, Jefferson and Cabell, *Early History of the University of Virginia*, 260; cf. Jefferson to William Short, 22 June and 31 October 1819, *Writings* 18:304–5 and 15:222–23.

32. Jefferson to Nathaniel Bowditch, 26 October 1818, *Writings* 19:267; Jefferson to Cabell, 22 December 1824, Jefferson and Cabell, *Early History of the University of Virginia*, 324; Resolutions of the Board of Visitors, 4 October 1824, in Jefferson, *Writings* 19:441; Honeywell, *Educational Work*, 99–100 and 89–92; Bruce, *University of Virginia* 1:200–206.

33. Jefferson to Cabell, 28 December 1822, Jefferson and Cabell, *Early History of the University of Virginia*, 260; Jefferson to Priestley, 18 January 1800, *Works* 9:98; Rockfish Gap report, in Honeywell, *Educational Work*, 256.

34. Ibid., 251; Jefferson to Priestley, 18 January 1800, *Works* 9:97; Jefferson to George Ticknor, 16 July 1823, *Writings* 15:455.

35. Resolutions of the Board of Visitors, 4 October 1824, in Jefferson, *Writings* 19:442–44.

36. Jefferson to the Trustees for the Lottery of East Tennessee College, 6 May 1810, *Complete Jefferson*, 1063–64. Bruce has a helpful discussion of the important suggestions Jefferson received from the architects William Thornton and Benjamin Latrobe: see *University of Virginia* 1:178–87. For bringing out the importance of close teacher-student relations, or "affectionate pedagogy," in Jefferson's educational ideas, we are indebted to Harold Hellenbrand, *The Unfinished Revolution: Education and Politics in the Thought of Thomas Jefferson* (Newark: University of Delaware Press, 1990).

37. Jefferson to Madison, 20 September 1785, *Papers* 8:535; comment on painting and sculpture quoted in Malone, *Jefferson and His Time*, vol. 2, *Jefferson and the Rights of Man*, 116.

38. Jefferson to Madison, 20 September 1785, *Papers* 8:534–35; Malone, *Jefferson and His Time*, vol. 2, *Jefferson and the Rights of Man*, 88, 91.

39. Jefferson to L'Enfant and Jefferson to Washington, 10 April 1791, *Writings* 8:163, 166.

40. Honeywell, *Educational Work*, 126; Enactment of the Board of Visitors, 7 April 1824, in Jefferson, *Writings* 19:434; Jefferson to William C. Rives, quoted in Bruce, *University of Virginia* 1:242–43; Malone, *Jefferson and His Time*, vol. 6, *The Sage of Monticello*, 259.

41. Jefferson to George Ticknor, 16 July 1823, *Writings* 15:455–56; Rockfish Gap report, in Honeywell, *Educational Work*, 257.

42. Jefferson to Cabell, 24 January 1816, *Writings* 14:412–13; Minutes of the Board of Visitors, 4 October 1824, 4 March 1825, and 3 October 1825, in Jefferson, *Writings* 19:449, 460, 468–70.

43. Regulations Adopted by the Board of Visitors, 4 October 1824, in Jefferson, *Writings* 19:444–48; cf. the regulations of Harvard and South Carolina College, in Honeywell, *Educational Work*, 279–80. See also Minutes of the Board of Visitors, 3–6 October

1825, in Jefferson, *Writings* 19:468–70, 473–74, 478–79; cf. Honeywell, *Educational Work,* 136–37 and 139–40.

44. Minutes of the Board of Visitors, 3, 5, and 7 October 1825, in Jefferson, *Writings* 19:472–73, 474–75, 477, 480; Jefferson to Ellen Coolige, 14 November 1825, *Writings* 18:347–48; cf. Jefferson to Joseph Coolige, 4 June 1826, ibid., 356.

45. Rockfish Gap report, in Honeywell, *Educational Work,* 252–53; Enactment of the Board of Visitors, 7 April 1824, in Jefferson, *Writings* 19:433–34.

46. Jefferson to John Emmett, 2 May 1826, *Writings* 16:170.

47. A Course of Reading for a Student of Law, in Honeywell, *Educational Work,* 217–21; Jefferson to Thomas Mann Randolph, 27 August 1786, *Papers* 10:306–7; Jefferson to Francis Wayles Eppes, 13 December 1820, *The Family Letters of Thomas Jefferson,* ed. Edwin M. Betts and James A. Bear (Columbia: University of Missouri Press, 1966), 437; cf. Jefferson to Eppes, 6 October 1820, and Eppes to Jefferson, 31 October 1820, ibid., 433–36. On the botanical garden, see Jefferson to John Emmett, 27 April 1826, *Writings* 16:167; on an observatory, see Rockfish Gap report, in Honeywell, *Educational Work,* 260; on a model of the solar system, see Jefferson's Bill for Amending the Constitution of the College of William and Mary, *Papers* 2:541; on the chemical laboratory, see Enactment of the Board of Visitors, 4 October 1824, in Jefferson, *Writings* 19:450; on the dispensary, see Minutes of the Board of Visitors, 3 and 4 April 1826, in ibid., 489–90.

48. Jefferson to John Emmett, 2 May 1826, *Writings* 16:168–72; Jefferson to David Williams, 14 November 1803, quoted in Honeywell, *Educational Work,* 117.

49. Rockfish Gap report, in Honeywell, *Educational Work,* 250; Minutes of Board of Visitors, 7 April 1824, in Jefferson, *Writings* 19:436; Jefferson to Joseph Cabell, 3 February 1825, Jefferson and Cabell, *Early History of the University of Virginia,* 339.

50. Jefferson to Madison, 1 and 12 February 1825, summarized in Honeywell, *Educational Work,* 97; Madison's response in ibid., 122; Resolutions of the Board of Visitors, 4 March 1825, in Jefferson, *Writings* 19:460–61.

51. Jefferson to Madison, 17 February 1826, ibid. 16:156–57.

52. Jefferson to William Smith, 13 November 1787, *Papers* 12:356; cf. Jefferson to Madison, 30 January 1787, ibid. 12:92–94. Jefferson to Madison, 6 September 1789, ibid. 15:392–97; cf. Jefferson to John Cartwright, 5 June 1824, *Complete Jefferson,* 296. Jefferson to Samuel Kercheval, 12 July 1816, *Works* 12:11–13.

53. Jefferson to Kercheval, 8 October 1816, ibid. 12:17; A Bill for Establishing Religious Freedom, *Papers* 2:546–47; cf. *Notes on the State of Virginia,* query 17, p. 161.

54. Jefferson to Peter Carr, 10 August 1787, *Papers* 12:18.

55. Jefferson to Martha Jefferson Randolph, 8 June 1797, *Family Letters,* 146; see chap. 6.

56. Abraham Lincoln, "The Perpetuation of Our Political Institutions: Address before the Young Men's Lyceum of Springfield, Illinois," 27 January 1838, *Abraham Lincoln: His Speeches and Writings,* ed. Roy P. Basler (Cleveland, Ohio: World Publishing, 1946), 76–85. For an eloquent statement on the necessity for instilling reverence especially in democratic education, with a view not only to political stability but above all to "human serenity," see Brann, *Paradoxes of Education,* 101–2.

57. Jefferson to John Taylor, 14 February 1821, *Writings* 18:312; see also Honeywell, *Educational Work,* 150–53.

58. For a succinct and profound discussion of the relation between liberal and civic education, see Christopher Bruell, "Liberal Education and Education for Citizenship," in *The Recovery of American Education: Reclaiming a Vision,* ed. Stephen N. Kranson (Lanham, Md.: University Press of America, 1991), 75–86.

59. James Wilson, "Of the Study of Law in the United States," in *Selected Political Essays of James Wilson,* 185ff.; quotations are from 200.

60. Edward Everett, "University of Virginia," *North American Review* 10 (1820): 115–37; Enactment of the Board of Visitors, 7 April 1824, in Jefferson, *Writings* 19:434; for entrance requirements, see Regulations Adopted by the Board of Visitors, 4 October 1824, in ibid., 442; for the level of classical teaching, see also Rockfish Gap report, in Honeywell, *Educational Work*, 254; Jefferson to John Emmett, 2 May 1826, *Writings* 16:170.

61. Rockfish Gap report, in Honeywell, *Educational Work*, 252; Everett, "University of Virginia," 120–21, 125.

62. Rockfish Gap report, in Honeywell, *Educational Work*, 252, 254–55; "Essay on the Anglo-Saxon Language," in *Complete Jefferson*, 855–82; Everett, "University of Virginia," 123—but see Jefferson's reaction to the unsigned Everett review of the university in his letter to John Adams, 15 August 1820, *Adams-Jefferson Letters* 2:565–66.

63. Bruce, *University of Virginia* 1:30; cf. 2:92–94, 188–89 on the "starved and spindling" English literature selection in the original library of the university.

64. On Jefferson's preference for history over literature, see, for example, the reading list enclosed in Jefferson's letter to Peter Carr, 10 August 1787, *Papers* 12:18–19. Locke, *Some Thoughts Concerning Education*, sec. 186; Jefferson to Nathaniel Macon, 12 January 1819, *Works* 12:110–11; Jefferson to Anne Randolph Bankhead, 8 December 1808, *Family Letters*, 370; Jefferson to Thomas Mann Randolph, 27 August 1786, *Papers* 10:306–7. See also Jefferson to William Duane, 4 April 1813, *Writings* 13:230, and Malone, *Jefferson and His Time*, vol. 6, *The Sage of Monticello*, chap. 14 (entitled "The Uses of History").

65. For the curriculum of the school of moral philosophy, see Enactment of the Board of Visitors, 7 April 1824, in Jefferson, *Writings* 19:434. Jefferson to Short, 31 October 1819, *Life and Selected Writings*, 693; Jefferson to Adams, 5 July 1814, *Adams-Jefferson Letters* 2:433; for the attack on Plato, see also Jefferson to Short, 4 August 1820, *Writings* 15:257–59. For the judgment on Aristotle's *Politics*, see Jefferson to Isaac Tiffany, 26 August 1816, *Writings* 15:65–66. A Course of Reading for a Student of Law, in Honeywell, *Educational Work*, 218. Jefferson recommended both Lucretius and the "Socratic dialogues" in a letter to the young Peter Carr, 10 August 1787, *Papers* 12:14–17.

66. Jefferson to Carr, 10 August 1787, *Papers* 12:14–17; Jefferson to Thomas Cooper, 14 August 1820, *Writings* 15:265; cf. Jefferson to Francis Wayles Eppes, 27 June 1821, *Family Letters*, 439–40; Everett, "University of Virginia," 127.

67. On Jefferson's library holdings, see Arrowood, *Thomas Jefferson and Education in a Republic*, 55, and Douglas L. Wilson, "Jefferson's Library," in Peterson, ed., *Thomas Jefferson: A Reference Biography*, 157–79, esp. 170, 177. On Jefferson's attitude toward the classical world, see Meyer Reinhold, in ibid., 135–56, esp. 149; and Brann, *Paradoxes of Education*, 82–86, 95–99. On Xenophon's Socrates, see Jefferson to Rush, 21 April 1803, and Jefferson to William Short, 31 October 1819, *Life and Selected Writings*, 569, 694. On the limitations on what can be learned from Roman political history, see esp. Jefferson to Adams, 10 December 1819, *Adams-Jefferson Letters* 2:548–50. On the limitations of Greek political history, see Jefferson to Isaac Tiffany, 26 August 1816, *Writings* 15:65–66.

68. Honeywell, *Educational Work*, 153.

69. Tewksbury, *Founding of American Colleges*, 56–57, 66–67; cf. 60–61 and 148–54.

70. Ibid., 65. Key excerpts from Webster's argument before the court and Marshall's decision may be found in Hofstadter and Smith, *American Higher Education* 1:202–19; see also Jefferson to New Hampshire Governor Plumer, 21 July 1816, *Writings* 15:46–47. Chancellor Kent is quoted in Tewksbury, *Founding of American Colleges*, 151.

71. Benjamin Rush, "Hints for Establishing a College at Carlisle in Cumberland County, Pennsylvania," is excerpted in Goode, *Benjamin Rush and His Services to American Education*, 102. Frederick Rudolph, *The American College and University: A History* (New York: Alfred A. Knopf, 1962), 69; as Rudolph indicates on 189, the denomina-

tional colleges frequently received public financial assistance. See also Brann, *Paradoxes of Education*, 49–50.

72. There has been considerable speculation as to who introduced the idea of an elective curriculum to the United States. Butts argues that Jefferson never discussed the idea until 1823, two years after Ticknor had proposed it at Harvard (*The College Charts Its Course*, 93–94; 107–8). In fact, Jefferson was writing about the importance of students' choosing their own courses in 1820; see Jefferson to Francis Wayles Eppes, 13 December 1820, *Family Letters*, 436. Even earlier, in his critique of the Rockfish Gap report, Edward Everett had censured the American custom of making students proceed lockstep through the whole curriculum, but it is not clear that Jefferson did not already have an elective program in mind. The idea was in the air; it was practiced in all the German universities Ticknor had visited as well as at the University of Edinburgh, which Jefferson admired above all others, and it was only a matter of time before it would be advocated in the United States. On Ticknor's reforms, see Morison, *Three Centuries of Harvard*, 230–38. On the surprisingly slight influence of German educational ideas in America before 1870, see Carl Diehl, *Americans and German Scholarship 1770-1870* (New Haven, Conn.: Yale University Press, 1978).

73. "Original Papers in Relation to a Course of Liberal Education [Yale report]," *American Journal of Science and Arts* 15 (January 1829): 300–302, 308–9, 323–24. Portions of this report are also reprinted in Hofstadter and Smith, *American Higher Education* 1:275–91. For a recent defense of the principles of the Yale report and of the spirit of the denominational colleges of the nineteenth century, against Jeffersonian educational principles, see Brann's *Paradoxes of Education*.

74. Yale report, 329, 330, 345, 347–48.

75. "Julian M. Sturtevant on the quality of teaching at Yale in the 1820s" in Hofstadter and Smith, *American Higher Education* 1:274–75.

76. Morison, *Three Centuries of Harvard*, chaps. 14 and 15.

Chapter 9. Religion

1. We refer in parentheses to the section numbers of the "Memorial and Remonstrance" and use the text printed in *The Mind of the Founder*, ed. Marvin Meyers (Indianapolis: Bobbs-Merrill, 1973), 8–16.

2. Lee to Madison, 26 November 1784, *The Letters of Richard Henry Lee*, ed. James Curtis Ballagh, 2 vols. (New York: Macmillan, 1911-1914), 2:304–5.

3. "As a leader among Virginia Baptists in the 1780s, Leland had been influential in petitioning the legislature on behalf of Jefferson's bill for religious freedom," and "there is strong evidence that James Madison personally sought his support of the federal constitution, which Leland had first opposed": Nathan O. Hatch, *The Democratization of American Christianity* (New Haven, Conn.: Yale University Press, 1989), 95–96; for discussion of the emerging evangelical sects' Jeffersonian attitudes on church-state relations, see also 76–78, 81, 97–98, and 101.

4. Madison to Edward Livingston, 10 July 1822, *The Mind of the Founder*, 432–33; veto of land grant in Madison, *Writings* 8:132–33. The veto message on the incorporation of the Episcopal church and the debate it stirred in Congress are quoted from the *Annals of Congress* 22:982–97, in Philip Kurland and Ralph Lerner, eds., *The Founders' Constitution*, 5 vols. (Chicago: University of Chicago Press, 1987), 5:99–100. For Madison's later views, see "detached memoranda ca. 1817" as printed in ibid. 5:103–4.

5. *Federalist Papers*, no. 69 (p. 422); Jefferson to Rev. Samuel Miller, 23 January 1808, *Works* 11:7–9; but contrast Bruce, *History of the University of Virginia* 1:26–27. Washing-

ton's proclamation in Kurland and Lerner, *Founders' Constitution* 5:94; see Madison's equally pious presidential proclamation of 16 November 1814, ibid. 5:102–3.

6. Jefferson to Danbury Baptist Association, 1 January 1802, *Writings* 16:281; Jefferson, A Bill for Establishing Religious Freedom, 12 June 1779, in Kurland and Lerner, *Founders' Constitution* 5:77; cf. the bill as enacted in 1785, in ibid., 84–85, and *Notes on the State of Virginia*, query 17, p. 159.

7. *Notes on the State of Virginia*, query 18, p. 163; for the Voltairean "spark of fanaticism" that "may have been in" Jefferson's "heterodoxy," see Malone, *Jefferson and His Time*, vol. 6, *The Sage of Monticello*, 249–50.

8. Jefferson to Joseph Delaplaine, 25 December 1816, quoted in Eugene R. Sheridan, introduction to *Jefferson's Extracts from the Gospels: "The Philosophy of Jesus" and "The Life and Morals of Jesus,"* ed. Dickinson W. Adams et al., *The Papers of Thomas Jefferson*, 2d ser., ed. Charles T. Cullen (Princeton, N.J.: Princeton University Press, 1983–), 4 n. 5; see also the quotation from Jefferson's grandson Thomas Jefferson Randolph in n. 4: "Of his peculiar religious opinions, his family know no more than the world." Miller and Johnson, *The Puritans* 1:186.

9. See the crucial texts and the valuable appendix of letters both to and from Jefferson in *Jefferson's Extracts from the Gospels*—especially "Syllabus of an Estimate of the Merit of the Doctrines of Jesus, Compared with Those of Others," in letter to Benjamin Rush, 21 April 1803, 332–34. In considering this "Syllabus," which Jefferson circulated rather widely, it is important not to make the mistake often made, of assuming that Jefferson himself agreed with all the admirable teachings he ascribes to Jesus. Jefferson warns against this mistake in his letter to William Short, 13 April 1820: "The Syllabus is therefore of *his* doctrines, not *all* of *mine*. . . . I read them . . . with a mixture of approbation and dissent" (p. 392). See also Jefferson to Benjamin Rush, 23 September 1800, to William Short, 31 October 1819, and to James Smith, 8 December 1822, ibid., 320, 388–89, 409; *Notes on the State of Virginia*, query 17, p. 161; letter to Joseph Priestley, 21 March 1801, *Life and Selected Writings*, 562; and letters to John Adams, 22 August 1813, and 15 August 1820, *Adams-Jefferson Letters* 2:368–69, 567–69.

10. "Syllabus of an Estimate of the Merit of the Doctrines of Jesus" and letters to Joseph Priestley, 9 April 1803; to Thomas Law, 13 June 1814; to Charles Thomson, 29 January 1817; to William Short, 4 August 1820; to Benjamin Waterhouse, 26 June 1822; and to George Thatcher, 26 January 1824, *Jefferson's Extracts from the Gospels*, 328, 334, 357, 384, 396, 405, 414.

11. See letter to Major John Cartwright, 5 June 1824, *Life and Selected Writings*, 714, and letters to John Adams, 14 March 1820, 15 August 1820, 11 April 1823, and 8 January 1825, *Adams-Jefferson Letters* 2:562, 567–69, 592–94, 606; Sheridan (*Jefferson's Extracts from the Gospels*, 41 n. 139) notes the "ambiguity" in a poem Jefferson wrote shortly before his death for his daughter Martha: "I go to my fathers; I welcome the shore, / which crowns all my hopes, or which buries my cares." The classic theology that combines materialism, a denial of the immortality of the soul, and an ostensible faith in a life after death through corporeal resurrection is that of Thomas Hobbes, as elaborated in *Leviathan*, parts 3 and 4; for a suggestive discussion of the intellectual lineage that may lead from Hobbes to Jefferson's religious teacher and confidant Joseph Priestley, see Basil Willey, *The Eighteenth-Century Background: Studies on the Idea of Nature in the Thought of the Period* (Harmondsworth: Penguin Books, 1962), chaps. 8 and 10, esp. p. 169.

12. Herbert J. Storing, ed., *The Complete Anti-Federalist*, 7 vols. (Chicago: University of Chicago Press, 1981), vol. 5, document 8, paragraphs 3–4 (or 5.8.3–4; subsequent references to this collection will be by this citation system, which Storing indicates in the margins of the volumes).

13. "Letter by David," in Storing, *Complete Anti-Federalist* 4.24.2.

14. Storing, *What the Anti-Federalists Were For*, vol. 1 of *Complete Anti-Federalist*, 23. To be sure, there were Anti-Federalist writers who made both of these complaints at once. Most striking is "A Watchman," who protests in practically the same breath that "there is no liberty given to the people to perform religious worship according to the dictates of their consciences" and that "there is a door opened for the Jews, Turks, and Heathen to enter into publick office, and be seated at the head of the government of the United States" (Storing, *Complete Anti-Federalist* 4.22.4). That the door of public office was indeed to be "open to all," "without regard to . . . any particular profession of religious faith," was stressed by both Hamilton and Madison in the *Federalist Papers*, nos. 36 (p. 217), 52 (p. 326), and 57 (p. 351). See also the airing of the issue in the debate in the North Carolina ratifying convention, 30 July 1788, in Jonathan Eliot, ed., *The Debates in the Several State Conventions on the Adoption of the Federal Constitution*, 5 vols. (Philadelphia: J. B. Lippincott, 1907), 4:191–200.

15. Patrick Henry, in Storing, *Complete Anti-Federalist* 5.16.24; "Essays of an Old Whig," ibid. 3.3.29; Storing, *What the Anti-Federalists Were For*, 23. See, for other examples of this position, "Letters from a Countryman" (perhaps DeWitt Clinton), in *Complete Anti-Federalist* 6.7.13; "Letters of Centinel" (probably Samuel Bryan), ibid. 2.7.55 and 109; "Essays by Cincinnatus," ibid. 6.1.19; "Essay by Deliberator," ibid. 3.13.5; "Letters from the Federal Farmer" (perhaps Richard Henry Lee), ibid. 2.8.53 and 86; "Address of the Albany Antifederal Committee," ibid. 6.10.6.

16. "Letters of Agrippa," in Storing, *Complete Anti-Federalist* 4.6.48; "Letters from a Customer," ibid. 4.16.1; "The Government of Nature Delineated, or An Exact Picture of the New Federal Constitution, by Aristocrotis," ibid. 3.16.14.

17. Ibid. 3.16.14–15; "Essay by Samuel," ibid. 4.14.7; "A Friend to the Rights of the People," ibid. 4.23.3, remark 9. Luther Martin, who had been a delegate to the Constitutional Convention from Maryland, complained of the thoughtless lack of debate with which the convention had passed the prohibition on religious tests for office, in "The Genuine Information Delivered to the Legislature of the State of Maryland Relative to the Proceedings of the General Convention Lately Held at Philadelphia," ibid. 2.4.108. The prohibition, introduced by Pinckney, was indeed adopted almost without discussion: see Farrand, *Records of the Federal Convention* 2:342, 468.

18. Charles Turner, in Storing, *Complete Anti-Federalist* 4.18.2.

19. "Address by Denatus," ibid. 5.18.9–12.

20. Walter Berns, *The First Amendment and the Future of American Democracy* (New York: Basic Books, 1976), 7–8. The text of the ordinance is taken from Kurland and Lerner, *Founders' Constitution* 1:27–29.

21. Debate in the House of Representatives, 15, 17, and 20 August 1789, in Kurland and Lerner, *Founders' Constitution* 5:92–94; Michael J. Malbin, *Religion and Politics: The Intentions of the Authors of the First Amendment* (Washington, D.C.: American Enterprise Institute, 1978), 5–6. We have profited from the excellent discussion in this work as well as in chap. 1 of Berns, *The First Amendment and the Future of American Democracy*.

22. Malbin, *Religion and Politics*, 7, 14–15; Kurland and Lerner, *Founders' Constitution* 5:92–93.

23. Kurland and Lerner, *Founders' Constitution* 5:93–94.

24. Tench Coxe, "Notes Concerning the United States of America" (1790), ibid. 5:94.

25. Washington, *Writings* 35:229.

Chapter 10. Economic and Political Life
as Sources of Moral Education

1. Jefferson, *Notes on the State of Virginia*, query 19, pp. 164–65.

2. Franklin to John Wright, 4 November 1789, *The Writings of Benjamin Franklin*, ed.

Albert Henry Smyth, 10 vols. (New York: Macmillan, 1905–1907), 10:61; Franklin to Catherine Green, 2 March 1789, ibid. 10:3.

3. Noah Webster, *Sketches of American Policy* (1785), as quoted in Drew McCoy, *The Elusive Republic: Political Economy in Jeffersonian America* (Chapel Hill: University of North Carolina Press, 1980), 111–12.

4. "Letters of Centinel," in Storing, *Complete Anti-Federalist* 2.7.126 (see also 2.7.127); "Letters of Agrippa," ibid. 4.6.6, 4.6.31 (cf. 4.6.30–33 and "Essays by Candidus" [Samuel Adams or his follower] in ibid. 4.9.13–15); "Essays by a Farmer," ibid. 5.1.78; "Essays by a Newport Man," ibid. 4.25.3; John Adams, *Defence of the Constitutions*, in *Works* 4:309–10.

5. Franklin to Benjamin Vaughan, 26 June 1784, *Writings* 9:243; Drew McCoy, "Benjamin Franklin's Vision of a Republican Political Economy for America," *William and Mary Quarterly*, 3d ser., 35 (1978): 626–27; Jefferson, First Inaugural Address, *Life and Selected Writings*, 342.

6. Frederick Jackson Turner, *The Frontier in American History* (New York: Holt, Rinehart, and Winston, 1920), 1, 248–52; Jefferson to Madison, 20 December 1787, *Papers* 12:442. On Jefferson's deliberate efforts to root out the "pseudo-aristocracy" of Virginia and replace it with a natural aristocracy based on virtues and talents, see esp. Jefferson to John Adams, 28 October 1813, *Adams-Jefferson Letters* 2:387–92, and Jefferson's *Autobiography*, in *Complete Jefferson*, 1150.

7. Alexander Hamilton, "Report on Manufactures," in *Papers* 10:252, 270. Cf. Joyce Appleby's "Commercial Farming and the 'Agrarian Myth' in the Early Republic," *Journal of American History* 68 (1982): 833–49; "What Is Still American in the Political Philosophy of Thomas Jefferson?" *William and Mary Quarterly*, 3d ser., 39 (1982): 287–309; and *Capitalism and a New Social Order: The Republican Vision of the 1790s* (New York: New York University Press, 1984); Drew McCoy, *The Elusive Republic*; John R. Nelson, *Liberty and Property: Political Economy and Policymaking in the New Nation, 1789–1812* (Baltimore: Johns Hopkins University Press, 1987); and the critical review of the last by David N. Mayer, "Policy and Principles in the Age of Jefferson," *Humane Studies Review* 5 (1988): 9–11, 16–17.

8. Melancton Smith, Speech in the New York State Ratifying Convention, 21 June 1788, in Storing, *Complete Anti-Federalist*, 6.12.20.

9. "Letter from A Delegate Who Has Catched Cold," ibid. 5.19.16; "Letters from the Federal Farmer," ibid. 2.8.196.

10. Ibid. 2.8.190; cf. 2.8.54–55, and "Essays by a [Maryland] Farmer," 5.1.65–67.

11. Wilson, introductory lecture to *Of the Study of the Law in the United States*, in *Selected Political Essays of James Wilson*, 189.

12. Wilson, "A Charge Delivered to the Grand Jury in the Circuit Court of The United States, for the District of Virginia," in *The Works of James Wilson*, ed. Robert McCloskey, 2 vols. (Cambridge: Harvard University Press, 1967), 2:803–23. Other judges and justices in the Founding era also used their duty to instruct juries as an opportunity to teach more general political lessons. The early judges, all Federalists or supporters of the Constitution, joined Wilson in arguing that liberty is best protected by the firm rule of law, and they urged juries to act in a spirit of lawful self-restraint and give the new Constitution a chance. Several echoed the Anti-Federalist desire to make jury service a means of keeping the people informed about the law and their duties as citizens. But others, Federalists in a more narrow and partisan sense, carried their political disputes into the courtroom and brought the practice of political instruction from the bench into general disrepute. Yet as Ralph Lerner has argued, if the political jury charge was short-lived, it was but one part, and never the most important part, of the federal judiciary's function as educator. This is a function best performed, then as now, through the instruction

in constitutional principles and legal reasoning contained in the best written opinions of Supreme Court justices, in a tradition spearheaded by Chief Justice John Marshall. See Ralph Lerner, "The Supreme Court as Republican Schoolmaster," chap. 3 in *The Thinking Revolutionary: Principle and Practice in the New Republic* (Ithaca, N.Y.: Cornell University Press, 1987).

13. Wilson, introductory lecture, in *Selected Political Essays of James Wilson*, 190; Wilson to the Speaker of the Pennsylvania House of Representatives, 24 August 1791, *Works* 1:62. As the editor McCloskey points out, Wilson himself often fell prey to the temptation to display his erudition in verbose digressions: on his style in writing Supreme Court decisions, see *Works* 1:36.

14. For a contemporary account of the way law functions—deliberately in many places, but now mostly inadvertently in the United States—to tell the story of how a society conceives of itself and what it aspires to be, see Mary Ann Glendon, *Abortion and Divorce in Western Law* (Cambridge: Harvard University Press, 1987).

15. "Letters from the Federal Farmer," in Storing, *Complete Anti-Federalist*, 2.8.95 (cf. 2.8.95, 97, and 190); "Essays of Brutus," ibid. 2.9.49 (cf. 2.9.18 and 2.9.48); Melancton Smith, 21 June 1788, ibid. 6.12.17 (cf. 6.12.15); see also "The Address and Reasons of Dissent of the Minority of the Convention of Pennsylvania to Their Constituents," ibid. 3.11.50. Some Federalists questioned whether the Anti-Federalist concern with winning the affections of the people to the support of the government, while perfectly valid, was not somewhat misdirected or based on faulty political judgment. Charles Pinckney, for example, argues that the distinction between governments that rest on force and those that rest on voluntary affection is chimerical: "All government is a kind of restraint" (Eliot, *Debates in the Several State Conventions* 4:261). As the Federalists saw it, the most steady attachment of the people to government is the *result* of a firm and uniform enforcement of the laws.

16. "Essays by a [Maryland] Farmer," in Storing, *Complete Anti-Federalist* 5.1.76–78, 82. On sumptuary laws, cf. the speeches of George Mason, 20 August and 13 September 1787, in Farrand, *Records of the Federal Convention* 2:344, 606. On the tendency of popular involvement in government to increase patriotism, see Jefferson to Joseph Cabell, 2 February 1816, *Life and Selected Writings*, 661.

17. "Letters of Cato," in Storing, *Complete Anti-Federalist* 2.6.36 and n. 24; ibid. 2.6.13 (quoting, with small changes, Montesquieu, *Spirit of the Laws*, bk. 8, chap. 16).

18. "Essays by a [Maryland] Farmer," in *Complete Anti-Federalist* 5.1.53; "Letters of Cato," ibid. 2.6.27 (quoting Montesquieu, *Spirit of the Laws*, bk. 3, chap. 5); "Review of the Constitution Proposed by the Late Convention by a Federal Republican," in *Complete Anti-Federalist* 3.6.21 (see Storing's note 19 ad loc.). On centralized government see also Melancton Smith, ibid. 6.12.20. On the federal capital see also "Observations on the New Constitution, and on the Federal and State Conventions, by a Columbian Patriot" (probably Mercy Warren), ibid. 4.28.8. On standing armies see "Essays by the Impartial Examiner," ibid. 5.14.8.

19. "Letters of Centinel," ibid. 2.7.101; Patrick Henry, Speech in the Virginia State Ratifying Convention, 5 June 1788, ibid. 5.16.3; cf. "Essays of Brutus," ibid. 2.9.20, and "Essays of John De Witt," ibid. 4.3.17. The Federalists strike a much more classical tone on this crucial point. Wilson, for example, speaks of the need to encourage the "laudable emulation" that prompts men to seek the highest offices in their country (*Works* 1:75). See Storing, *Complete Anti-Federalist* 1:41–47, and the revealing debate in the Constitutional Convention, 23 June 1787, in Farrand's *Records of the Federal Convention* 1:386–94.

20. When Jefferson's ward system was in fact tried in Virginia in 1850, the effect was to drain interest away from citizens' meetings at the county level, without creating a vital public life in the wards: see Honeywell, *Educational Work*, 149.

21. Alexis de Tocqueville, *Democracy in America*, vol. 2, pt. 2, chaps. 5 and 7; our translation from *De la Démocratie en Amérique*, in *Oeuvres, Papiers et Correspondances*, ed. J.-P. Mayer, 5th ed. (Paris: Gallimard, 1951), vol. 1, pt. 2, 115–16, 123.

22. Ibid., 122.

Chapter 11. Education through the Free Exchange of Ideas

1. Jefferson to Adamantios Coray, 31 October 1823, *Writings* 15:489; see also Jefferson to Edward Carrington, 16 January 1787, *Life and Selected Writings* 411–12.

2. Tocqueville, *Democracy in America*, vol. 2, pt. 2, chap. 6, in Mayer edition, 2:119.

3. Jefferson, *Notes on the State of Virginia*, query 17, p. 159; see also A Bill for Establishing Religious Freedom, *Papers* 2:545.

4. Quoted by Leonard Levy, *Freedom of Speech and Press in Early American History: Legacy of Suppression* (New York: Harper and Row, 1963), 180.

5. Franklin, *Writings* 10:36–40. Levy, in a characteristically humorless reading of this passage, seems to miss Franklin's irony, as well as his argument that the entire community has a stake in preventing libels against any individual. Levy assumes that "when the public is affronted" can mean only "when the government's reputation is affronted," and he denies the community any right to punish this injury (*Freedom of Speech and Press*, 187). Jefferson to John Norville, 14 June 1807, *Works* 10:417–18; cf. Jefferson to Thomas McKean, 19 February 1803, ibid. 9:451–52, and Jefferson to Thomas Seymour, 11 February 1807, ibid. 10:367–69.

6. Levy, *Freedom of Speech and Press*, 6.

7. Ibid., 13.

8. *Cato's Letters* 1:97 (letter no. 15).

9. James Madison, Report on the Virginia Resolutions, in Kurland and Lerner, *Founders' Constitution* 5:144, 142.

10. Walter Berns, *The First Amendment and the Future of American Democracy*, 143–46; *People v. Croswell*, 3 Johns. Cas. 337 (New York 1804), in Kurland and Lerner, *Founders' Constitution* 5:160, 162.

11. Jefferson to Abigail Adams, 11 September 1804, *Adams-Jefferson Letters* 1:297. Despite Washington's standing as the greatest hero of all, he was sensitive about his reputation and gave as one reason for retiring "a disinclination to be longer buffetted in the public prints by a set of infamous scribblers" (Washington to Hamilton, 26 June 1796, *Writings* 35:102).

12. *Abrams v. United States*, 250 U.S. 616, 630 (1919).

13. Walter Berns, *The First Amendment and the Future of American Democracy*, chap. 4.

14. On public opinion and mobs, see esp. *Federalist Papers*, nos. 55 (p. 342), 63 (p. 384), 73 (p. 443), 78 (p. 470); see also Hamilton's 1794 comments on the French Revolution, *Papers* 17:586–88 and 26:738–41. For Jefferson on monarchists, see *Notes on the State of Virginia*, query 8, pp. 84–85.

15. Levy reads this into Madison's 1800 report, but Madison does not go this far: *Freedom of Speech and Press*, 273.

16. Jefferson, First and Second Inaugural Addresses, *Life and Selected Writings*, 322, 343–44.

17. *The Works of Fisher Ames* 1:134, 185.

18. Ibid. 1:12–16, 2:1411, 1416. Madison also had little hope for a nonpartisan press, though he wished it could be brought into being. See Madison to N. P. Trist, 23 April 1826, *Letters and Other Writings* 3:630.

19. *Gazette of the United States*, 4 March 1799, quoted in Willard Bleyer, *Main Currents in the History of American Journalism* (Boston: Houghton Mifflin, 1927), 126. Of the hand-

ful of complete histories of American journalism, this remains the most useful in relating the development of journalism to the important political, moral, and educational issues of the Founding era. Bleyer also quotes at length from the editors themselves to show their understanding of their function in society. Also useful is Frank Luther Mott, *American Journalism*, 3d ed. (New York: Macmillan, 1962), which has an especially good account of the politicization of the press during the American Revolution.

20. *Boston Daily Advertiser*, 7 April and 6 December 1814, quoted in Bleyer, *American Journalism*, 142–43.

21. *Minerva*, 9 December 1793, reproduced in Bleyer, *American Journalism*, 113.

22. Franklin, *Autobiography*, 165.

23. Gordon Wood, "The Democratization of Mind in the American Revolution," in Robert Horwitz, ed., *The Moral Foundations of the American Republic*, 3d ed. (Charlottesville: University Press of Virginia, 1986), 110, 117.

24. On the Library of Congress, see Douglas L. Wilson, "Jefferson's Library," in Peterson, ed., *Thomas Jefferson: A Reference Biography*, 157–59; Jefferson, A Bill for Establishing a Public Library, *Papers* 2:544; Jefferson, *Autobiography*, in *Works* 1:75; see also Jefferson to John Wyche, 19 May 1809, *Writings* 12:283.

25. Franklin, *Autobiography*, 142; Cremin, *American Education: The Colonial Experience, 1607–1783*, 338–41, 398–99.

26. Franklin, *Papers* 2:378–83; Cremin, *American Education: The Colonial Experience, 1607–1783*, 408–11.

27. Franklin, *Autobiography*, 164. For his charming frankness about his profit motives, see also the prefaces to *Poor Richard* for 1733 and 1734, *Papers* 1:311, 349–51. Franklin was, however, by no means the first to employ almanacs as a vehicle for popular education: see Cremin, *American Education: The Colonial Experience, 1607–1783*, 389–91.

Chapter 12. George Washington and the Principle of Honor

1. For an illuminating exploration of Jefferson as a writer, see Robert Dawidoff, "Man of Letters," in Peterson, ed., *Thomas Jefferson: A Reference Biography*, 181–98.

2. Washington to George Steptoe Washington, 23 March 1789, *Writings* 30:248; Washington to George Washington Parke Custis, 28 November 1796, ibid. 35:295.

3. Washington to George Washington Parke Custis, 15 and 28 November 1796, ibid. 35:282, 295; Washington to George Steptoe Washington, 23 March 1789, ibid. 30:246.

4. Washington to John Boucher, 9 July 1771, ibid. 3:50; Washington to Nicholas Pike, 20 June 1788, ibid. 30:2–3.

5. Jefferson's comment quoted in James Thomas Flexner, *George Washington*, 4 vols. (Boston: Little, Brown, 1965–1969), 3:46.

6. Washington to James Anderson, 21 December 1797, *Writings* 36:113; James Thomas Flexner, *Washington: The Indispensable Man* (New York: New American Library, 1969), 194; Washington, Farewell Address, *Writings* 35:231–37. For a useful introduction to Washington's character and especially his sense of honor, see Edmund S. Morgan, *The Meaning of Independence* (New York: W. W. Norton, 1976), chap. 2 (entitled "George Washington").

7. 1759 Farewell Address of Washington's officers, reprinted in John Marshall, *The Life of George Washington*, 2d ed., 2 vols. (Philadelphia: James Crissy, 1832), vol. 1, pp. 12–13 of notes.

8. This is the way Weems's portrait of Washington is characterized in Beveridge's *Life of John Marshall* 3:231–232n.

9. Charles Beard, *An Economic Interpretation of the Constitution of the United States*

(New York: Macmillan, 1913); Douglass Adair, _Fame and the Founding Fathers_, ed. Trevor Colbourn (New York: W. W. Norton, 1974), chap. 1; _Federalist Papers_, no. 72 (p. 437).

10. See especially Aristotle, _Nicomachean Ethics_, 1123a34– 1125a35.

11. Washington to Warner Lewis, 14 August 1755, _Writings_ 1:162; Washington to Mary Washington, 14 August 1755, ibid. 1:159.

12. Washington to Benjamin Harrison, 22 January 1785, ibid. 28:34–37; Washington to Jefferson, 25 February 1785, ibid. 28:80; to Edmund Randolph, 30 July 1785, ibid. 28:214–16; to Patrick Henry, 29 October 1785, ibid. 28:303–4. As we have indicated in an earlier context, Washington's solution was to accept the shares but designate them for a charity school and a national university.

13. Washington to Lafayette, 1 February 1784 and 29 January 1789, ibid. 27:316–18 and 30:186; Washington to Henry Lee, 22 September 1788, ibid. 30:97–98; see also Jefferson to Washington, 10 May 1789, _Works_ (of Jefferson), 5:475. Washington had undergone similar qualms before deciding to attend the Constitutional Convention, particularly since he had used his own promise to remain in private life as proof of his disinterestedness in calling for a stronger central government. See "Circular to the States," 8 June 1783, _Writings_ 26:486–87.

14. Forrest McDonald, _Novus Ordo Seclorum: The Intellectual Origins of the Constitution_ (Lawrence: University Press of Kansas, 1985), 186–99.

15. Jefferson, _Life and Writings_, 173–74; Washington, First Inaugural Address, _Writings_ 30:294. See also Jefferson's comment in the _Anas_, in _Works_ 1:165: "[Washington's] passions were naturally strong; but his reason, generally, stronger." Also of interest here is Gouverneur Morris's eulogy of Washington: "Heaven, in giving him the higher qualities of the soul, had given also the tumultuous passions which accompany greatness, and frequently tarnish its lustre. With them was his first contest, and his first victory was over himself": _Eulogies and Orations on the Life and Death of George Washington_ (Boston: Manning and Loring, 1800), 44. Some years later, Morris was to comment that "perhaps no one" had ever existed "who so completely commanded himself": Morris to John Marshall, 26 June 1807, excerpt in _The Diary and Letters of Gouverneur Morris_, ed. Anne Cary Morris, 2 vols. (London: Kegan Paul, 1889), 2:492.

16. Forrest McDonald, _Novus Ordo Seclorum_, 195–99; Fredric M. Litto, "Addison's _Cato_ in the Colonies," _William and Mary Quarterly_, 3d ser., 23 (1966): 431–49.

17. _Cato_, in _The Works of the Right Honorable Joseph Addison_, ed. Richard Hurd, 6 vols. (London: Henry G. Bohn, 1854), 1:177.

18. Ibid., 182, 198.

19. Ibid., 207.

20. Ibid., 188, 189.

21. Ibid., 176, 194, 216; but cf. 219.

22. Addison, _Works_ 4:308–9; cf. again Aristotle's treatment of greatness of soul in _Nicomachean Ethics_ 1123a34–1125a35.

23. McDonald, _Novus Ordo Seclorum_, 198. This error begins when McDonald quotes as Addison's a rather misleading note by Addison's editor Hurd, characterizing honor as "the love of honest fame" or "the esteem of wise and good men" (see Addison, _Works_ 4:309–10), but McDonald carries this idea much further than Hurd does.

24. For the discussion that follows, see especially _Spirit of the Laws_, bk. 2, chaps. 4–5; bk. 3, chaps. 1–2 and 5–10; bk. 4, chaps. 2–4; bk. 5, chaps. 9–12; bk. 6, chaps. 1–2; bk. 8, chaps. 6–9; bk. 19, chaps. 5–9.

25. Ibid., bk. 4, chap. 2; bk. 3, chap. 5; bk. 7, chap. 8; bk. 28, chap. 22; cf. bk. 19, chaps. 5–10; bk. 20, chaps. 4 and 22. On the vices of courts, see chap. 10 in this book; cf. also Jefferson's assessment of the merits and deficiencies of the French spirit, especially as

regards sexual mores, in his letter to Charles Bellini, 30 September 1785, *Life and Selected Writings*, 382–83.

26. Montesquieu, *Spirit of the Laws*, bk. 4, chap. 2.

27. Jean-Jacques Rousseau, *Emile, or On Education*, trans. Allan Bloom (New York: Basic Books, 1979; orig. pub. 1762), index entries under "amour-propre," "amour de soi"; *Discourse on the Origin and Foundations of Inequality among Men*; Montesquieu, *Spirit of the Laws*, bk. 3, chap. 7 (entitled "On the Principle of Monarchy"); cf. bk. 5, chap. 12.

28. *Federalist Papers*, no. 39 (p. 240). For a good comparison of Washington, as portrayed in Marshall's biography, with the classical image of the gentleman-statesman, see Robert K. Faulkner, *The Jurisprudence of John Marshall* (Princeton, N.J.: Princeton University Press, 1968), 127–30.

29. See Flexner, *Washington: The Indispensable Man*, 110, and *George Washington* 2:251, 533. On the treatment of Tories, see, e.g., Washington to Joseph Reed, 1 April 1776, *Writings* 4:456: "Unhappy wretches! Deluded mortals! Would it not be good policy to grant a generous amnesty, and conquer these people by a generous forgiveness?"

30. On the Newburg conspiracy, see esp. Richard H. Kohn, *Eagle and Sword: The Federalists and the Creation of the Military Establishment in America, 1783–1802* (New York: Free Press, 1975), chap. 2. Jefferson to Washington, 16 April 1784, *Papers* 7:106–7; Washington to the Secretary for Foreign Affairs, 18 July 1788, *Writings* 30:16.

31. Letter of Reverend William Emerson, in *The Writings of George Washington*, ed. Jared Sparks, 12 vols. (Boston: Little, Brown, 1833–1837), 3:491.

32. Washington to Patrick Henry, 5 November 1776, *Writings* (Fitzpatrick ed.), 6:167; see also Washington to Col. William Woodford, 10 November 1775, ibid. 4:81; cf. Washington to William Pearce, 18 December 1793, ibid. 33:194.

33. Washington to the President of Congress, 24 September 1776, *Writings* 6:107–9; see also Washington to John Bannister, 21 April 1778, ibid. 11:286.

34. Washington to David Stuart, 26 July 1789, ibid. 30:361; Washington to Catherine Macaulay Graham, 9 January 1790, ibid., 498; Leonard White, *The Federalists*, 108. See also Flexner, *George Washington* 3:16; White, *The Federalists*, chaps. 21, 22, 25; White, *The Jeffersonians, 1801–1829*, 356–68, 547–49; White, *The Jacksonians: A Study in Administrative History 1829–1861* (New York: Macmillan, 1954), 316–24, 347, 411–12, 418–19, 430, 552–53.

35. On Jefferson's return from France to assume the duties of secretary of state, he was surprised at how quickly the opposition to the Constitution had subsided, and he largely credited Washington with the change (Jefferson to Lafayette, 2 April 1790, *Works* 6:40).

36. Addison, *Works* 1:219. As Aristotle has shown, such virtue poses a delicate problem for friendship: in seeking to benefit one another, friends are also inevitably competing to get a larger share of the noble; see *Nicomachean Ethics* bk. 9.

37. Washington, First Inaugural Address, *Writings* 30:294.

Chapter 13. Thomas Jefferson and the Natural Basis of Moral Education

1. Jefferson to Peter Carr, 10 August 1787, *Papers* 12:14–15.

2. Jefferson to Thomas Law, 13 June 1814, *Complete Jefferson*, 1032–34; here and elsewhere, Jefferson uses the terms *morality* and *virtue* interchangeably.

3. Jefferson to Mrs. Trist, 18 August 1785, *Life and Selected Writings*, 371–72. On Jefferson's dim view of the moral code of the Hebrews, see Jefferson to Adams, 12 October

1813, *Adams-Jefferson Letters* 2:383–84. In this letter Jefferson introduces another unfortunate source of variety in moral codes: the ascendancy of corrupt priests.

4. Jefferson, *Notes on the State of Virginia*, query 14, p. 147.

5. Quoted in Malone, *Jefferson and His Time*, vol. 2, *Jefferson and the Ordeal of Liberty*, 126.

6. Jefferson to Martha Jefferson Randolph, 26 April 1790, *Family Letters*, 54; Jefferson to Martha Jefferson, 28 March 1787, ibid., 34.

7. Jefferson to Martha Jefferson, 5 May 1787, *Family Letters*, 40; cf. Jefferson to same, 28 March 1787, ibid., 36; Jefferson to Mary Jefferson, 11 April and 13 June 1790, ibid., 52, 58–59.

8. Jefferson to Carr, 10 August 1787, *Papers* 12:16; Jefferson to Carr, 19 August 1785, ibid. 3:406.

9. Jefferson to John Banister, 15 October 1785, *Papers* 8:635–37. But cf. Malone, *Jefferson and His Time*, vol. 2, *Jefferson and the Ordeal of Liberty*, 149; without endorsing foreign education for young Americans, Jefferson later begins to speak positively about the advantages they might gain from European travel.

10. Jefferson to Nathaniel Burwell, 14 March 1818, *Works* 12:91. This concern may seem quaint when compared with the radical corrosiveness of contemporary television, but Jefferson points to the central issue that critics of the modern media often miss. What is most damaging about the addiction to television is not the taste for sex and violence that it may engender, but the consequent numbing of the soul to pleasures of a more rational or a more sublime nature. As Jefferson saw it, a fascination with romantic novels and their stormy, dramatic love affairs may leave one insensitive to the quiet happiness of marriage between good-hearted, sensible partners. A constant overindulgence in the cheap thrills of television may go further, leaving one a relative stranger to the pleasures of rational conversation, to sublime poetry, and to habits of persistence in great and difficult undertakings. It may therefore in some measure impede the capacity to love with the depth and commitment of soul needed for either a great love affair or a solid marriage.

11. Jefferson to Peter Carr, 10 August 1787, *Papers* 12:15–16; Laurence Sterne, *The Sermons of Mr. Yorick*, 2 vols. (London: Basil Blackwell, 1927; orig. pub. 1760–1769), 1:84 and 82. For Sterne's treatment of the themes of this chapter, see esp. sermon 3, "Philanthropy Recommended," and sermon 7, "Vindication of Human Nature."

12. Jefferson to Martha Jefferson, 11 December 1783, 6 March 1786, and 7 April 1787, *Family Letters*, 21, 30, 36–37; Jefferson to Martha Jefferson Randolph, 28 April 1793, ibid., 116; Jefferson to Mary Jefferson, 11 April 1790, ibid., 52; cf. Jefferson to Martha Jefferson, 28 November 1783, ibid., 20.

13. Jefferson to Thomas Jefferson Randolph, 24 November 1808, *Life and Selected Writings*, 590–91.

14. Jefferson to Law, 13 June 1814, *Complete Jefferson*, 1034; Jefferson to Martha Jefferson, 15 January 1784, *Family Letters*, 23.

15. Rockfish Gap report, *Complete Jefferson*, 1105.

16. "Syllabus of an Estimate of the Merit of the Doctrines of Jesus, Compared with Those of Others," *Complete Jefferson*, 949; Jefferson to William Short, 31 October 1819, *Life and Selected Writings*, 693–97.

17. Jefferson to Maria Cosway, 12 October 1786, *Life and Writings*, 395–407.

18. Jefferson to Martha Jefferson Randolph, 8 June 1797, *Family Letters*, 146; Jefferson to David Rittenhouse, 19 June 1778, *Papers* 2:203.

19. Jefferson to Law, 13 June 1814, *Complete Jefferson*, 1033; Jefferson to Mary Jefferson Eppes, 1 January 1799, *Family Letters*, 170.

20. Aristotle, *Nicomachean Ethics* 1142a25–30, 1143a35–b7, 1147a26; see also Brann, *Paradoxes of Education*, 26.

21. Jefferson to Carr, 19 August 1785, *Life and Selected Writings*, 373–74.

Chapter 14. Benjamin Franklin and the Art of Virtue

1. Benjamin Franklin, *Autobiography*, 133–40. Further quotations from Franklin's *Autobiography* are cited in the text, using page numbers from the Labaree edition.

2. See, for example, the stories of Collins, Rogers, and Keimer, in *Autobiography*, 84–86, 107, 126.

3. Alexander Solzenitsyn, *One Day in the Life of Ivan Denisovich*, trans. Ralph Parker (New York: Penguin Books, 1963), 79–92.

4. For Franklin's sense of the all-important human need for friendship and society, see esp. his journal entry of 25 August 1726, *Papers* 1:85–86.

5. Max Weber, *The Protestant Ethic and the Spirit of Capitalism*, trans. Talcott Parsons (New York: Charles Scribner's Sons, 1958), 48–54, 78; cf. Thomas Pangle, *The Spirit of Modern Republicanism*, 16–19.

6. Poor Richard, 1738, *Papers* 2:197. On Franklin's interest in science, see esp. Franklin to Peter Collinson, 28 March 1747, *Papers* 3:118–19, and also Carl Becker's assessment: "One exception there was [to Franklin's detached stance toward life]—science: one activity which Franklin pursued without outward prompting, from some compelling inner impulse; one activity from which he never wished to retire, to which he would willingly have devoted his life, to which he always gladly turned in every odd day or hour of leisure, even in the midst of the exacting duties and heavy responsibility of his public career. Science was after all the one mistress to whom he gave himself without reserve and served neither from a sense of duty nor for any practical purpose" (Carl Becker, *Benjamin Franklin: A Biographical Sketch* [Ithaca, N.Y.: Cornell University Press, 1946], 36). For Franklin's feelings about business at the time of his retirement, see esp. Franklin to Cadwallader Colden, 29 September 1748, *Papers* 3:317–20. On his financial support of the army, see *Autobiography*, 217–23, 228, 254–55.

7. "A Proposal for Promoting Useful Knowledge among the British Plantations in America," 14 May 1743, *Papers* 2:380; "On the Need for an Academy," 24 August 1749, *Papers* 3:385–86.

8. Ralph Lerner, "Franklin, Spectator," chap. 1 in *Thinking Revolutionary*, 48. The subtle observations of this chapter have given us invaluable guidance in understanding the *Autobiography*.

9. "Proposals Relating to the Education of Youth in Pennsylvania" (1749), *Papers* 3:412, 419. On the service that Franklin argued a talented man owed his country in times of crisis, see also Franklin to Samuel Johnson, 23 August 1750, *Papers* 4:40–42.

10. Franklin to Peter Collinson, 9 May 1753, *Papers* 4:479–83; Franklin to Benjamin Vaughan, 26 July 1784, *Writings* 9:243.

11. *Papers* 1:57–71.

12. Ibid., 61.

13. Franklin to Benjamin Vaughan, 9 November 1779, *Writings* 7:412.

14. *Papers* 1:213; *Autobiography*, 146, 162.

15. Franklin to Ezra Stiles, 9 March 1790, *Writings* 10:84–85.

16. See, for example, *Autobiography*, 213–14, 239–40; Lerner, *Thinking Revolutionary*, 56.

17. Verner W. Crane, *Benjamin Franklin and a Rising People* (Boston: Little, Brown,

1954), 135; *Autobiography*, 196 n.7, 197 n.4, 208, 213; Franklin to William Franklin, 16 August 1784, *Writings* 9:252–54.

18. "Articles of Belief and Acts of Religion" (dated 1728, when Franklin was 22), *Papers* 1:101–9.

19. Matt. 9:13; Franklin to Joseph Huey, 6 June 1753, *Papers* 4:504–6.

20. Jonathan Edwards, *Personal Narrative*, reprinted in David Levin, ed. *The Puritan in the Enlightenment* (Chicago: Rand McNally, 1963), 10–12.

21. "Father Abraham's Speech," printed as the preface to *Poor Richard Improved* (1758), in *Papers* 7:350; "A Man of Sense," *Pennsylvania Gazette*, 11 February 1735, in *Papers* 2:17–18.

22. See, for example, *Autobiography*, 85–86, 90–91, 122–23, 189–90, 212–14, 250–51; cf. Lerner, *Thinking Revolutionary*, 55.

23. See, for example, *Autobiography*, 64–65, 66, 68, 75, 159–60, and Lerner, *Thinking Revolutionary*, 53; cf. the rather envious spirit of John Adams's assessment of Franklin's fame, in *Works* 1:659–64.

24. Lawrence's two essays on Franklin, both entitled "Benjamin Franklin," were first published in the *English Review* 27 (1918): 397–408, and in D. H. Lawrence, *Studies in Classic American Literature* (New York: Viking Press, 1961; orig. pub. 1923), 9–21; both are reprinted in Melvin H. Buxbaum, ed. *Critical Essays on Benjamin Franklin* (Boston: G. K. Hall, 1987), 41–60; passages quoted are from 44 and 58.

25. Franklin, *Autobiography*, 149–50; Lawrence, "Benjamin Franklin," in *Critical Essays on Benjamin Franklin*, 52, 56–58.

26. Charles Angoff, *A Literary History of the American People*, 2 vols. (New York: Tudor, 1935), 2:296.

27. Lawrence, "Benjamin Franklin," in *Critical Essays on Benjamin Franklin*, 57, 56.

28. Ormond Seavey, "Benjamin Franklin and D. H. Lawrence as Conflicting Modes of Consciousness," in Buxbaum, ed., *Critical Essays on Benjamin Franklin*, 71.

Conclusion

1. Jefferson, *Notes on the State of Virginia*, query 14, p. 147.

Bibliography

Adair, Douglass. *Fame and the Founding Fathers*. Edited by Trevor Colbourn. New York: W. W. Norton, 1974.

Adams, John. *The Works of John Adams, Second President of the United States*. Edited by Charles Francis Adams. 10 vols. Boston: Little, Brown, 1851–1856.

Adams, John, and Thomas Jefferson. *The Adams-Jefferson Letters*. Edited by Lester J. Cappon. 2 vols. Chapel Hill: University of North Carolina Press, 1959.

Adams, John Quincy, and Charles Francis Adams. *John Adams*. 2 vols. New York: Chelsea House, 1980.

Adams, Samuel. *The Writings of Samuel Adams*. Edited by Harry Alonzo Cushing. 4 vols. New York: G. P. Putnam's Sons, 1904–1908.

Addison, Joseph. *The Works of the Right Honorable Joseph Addison*. Edited by Richard Hurd. 6 vols. London: Henry G. Bohn, 1854.

Ambrose, Stephen E. *Duty, Honor, Country: A History of West Point*. Baltimore: Johns Hopkins University Press, 1966.

Ames, Fisher. *The Works of Fisher Ames*. Edited by Seth Ames; ed. and enlarged by W. B. Allen. 2 vols. Indianapolis: Liberty Classics, 1983.

Angoff, Charles. *A Literary History of the American People*. 2 vols. New York: Tudor, 1935.

Appleby, Joyce. *Capitalism and a New Social Order: The Republican Vision of the 1790s*. New York: New York University Press, 1984.

———. "Commercial Farming and the 'Agrarian Myth' in the Early Republic." *Journal of American History* 68 (1982): 833–49.

———. "What Is Still American in the Political Philosophy of Thomas Jefferson?" *William and Mary Quarterly*, 3d. ser., 39 (1982): 287–309.

Aristotle. *Ethica Nicomachea*. Edited by I. Bywater. Oxford: Clarendon Press, 1962.

———. *The Politics of Aristotle*. Edited by W. L. Newman. 4 vols. New York: Arno Press, 1973.

Arrowood, Charles Flinn. *Thomas Jefferson and Education in a Republic*. New York: McGraw-Hill, 1931.

Bacon, Francis. *The Advancement of Learning and New Atlantis*. London: Oxford University Press, 1974.

———. *The New Organon*. Edited by Fulton H. Anderson. Indianapolis: Bobbs-Merrill, 1960.

Bailyn, Bernard. *Education in the Forming of American Society*. New York: W. W. Norton, 1972.

Baldwin, Alice M. *The New England Clergy and the American Revolution.* Durham, N.C.: Duke University Press, 1928.

Barlow, Joel. *The Works of Joel Barlow.* 2 vols. Gainesville, Fla.: Scholars' Facsimiles and Reprints, 1970.

Beard, Charles. *An Economic Interpretation of the Constitution of the United States.* New York: Macmillan, 1913.

Becker, Carl L. *Benjamin Franklin: A Biographical Sketch.* Ithaca, N.Y.: Cornell University Press, 1946.

Berns, Walter. *The First Amendment and the Future of American Democracy.* New York: Basic Books, 1976.

————. *Taking the Constitution Seriously.* New York: Simon and Schuster, 1987.

Beveridge, Albert. *The Life of John Marshall.* 4 vols. Boston: Houghton Mifflin, 1916–1919.

Blackstone, William. *Commentaries on the Laws of England.* 4 vols. Oxford: Clarendon Press, 1765–1769. Facsimile reprint. Chicago: University of Chicago Press, 1979.

Bleyer, Willard. *Main Currents in the History of American Journalism.* Boston: Houghton Mifflin, 1927.

Blinderman, Abraham. *American Writers on Education before 1865.* Boston: Twayne Publishers, 1975.

Brann, Eva T. H. *Paradoxes of Education in a Republic.* Chicago: University of Chicago Press, 1979.

Bridenbaugh, Carl, and Jessica Bridenbaugh. *Rebels and Gentlemen: Philadelphia in the Age of Franklin.* New York: Oxford University Press, 1962.

Bruce, Philip Alexander. *History of the University of Virginia 1819–1919: The Lengthened Shadow of One Man.* 5 vols. New York: Macmillan, 1920–1922.

Bruell, Christopher. "Liberal Education and Education for Citizenship." In Stephen N. Kranson, ed., *The Recovery of American Education: Reclaiming a Vision.* Lanham, Md.: University Press of America, 1991.

Burke, Edmund. *Reflections on the Revolution in France.* Garden City, N.Y.: Doubleday, 1961.

Butts, R. Freeman. *The College Charts Its Course: Historical Conceptions and Current Proposals.* New York: McGraw-Hill, 1939.

Buxbaum, Melvin H., ed. *Critical Essays on Benjamin Franklin.* Boston: G. K. Hall, 1987.

Calvin, John. *The Institutes of the Christian Religion.* 2 vols. Translated by John Allen, as revised and corrected by Benjamin B. Warfield. Philadelphia: Westminister Press, 1945.

Clarke, John. *An Essay Upon the Education of Youth in Grammar-Schools. In Which the Vulgar Method of Teaching Is Examined, and a New One Proposed, for the More Easy and Speedy Training Up of Youth to the Knowledge of the Learned Languages; Together with History, Chronology, Geography, &c.* 2d ed. London: Arthur Bettesworth, 1730; orig. pub. 1720.

Cohen, Sheldon S. *A History of Colonial Education, 1607–1776.* New York: John Wiley and Sons, 1974.

Crane, Verner W. *Benjamin Franklin and a Rising People.* Boston: Little, Brown, 1954.

Cremin, Lawrence A. *American Education: The Colonial Experience, 1607–1783.* New York: Harper and Row, 1970.

————. *American Education: The National Experience, 1783–1876.* New York: Harper and Row, 1980.

————. "Reading, Writing, and Literacy." *Review of Education* 1 (1975): 517–21.

————. *Traditions of American Education.* New York: Basic Books, 1977.

Cubberly, Ellwood P. *Readings in Public Education in the United States.* Boston: Houghton Mifflin, 1934.

Diehl, Carl. *Americans and German Scholarship 1770-1870*. New Haven, Conn.: Yale University Press, 1978.

Dworetz, Steven M. *The Unvarnished Doctrine: Locke, Liberalism, and the American Revolution*. Durham, N.C.: Duke University Press, 1990.

Eliot, Jonathan, ed. *The Debates in the Several State Conventions on the Adoption of the Federal Constitution*. 5 vols. Philadelphia: J. B. Lippincott, 1907.

Epstein, David. *The Political Theory of the Federalist*. Chicago: University of Chicago Press, 1984.

Eulogies and Orations on the Life and Death of George Washington. Boston: Manning and Loring, 1800.

Everett, Edward. *Orations and Speeches on Various Occasions*. 2 vols. Boston: Little, Brown, 1878.

———. "University of Virginia." *North American Review* 10 (1820): 115-37.

Farrand, Max, ed. *The Records of the Federal Convention of 1787*. 4 vols. New Haven, Conn.: Yale University Press, 1966.

Faulkner, Robert K. *The Jurisprudence of John Marshall*. Princeton, N.J.: Princeton University Press, 1968.

———. *Richard Hooker and the Politics of a Christian England*. Berkeley and Los Angeles: University of California Press, 1981.

Flexner, James Thomas. *George Washington*. 4 vols. Boston: Little, Brown, 1965-1969.

———. *Washington: The Indispensable Man*. New York: New American Library, 1969.

Ford, Paul L. ed. *The New England Primer: A History of Its Origins and Development, with a Reprint of the Unique Copy of the Earliest Known Edition*. New York: Teachers College, Columbia University, 1962.

Ford, Worthington C., et al., eds. *Journals of the Continental Congress, 1774-1789*. 34 vols. Washington, D.C.: Government Printing Office, 1904-1937.

Fox-Bourne, Henry R. *The Life of John Locke*. 2 vols. New York: Harper and Brothers, 1876.

Franklin, Benjamin. *The Autobiography of Benjamin Franklin*. Edited by Leonard W. Labaree. New Haven, Conn.: Yale University Press, 1964.

———. *The Papers of Benjamin Franklin*. Edited by Leonard Labaree et al. 28 vols. to date. New Haven, Conn.: Yale University Press, 1959-.

———. *The Works of Benjamin Franklin*. Edited by Jared Sparks. 10 vols. London: B. F. Stevens, 1882.

———. *The Writings of Benjamin Franklin*. Edited by Albert Henry Smyth. 10 vols. New York: Macmillan, 1905-1907.

Goode, Harry G. *Benjamin Rush and His Services to American Education*. Berne, Ind.: Witness Press, 1918.

Glendon, Mary Ann. *Abortion and Divorce in Western Law*. Cambridge: Harvard University Press, 1987.

Gribbin, William. "Rollin's Histories and American Republicans." *William and Mary Quarterly*, 3d ser., 29 (1972): 611-22.

Gummere, Richard M. *The American Colonial Mind and the Classical Tradition*. Cambridge: Harvard University Press, 1963.

Hamilton, Alexander. *The Papers of Alexander Hamilton*. Edited by Harold C. Syrett et al. 27 vols. New York: Columbia University Press, 1961-1987.

Harrison, Lowell H. *The Antislavery Movement in Kentucky*. Lexington: University Press of Kentucky, 1978.

Hatch, Nathan O. *The Democratization of American Christianity*. New Haven, Conn.: Yale University Press, 1989.

Hellenbrand, Harold. *The Unfinished Revolution: Education and Politics in the Thought of Thomas Jefferson.* Newark: University of Delaware Press, 1990.

Hill, Christopher. *Society and Puritanism in Pre-Revolutionary England.* 2d ed. New York: Schocken Books, 1972.

Hofstadter, Richard, and Wilson Smith, eds. *American Higher Education: A Documentary History.* 2 vols. Chicago: University of Chicago Press, 1961.

Honeywell, Roy. *The Educational Work of Thomas Jefferson.* Cambridge: Harvard University Press, 1931.

Hooker, Richard. *The Works of That Learned and Judicious Divine Mr. Richard Hooker.* Edited by J. Keble. 3 vols. 7th ed. New York: Burt Franklin, 1970.

Horwitz, Robert H., and Judith B Finn. "Locke's Aesop's Fables." *Locke Newsletter* 6 (1975): 71–88.

Hume, David. *Enquiries Concerning the Human Understanding and Concerning the Principles of Morals.* Edited by L. A. Selby-Bigge. Oxford: Clarendon Press, 1955.

———. *Essays: Moral, Political, and Literary.* Edited by Eugene F. Miller. Indianapolis: Liberty Press, 1985.

———. *History of England from the Invasion of Julius Caesar to the Revolution in 1688.* 6 vols. New York: John W. Lovell, n.d.

Hutchinson, Thomas. *History of the Colony and Province of Massachusetts-Bay.* Edited by Lawrence Mayo. 3 vols. Cambridge: Harvard University Press, 1936.

Hyneman, Charles S., and Donald S. Lutz, eds. *American Political Writing during the Founding Era, 1760–1805.* 2 vols. Indianapolis: Liberty Press, 1983.

Jefferson, Thomas. *The Complete Jefferson.* Edited by Saul Padover. New York: Duell, Sloan, and Pearce, 1943.

———. *The Family Letters of Thomas Jefferson.* Edited by Edwin M. Betts and James A. Bear. Columbia: University of Missouri Press, 1966.

———. *Jefferson's Extracts from the Gospels: "The Philosophy of Jesus" and "The Life and Morals of Jesus."* Edited by Dickinson W. Adams et al. *The Papers of Thomas Jefferson*, 2d ser. Edited by Charles T. Cullen. Princeton, N.J.: Princeton University Press, 1983–.

———. *The Life and Selected Writings of Thomas Jefferson.* Edited by Adrienne Koch and William Peden. New York: Random House, Modern Library, 1944.

———. *Notes on the State of Virginia.* Edited by William Peden. New York: W. W. Norton, 1972.

———. *The Papers of Thomas Jefferson.* Edited by Julian P. Boyd et al. 22 vols. to date. Princeton, N.J.: Princeton University Press, 1950–.

———. *The Works of Thomas Jefferson.* Edited by Paul L. Ford. 12 vols. Federal Edition. New York: G. P. Putnam's Sons, 1905.

———. *The Writings of Thomas Jefferson.* Edited by Andrew A. Lipscomb and Albert E. Bergh. 20 vols. Washington, D.C.: Thomas Jefferson Memorial Association, 1903 (cited as *Writings*).

———. *The Writings of Thomas Jefferson.* Edited by Henry A. Washington. 9 vols. New York: Riker, Thorne, 1853–54.

Jefferson, Thomas, and Joseph Cabell. *Early History of the University of Virginia as Contained in the Letters of Thomas Jefferson and Joseph C. Cabell.* Edited by Nathaniel Francis Cabell. Richmond, Va.: J. W. Randolph, 1856.

Juvenal [Junius Juvenalis]. *Satires.* In *Juvenal and Persius*, edited by G. G. Ramsay, rev. Cambridge: Harvard University Press, Loeb Library, 1950.

Karier, Clarence J. *The Individual, Society, and Education: A History of American Educational Ideas.* 2d ed. Urbana: University of Illinois Press, 1986.

Katz, Michael B. *Reconstructing American Education.* Cambridge: Harvard University Press, 1987.

Kerber, Linda K. "Daughters of Columbia: Educating Women for the Republic 1787–1805." In Stanley Elkins and Eric McKitrick, eds., *The Hofstadter Aegis: A Memorial.* New York: Alfred A. Knopf, 1974.

———. *Federalists in Dissent: Imagery and Ideology in Jeffersonian America.* Ithaca, N.Y.: Cornell University Press, 1970.

———. *Women of the Republic.* Chapel Hill: University of North Carolina Press, 1980.

Knight, Edgar W. *A Documentary History of Education in the South before 1860.* 5 vols. Chapel Hill: University of North Carolina Press, 1950.

Koch, Adrienne. *Jefferson and Madison: The Great Collaboration.* New York: Oxford University Press, 1964.

Kohn, Richard H. *Eagle and Sword: The Federalists and the Creation of the Military Establishment in America, 1783–1802.* New York: Free Press, 1975.

Kurland, Philip, and Ralph Lerner, eds. *The Founders' Constitution.* 5 vols. Chicago: University of Chicago Press, 1987.

Lee, Richard Henry. *The Letters of Richard Henry Lee.* Edited by James Curtis Ballagh. 2 vols. New York: Macmillan, 1911–1914.

Lerner, Ralph. *The Thinking Revolutionary: Principle and Practice in the New Republic.* Ithaca, N.Y.: Cornell University Press, 1987.

Levin, David, ed. *The Puritan in the Enlightenment.* Chicago: Rand McNally, 1963.

Levy, Leonard. *Freedom of Speech and Press in Early American History: Legacy of Suppression.* New York: Harper and Row, 1963.

Lincoln, Abraham. *Abraham Lincoln: His Speeches and Writings.* Edited by Roy P. Basler. Cleveland, Ohio: World Publishing, 1946.

Litto, Fredric M. "Addison's *Cato* in the Colonies." *William and Mary Quarterly,* 3d ser., 23 (1966): 431–49.

Locke, John. *The Educational Writings of John Locke: A Critical Edition with Introduction and Notes.* Edited by James L. Axtell. Cambridge: Cambridge University Press, 1968.

———. *An Essay Concerning Human Understanding.* Edited by Peter H. Nidditch. Oxford: Clarendon Press, 1979.

———. *A Letter Concerning Toleration: Latin and English Texts Revised.* Edited by Mario Montuori. The Hague: Martinus Nijhoff, 1963.

———. *Two Treatises of Government.* Edited by Peter Laslett. New York: New American Library, 1965.

Lowrie, Walter, and Matthew Clark, eds. *American State Papers: Documents, Legislative and Executive, of the Congress of the United States.* Military Affairs. 2 vols. Washington, D.C.: Gales and Seaton, 1832.

McClellan, B. Edward, and William J. Reese, eds. *The Social History of American Education.* Urbana: University of Illinois Press, 1988.

McColley, Robert. *Slavery and Jeffersonian Virginia.* 2d ed. Urbana: University of Illinois Press, 1973.

McCoy, Drew. "Benjamin Franklin's Vision of a Republican Political Economy for America." *William and Mary Quarterly,* 3d ser., 35 (1978): 605–28.

———. *The Elusive Republic: Political Economy in Jeffersonian America.* Chapel Hill: University of North Carolina Press, 1980.

———. *The Last of the Fathers: James Madison and the Republican Legacy.* Cambridge: Cambridge University Press, 1989.

McDonald, Forrest. *Novus Ordo Seclorum: The Intellectual Origins of the Constitution.* Lawrence: University Press of Kansas, 1985.

MacLean, Kenneth. *John Locke and English Literature of the Eighteenth Century.* New York: Russell and Russell, 1962.

McWilliams, Wilson Carey. "Civil Religion in the Age of Reason: Thomas Paine on Liberalism, Redemption, and Revolution." *Social Research* 54 (1987): 447–90.

Madison, James. *Letters and Other Writings of James Madison.* 4 vols. Philadelphia: J. B. Lippincott, 1865.

————. *The Mind of the Founder.* Edited by Marvin Meyers. Indianapolis: Bobbs-Merrill, 1973.

————. *The Writings of James Madison.* Edited by Gaillard Hunt. 9 vols. New York: G. P. Putnam's Sons, 1908.

Madison, James, Alexander Hamilton, and John Jay. *The Federalist Papers.* Edited by Clinton Rossiter. New York: New American Library, Mentor Books, 1961.

Madsen, David L. *Early National Education, 1776–1830.* New York: John Wiley and Sons, 1974.

————. *The National University: Enduring Dream of the USA.* Detroit, Mich.: Wayne State University Press, 1966.

Malbin, Michael J. *Religion and Politics: The Intentions of the Authors of the First Amendment.* Washington, D.C.: American Enterprise Institute, 1978.

Malone, Dumas. *Jefferson and His Time.* 6 vols. Boston: Little, Brown, 1948–1981.

Marshall, John. *The Life of George Washington.* 2 vols. 2d ed. Philadelphia: James Crissy, 1832.

Mather, Cotton. *The Diary of Cotton Mather.* 2 vols. New York: Frederick Ungar, 1957.

Mayer, David N. "Policy and Principles in the Age of Jefferson." Review of *Liberty and Property: Political Economy and Policymaking in the New Nation, 1789–1812,* by John R. Nelson. *Humane Studies Review* 5 (1988): 9–11, 16–17.

Middlekauf, Robert. "A Persistent Tradition: The Classical Curriculum in Eighteenth-Century New England." *William and Mary Quarterly,* 3d ser., 18 (1961): 54–67.

Miller, Eugene. "On the American Founders' Defense of Liberal Education in a Republic." *Review of Politics* 46 (1984): 65–90.

Miller, Perry, and Thomas H. Johnson, eds. *The Puritans: A Sourcebook of Their Writings.* 2 vols. rev. ed. New York: Harper and Row, 1963.

Milton, John. *Areopagitica and Of Education.* Edited by George H. Sabine. Northbrook, Ill.: AHM Publishing, Crofts Classics, 1951.

————. *Paradise Lost: A Poem in Twelve Books.* Edited by Merritt Y. Hughes. Indianapolis: Bobbs-Merrill, 1975.

Monaghan, E. Jennifer. *A Common Heritage: Noah Webster's Blue-Back Speller.* Hamden, Conn.: Archon Press, 1983.

Montesquieu. *Oeuvres complètes.* Edited by Roger Caillois. 2 vols. Paris: Gallimard, Pléiade Edition, 1949–1951.

Morgan, Edmund S. *The Meaning of Independence.* New York: W. W. Norton, 1976.

————. *The Puritan Dilemma: The Story of John Winthrop.* Boston: Little, Brown, 1958.

————. *The Puritan Family: Religion and Domestic Relations in Seventeenth-Century New England.* Rev. and enl. New York: Harper and Row, 1966.

Morison, Samuel Eliot. *The Intellectual Life of Colonial New England.* 2d ed. Ithaca, N.Y.: Cornell University Press, 1980.

————. *Three Centuries of Harvard: 1636–1936.* Cambridge: Harvard University Press, 1965.

Morley, John. *Oliver Cromwell.* New York: Century Co., 1900.

Morris, Gouverneur. *The Diary and Letters of Gouverneur Morris.* Edited by Anne Cary Morris. 2 vols. London: Kegan Paul, 1889.

Mott, Frank Luther. *American Journalism.* 3d ed. New York: Macmillan, 1962.

Nelson, John R. *Liberty and Property: Political Economy and Policymaking in the New Nation, 1789–1812*. Baltimore: Johns Hopkins University Press, 1987.

Newlin, Claude M. *Philosophy and Religion in Colonial America*. New York: Philosophical Library, 1962.

"Original Papers in Relation to a Course of Liberal Education." *American Journal of Science and Arts* 15 (January 1829): 297–351.

Paine, Thomas. *The Rights of Man*. Garden City, N.Y.: Doubleday, 1961.

Pangle, Thomas L. *The Spirit of Modern Republicanism: The Moral Vision of the American Founders and the Philosophy of Locke*. Chicago: University of Chicago Press, 1988.

Peterson, Merrill D., ed. *Thomas Jefferson: A Reference Biography*. New York: Charles Scribner's Sons, 1986.

Plato. *The Laws of Plato, Translated with Notes and an Interpretive Essay*. Edited by and translated by Thomas L. Pangle. New York: Basic Books, 1980.

_____. *Opera*. Edited by John Burnet. 5 vols. Oxford: Clarendon Press, 1961.

Pliny the Younger [Caius Plinius Caecilius Secundus]. *Letters, in the Translation of Melmoth*. Edited by F. C. T. Bosanquet. London: George Bell and Sons, 1878.

[Plutarch?]. "On the Education of Children." In *Moralia*, vol. 1, edited by Frank Babbitt. Cambridge: Harvard University Press, Loeb Library, 1960.

Quintilian [Marcus Fabius Quintilianus]. *Institutio Oratorio* [The Education of the Orator]. Edited by H. E. Butler. 4 vols. Cambridge: Harvard University Press, 1921.

Reinier, Jacqueline S. "Rearing the Republican Child: Attitudes and Practices in Post-Revolutionary Philadelphia." *William and Mary Quarterly*, 3d ser., 39 (1982): 150–63.

Rollin, Charles. *Ancient History of the Egyptians, Carthaginians, Assyrians, Babylonians, Medes & Persians, Macedonians, and Grecians*. 13 vols. London: James, John, and Paul Knapton, 1734–1739.

_____. *The Method of Teaching and Studying the Belles Lettres; or An Introduction to Languages, Poetry, Rhetorick, History, Moral Philosophy, Physicks, etc., with Reflections on Taste; and Instructions with Regard to the Eloquence of the Pulpit, the Bar, and the Stage. The Whole Illustrated with Passages from the Most Famous Poets and Orators, Ancient and Modern, with Critical Remarks on Them, Designed More Particularly for Students in the Universities*. 4 vols. 7th ed. London: W. Strahan et al., 1770 (orig. pub. 1731).

Rollins, Richard. *The Long Journey of Noah Webster*. Philadelphia: University of Pennsylvania Press, 1980.

Rousseau, Jean-Jacques. *Emile, or On Education*. Translated by Allan Bloom. New York: Basic Books, 1979 (orig. pub. 1762).

_____. *Oeuvres complètes*. Edited by Bernard Gagnebin et al. 4 vols. to date. Paris: Gallimard, Pléiade Edition, 1959–.

Rudolph, Frederick. *The American College and University: A History*. New York: Alfred A. Knopf, 1962.

Rudolph, Frederick, ed. *Essays on Education in the Early Republic*. Cambridge: Harvard University Press, 1965.

Rush, Benjamin. "Enquiry into the Utility of a Knowledge of the Latin and Greek Languages, as a Branch of Liberal Education, with Hints of a Plan of Liberal Instruction without Them." *American Museum* 5 (June 1789): 525–35.

_____. *Essays, Literary, Moral, and Philosophical*. Schenectady, N.Y.: Union College Press, 1988 (orig. pub. 1798).

_____. *Letters of Benjamin Rush*. Edited by L. H. Butterfield. 2 vols. Princeton, N.J.: Princeton University Press, 1951.

_____. *The Selected Writings of Benjamin Rush*. Edited by Dagobert D. Runes. New York: Philosophical Library, 1948.

Sigmund, Paul E. "The Catholic Tradition and Modern Democracy." *Review of Politics* 49 (1987): 530–48.

Smith, Adam. *An Enquiry into the Nature and Causes of the Wealth of Nations.* Edited by R. H. Campbell et al. 2 vols. Indianapolis: Liberty Press, 1981.

Smith, Wilson, ed. *Theories of Education in Early America 1655–1819.* Indianapolis: Bobbs-Merrill, 1973.

Solzenitsyn, Alexander. *One Day in the Life of Ivan Denisovich.* Translated by Ralph Parker. New York: Penguin Books, 1963.

Sterne, Laurence. *The Sermons of Mr. Yorick.* 2 vols. London: Basil Blackwell, 1927 (orig. pub. 1760–1769).

Storing, Herbert J., ed. *The Complete Anti-Federalist.* 7 vols. Chicago: University of Chicago Press, 1981.

Strauss, Leo. *The Rebirth of Classical Political Rationalism: An Introduction to the Thought of Leo Strauss.* Edited by Thomas L. Pangle. Chicago: University of Chicago Press, 1989.

Tarcov, Nathan. *Locke's Education for Liberty.* Chicago: University of Chicago Press, 1984.

Taylor, A. J. P. *Bismarck: The Man and the Statesman.* New York: Random House, Vintage Books, 1967.

Tewksbury, Donald G. *The Founding of American Colleges and Universities before the Civil War: With Particular Reference to the Religious Influences Bearing upon the College Movement.* New York: Teachers College, Columbia University, 1932.

Thayer, Theodore. *Pennsylvania Politics and the Growth of Democracy 1740–1776.* Harrisburg: Pennsylvania Historical and Museum Commission, 1953.

Thomas Aquinas, St. *Commentary on the Nicomachean Ethics.* Translated by C. I. Litzinger. 2 vols. Chicago: Henry Regnery, 1964.

Tocqueville, Alexis de. *De la Démocratie en Amérique* [Democracy in America]. Vol. 1, pts. 1 and 2 of *Oeuvres, Papiers et Correspondances.* Edited by J.-P. Mayer. 5th ed. Paris: Gallimard, 1951.

Todd, Charles Burr. *The Life and Letters of Joel Barlow.* New York: G. P. Putnam's Sons, 1886.

Trenchard, John, and Thomas Gordon. *Cato's Letters or, Essays on Liberty, Civil and Religious, and Other Important Subjects.* 4 vols. 3d ed. New York, Russell and Russell, 1733 (facsimile reprint, 1969).

Troeltsch, Ernst. *The Social Teaching of the Christian Churches.* Translated by Olive Wyon. 2 vols. Chicago: University of Chicago Press, 1976.

Turner, Frederick Jackson. *The Frontier in American History.* New York: Holt, Rinehart, and Winston, 1920.

Tyack, David B. "The Spread of Public Schooling in Victorian America: In Search of a Reinterpretation." *History of Education* 7 (1978): 173–82.

———. *Turning Points in American Educational History.* Waltham, Mass.: Blaisdell, 1967.

Walker, Obadiah. *Of Education, Especially of Young Gentlemen.* 2d ed. Oxford: n.p., 1673. Facsimile reprint. Menston, England: Scolar Press, 1970.

Walzer, Michael. *The Revolution of the Saints: A Study in the Origins of Radical Politics.* New York: Atheneum, 1973.

Warfel, Harry R. *Noah Webster: Schoolmaster to America.* New York: Macmillan, 1936.

Washington, George. *The Writings of George Washington.* Edited by Jared Sparks. 12 vols. Boston: Little, Brown, 1833–1837.

———. *The Writings of George Washington from the Original Manuscript Sources.* Edited by John C. Fitzpatrick. 39 vols. Washington, D.C.: Government Printing Office, 1931–1940 (cited as *Writings*).

Watts, Isaac. *The Improvement of the Mind: With a Discourse on the Education of Children and Youth*. London: T. Nelson, 1849 (orig. pub. 1741, 1751).

Weber, Max. *The Protestant Ethic and the Spirit of Capitalism*. Translated by Talcott Parsons. New York: Charles Scribner's Sons, 1958.

Webster, Noah. *An American Selection of Lessons in Reading and Speaking*. Philadelphia: David Hogan, 1810.

_____. *The American Spelling Book*. Boston: Isaiah Thomas and Ebenezer T. Andrews, 1794.

_____. *A Collection of Essays and Fugitiv Writings*. Boston: Thomas Andrews, 1790.

_____. "An Examination into the Leading Principles of the Federal Constitution Proposed by the Late Convention Held at Philadelphia. With Answers to the Principal Objections that Have Been Raised Against the System." In Paul L. Ford, ed., *Pamphlets on the Constitution of the United States Published during Its Discussion by the People, 1787–1788*. Brooklyn, N.Y.: n.p., 1888.

_____. *A Grammatical Institute, of the English Language, Comprising, an Easy, Concise, and Systematic Method of Education, Designed for the Use of English Schools in America. In Three Parts*. Pts. I and 2. Hartford, Conn.: Hudson and Goodwin, 1783 and 1784. Facsimile reprints. Menston, England: Scolar Press, 1968.

_____. *The Little Reader's Assistant*. Hartford, Conn.: Babcock, 1790.

_____. *Noah Webster's Elementary Spelling Book, with a Facsimile of the 1831 Edition*. Edited by Henry Steele Commager. New York: Teachers College, Columbia University, 1958.

Weems, Mason L. *The Life of Washington*. Cambridge: Harvard University Press, 1962.

Welter, Rush. *Popular Education and Democratic Thought in America*. New York: Columbia University Press, 1962.

White, Leonard. *The Federalists: A Study in Administrative History 1789–1801*. New York: Macmillan, 1948.

_____. *The Jacksonians: A Study in Administrative History 1829–1861*. New York: Macmillan, 1954.

_____. *The Jeffersonians: A Study in Administrative History 1801–1829*. New York: Macmillan, 1951.

Willey, Basil. *The Eighteenth-Century Background: Studies on the Idea of Nature in the Thought of the Period*. Harmondsworth: Penguin Books, 1962.

Wilson, James. *Selected Political Essays of James Wilson*. Edited by Randolph G. Adams. New York: Alfred A. Knopf, 1930.

_____. *The Works of James Wilson*. Edited by Robert McCloskey. 2 vols. Cambridge: Harvard University Press, 1967.

Wood, Gordon. *The Creation of the American Republic, 1776–1787*. New York: W. W. Norton, 1972.

_____. "The Democratization of Mind in the American Revolution." In *The Moral Foundations of the American Republic*, edited by Robert Horwitz. 3d ed. Charlottesville: University Press of Virginia, 1986.

Woodress, James. *A Yankee's Odyssey: The Life of Joel Barlow*. Philadelphia: J. B. Lippincott, 1958.

Woodson, G. C. *The Education of the Negro prior to 1861*. New York: Arno Press, 1968.

Wright, Louis B. *The Cultural Life of the American Colonies 1607–1763*. New York: Harper and Brothers, 1957.

_____. "Thomas Jefferson and the Classics." In Merrill Peterson, ed., *Thomas Jefferson: A Profile*. New York: Hill and Wang, 1967.

Xenophon. *Opera*. Edited by E. C. Marchant. 5 vols. Oxford: Clarendon Press, 1969.

Index